Errors in Language Learning and Use

Exploring Error Analysis

Carl James

Longman

London and New York

Addison Wesley Longman Limited
Edinburgh Gate
Harlow, Essex CM20 2JE
England

and Associated Companies throughout the world

*Published in the United States of America
by Addison Wesley Longman Inc., New York*

First published 1998

ISBN 0 582 25763-8   Paper

British Library Cataloguing-in-Publication Data

A catalogue record for this book is
available from the British Library

Library of Congress Cataloging-in-Publication Data

James, Carl, 1939–
    Errors in language learning and use: exploring error analysis /
Carl James.
        p.   cm. — (Applied linguistics and language study)
    Includes bibliographical references and index.
    1. Language and languages—Study and teaching—Error analysis.
I. Title. II. Series.
    P53.3.J36 1998
    418'.007—dc21   97–34548
                                                                CIP

Set by 35 in 10/12 pt Baskerville

Produced through Longman Malaysia, PA

Errors in Language Learning and Use

APPLIED LINGUISTICS AND LANGUAGE STUDY

General Editor
PROFESSOR CHRISTOPHER N. CANDLIN,
MACQUARIE UNIVERSITY, SYDNEY

For a complete list of books in this series see pages v–vi

APPLIED LINGUISTICS AND LANGUAGE STUDY

GENERAL EDITOR

PROFESSOR CHRISTOPHER N. CANDLIN

Macquarie University, Sydney

Contents

vii

Publisher's Acknowledgements

We are indebted to the very Revd. Dr. N T Wright for permission
to reproduce an extract from his letter to *The Times* 7 December
1996.

Author's Preface

I notice on my travels that students on TEFL and Applied Linguistics courses, in the UK and beyond, study not only the Interlanguage paradigm of foreign language learning. Courses in Contrastive Analysis are still generally offered, and Error Analysis (EA) continues to enjoy widespread appeal. The explanation is not hard to find: teachers cannot escape from a preoccupation with learners' errors, and they are attracted towards EA by its promise of relevance to their everyday professional concerns. Students, for their part, enjoy the 'hands on' contact with real data that EA provides. As Vivian Cook puts it, Error Analysis is 'a methodology for dealing with data, rather than a theory of acquisition' (1993: 22). In fact, while some people want theory of Second Language Acquisition (SLA), I am convinced that many others want methodology for dealing with data.

Though there are a number of books available on Contrastive Analysis (or 'Language Transfer' as it is now called) and on Interlanguage study, there is no well-documented and reasonably comprehensive monograph on EA. This is all the more surprising when you consider that Bernd Spillner's diligent *Comprehensive Bibliography of Error Analysis* carried, back in 1991, a staggering 5,398 entries. We have only the excellent but short handbooks for teachers by John Norrish: *Language Learners and their Errors* (1983) and by J. Edge: *Mistakes and Correction* (1989). The only other books available on EA are the edited anthologies by J.C. Richards: *Error Analysis: Perspectives on Second Language Acquisition* (Longman, 1974), and that by R. Freudenstein: *Error in Foreign Languages* (1989). Nickel's *Fehlerkunde* (1972) did much to define parameters of the field, especially that of error evaluation, and S.P. Corder's *Error Analysis and Interlanguage* (1981) is a collection of his seminal papers, wherein one can trace his developing thoughts. But some of these collections are to some extent dismissive of EA and defend the Interlanguage approach. The would-be student of EA therefore has no option but to seek out individual articles published by the thousands in a wide range of journals. This is an unsatisfactory situation at a time when the rising cost of journals, tougher copyright law enforcement and higher numbers of students make easier access to study materials a high priority.

EA used to be associated exclusively with the field of foreign language teaching, but it has recently been attracting wider interest, having become associated with other domains of language education: mother-tongue literacy, oracy and writing assessment; language disorders and therapy work; and the growing field of forensic linguistics. In fact, it was in the course of a friendly conversation that Malcolm Coulthard, doyen of forensic linguistics, bemoaning the lack of a solid monograph on EA for people in his field to train on, suggested I write this book.

There is also an increased interest in error among cognitive and educational scientists outside the field of language: Pickthorne's work on Error Factors in children's arithmetic is an example, while the Chomskian discussion of the roles of 'evidence' (especially negative evidence in the form of error) and the renewed interest in feedback (now delivered to the learner by computer) in language acquisition all point to a revival of interest in EA. I therefore believe the time is ripe for a publication on Error Analysis, and the best channel must be Chris Candlin's Applied Linguistics and Language Study series with Longman.

I published *Contrastive Analysis* with Longman in 1980, and one of the reviews it received in particular (that written by my good friend Eddie Levenston), has been giving me food for thought for 17 years. Eddie wrote that *Contrastive Analysis* was a book that anyone could have written but only Carl James did. Did he mean I was an opportunistic carpetbagger who saw a chance and grabbed it? Or that the book wasn't really worth writing because it said nothing new – nothing at least to the scores of applied linguists who *could* have written it? Criticism on this score would be invalid, since the book was not written for my peers and was not intended as an advancement of human knowledge, but rather it was a textbook, written to clarify the field to students and to serve as a set text and catalyst of discourse for applied linguistics classes. Now though I believe I know what Eddie was 'saying', in his very subtle way, and he hit the nail right on the head: that this book was in fact written by others, all of them acknowledged in the Bibliography of course. I had merely been the agent, organizing and putting their original ideas into one, I hope, coherent text. I would not be disappointed if the present volume were to receive the same judgement from the same eminences.

We have seen in recent years a plethora of publication of encyclopaedias of language, linguistics and applied linguistics. The present volume is a non-alphabetic and non-thematic, but perhaps a procedurally organized encyclopaedia of Error Analysis. I certainly have tried to be encyclopaedic (in the sense of comprehensive), in my coverage of the subject matter. Its principal merits: it seeks coherence; it is wide-ranging; it is balanced; and, most important, I am riding no bandwagon. At the very least, the book can be used as an annotated bibliography.

The present book, *Errors in Language Learning and Use*, is conceived as a companion volume to *Contrastive Analysis*, and is similarly a compendium, a digest and a history of the vast and amorphous endeavours that hundreds of scholars and teachers have made over the years in trying to grapple with foreign language learners' learning difficulties and the inadequacies in their repertoires that bear testimony to the daunting undertaking of foreign language learning.

I am indebted to many people, too numerous to name. But I could never have witten this book without the generosity of the Government of Brunei Darussalam, whose Visiting Professorship at the University of Brunei offered me a year's academic asylum in that veritable 'Abode of Peace' from the numbing 60-hour working weeks endemic to British universities.

Special thanks and admiration are due also to Chris Candlin, General Editor of the Longman *Applied Linguistics and Language Study* series, for his constant encouragement of the author at times of self-doubt and for his advanced insights into the most intricate subject matter: long may he maintain his genius – and his stamina!

Carl James
Bangor, Wales

Abbreviations

Applied linguistics has spawned its myriad of specialist jargon terms, many of which have been abbreviated and some expressed as acronyms. While the newcomer might be daunted by their use, I have tried to define them by use in context. There follows a grouped listing of the most common:

NL (native language), MT (mother tongue), L1 (first language): synonyms here

FL (foreign language): unlike SL/L2 in being learnt/used solely in class
SL or L2 (second language): synonyms here
TL (target language), language (FL or SL/L2) being learnt
(T)ESL/EL2 (Teaching) (English as a second language)
(T)EFL (Teaching) (English as a foreign language)
ELT (English Language teaching)

SLA (second language acquisition) cf. FLL (foreign language learning)

NS (native speaker); NNS (non-native speaker), NrNS (near-native speaker)

CA (Contrastive analysis: contrasting MT and TL of the learner)
EA (Error analysis)
TA (Transfer analysis)
IL (Interlanguage: the version of the TL used or known by the learner)
ID (idiosyncratic dialect: near-synonym for IL, q.v.)

EIL (English as an international language)
WSE (World standard English: an ideal global norm for English)

LA (Language awareness: a person's explicit knowledge about their linguistic competence)
CR (Consciousness raising: drawing learners' attention to forms of the TL)

Two common bracketing conventions are used: [...] enclose phonetic elements; < ... > enclose spellings.
The asterisk * signals error, while the tick √ indicates well-formedness. * and √ are often juxtaposed.

The question mark ? indicates linguistic strangeness.

Bold type indicates key concepts in the text.
Italic type is used for emphasis and examples.

Dedicated to my Dear Friend
der Allendörfer Jugendjahre:

Dr. med. Wolfgang Reichel

1941–1975

1

Definition and Delimitation

Es irrt der Mensch, so lang' er strebt.

If you try to better yourself, you're bound to make the odd mistake.
(Goethe, *Prolog im Himmel, Faust Part 1*, eds R. Heffner,
H. Rehder and W.F. Twaddell. Boston: D.C. Heath and
Co., 1954 p. 17)

Human error

Much effort has gone into showing the uniqueness of language to
humans: *homo sapiens* is also *homo loquens*, and humans' wisdom is
the consequence of their gift of language. Linguistics is, by this fact,
the direct study of humankind, and ought to be the most human-
istic of all disciplines. Error is likewise unique to humans, who are
not only *sapiens* and *loquens*, but also *homo errans*. Not only is to err
human, but there is none other than human error: animals and
artifacts do not commit errors. And if to err and to speak are each
uniquely human, then to err at speaking, or to commit **language
errors**, must mark the very pinnacle of human uniqueness. Language error is the subject of this book. The first thing we need is
a provisional definition, just to get us started on what will in fact
be an extended definition of our topic. Let's provisionally define a
language error as an unsuccessful bit of language. Imprecise though
it sounds, this will suffice for the time being. It will also allow us
to define Error Analysis: Error Analysis is the process of determining the incidence, nature, causes and consequences of unsuccessful language. I shall presently return to dissect this definition.

In Chapter 2 we shall explore the scope of Error Analysis (EA)
within the many disciplines that have taken on board the notion

1

of error. Indeed, the very idea of 'discipline' suggests recognition of the need to eliminate or minimize error. In this book, however, we focus on errors and their analysis in the context of foreign language (FL) and second language (SL or synonymously L2) learning and teaching. Doing this is quite uncontentious: a recent statement implying that error is an observable phenomenon in FL/SL learning that has to be accounted for is Towell and Hawkins: 'Second language learners stop short of native-like success in a number of areas of the L2 grammar' (1994: 14). They stop short in two ways: when their FL/SL knowledge becomes fixed or '**fossilized**', and when they produce errors in their attempts at it. Both of these ways of stopping short add up to failure to achieve native-speaker competence, since, in Chomsky's words, native speakers (NSs) are people who know their language perfectly. While we shall focus on FL/SL error, we shall, especially in Chapter 2 which explores the scope – the breadth rather than depth – of EA, refer to errors in other spheres.

In the rest of this chapter we shall attempt to contextualize EA: first, historically, showing the course of development of ideas about learners' less-than-total success in FL/SL learning; and secondly, by looking at EA as a '**paradigm**' or approach to a field of study (FL/SL learning) and seeing how that one of several options relates to alternative options. In fact, since paradigms, like fashions, have their heyday in strict succession, any account of them tends also to be historical.

Successive paradigms

Notwithstanding our claim that the study of human error-making in the domain of language Error Analysis is a major component of core linguistics, Error Analysis is a branch not of linguistic theory (or 'pure' linguistics) but of **applied linguistics**. According to Corder's (1973) account of applied linguistics, there are four 'orders of application', only the first two of which will concern us here. The 'first-order' application of linguistics is **describing** language. This is a necessary first step to take before you can move on to the 'second-order' application of **comparing** languages.

In the applied linguistics of FL/SL learning there are three 'codes' or languages to be described. This becomes clear when we describe the typical FL/SL learning situation. In terms of

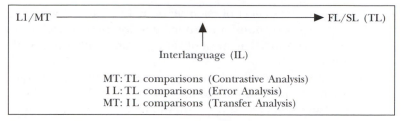

Figure 1.1   Points of comparison for successive FL learning paradigms

Figure 1.1, at the start of their FL/SL learning, the learners are monoglots, having no knowledge or command of the FL/SL, which is a distant beacon on their linguistic horizon. They start, and tortuously, with frequent backtrackings, false starts and temporary stagnation in the doldrums, gradually move towards their FL/SL goals. This is the complex situation: what are the language codes involved which need to be described?

First, language teaching calls for the description of the language to be learnt, the FL/SL. Let us use a term that is neutral between these two: **target language** or TL. This is a particularly useful label in the way it suggests **teleology**, in the sense of the learners actually wanting or striving to learn the FL/SL. It may even be extended to include the learners setting themselves goals. Without that willingness, there is of course no learning.

The second code in need of description in the teaching enterprise is the learners' version of the TL. Teachers are routinely called upon to do this when they decide whether the learners have produced something that is right or wrong. This requires them to describe the learners' version of TL, or, as it is called by Selinker (1972, 1992), their **Interlanguage** (IL), a term suggesting the halfway position it holds between knowing and not knowing the TL. Corder (1971) prefers to call it the learners' **idiosyncratic dialect** of the TL standard, a label that emphasizes other features it has. Another label that has been applied to description of the learners' set of TL-oriented repertoires is **performance analysis**. Færch (1978) attributes to Corder (1975) a conceptual distinction which is relevant here. Performance analysis is 'the study of the whole performance data from individual learners' (Corder, 1975: 207), whereas the term EA is reserved for 'the study of erroneous utterances produced by groups of learners' (ibid.: 207). Note the consistency in Corder's equation of performance analysis with the study of the **idiosyncratic** dialect of each learner. In that case we need to ask what sorts of 'groups of learners' develop systems that have something in common. The most obvious group is of learners with a common L1.

There is at least one other language involved in the FL learning operation: the learner's mother tongue (MT) or L1. This should be described also. I said at least one other language, but there might be more: people who know many languages already might want to learn even more, in which case we should describe the totality of the TL learner's **prior linguistic knowledge**, whether this be one or many languages, to varied degrees of mastery.

Moving on to the **second-order applications** of linguistics, which is **comparisons**, we can compare these three (MT, IL, TL) pairwise, yielding three paradigms – (a), (b) and (c). By 'paradigm' here we mean something like 'fashion': the favoured or orthodox way, at a certain period, of viewing an enterprise. The enterprise in this case is FL/SL teaching and learning.

(a)   Contrastive Analysis

In the 1950s and 1960s the favoured paradigm for studying FL/SL learning and organizing its teaching was Contrastive Analysis (James, 1980). The procedure involved first describing comparable features of MT and TL (e.g. tense, cooking verbs, consonant clusters, the language of apologizing), and then comparing the forms and resultant meanings across the two languages in order to spot the mismatches that would *predictably* (with more than chance probability of being right) give rise to interference and error. In this way you could predict or explain, depending on the degree of similarity between MT and TL, up to 30 per cent of the errors that learners would be likely or disposed to make as a result of wrongly transferring L1 systems to L2. By the early 1970s, however, some misgivings about the reliability of Contrastive Analysis (CA) began to be voiced, mainly on account of its association with an outdated model of language description (Structuralism) and a discredited learning theory (Behaviourism). Moreover, many of the predictions of TL learning difficulty formulated on the basis of CA turned out to be either uninformative (teachers had known about these errors already) or inaccurate: errors were predicted that did not materialize in Interlanguage, and errors did show up there that the CA had not predicted. Despite some residual enthusiasm and some attempts to formulate more modest claims for CA (James, 1971), the paradigm was generally jettisoned.

(b)   Error Analysis

The next paradigm to replace CA was something that had been around for some time (as we shall presently see): Error Analysis (EA). This paradigm involves first independently or 'objectively' describing the learners' IL (that is, their version of the TL) and the TL itself, followed by a comparison of the two, so as to locate mismatches. The novelty of EA, distinguishing it from CA, was that the mother tongue was not supposed to enter the picture. The claim was made that errors could be fully described in terms of the TL, without the need to refer to the L1 of the learners.

(c)   Transfer Analysis

It has, however, proved impossible to deny totally the effects of MT on TL, since they are ubiquitously and patently obvious. Where CA failed was in its claim to be able to predict errors on the basis of compared descriptions. This shortcoming had been noticed by Wardhaugh (1970), who suggested that the CA hypothesis should be thought of as existing in two versions, a 'strong' version that claims to be able to predict learning difficulty on the basis of a CA of MT and TL, and a 'weak' version that makes the more cautious claim of merely being able to explain (or diagnose) a subset of actually attested errors – those resulting from MT interference. In its strong version, CA is no longer much practised in *applied* linguistics. This is not surprising, since the alternative, diagnostic CA, is compatible with and easily incorporated into EA, as a way of categorizing those errors that are caused by interference from the MT.

Predictive CA has had to give way to the description and explanation of actually occurring MT transfers. This has led to some contentious relabelling as CA got swept under the carpet, and it is now more politic to talk of '**crosslinguistic** influence' (Kellerman and Sharwood Smith, 1986) or of '**language transfer**' (Gass and Selinker, 1983; Odlin, 1989). The term I reserve for this enterprise is **transfer analysis** (TA) (James, 1990: 207). It must be emphasized, however, that this TA is no longer CA, since the ingredients are different in that when you conduct Transfer Analysis, you are comparing IL with MT and not MT with TL. Nor are you comparing IL and TL, so you are not doing EA proper. TA is a subprocedure applied in the diagnostic phase of doing EA. TA is not a credible alternative paradigm but an ancillary procedure within EA for dealing with those IL:TL discrepancies (and the associated errors) that are assumed to be the results of MT transfer or interference. In so far as TA is something salvaged from CA and added to EA, the balance has shifted.

Interlanguage and the veto on comparison

The third paradigm for the study of FL learning that has been widely embraced is the Interlanguage hypothesis propounded by Selinker (1972). Its distinctiveness lies in its insistence on being wholly descriptive and eschewing comparison. It thus tries to avoid what Bley-Vroman has called 'the comparative fallacy in FL learner research', that is 'the mistake of studying the systematic character of one language by comparing it to another' (1983: 15). This veto on comparison is probably aimed at CA, but it is not wholly justified. The practitioners of CA similarly stressed the desirability of not allowing the descriptive categories of one language to colour what should be an objective, independent description of another. The idea of describing a learner's language in its own terms without reliance on the descriptive categories derived from the analysis of another language (the technical term is *sui generis*) is not new: the Structuralists of the 1950s warned against proscribing sentence-final prepositions in English merely because putting them in this position broke a rule – not of English, but of Latin. There are even echoes of anthropological linguistic fieldwork methods in the comparative prohibition too: study your learner 'objectively', much like the anthropological field linguists, missionaries and Bible translators did their native informants.

IL, or what the learner actually says, is only half of the EA equation. Meara (1984) set out to explain why the learning of lexis has been so neglected in IL studies. His diagnosis is illuminating: it is because IL studies have concentrated almost exclusively on the **description** of ILs, on what Meara refers to as 'the tools'. And there has been widespread neglect of the comparative dimension. This is regrettable since, 'we are interested in the difference between the learner's internalized description of his L2 and the internalized descriptions that native speakers have' (Meara, 1984: 231). We do have to have a detailed and coherent description of the learners' repertoires, but we cannot stop there, as Bley-Vroman would have us stop. This is not to say that his directive is misguided: it is necessary to be 'objective' and non-derivative in one's linguistic description, and take care not to describe X in terms of Y. With one exception: when you are doing EA! The reason is obvious. The learners' errors are a register of their current perspective on the TL.

There is a constant tension between, on the one hand, the long-term descriptive and explanatory priorities of people engaged in IL studies and dedicated to Second Language Research (SLR) and, on the other hand, the shorter-term pedagogic priorities of foreign language educators who do EA. One is tempted at times to conclude that SLR is not a part of applied linguistics, and is not interested in language teaching, but is a branch of pure linguistics, interested in the properties of languages rather than the problems of learners, in language **learnability** rather than the processes of teaching. There does not have to be tension if we agree that the SLR and EA enterprises are different and have different goals. After all, as Cook puts it: 'Error Analysis was [and still is! CJ] a methodology for dealing with data, rather than a theory of acquisition' (1993: 22). Let those who want theory have theory, and those who want them, ways of 'dealing with data'.

In one sense, however, SLA Interlanguage research is inescapably comparative. There are two ways to conceptualize 'IL'. First, it can refer to the abstraction of learner language, the aggregate of forms, processes and strategies that learners resort to in the course of tackling an additional language. This concept is similar to de Saussure's **langue**. Alternatively, 'IL' can be used to refer to any one of a number of concretizations (cf. de Saussure's **parole**) of the underlying system. These are sequenced in time: IL1 develops after 100 hours of exposure, IL2 after 200 hours, and so on. The SLA researcher who studies IL developmentally or longitudinally, like the historical linguist, will be forced to make comparisons of these successive stages.

In fact, this 'successive steps' view of FL learning is not unproblematic for EA as we have defined it. It is plausible to suggest that it has some psychological reality, in that the learners at the learning stage of ILn, shall we say, are in fact aiming at linguistic forms that are not at the *end* of the IL continuum, not TL forms, but forms that are but one stage *nearer* to TL than their IL competence is currently located. In that case, we would define errors in terms of the discepancy between what they are aiming at (IL n+1) and ILn, not in tems of ILn and TL as suggested above.

At least one objective observer has no difficulty with the comparative definition of error. John Hawkins could not have been clearer when he stated: 'The whole concept of error is an intrinsically relational one. A given feature of an [IL] is an error *only* by comparison with the corresponding TL: seen in its own terms the [IL] is a completely well-formed system' (1987: 471). There are even times when the SLA theorists are caught off their guard, when they too admit the need to compare IL with the TL. Ellis (1992: 232 ff.), for example, undertakes to define, exemplify and compare two language-teaching techniques – language practice and consciousness-raising. The latter, he contends, constitutes gaining **explicit** knowledge, while practice is aimed at making knowledge **implicit**. Now according to Ellis 'the acquisition of implicit knowledge involves three processes: noticing, . . . comparing, . . . and integrating' (ibid.: 238). Ellis's definition of comparing runs as follows: 'the learner compares the linguistic features noticed in the input with her own mental grammar, registering to what extent there is a "gap" between the input and her grammar' (ibid.: 238). I believe that what Ellis intends here by 'her grammar' is not the learner's NL but the learner's representation of the TL – that is, her IL. What the learner is engaged in therefore, if Ellis is right, is no other than EA, as we have defined it – comparing one's IL with TL and noticing the discrepancies between the two.

Ellis develops this idea and gives it a label: **cognitive comparison**, which he recommends enthusiastically, since 'intake is enhanced when learners carry out a second operation – comparing what they have noticed in the input with what they currently produce in their own output' (1995b: 90). And, Ellis declares: 'One way of fostering this is to draw learners' attention to the kinds of errors learners typically make' (ibid.: 95). This is by no means a new idea. Harlow (1959) defined all learning as a process of progressive and cumulative error-correction. Clark (1982) had the same idea in mind when she formulated **coordination theory**, since it is a process whereby language production is brought more and more into line (that is, coordinated) with what children hear, and the gap between these two is closed as children compare their output with available input and proceed to narrow the gap between these two. Not only does Ellis appear to be unaware of this tradition, he even forgets to acknowledge those many practical error analysts who have collected common errors (Turton, 1995) or region-specific errors (Crewe, 1977), the purpose of such collections being to guide learners in making their (often complex) 'cognitive comparisons'. Ellis might argue that it is desirable for the learner to do EA but not for the teacher. He might argue further that the learners are not just comparing actual erroneous forms with TL input data, but rather their total grammar, and that the comparison will therefore not be arbitrarily limited to erroneous forms but will also include correct forms. These arguments would not alter the fact that we have here an admission of the utility of EA.

Having shown that EA still justifies itself today, we shall now take a brief retrospective look at early foundation work in EA.

Learners and native speakers

Concern with the errors of FL learners and with those of native speakers (NS) have run in tandem. Early work in FL learners' EA was **taxonomic**, by which we mean it concentrated on the collection and classification of errors, much as the lepidopterist would organize a collection of butterflies. By contrast, early native speakers' EA was more interested in identifying cause and system. The two approaches appear to have coexisted side by side for some time, with little or no cross-fertilization. An early influential native-speaker EA was S.A. Leonard's *The Doctrine of Correctness in English Usage, 1700–1800* (1929), following the pioneering book by Henri Frei, *Grammaire des Fautes* (Paris, 1929). Frei contrasted normative and functional approaches to NS error. The former has to do with attitudes and standards, the latter with clarity, economy and expressiveness: it is in this latter context alone, Frei suggests, that we can talk of error in terms of deficiency. Frei also discusses the connection between 'rule' of grammar and the rules (laws) of society. Finally, he relates error to linguistic change, distinguishing linguistic **change** (which is reversible) from linguistic **evolution** (which is irreversible). Frei quotes the perceptive observation of Claude Bernard: 'le pathologique n'est que l'exagération du normal' (The pathological is merely exaggerated normality), the significance of which is its claim that it is only by having to decide what is wrong that we come to terms with what is right.

An informative account of eighteenth-century attitudes to native language (NL) errors is to be found in the *Dictionary of English Normative Grammar* (*DENG*) developed by Sundby and his colleagues at the University of Bergen, accounts of which are available in Sundby (1987) and Sundby and Bjørge (1983). Building on S.A. Leonard's classic account of the doctrine of correctness as it prevailed in eighteenth-century England, they analysed the metalanguage used by prescriptive grammarians of the period like Priestley (1761), Sedger (1798), and Wood (1777). *DENG* is consequently not only a dictionary of errors, but also a compendium of terms used over the course of a century to describe and evaluate errors. It is an account of the **metalanguage** or the **register** used by people of influence when they were called upon (or moved) to discuss language error. We shall return to this second feature of *DENG* in Chapter 4 when looking at ways of classifying errors. The finding I wish to focus upon here is that 'The "bad" forms are in focus, not the "good" usage itself. Prescriptive grammar virtually becomes a grammar of errors' (Sundby, 1987: 3). He goes on to quote Sedger, who wrote at the end of the century: 'most of our grammarians [have] written rather with a view to point out the common errors of speech than minutely to investigate the genius of the tongue'. In other words, there was a time when the role of the grammarian was seen to be that of custodian of the language, as the proscriber of error.

Among the taxonomic second language EA publications the best known is Brown and Scragg, *Common Errors in Gold Coast English* (1948). They assume mother tongue (MT) interference to be the source of these errors. Some of their assumptions are questionable, however. For example, they categorize some forms as erroneous which occur in British English: *That's the *(!)very man I was talking about.* They also label as errors some forms that are standard West Africa English such as: *We reached *at Accra.* It was not until Kofi Sey published *Ghanaian English* (1973) that the idea of such a named variety of English was mooted. Other works that focus on the typical errors of learners with a particular MT include Ishiyama (1982) and Petersen (1988). C.L. Holden's *An Enquiry into the Written English at Secondary Level in Sierra Leone* (1960) raises some interesting questions still central to EA today, such as the role of attitudes in the assessment of error, the existence of regional standards of English (the 'New Englishes'), and the elusiveness of useful classificatory systems.

Pioneering work in EA was done in the 1960s in the form of Masters' theses written by highly experienced teachers of English as a FL/SL, taking advantage of the development of applied linguistics courses that were being instituted at the time in several British universities. Two of these are well worthy of mention: D.A.L. Harper's Diploma dissertation in applied linguistics, done at Edinburgh University in 1962, sifts the available EA literature, pinpoints the deficiencies noted above, and proposes a revised approach. This approach sees no need to consider the MT, since 'once a mistake has been made in an L2, to describe it and tabulate it and describe it is possible in terms of the L2 alone' (Harper, 1962: 19). The approach makes use of a powerful model of language description, namely Halliday's, which offered the category of **delicacy** as a way to avoid rigidity in descriptions of errors, and offered the more fully defined categories of **style** and **register** as additional classificatory tools.

A.L. Jones's Manchester MEd dissertation was '*The written English of Malayan teacher training college students*' (1966). He assembled a 221,000-word corpus of 386 essays written by these students and set out 'to detect all the non-Standard-British-English features which occurred in the corpus'. The problems were many, but perhaps the most interesting was the failure of the native-speaker judges to agree on the deviance or nondeviance of certain features in the students' English. So, for instance, 32 of 128 items stigmatized by one NS judge were acceptable to the other five. A review revealed that no fewer that 265 of 4,530 original 'deviances' were in fact acceptable. The NS judges also failed to reach consensus on the ideal correction of most errors. For instance, suggestions as to how to correct the sentence *The price tags on the list are a great advantage* included: *The prices are . . . , The price list is . . . , The list of prices . . . , The prices in the list. . . .* Such indeterminacy of error and indecision of the NS remains a problem in EA, as we shall see.

The heyday of Error Analysis

By the late 1960s EA had become the acceptable alternative to the Behaviourism-tainted CA of the 1950s. In 1977, Schachter and Celce-Murcia could say: 'EA currently appears to be the "darling" of the 70s' (Schachter and Celce-Murcia, 1977: 442), lamenting the fact that the pendulum had swung too far in its favour and therefore feeling it was time to take stock and expose some of its weaknesses. A sort of competition went on to establish the supremacy of CA over EA or the converse. We shall turn to the weaknesses later. First let us see what kind of a heyday EA was having.

It was the late S. Pit Corder who, over a short, four- year period, first revived and then abandoned EA. In his seminal 1967 paper 'The significance of learners' errors', he made five crucial points:

(i)   We should look for parallels between L1 acquisition and L2 learning, since these are governed by the same underlying mechanisms, procedures and strategies. However, one difference between the two is that L2 learning is probably facilitated by the learner's knowledge of the MT. Note Corder's optimistic view of the role of the L1, a view more recently corroborated by research undertaken by Ringbom (1987) working with Finnish learners of English.

(ii) Errors are evidence of the learners' in-built syllabus, or of what they have taken in, rather than what teachers think they have put in: **intake** should not be equated with **input**.

(iii) Errors show that L1 and L2 learners both develop an independent system of language, 'although it is not the adult system . . . nor that of the second language' (Corder, 1967: 166) but is evidence of a '**transitional competence**'.

(iv) Errors should be distinguished from **mistakes** (see Chapter 3).

(v)   Errors are significant in three respects: they tell the teacher what needs to be taught; they tell the researcher how learning proceeds; and they are a means whereby learners test their hypotheses about the L2. This is patently a very positive assessment of EA, announcing a programme that might well take several decades and not just a heyday to complete.

The two most significant single taxonomic publications were H.V. George (1972) and M. Burt and C. Kiparsky (1972). George's is a remarkably perceptive account of the major causes and types of learner error, full of suggestions for ways to avoid or remedy errors. In fact this book could stand as a methodology manual in its own right. It is theoretically well-informed and still up to date, for example in its discussion of the role of pairing **marked** and **unmarked** options in the teaching programme. There are also several places in George's book where he anticipates current discussion of the role of **noticing** features of the TL that need to be learnt (see George, 1972: 99–109). Reference is made to Corder as well as to Chomsky, without however overlooking the insights into error gained by the older grammarians, notably Jesperen and Kruisinga. It is also an eminently practical work, written by an accomplished English as a second language (EL2) teacher reflecting on a lifetime's experience in teaching and teacher training. In fact, it anticipates some of the features of a 'reflective' approach to teacher training recently proposed by Wallace (1991).

The three principal causes of learners' FL errors are, according to George: **redundancy** of the code, unsuitable **presentation** in class (see 'Induced errors' in Chapter 6), and several sorts of **interference**. Each cause is discussed and illustrated at length, with suggestions following for countering these forces in class. George even launched a vigorous attack on audiolingual teaching methodology, suggesting that in the abandonment of the old grammar-translation approach, the baby had been thrown out with the bath water. One of the tenets of audiolingualism was (and still is) **automaticity of response**, otherwise termed fluency, which was/is seen as a necessary component in communicative activity. Now, while translation was slow and did not promote fluency, it promoted something that is arguably just as vital: 'time for reflection' (George, 1972: 180). Not just reflecting on the TL, noticing its features and their degree of complexity and familiarity to the learner, but also noticing and reflecting upon the relations between unknown TL features and their known MT near-equivalents: something we return to in Chapter 8, where we outline the role that can be played by **Contrastive Analysis** in **Consciousness Raising.** Indubitably, George's book is still the best ever published on EA, and one well worth reprinting.

Burt and Kiparsky (1972) entitle their book *The Gooficon*, which they define as 'a collection of goofs and their explanations, *from the point of view of English grammar*' (1972: 1, my emphasis). This stance echoes that of F.G. French's *Common Errors in English* (1949) which anticipated the more modern universalist view, minimizing the effects of MT transfers, and claiming that the MT does not have any significant effect.

Note though that there is no insistence on the integrity of IL in Burt and Kiparsky, since the errors are all juxtaposed alongside the correct forms. The errors they assemble are from all over the world, and they find it unnecessary to refer to the learners' L1s. They justify this on the grounds that 'we have not found that the majority of the syntactical goofs are due to the native language syntax of the learner' (Burt and Kiparsky, 1972: 3). Nevertheless they do frequently refer to L1 influence, for instance on page 57 and elsewhere. This is an early consciousness-raising book, where teachers are shown in what systematic ways English can be got wrong, and what criteria are relevant to deciding correction priorities. One of its merits is to group together closely related goofs so that the correction of errors is at least as systematic as was their commission. Useful teaching suggestions are provided, and there is an attempt to relate error to 'rules'. The rules are those of the now obsolete transformational-generative (T-G) grammatical format, where the assumption is made that elements move out of one phrase or clause into another by processes called transformations: so, on page 90ff. we see noun phrases in subordinate clauses becoming 'snatched subjects' of the main clause. When it comes to explanations and the formulation of rules to facilitate learning, they are prepared to tell 'white lies' or 'to express a partial truth' (ibid.: 9). Such a 'white lie' is: *'Do' never appears in the same clause with an auxiliary.* Applying this rule will have the desired effect of discouraging *Do I must go? but only at the cost of 'ruling out' the well-formed √Must I do that? √Do be working (when the inspectors arrive)!, where auxiliaries do cooccur with do. I admit, however, that beginners would be unlikely to want to attempt these two sentences. Grammar 'white lies' have been recommended by other teaching experts: Holley and King (1971), in the context of teachers' explanation of German word order in subordinate clauses, applaud the teacher who 'did not provide a complete explanation' but promoted 'an interim rule which would have to be modified later'. This practice is made more acceptable if the rule formulation is one that can be progressively modified to suit new instances, and does not have to be rejected in its entirety.

Most interesting is the organization of the errors. They are categorized into the following six types: clausal, auxiliary, passive, temporal conjunctions, sentential complements and psychological predicates. This organization reflects the main preoccupations of early T-G syntax, and one occasionally has the impression that a few of the putative errors analysed were probably not attested from learners but 'generated' by intentionally relaxing a rule of the grammar. For example, do learners really systematically produce forms like **Talmy was painful that his mother was crying* or **He admits me hard to learn quickly?* I think not, and do not recollect having seen or heard real learners making such errors. Some errors, as we shall see later, are feasible if a rule of the particular language is infringed, but are in fact ruled out by Universal Grammar (UG). In other words, people's intuitions tell them that such things cannot be said in such ways in human languages. I suspect that the above two fall into this category.

The taxonomic tradition has been perpetuated at another level. I refer to the FL learners' guides. A good example is J.B. Heaton and N.D. Turton, *Longman Dictionary of Common Errors* (1987). This is an alphabetically ordered listing of the 1,700 errors in English most commonly made by foreign learners. The book is based on a sample of errors taken from Cambridge First Certificate in English answer papers. A randomly selected entry is:

English   *Our teacher is a typical English.
    Our teacher is a typical Englishwoman.*
    the English (= English people) but NEVER **an English**

Of course not all errors are universal: some selectively afflict learners having a certain L1. On the lexical level in particular, MT interference produces errors known as '**false friend**' errors. These tend to occur when a MT word and a TL word are identical or similar in form but different in meaning. For example, German *Baracken* does not mean *barracks* (which is *Kaserne* in German), but *shacks* or *hovels*. Instances of such relationships between parts of the word-stocks of cognate languages can be collected as learner aids: one such is Margaret Helliwell, *Can I become a beefsteak?* (1989). They are often amusing in as much as the errors caused by these cross-language asymmetries of form and meaning often lead to embarrassing or absurd incidents.

Crewe (1977) is a collection of errors collected from Singaporean learners of English, forms that might be appropriate for use in informal in-group settings in Singapore but which are considered unsuitable for use in formal settings or on the international scene.

Mounting criticism of Error Analysis

The heyday of EA was short-lived, however. In 1971 Corder had published a paper entitled 'Idiosyncratic dialects and error analysis'.

The concept of **idiosyncratic dialect** (ID) is a development of the 1967 concept of '**transitional competence**'. It also has strong affinities to Selinker's '**Interlanguage**' (1972) and an uncanny resemblance to Nemser's '**approximative system**' (1971). For Corder, an ID is 'a special sort of dialect', special in that while some of its rules are held in common with speakers of other dialects of the TL (or target dialect), these are too few to ensure interpretability of the learners' utterances by others. There are also too few individuals sharing the rules of any one ID to allow us to say that it has a community of speakers. In other words, it is not a **social** dialect but an **idiosyncratic** one. Some of these claims have gone unchallenged. It is, for example, demonstrable that learners of any given FL who share the same L1 and have been taught under similar conditions with the same texts and syllabus do emerge speaking the same 'social' dialect of that FL. They encounter few problems understanding each other's utterances rendered in that dialect, but outsiders, including speakers of the target dialect, that is 'native speakers', find it unintelligible (see Lane, 1963).

Corder, like Nemser, proceeds to argue that there are other sorts of ID besides those of FL learners: the language of poets and poetry, aphasic language, child language. But he insists that there is a difference, and this is where EA goes to the gallows. It is legitimate, Corder contends, to compare a poet's or an aphasic's ID to 'normal' dialect of a prose writer and a neurologically healthy person, using an 'approach that is essentially that of "error analysis", *a type of bilingual comparison*' (Corder, 1971: 150, my emphasis). It is not deemed legitimate, on the other hand, to compare the child's or the FL learner's ID to the dialect of adults or of native speakers of the FL respectively. The reason, Corder argues, is that the poet and the aphasic are – or once were – speakers of the standard dialect, and their deviance from the standard deserves the label because it is deliberate or pathological respectively. On the other hand, the child or the FL learner are neither deliberately nor pathologically deviant in their language, so it would be wrong to refer to their repertoires as erroneous. In the case of the FL learner, use of the label 'error' would be particularly inappropriate 'because it implies wilful or inadvertent breach of rules which, in some sense, ought to be known' (ibid.: 152). Reference to 'error' would only be justifiable if the rules had been deliberately flaunted or caused by performance factors, that is, if they were 'cases of *failure*... to follow a *known* rule' (ibid.: 152).

Corder uses two further arguments against calling the FL learner's ID 'erroneous', 'deviant' or 'ill-formed'. First, he objects that to do so is 'to prejudge the explanation of the idiosyncrasy' (ibid.: 152). We study an ID or IL in order 'to discover why it is as it is . . . to explain it' (ibid.: 153). However, as we shall presently see, it is not the ambition of EA to jump to conclusions in the way Corder implies. The explanation (or 'diagnosis') of a unit of learner language that does not match its equivalent in the TL is in no way prejudged by the simple act of calling it an error. Corder's second argument is aimed at those who call a learner's sentences 'ungrammatical': this is wrong, he insists, since 'they are in fact *grammatical* in terms of the learner's language' (ibid.: 153), that is in terms of the learner's IL or ID grammar. This is uncontentious: when we say that something is 'ungrammatical' we assume that this means ungrammatical in terms of the grammar of the language which the learners claim or believe themselves to have been speaking or writing at the time. Certainly everything is true 'unto itself', but this is a truism that won't take the learner very far. An analogy might help clarify the point. The mafia is said to have its own rules of conduct. We see it in operation in a novel like *The Godfather*. These rules are perfectly acceptable to the mafia, of course, and if this were not the case, it would amend them. But they are not acceptable to society at large, beyond the mafia: they are seen to be 'wrong', in fact criminally and wilfully wrong, and those who use them are required to mend their ways, or face dire penalties. A telling difference between mafiosi and FL learners is that the former do not want their behaviour to conform to the standard, whereas most FL learners do. For as long as FL learners are prepared to see and call themselves learners, the assumption that they wish to conform is surely a reasonable one to make.

Other, more direct, criticism of EA followed Corder's. Bell refers to EA as 'a recent pseudoprocedure in applied linguistics' (1974: 35), and attacks EA for its poor statistical inference, the subjectivity of its interpretations of errors, and its lack of any predictive power (something any scientific procedure must have). There was more emphasis on such statistical and objective rigour when Bell wrote than there is now, and we have become more realistic and modest in our demands of a science. Hammarberg points to the 'insufficiency of error analysis', which for him lies in its one-sided practice of 'analyzing out the errors and neglecting the careful description of the non-errors' (Hammarberg, 1974: 185). This is short-sighted, he claims, because it conceals from teachers exactly the information they could put to good use, information about potential errors that the learners somehow manage to avoid committing. Knowing how learners avoid certain likely errors is the first step to discovering how to help the same learners avoid the errors they fail successfully to avoid. This is a valid point of course, and is related to research (Cohen, forthcoming) that seeks to identify the strategies used by good FL learners so that these same strategies can be taught to not-so-good learners. Schachter (1974) also discovered what she saw as a fundamental flaw in EA – a failure to recognize that learners have a tendency to avoid TL items they are not sure about, and so not to commit errors which they would be expected to commit. By 1977 Schachter and Celce-Murcia were entertaining a number of reservations about EA. We return presently to the strategy of **avoidance** and those other reservations.

It seems, then, that EA was earmarked for obsolescence by the mid-1970s, and the theoretical ground was being cleared for the new IL paradigm. However, work in EA did not come to a sudden halt – as the rest of this book testifies. People continued to do EA despite the odds. Some fought a rear-guard action: Zydatiß (1974) offered a 'kiss of life' for EA. Rocha (1980) suggested that 'objectivity' can be salvaged in EA by submitting putative errors to panels of judges. Abbott (1980) answered some of Bell's worries by suggesting ways to increase the rigour of EA. Færch (1978), as if responding to Hammarberg (1974), offered **Performance Analysis** as an alternative to EA that does take into account both errors and non-errors.

Others were content to work in a theoretical vacuum, for the sake of doing something of practical value: I refer here to work on error gravities (James, 1974, 1977; Johansson, 1978; Hughes and Lascaratou, 1982; Davies, 1983; McCretton and Rider, 1993). Norrish (1983) produced an excellent account of EA for teachers. Others played safe and aligned themselves on the new IL paradigm, and, encouraged by the parallel communicative movement in FL teaching methodology, argued that errors and their 'creative' authors have to be treated with due respect (Edge, 1989; Page, 1990). It has also been a period for publishing collected papers on EA: Richards (1974), Svartvik (1973), Page, Harding and Rowell (1980). It is my contention that EA has become a more widespread practice than it is given credit for. The main objective of the next chapter will be to show just how wide the scope of EA is.

Data collection for Error Analysis

We have so far addressed two 'preliminaries' to our account of EA. First, we suggested where EA is located within the succession of paradigms for applied linguistics. Secondly, we gave an historical sketch of the recent development of EA, up to and beyond its brief official heyday, suggesting that EA as never been abandoned, but has rather lain in the doldrums perhaps awaiting the signal to ply the main. However, there is one further preliminary to EA, and this is getting the errors to analyse.

For most practising teachers the idea that somebody should waste ink on describing how to come by errors must be hilarious. After all, do not FL learners supply a seemingly endless torrent of errors in their work? And are not these learners unstinting in their invention of new ways of getting it wrong? So it would seem. Indeed, I would maintain that most teachers can dispense with the first of the two steps in **error elicitation** that I shall outline. This first elicitation, which is done as a matter of course in all classrooms, I shall call the **broad trawl**. The metaphor is one of casting one's net to catch all and any sorts of errors that happen to be at large, indiscriminately. The purpose of the broad trawl is to gain a first impression of the learner's capacities and limitations, to identify the areas of TL competence where they are most susceptible to error. The broad trawl is thus the source of the analyst's initial hypotheses about the learner's state of knowledge of the TL. It resembles the **scheduled elicitation** done by field linguists working in jungle and on steppe with a native informant to compile the first accounts of unrecorded languages: 'Scheduled elicitation starts with relative or complete ignorance about the language under investigation' (Samarin, 1967: 108). One good use of Contrastive Analysis is as a tool serving to pre-identify the probable areas of learning difficulty, with a given TL and learners speaking a given L1.

Once the analyst has identified significant areas of error-proneness, where a closer examination would appear to be called for, it is time to do **targeted elicitation**, which corresponds to Samarin's **analytical elicitation** (ibid.: 112). To target means to make decisions about the levels and systems (even subsystems) of the TL to be sampled: the receptive modality or the productive; the written or the spoken medium. Combinations of these two parameters will allow choices of addressing any of the **four skills**: listening, speaking, reading and writing.

Earlier on we referred to Performance Analysis, and this has relevance to elicitation, since what we elicit from learners are samples, which we hope are representative and rich, of the learner's TL performance. This performance will be a mix of right and wrong, nondeviant alongside erroneous. The point is that EA has traditionally based itself on such performance data. As Selinker puts it: 'the utterances which are produced when the learner attempts to say sentences of a language' are the main source of data for EA (1972: 213).

There have been attempts to systematize the different methods of data collection, and a workable but not totally watertight classification of elicitation modes is tripartite. Initially, a distinction is drawn between **observational** and **experimental** studies, the difference between these two residing mainly in the naturalness of the former compared to the manipulative nature of the second. The distinction is very close to the one we have drawn between broad trawl and targeted **elicitation**. The classroom activities developed in Communicative Language Teaching (see Littlewood, 1981) are eminently suitable observational instruments: **role play**, **information gap activities**, **simulations**, involving pairs and groups of learners, can all be used. Among the less clear-cut observational techniques, we have first **longitudinal** studies, which take their name from the practice of target-sampling the performance of the same population of learners on a series of separate successive occasions, usually listed as 'time 1', 'time 2', and so on. The aim is to trace development of learning over time. The alternative is the **cross-sectional** study, where at one and the same time (time x) different representative subpopulations have their performance sampled by elicitation: one hopes to be able to infer something about language development without having to invest time waiting for the longitudinal group to progress. Another sort of observational study is **classroom observation**, using an observation sheet to record errors that occur during a lesson, for instance. Of course, if the observation sheet is open-ended, we have a broad trawl, whereas if the categories are predetermined, the recording is of 'targeted' forms. The same distinction cuts across the longitudinal and cross-sectional studies as well. What they have in common as 'observational' is their non-intervention.

The **experimental** techniques are by contrast interventionist. They take the learners aside and give them tasks to do, the sole purpose of which is to elicit targeted forms which the Error Analyst is interested in. Simple **imitation** is an experimental technique: it was used effectively in the Ontario study of the good language learner (Naiman *et al.*, 1978) to identify the limits of L2 French learners' knowledge of articles, pronouns, adverb order, and so on. **Stimulus modification** involves not verbatim repetition but changing an input along certain determined parameters, for example negativizing an affirmative, passivizing an active, inverting a cleft. **Controlled elicitation** is another technique, involving the use of **cloze** tests, **dictations**, and even **multiple choice** items.

More recently, a third source of data for EA has come to the fore: **introspection**. This approach means getting the learner's cooperation in order to discover what is going on in that 'black box' (George, 1972: 5) which is the language learner's mind. Under Behaviourism the workings of the mind had to be inferred from measurements of the differences between inputs and outputs, but, as Chomsky observed, 'Behavior is only one kind of evidence, sometimes not the best, and surely no criterion for knowledge' (Chomsky, 1980: 54). This prompted researchers to identify other sources of data (or 'evidence') and we have witnessed a return to pre-Behaviourist ways of accessing mental processes that were prevalent in the nineteenth century but had survived only in the field of psychoanalysis. The central assumptions of introspection research (Færch and Kasper, 1987) are that language learners and users have access to – and therefore can observe – the mental processes that govern their language activities, and that they can be encouraged to articulate their observations, using some sort of **metalanguage**. That learners do have access to mental representations is undeniable. Zoila, studied by Shapira (1978: 254) is a 25-year-old Venezuelan immigrant to the USA whose English has fossilized for socio-motivational reasons. Nevertheless, she can talk about her English most revealingly. She says:

> I never listen . . . the words little . . . for continue my conversation . . . I'm hear and put more attention the big words . . . I know 'house' is the *casa* for me. And [eses] and little words no too important for me.

Notice her remarkable perception of the distinction between function ('little') words and lexical words. Notice her ability to isolate the –s morpheme, and her insight into her tendency to equate L1 items and their translations (*house* = *casa*)

It would not be true to say that this source was completely untapped hitherto, however. At least two sorts of introspection have a long history in language study. First, **learner diaries** had been widely used even before the Schumanns (Schumann and Schumann, 1977) recounted their experiences as learners of Hebrew after arriving to live in Israel. They invoked, for example, the socio-psychological concept of 'nesting' to explain that before they had found a secure home they felt it impossible to embark wholeheartedly on their learning. Students following Master's courses at some British universities in the 1960s and 1970s were encouraged to learn a new (often exotic) language and to keep a diary of their learning experience. **Questionnaires** were used also, both formal ones and informal prompting ones of the type that Pickett (1978) devised. He wrote to 30 successful FL learners, inviting them to write 2,000 to 8,000 words in the form of 'an impressionistic ramble' addressing a range of topics related to their FL learning: their preferred learning styles, their perception of difficulty and its sources, the roles of teachers, tapes, texts, tests – in fact any matter of potential relevance.

A second sort of introspection, loosely defined, is exploited in the language judgement tests of the sort described by Greenbaum and Quirk (1970). These were an attempt to refine, formalize and operationalize the procedures used by generative grammarians for consulting their **intuitions** as to the well-formedness of some sentences that they had thought up as a test-case of their latest theory. The judgement tests constitute a class distinct from performance tests in the Greenbaum and Quirk system. Judgements are of three kinds: they may involve **evaluation** (it is or is not 'good'), **preference** (x is better than y), and **similarity** perception (z is more like x than y).

What characterizes such techniques is that they address pre-identified problem areas. Therefore, they are of the targeted elicitation type. In this respect they resemble the techniques for linguistic fieldwork described by Samarin (1967). More important for us, however, is the role they can play in EA, a role identified and exploited by Kellerman under the rubric of **lateralization**. This label is informative, suggesting that once a TL problem area is identified in learner error, the analyst indulges – and invites the learners who produced that error to indulge – in some 'lateral thinking', exploring as many facets of the problem from as many angles as possible. In fact, the learners are being asked to try to

explain why they decided to produce form *x and not alternative forms y or z. So, for example, a learner's error is identified, say *Arrived at Dover, the first thing I saw was. . . .* The first step is for the analyst to construct analogous examples, in order to see if the rule misapplication is specific to this one situation (a **nonce** error) or is systematic and recurrent for this learner. The question is resolved by finding out whether the learner accepts analogues like *Sat down, I asked for a drink* or *Eaten the sandwich, the waiter brought me another.* Readers might care to consider how they would lateralize an error from Portuguese learners who wrote: *Portugal is not a so developed country.* Would the learners be prepared to substitute *such* and *that* for *so*? And what movements of *so* would they be prepared to accept? How would we take account of the learners' MT, Portuguese?

The form of introspection on the part of FL learners that is now most widely practised in FL learning research is the **protocol**, which is a usually oral report rendered by the learner. The use of protocols to investigate FL learners' strategies of learning is discussed at length in Cohen (forthcoming). There are three types of report. First, a **self-report**, which is a collection of generalizations about oneself as a learner, such as '*I am prepared to make guesses at meanings*' or '*I learn FL vocabulary from lists of target words and their translations in my MT*'. Pickett (1978) based his research on self-report, delivered in writing. The second sort of report is **self-revelation**, which involves spontaneous 'stream-of-consciousness' disclosure strongly reminiscent of psychoanalysis. This is difficult for most learners to do, since it involves them in carrying out at least two and possibly three activities simultaneously: doing the learning; observing that learning; and formulating commentary on that learning. There is also the problem of which language (L1 or TL) the commentary is to be in.

The third sort of protocol, **self-observation**, lies somewhere between the other two. Unlike self-report, which elicits generalizations, self-observation involves a specific learning task. Unlike self-revelation, which runs in tandem with the learning task under investigation, self-observation allows a time lag between task completion and articulation, time to collect one's thoughts, but not time enough to resort to plausible but fabricated *post hoc* rationalizations of one's learning behaviour. The whole methodology of protocol elicitation raises the question of the relationship between foreign language **learning** which is done consciously, and second language **acquisition**, which is largely unconscious. The specific question is: is learning more accessible to introspection than acquisition by virtue of the different levels of consciousness operative at the time they were effected? Or, once assimilated in the mind, does the distinction, and therefore also their accessibility to introspection, evaporate? For some discussion of this, see James (1991a)

So, our errors are in the bag and we can start to do EA. First though, we shall consider two more essential matters. In Chapter 2 we shall consider the **scope** of EA, and in Chapter 3 we shall get our definitions agreed, so as to be sure that when we talk about errors and related language phenomena, we shall not be talking from different perspectives.

2

The Scope of Error Analysis

We've allowed so many standards to slip. . . . Teachers weren't
bothering to teach kids to spell and to punctuate properly. . . . If
you allow standards to slip to the stage where good English is no
better than bad English, where people turn up filthy . . . at school.
. . . All those things tend to cause people to have no standards at
all, and once you lose standards then there's no imperative to stay
out of crime.

(Lord Tebbitt, former Conservative MP Mr Norman Tebbitt,
BBC Radio 4, November 1985)

The purpose of this chapter is to dispel any remaining miscon-
ceptions about EA being a narrow academic pursuit. This is far
from the truth, and the scope of EA is wide and widening. EA is
of relevance to a good many important and vexatious issues. These
fall into two categories: first, those relevant to native speakers of
English, whom Kachru (1985) calls the 'Inner Circle' speakers of
English and who are estimated to number between 350 and 450
million. Issues concerning these include: the perennial debate
about 'good English' and the purported decline in standards of
correctness; social elitism and linguistically sanctioned power assignment in society; a wide range of concerns touching on aspects
of language education and training, ranging from the teaching of
basic literacy to the training of touch-typists. The second group
of issues are those which concern people who speak English as
a second language (EL2) (either as a second or as a foreign language) who probably outnumber the native speakers by two to
one: there are around 800 million in this category. The questions
that exercise this group include: whether there are limits to the
degree of perfection or 'nativeness' that a learner can or ought to
try to achieve in EL2; and the status we should accord to those

(now institutionalized) overseas varieties of English – now called the 'new Englishes' – that have developed throughout the world. Finally, we shall consider a third area of miscellaneous concerns impinging on error beyond language learning, broadening the notion of error as it applies to doing activities as remote as sport or mathematics.

Good English for the English

Throughout the 1980s there was public concern in Britain about purported declining standards of literacy – and oracy. Teachers and liberal 'leftist' local educational committees were blamed, occasionally with an irrational fervour close to that of Lord Tebbitt's. These outbursts were overtures to a review of the National Curriculum, the commissioning of the *Kingman Report* (1988) and the *Cox Report* (1989) ostensibly to make objective and authoritative recommendations on how to put matters right in English mother-tongue teaching. These reports were subsequently rejected by the British government for being insufficiently radical: they failed to advocate a full-scale return to the educational basics of the 'three Rs' (reading, [w]riting and [a]rithmetic). The applied and educational linguistics community was outraged and alienated by the British government's refusal to listen to expert advice and its unwillingness to temper its obvious determination to put spelling and punctuation – the basic mechanics of written English – at the head of the English curriculum. Fortunately, some linguists' opinions appeared in print, both during and after the heated public debate, and it is possible to distil from these statements their informed stance to the issue of error. For error is what the debate was (and still is) about; it is about children not conforming to 'standards' and therefore committing errors. Andersson and Trudgill make this link clear: the argument is 'between different types of error – different types of "bad language"' (1990: 173).

   Concern about low-grade English (or other languages) does not have to be as petulant as Lord Tebbitt's, and the causal link he sees between punctuation and delinquency is tenuous at the very least. Nonetheless, everybody wonders at times about the correctness of some item of language, and this is a natural and legitimate thing to do. It testifies to people's language awareness. I have before me today's *Borneo Bulletin* (5 December 1994), which carries the headline: '*Yearend rush at airport*', and I cannot help wondering about the correctness of the first word. It seems 'odd' to use as neutral an epithet as possible. Innumerable English-medium newspapers and magazines throughout the world have a 'Watch your language' column, such as that written by James Nation in the weekly *Asia Magazine*. Over a period of six weeks in 1994 he addressed issues including: verbless sentences in advertizing language; pleonastic combinations such as *free gift, end user, new innovation*; confusibles like *orientate* and *orient*; using nouns as verbs, as in *He revenged himself*, where the noun has indeed been 'verbed', the standard verb '*avenged*' seemingly avoided, and so on.

It is important to emphasize that such columnists do not sit in offices inventing these linguistic bones of contention and fomenting public unrest over disputed usage. It would be unreasonable to suggest that the 'demand' is artificially created. There is no backstreet industry turning out shibboleths by the score, to be circulated among the usage columnists. Nor is it just a handful of eccentrics who become alarmed about language. Presumably, publishers of magazines know that there is sufficient interest in language correctness to justify dedicating a column to it. Minority interests tend not to get media coverage, which suggests that these are not minority concerns. These editors are responding to public concern, one might say providing a 'customer service'. The point I wish to make here is that there is a demand from the public for error analysts to consult on disputed matters of usage. Further evidence for this market is the steady stream of books that are published on purported language decline and how it might be arrested. I mean books about the shibboleths, about what should be seen as 'right' and 'wrong' in English. They are a part of the infrastructure of EA inasmuch as they are concerned with the evaluation of language. Fowler's *The King's English* (1906) was an early and august example of a campaign to de-Americanize British English, Americanisms being 'foreign words and should be so treated'. A recent addition to this library is Godfrey Howard, *The Good English Guide* (1992). I assume Howard not to be a professional – at least not an 'academic' – linguist, but more of a publicist, a fact which gives his ideas more than academic interest. He reviews his own book in a short paper published in *The Author* (Howard, 1993), revealing, for example, that he received 'conflicting advice from a panel of writers, editors, broadcasters and other consultants' (1993: 97). None of these appear to have been linguists.

It is obvious that Howard is seeking to define and purify *written* English. Milroy and Milroy see some justification for this stalwart defence of writing on the grounds that 'written language . . . has to be more careful and precise than spoken' (1985: 43). Howard takes his criteria for passing linguistic judgement from 'a balance between conventional wisdom and a response to the way established *writers* use the language' (1993: 97, my emphasis). About the 'set-piece grammatical chestnut . . . "*for my husband and I*"' he admits that 'We hear this occasionally even *in the best literary circles*' (1993: 98, my emphasis). One wonders whether he has talking books in mind! 'Sloppy and slipshod' though it may be, it is already 'the Queen's English' he claims, since 'Her Majesty has been heard to say it' (ibid.). You won't see a more literal definition of 'The Queen's English' than this one. But notice how his professed defence of written standard has subtly been extended to speech.

Howard claims that when we evaluate language, we need to distinguish between 'expressions that are taking root' and 'easy-come-easy-go words'. The latter do not pose a serious threat to the language, being ephemeral passing fancies: slang is a case in point. The former category is to be taken more seriously and treated more radically. The problem with exercising this distinction is that we have no way of knowing in advance to which category any particular innovation belongs. Should we wait until a form has entered the language before purging it? Or should we 'gate keep' to make sure that undesirable forms are kept out? Would this be prejudicial? For example, it is apparent that Progressive *-ing* forms have become normal in English, continuing a trend that began in Early Modern English (Quirk *et al.*, 1985: 202). Potter (1975: 118–22) illustrates the growing tendency for stative verbs to occur combined with the progressive, yielding forms like the following from a satisfied choirmaster: *At last it's sounding good: I'm liking what I'm hearing.* Today even present progressive passives are common: *My father has been being treated for gallstones.* Can turning a blind eye to a passing fancy bring about radical grammatical shifts in English of this nature? The issue is related to the pedagogic option of whether to allow the learner to make mistakes, which we then correct, or to prevent them from occurring in the first place.

We see here a harmless, even if dilettante, inquisitiveness about usage. This can very quickly be transformed, however, into what Milroy and Milroy (1985: 30–8) call the **complaints tradition**. They suggest that it manifests itself in two forms: **Type 1 complaints**, which date back at least to Swift (1712), are concerned with up-holding standards of correctness and with discouraging speakers' misuse of specific systems of English. Such complaints are 'ded-icated to the maintenance of the norms of standard English in preference to other varieties' (Milroy and Milroy, 1985: 38). They are targeted at a few stigmatized nonstandard forms. These are the shibboleths I have mentioned. In fact, a major function of English lessons taught by purist language teachers has been to articulate a small set of **proscriptions**, that is, usages (or 'abusages') to be avoided. What is particularly irksome about these proscrip-tions is their negativity: a Baedecker of places to avoid, as someone once described them. Their aim is to root out linguistic usage that stigmatizes those who use it, like split infinitives, sentence-final prepositions, double negatives, dangling participles, stranded pre-positions and two score of the same order. Most of these shibboleths are written forms, but latterly spoken ones have been added: [h]-dropping of course, then glottal stopping, *runnin'* for *running*. The author, who went to school in the English Midlands, remembers clearly an incident in an English lesson in his first term at gram-mar school, when he was aged eleven. The teacher was Miss Jones (MJ) and CJ was caught eating the remains of a sandwich in class:

MJ: What are you eating, James?
CJ: [mi bred ǝn bʊtǝ] Miss.
MJ: [bʊtǝ].... [bʊtǝ]? Do you always say [bʊtǝ] James?
CJ: No: [djʊst sʊmtaimz] Miss.

Most professional 'structural' linguists would have seen Miss Jones as an enemy of the people and defended CJ to the death. They disapproved strongly of Type 1 complaints, arguing for the equal-ity of all languages and dialects. They have therefore given the impression that they condone 'bad' language.

Here we shall concentrate on Type 1 complaints, but first let us briefly consider the other sort, what the Milroys (1985) call **Type 2 complaints**. These are seen positively by the linguists, who tend to endorse them. They suggest calling them 'moralistic', since they typically 'recommend clarity in writing and attack what appear to be abuses of language that may mislead and confuse the public' (1985: 38). The concern now is with 'clarity, effectiveness, moral-ity and honesty in the public use of the standard language' (ibid.). George Orwell was one non-linguist dedicated to this 'consumer protection' type of language vigilance. More recently, Bolinger's *Language: The Loaded Weapon* (1980) continued this tradition, but he was for a long time a minority voice. Others have issued appeals for linguists to do their public duty by invigilating the manipulative use of language. Philip Howard laments that 'the academics of English faculties have mostly retreated to their private fortress of Structuralism' (1984: xi) (which must include the linguists' edifice of Chomskian theory). One presumes that Andersson and Trudgill were responding directly to this exhortation when they resolved, with their book *Bad Language* (1990) to come down from their ivory tower to answer 'questions not normally considered in university linguistics programmes . . . [because] . . . the questions are either too hard or too trivial . . . [and] . . . unamenable to linguistic research' (Andersson and Trudgill, 1990: 6). Greenbaum (1988) took a similarly positive line, when he conceded that linguists have a social responsibility which they have neglected for too long. 'Grammarians have a responsibility, not yet generally acknowledged, to address students and the general public on such matters as linguistic etiquette' (Greenbaum, 1988: 35). Greenbaum pinpoints certain areas for linguists to address. These fall into the category of Type 2 complaints: 'condemn writing that is imprecise or unclear' and expose 'deception through euphemism, obfuscation, or grammatical manipulation . . . racist, sexist or other types of bias or stereotyping' (ibid.: 36). This sort of action is referred to by Philip Howard (1984: 35) and again by Cameron (1994: 19) as a commitment to **verbal hygiene**. It involves 'regulating language, cleaning it up, improving it' and attending to a range of practical language-based activities such as: 'campaigning for the use of plain language', 'advocating spelling reform, dialect preservation or artificial languages', 'editing prose in conformity with house style', 'producing guidelines on politically correct language', and 'regulating the use of swear words in the media'. All these share a vital feature: 'They are linked . . . by a very strong concern with value. Verbal hygiene comes into being when people reflect on language in a critical, in the sense of evaluative, way' (Cameron, ibid.: 19).

We have referred to two approaches to the evaluation of language done on behalf of native speakers. First, we considered the negatively valued Type 1 complaints tradition that focuses on a few dozen shibboleths, which can find expression as a harmless social activity no more insidious than a parlour game or a topic for phatic communion, but can be abused as a way of stigmatizing the disadvantaged or outsider. Then there are the more serious Type 2 complaints connected with protecting ourselves (and those unable to protect themselves) from jargon, media language and advertizers' deceit. But are these two types of complaint really so different? The bank interest rate notice below suggests not. Type 1 complaints consist in detecting error that is due to ignorance and testifies to a failed education or plain carelessness, while Type 2 complaints involve exposing the deliberate manipulation of language by those who are not ignorant, but just the opposite – too clever by half. Yet the two traditions have a great deal in common and cannot be easily separated. Both are committed to protecting those who cannot protect themselves: the proscriptivists' admonitions, if heeded, would protect the less well-educated from being devalued in society on the sole evidence of their language. The hygienists likewise seek to protect the vulnerable from linguistic exploitation by the unscrupulous. Not only are their aims similar, but their logic is also. The proscriptivist appeals to logic when condemning double negatives: *I haven't got none* must imply you have some in the same way as the hygienist points to the illogicality of *Persil washes whiter* or the illegitimacy of measuring size by the criterion of pleasure when advertizing new *fun-size Chokko bars*. Both groups are engaged in analysing language use and deciding on its acceptability. These decisions assume the existence and acceptance of criteria for deciding whether a piece of language is right or wrong, and the degree of its rightness or wrongness.

While conceding the usefulness of distinguishing these two types of complaint about language use, we should be aware that the distinction is not always clear-cut in practice. When we look closely we sometimes discover that not all Type 1 complaints are necessarily pedantic, and that there does not have to be a demonstrable wish to deceive through linguistic manipulation for misunderstanding to have potentially serious consequences. A real-life example will make this clear. In June 1994 at least one branch of a major British bank, located not 200 metres from a British university, displayed the notice:

*It's 1969 since mortgage rates were as low as they are today.

The educated non-linguist who spotted this strange form was prepared to admit that the meaning was 'more or less clear', and was able to formulate three possible grammatical reconstructions of the notice, namely:

(a) √*It was 1969 when interest rates were last as low as they are today.*
(b) √*It is 25 years since mortgage rates were as low as they are today.*
(c) √*Mortgage rates have not been as low as they are today since 1969.*

The point is, if it is not only possible, but also necessary, to associate three paraphrases with the notice, then the notice is either triply ambiguous or simply imprecise. The public can only guess at the intended precise meaning. There is no suggestion that there was a deliberate intent to mislead the public: it is not a Type 2 complaint therefore. An alternative and rather disturbing explanation is that the author of this notice simply had no precise idea in mind – just a fuzzy one. In that case what should our reaction be? Do we object, insisting that all ideas worth communicating should be formulated with precision, if the precision is linguistically viable and the idea not too complex to admit precision? Or do we admit that there are times when precision just isn't necessary, and when we can therefore afford to be fuzzy? If you choose the second option, the next question you will have to answer is whether a bank's campaign to advertize one of its most crucial achievements (low interest rates) is a suitably relaxed occasion for fuzziness. This relates to a point Howard makes: that 'standard English' should not be spelt with a capital 's' 'because there are a number of overlapping standards' (Howard, 1993: 97), and certainly we ought not to invoke a criterion of precision when discussing casual social interaction, say. This, however, is not such an occasion.

When one objector [not the author] complained to the bank in question, it was pointed out to him that nobody else had objected (though no research has been done to establish the truth of this claim), and that the notice was therefore 'acceptable'. He counterargued that if 'acceptable' is defined without reference to a criterion, then it must be a subjective concept. Since the formulation in question is not acceptable to him, and his subjective view counts, then it is not acceptable, especially if a paraphrase can be found (three have been) which is acceptable to him without being unacceptable to anyone else. More importantly, he felt, as a scientist, that it was not only convention that had been violated by this formulation but **truth**. Option (a) indicates a **point** in time, while paraphrases (b) and (c) indicate time **duration**. While linguists show interest in these notions when they describe the Tense and Aspect systems of languages, scientists in other fields recognize the practical real-world importance of the point versus duration of time distinction. For example, in his book *Time, Discounting and Value* (1993) the economist Colin Price points out that some of the reasons for discounting are to do with lapse of time (duration), but are applied in the banking system as though they were relevant to particular points of time in history: this is, in his view, a fundamental misconception and it confuses an important distinction. It is therefore ironic but consistent that the bank notice fudges this distinction too.

When John Honey published his book, *The Language Trap* (1983), he took the linguists to task for their commitment to impartial descriptivism and what he saw as their abdication of their public duty to draw a clear line between 'good' and 'bad' (standard and nonstandard) English. Descriptive linguists like R. Hall, in his *Leave Your Language Alone!* (1950), had tried to convince us of the illegitimacy of such complaints and the speciousness of these distinctions, showing them to be ill-founded in etymology, pedantry and preciosity. Linguists, so it seemed to Honey, believed too literally that all languages and dialects are 'equal', and they were wrong to adduce from this that a child's nonstandard 'home' dialect ought not to be standardized out of existence: perhaps it should be nurtured as a precious linguistic object, as another 'endangered species'. It is understandable that linguists should lament language death. Perhaps Honey had misread the linguists, or they really had failed to make it clear that they were talking about the **systemic** equivalence of all languages and dialects, not their **social** equivalence, which is a totally different matter. It is an objectively verifiable fact that any society – whatever the reasons are – usually favours one dialect to represent the 'best' face of its language (hereby elevating it to the 'standard') and through this discrimination stigmatizes all the others. Some have even argued that standard dialects are inherently better than nonstandard ones. Leith (1983: 32), as quoted by Milroy and Milroy (1985: 25), claimed that a standard dialect is one having the minimum of variation in form with the greatest possible range of functions. This, if true, does make the standard 'better' than nonstandards, in terms of efficiency and cost-effectiveness. But we must not confuse cause with effect. It is not the case that the candidate for standard status gets selected because it is the least variable and so the most efficient of all the contenders. Rather, it is as a result of it having been selected as the standard – for other, non-linguistic power-dynamic reasons – that it becomes the least variable and most efficient. Efficiency is not an inherent quality of any dialect but might follow on from its standardization.

The question is: what to teach native-speaking children in our schools? Should we encourage people to pursue the class struggle and argue that the standard was not selected objectively and 'fairly', and therefore we do not owe it any allegiance? In that case, which dialects should be elevated to the standard? It seems that any choice would be as arbitrary as the choice that has been made, since it would be impossible to motivate the preference for any one available dialect on grounds of inherent superiority, measured in terms of efficiency, beauty, or equality. After all, as the linguists maintain, all dialects are *linguistically* pretty much on a par.

We must first define linguistic norms and standards. A **norm** is defined by Milroy as 'What is agreed on by speakers in the community concerned' (1992: 7). It is therefore a democratic notion. First, in being egalitarian: all communities, whatever their status, prestigious or not, have their right to a norm. Nonstandard dialects also have their norms. Anyone trying to infiltrate a modern city street-gang would be well-advised, before doing so, to learn its linguistic norms to perfection! The second sense in which norming is democratic is that it is consensual: everyone has their say. The question that arises is: how do these speakers reach their consensus? What makes them agree? All kinds of social, affective and power-related forces operating at an unconscious level will determine which sets of forms they select to constitute their norm, especially the in-group 'local' and nonstandard norm. There are limits to the democracy though, in that it will be the subgroup within the community that is recognized as the elite whose language will determine the norm. Norms are everywhere consensual endorsements of elitism.

There is the 'official' or national norm. This is the norm that reflects the language of the elite holding power at national level: one might call it the 'power norm', but the label we use is the **standard**. It is the standard (norm) that the 'Mind your Language!' columnists and the style manuals answer questions about – questions put by puzzled and sometimes insecure aspirants to that norm. Posing and answering these questions is a way of codifying and defining this standard norm, an informal (yet at least democratic) way of doing through the media what other language communities do through the more authoritarian agency of a Language Academy. The institutional and formal agency for formulating and transmitting the national norm (standard) is the school. The National Curriculum and the back-to-basics prescriptivists see it as their duty to transmit standard English through the school, while those unwilling to accept such regulation see these efforts as an unwarranted centralist imposition of an arbitrary standard.

At its most radical, the question is: should there be a pedagogic norm of native-speaker (NS) English?, bearing in mind that: 'A pedagogic norm refers to the model that the students are to be taught, and to the particular variety of English that will provide a proficiency scale against which their performance can be measured' (Andreasson, 1994: 398). Or should children use in school whatever forms of language come naturally? This would be tantamount to abandoning the institution we call school. It would also be contrary to the concept of language education, because, as Andreasson (1994) argues, norm is central to linguistic form since without norms, language – being based on a set of arbitrary conventions – would break down.

Howard (1984: 8) sees three educational alternatives: (i) the elimination of the nonstandard 'home' language; (ii) its approval and reinforcement (and possible expansion) in school; and (iii) the stylistic and functional differentiation of home and school languages. This last approach would encourage **bidialectism**, a facility in switching from home to school dialect according to the setting. The *Cox Report* (1989: Para 4.32) initially recommended the third of these options, expressing this in five recommendations for teaching standard English (SE):

1. Respect for the pupil's home language.
2. Teaching SE for wider communication inside school.
3. Teaching SE for wider communication outside school.
4. Teaching the relation of SE to the literary heritage.
5. Teaching the relationship of SE to cultural power.

The National Curriculum solution was opposed by Rosen (1991) on the grounds that it implied something quite unacceptable to him, that 'all pupils must be taught to *speak* Standard English' (Rosen, 1991: 104). While the idea of every child learning to *write* SE is uncontroversial, not so the suggestion that they should also be made to *speak* it. This centralist imposition of uniformity Rosen brands the 'nationalization' of English, a policy to which the then Conservative government was obdurately opposed in the industrial sector, but one that it seemed to call for in the educational domain in particular.

I can see no point to Rosen's particular objection to the idea that at school – the institution dedicated to the transmission of the standard norm – children should be required to speak (as well as write) standard English. They will be free to use either the standard or their nonstandard dialect on the playground, but in the formal class setting should normally speak standard English. Their English will be less standard as the learning situation becomes less formal: in small group-work, for example, they will gravitate to a less standard style. It is a different matter when **accent** enters the picture, and possibly Rosen had this in mind. There is no justification whatsoever for requiring children to speak the standard elite accent we call RP (received pronunciation) unless that is the accent they have brought from home anyway, in which case it would be equally absurd to discourage its use in school.

We have begun to look at combinations of language options. A clear statement on the issue is Andersson and Trudgill, *Bad Language* (1990). They frame their statement in terms of four aspects of language variability: **style** (on a scale formal > neutral > informal); **accent** (high- or low-prestige); **register** (technical versus non-technical); and **dialect** (standard versus nonstandard), and say:

> It is important to appreciate the logical independence of dialect, accent, register and style. It *is* possible to speak Standard English with a Liverpool accent. It *is* possible to swear and use slang while speaking Standard English. *All* dialects are capable of being spoken in a whole range of formal and informal styles. There is *no* need to be a Standard English-speaker in order to acquire extensive technical vocabulary.   (Andersson and Trudgill, 1990: 172)

Note the combination that is conspicuously absent here: speaking nonstandard English in an RP accent. It does occur, but doing it is to invite ridicule, springing from the contradiction between these two coinciding: people privileged with RP must have received a standard English upbringing.

Andersson and Trudgill's is a statement of what is feasible, where we define feasibility in terms of what is tolerated. This is not a structural but a social matter, and lies at the very heart of the 'correctness' debate. People 'in power' tend to make value judgements about people 'out of power' (and vice versa also) on the basis of their language. Not long ago you would have had difficulty getting employed as a BBC reporter or an English teacher if you spoke with a regional accent. Your life would also – let's not forget this – have been made miserable if you were a standard English and RP-speaking bricklayer. It was people like Wilfred Pickles and J.B. Priestley who broke that ban, and broadcasted in their Northern England accents. Nowadays people with pronouncedly (!) regional accents even get appointed to teach English overseas. The bricklayers have not yet made a comparable breakthrough.

Rosen goes on to claim with authority that what he calls 'the additive principle' is flawed: one cannot 'bolt on' a second SE dialect and expect the home dialect to be unaffected. If one tries, then children will both lose confidence in their home dialect and lose respect for themselves, he suggests. I suggest that this is another manifestation of the British monolingual bias, a set of assumptions that reflect the experience – and colour the judgements – of people for whom monolingualism is the norm. In this context, let us call it the **monodialectal bias**. In the 1960s and 1970s there was a successful language education programme launched in the USA intended to help American Blacks and Hispanics (speakers of nonstandard American English dialects) to 'bolt on' a second, standard dialect to be used in appropriate settings. This programme was given the constructive label of **dialect expansion** to reflect the idea that in pursuing its goals, one added to one's repertoire of dialects and at the same time enlarged one's command of the dialects one spoke.

That first and second dialects can be successfully separated between 'home' and 'school' settings and between the spoken and written media is reasonably certain. There is recent research evidence (Williamson, 1990, 1995) that children's errors in their written English are not caused by interference from their spoken home dialects but by inadequate teaching of the writing conventions. Williamson analysed the written errors of two groups of Tyneside children, aged 11 and 16, speakers of the Geordie dialect. Of these errors 80 per cent were found to be attributable to ignorance of spelling, punctuation and other writing conventions. Only 6 per cent could be traced back to their home dialect, for example: *me and my brother as a sentence subject, He got the job *easy (adjective confused with adverb), and the first nine mile* (no plural marker). This was a small-scale study and one should not rush to global conclusions. At least it casts serious doubt on the claim made by Bloomfield that 'mistakes in language are simply dialect forms carried into the standard language' (1935: 50). Williamson's conclusion is: 'The problem for these children, and for their teachers, lies in the difficulty of mastering the writing system, not in dialect variation' (1990: 260).

We have spoken of the role of the school in a way that might give the wrong impression that the problems of semi-literacy get solved by the time English-speaking children leave school. They do not, and Wray (1996) reveals disturbingly low levels of achievement (high levels of error) even among British undergraduates, who have failed to master the genitive apostrophe, basic spelling rules and word-breaks. Their incompetence in written syntax, cohesion and coherence is even more alarming, but little researched and underdocumented.

An English curriculum should insist that all **functional** writing (formal or not, no matter how non-technical) should be in standard English. I cannot conceive of a use outside fiction for writing in the nonstandard dialect. One might, as an exercise in awareness-raising (James and Garrett, 1991), do some experimental writing that attempts to represent nonstandard dialect and local accent, and some people might want to present local dialect and accent poetry at the regional arts or folklore festival. There is much to recommend such an eisteddfod-like activity: it has, after all, contributed to the survival of the Welsh language. However, standard English literacy will be the institutional and national norm.

As for unscripted or impromptu speaking, there should be more scope for using a range of repertoires. In the playgrounds of the majority of day-schools – outside those 'leafy suburban' middle-class catchment areas – the nonstandard dialect and the local accent will be used, and children coming from homes where only SE and RP are used will have an opportunity to acquire the local nonstandard norms, and so to integrate socially. Inside school the child will encounter a wide range of situations and genres and will have to learn to select the appropriate dialect and accent mix to suit the formality and technicality of the speech situation. As Rosen (1991: 109) points out, it is not a matter of simply code-switching between the 'on' and 'off' options of two accents and dialects, but of code-sliding along a continuum of language optionality. Compare this with Howard's observation that 'standard' should not be written with a capital 's' 'because there are a number of overlapping standards (1993: 97). Learning to code-slide and select the standard appropriate for a given situation is a formidable task. It is conceivably a task compared with which the acquisition of a generative syntax of their language is child's play.

Lessons should be conducted in SE dialect because school is a preparation for life beyond one's origins, the first step in a process that is going to take the individual on to further or higher education and/or employment, usually involving a move away from home, to mix in subsequent settings with people from other areas. Some, of course, may do neither, and will not experience mobility. Such an eventuality is not predictable for each individual, however, and so should not be taken as the default or normal course of events. It is safer to err on the side of over-providing for the child with a range of linguistic resources rather than the opposite. The spoken discourse in school ought to draw on the local accent, which will be prestigious for as long as it is used here, just as RP will be non-prestigious here from the lips of 'locals'. Those parts of lessons where the whole class is involved, where speech is addressed to the group and the teacher, are more formal, and will draw less on local dialect and accent than small group-work interactions. The label for such adaptive language use is **speech accommodation** (Giles, 1979; James, 1993), and it is an apt label since it conjures up the image of the child developing a capacity to get along with others (and they reciprocally with him or her) with a minimum of friction. Where the child fails to make these accommodations successfully, we have errors to mark the failures: EA will be needed continually.

Good English for the FL/SL learner

I am here using the terms 'FL/SL' to contrast with 'L1', the term used to describe native speakers of English. The now broadly accepted division of non-L1 speakers of English into SL and FL speakers is clearly set out in Christophersen (1973), but a more recent framework for describing the different statuses of English in the world is that of Kachru (1985). He distinguishes three sorts of English:

(i) English of the **Inner Circle**: British, American, Canadian, Australian, and New Zealand. These are the older Englishes, usually equated with native-speaker English, and are the original norm-providers for those learning English as an L2.

(ii) English of the **Outer Circle**, including Ghanaian, Indian, Zambian, Philippino, Malaysian Englishes, and many more such 'colonial' varieties. These are 'nativized' Englishes, having official standing in those countries and coexisting alongside at least one other language spoken by its normally bilingual speakers. Norms here used to be based on Inner Circle English, but there is now a tendency for norms to be developed internally: **exonormative** standards are being challenged by **endonormative** ones.

(iii) **Expanding Circle** Englishes, as taught and spoken in countries such as China, Japan, Russia, Brazil – countries with no colonial links to the Inner Circle. Here there are no local norms developing, and the norms are derived from the Inner Circle.

There are problems surrounding the selection of norms in the Outer and Expanding Circles. In the Outer Circle the question is: which of the alternative Inner Circle standard varieties to take as the norm? The choice used to be between just the British and the American varieties: Malaysia took the former, the Philippines the latter, for different historical reasons in each case. Now the choice is getting wider, and South-East Asian countries are faced with an easily justified third choice – Australian English. In some locations, Indian English, not an Inner Circle variety at all but an Outer Circle variety, is becoming a *de facto* but unplanned norm by virtue of the large numbers of Indian teachers being recruited into the schools. One once-valid justification for limiting norms to those of the Inner Circle used to be that only Inner Circle speakers are native speakers of the language. This is no longer true, there being hundreds of thousands of Outer Circle speakers of English for whom English is at least one of their native languages. There are even Outer Circle monolingual native speakers of English today, though their numbers are smaller.

The crux of the problem is that English, in SL settings, has two conflicting roles. It must serve, on the one hand, as a language for international communication and, on the other hand, especially where there is a potentially divisive multiplicity of local languages, as a *lingua franca* and local agent and marker of national identity. Now, to serve as a vehicle for transnational communication on the global business scene, the SL (and FL) English must remain intelligible to outsiders (including the Inner Circle speakers). It must conform to World Standard English (WSE) norms. On the other hand, SL speakers in the Outer Circle (unlike FL learners in the Expanding Circle) wish to have an English that is their very own, and which is distinct from other varieties. When that happens, we have the emergence of a '**New English**' (Platt *et al.*, 1984). So, Singaporean English is a unifying symbol of Singaporean nationality, yet at the same time must remain efficient as a vehicle for international commerce. These two roles are often inimical, since the price you normally pay for making your language a convertible common currency is that it must shed its more private and therefore opaque local idiosyncrasies: it must conform to the norms of a World Standard English. When this conformity is neglected, there is code-conflict and miscommunication, as in the following brief exchange between A (a Singaporean) and B (an Australian), both living in Brunei:

> A: Yes, we're going to Labuan for Christmas.
> B: Oh. Where are you staying? (The intended *future* time reference being 'when in Labuan, temporarily – which hotel?')
> A: Jalan Gadong, Mile 2. (Interpreting the enquiry as one about his *permanent* residence in Brunei, and confusing the verbs *stay* and *reside*)

One solution to this kind of miscommunication would be for the Australian and the Singaporean to learn one another's dialects of English, at least receptively, if not for production. I believe that this happens to some extent, spontaneously, where speakers of different varieties have protracted contacts. The natural urge to accommodate linguistically on such occasions will be accompanied by a tendency, driven by the forces of prestige, to converge towards the Inner Circle variety. For more systematic learning to occur, there would have to be descriptions of the 'standard' forms of each New English, and short 'Teach Yourself' pocket books produced for the tourist or businessperson, sold at airport bookshops alongside those little books claiming to teach (or revive) Spanish in a few hours. This would represent a departure from present practice.

An alternative suggestion follows the spoken *versus* written division. This alternative is certainly valid for native English, since, as Milroy and Milroy point out, 'non-standard English is almost by

definition spoken rather than written' (1985: 70). The implication
is that the New Englishes ought to be encouraged to diverge from
the Older Englishes in their *spoken* manifestations, but ought to
observe international norms of English as an International Language (EIL) when *written*.

> If English is to retain its value as an international language it is
> important that the norms of written English in countries where
> English is a second language do not diverge too far from those of
> the international written standard.   (Greenbaum, 1988: 38)

There are parallels to be drawn with the native-speaker issues discussed earlier in this chapter. First, the National Curriculum Council has insisted that the norms of speech and of writing should be
uniform, which implies that children should be required to write
and speak standard English, and to eschew nonstandard speech as
well as nonstandard writing. In other words, neither to write nor
speak dialect, not to speak in a local accent, but to speak RP.
Compare this with the suggestion from Platt, Weber and Ho Mian
Lian (1984: 163) that for the New Englishes the *written* standard
will be exonormative but the *spoken* standard endonormative.
Crewe, writing about the use of Singaporean 'dialect' of English,
expresses this position clearly:

> What I am suggesting is that the dialect should be restricted to
> informal usage (conversation, letters, dialogue in novels etc.) but
> that for formal written purposes where communication is para-
> mount the more neutral international standard should be adopted,
> which is the system prevailing in Britain and the U.S.A.
>   (Crewe, 1977: 6)

The big problem with the New Englishes, though, is that as *developing* varieties they have speakers who are also learners, and
learners have to have a standard to which to conform. If an internal standard is to serve this purpose, as Platt, Weber and Ho Mian
Lian suggest, it should be the usage of the educated group in that
community. Now, it will be usual for the variety spoken by this
educated elite to be normed itself on an Inner Circle model, and
often to be indistinguishable from that. All we have accomplished
is to replace an external with a home-grown elite.

But even when that group has been identified and its norms
described and codified, there still remains the *pedagogic* requirements, the wherewithal to teach this variety. Not just textbooks,

syllabuses, readers, tests, etc., but 'above all they need *systematicity*'. This Platt, Weber and Ho Mian Lian define as: 'a model to which they can refer, a model which tells them what to regard as a "learner's mistake" and what to consider as a legitimate feature of the educated variety of the new English' (1984: 167). Crewe expresses a similar view: 'The line demarcating institutionalised from random usage is often very unclear' (1977: 7). It is clear that this model will have to be based on an Error Analysis. But it will be more of a 'retro' EA in that the aim will be 'to show that a language feature is not an idiosyncratic learner's error but part of the language system of a New English' (Platt *et al.*, 1984: 167). Or, in Crewe's words: 'The greater frequency of error, the more institutionalised the usage' (1977: 7).

This willingness to recognize as legitimate and inviolate 'new' Englishes (or any other language), both institutionalized and individual or 'idiosyncratic' (Corder, 1971, 1981), is a feature of the Interlanguage ethos. Interlanguage (IL) (Selinker, 1972, 1992) is defined as a version of a foreign language spoken by its learners (rather than its native speakers). An IL is a natural human language in its own right and should be respected as such and described independently or *sui generis*. Therefore it is considered linguistic malpractice even to compare the learner's IL with the native's version in order to find the misfit – which is exactly what EA is all about, of course. According to one writer: 'This is judging the students by what they are *not* – native speakers. L2 learning research considers that learners should be judged by the standards appropriate to *them*, not by those used for natives' (Cook, 1991: 6). I just cannot accept this argument. First, it seems to be based on the misconception that we *do* judge learners by the same standards as we judge native speakers, whereas we have a natural tendency to judge nonnative speakers by less rigid standards. Moreover, an entity is always judged by a standard external and independent of that entity: there is no point in judging something against itself, since this would not constitute judgement. I might concede that when IL users are speaking among themselves, they are using an intimate local variety, the function of which is as much to signal solidarity as to communicate, and there would be no point in comparing this to, say, the British standard. After all, intimate local varieties of British English are usually nonstandard also. But when they write anything any more ambitious than a shopping list they should write in standard English, and especially so if they are writing for a readership beyond the locality. As the sources quoted above indicate, there seems to be widespread agreement that it is in the *written* medium that both native and second language users need to conform to a standard.

The IL idea is not new. It cropped up under the more colourful label 'The British Heresy' in a paper by Prator (first published in 1968 and reprinted in 1992), in which he criticizes the British ELT 'doctrine of establishing local models for TESL':

> In a nutshell, the heretical tenet I feel I must take exception to is the idea that it is best, in a country where English is not spoken natively but is widely used as the medium of instruction, to set up the local variety of English as the ultimate model to be imitated by those learning the language.   (Prator, 1992: 11)

He traces this heresy back to Halliday, McIntosh and Stevens (1964: 294ff.), a book commonly regarded as an early milestone in British applied linguistics. So why does he object? He gives several reasons. First, flying in the face of those who see ILs as 'dialects' of the TL, he claims that such learner varieties are *not* dialects of English, but represent 'an utterly dissimilar tongue'. Secondly, the solution will be only local, since there will evolve a number of competing local varieties, not one. Thirdly, there will be 'progressive' deviation from the EIL norm, so that the solution will not only be local but also short-lived. Fourthly, speakers of the different local ILs (Tanzanian and Ghanaian or Malaysian and Singaporean) will understand one another's IL less easily than they understand the EIL norm. As we have seen above in statements from Platt, Weber and Ho Mian Lian, and Crewe, if the local variety is to be nurtured or at the very least respected, it will have to be monitored, and that is what EA is there to do.

The 'heresy' gets resurrected intermittently, then put to rest for a few years. In fact, Kachru (1985) aligns himself with those whom Prator takes to task, arguing that the Outer Circle Englishes must be given their autonomy, and be exempt from futile attempts to secure their standardization. This must happen, even if the degree of de-Englishization and nativization of these New Englishes sets them far apart from the Old World variety from which they originated. As he concludes: 'I do not believe that the traditional notions of codification, standardization, models and methods apply to English any more' (Kachru, 1985: 29).

Quirk (1985) takes the opposite view, and to some is thereby seen as promoting a new British heresy, the obverse of that which Prator targeted. Quirk attacks those who see no further place for the concept of standard, and warns that this 'anti-standard ethos' will lead to a diaspora of English into several mutually incomprehensible languages, and English will go the way Latin went after the fall of the Roman Empire, resulting in the different Romance languages. He objects to the 'fashionably unfashionable elitism' of the academic linguists who suggest that any variety is as good or correct as any other. A World Standard English (WSE) or a 'single monochrome standard that looks as good on paper as it sounds in speech' (Quirk, 1985: 6) is achievable. In fact, some examples of this WSE already exist: the BBC World Service, All India Radio, *The Straits Times*, and *The Japan Times*. These are understood and respected world-wide; they are uniform; and they represent the English of minorities in their own countries – which is a characteristic of standards anywhere, including the Inner Circle.

While Kachru's argument is persuasive for the English as a second language (ESL) speaker, it would be foolish to extend it to the English as a foreign language (EFL) learner. I have no sympathy with the idea that one should set out to 'teach Brazilian English' in Brazil for instance, a proposition with which I was once confronted. Baxter (1980) broadens the issue for discussion in a Japanese EFL or Expanding Circle context. Japanese learners of English 'do not perceive themselves as being speakers of English' (Baxter, 1980: 56) – which, of course, they are not, but presumably are striving to become. For the time being, while they are learners, they speak English 'Japanesely'. We are told that there is not strong support for 'adopting Japanese English as the form to be taught in schools' (ibid.: 59), which is reassuring, since that will (unfortunately) be the form learnt, even when it is not taught, as every teacher can testify. The solution that Baxter suggests is Quirk's: to teach the Japanese to 'speak internationally' rather than to speak Japanesely or Americanly. A good solution, but the means he proposes for its attainment are dubious: send the teachers not to Britain or America but to ESL countries like Ghana or Sierra Leone. I believe that Japanese–Ghanaian reciprocal intelligibility would be enhanced, but that the Japanese students would subsequently still have trouble when meeting an Indian or a Jamaican. Had they gone to the UK, the USA or Australia, they would have been better prepared to understand a wide range of

ESL variants. The reason for this is that all these SL speakers of English are oriented towards a common norm, which we have called the **Inner Circle** Englishes.

Note the use of the term 'orientation', which is intentionally vague. Abbott (1991) sees the future of English in the world either as **fission**, the break-up of English into a number of mutually unintelligible variants, in the way that Latin broke up into the modern Romance language 'family', or as **fusion**, the survival of one monolithic and colourless English (possibly American). Neither prospect is appealing. Abbott proposes a compromise, the plausibility of which depends on drawing a distinction between a **model** and a **goal** for learners. Any ESL country should select (according to the historical, economic, cultural and geographic affinities available) one of the standard Englishes of the Inner Circle. Schools and other institutions should then adopt this model, without, however, seeing it as a goal that must be attained: it would be a pity if it were attained, but it will not, short of some miraculous leap forward in language teaching and learning techniques. Only a few individuals, like the proverbial eccentric Danish professor of English, might totally naturalize and achieve RP, and wear bowler hats and carry tightly rolled umbrellas – and become honorary Native Speakers for their pains.

The native speaker and the power dimension

We referred earlier to the utility of having 'natural' international norms for English (Crewe, 1977). Now one of the virtues of these international norms is their neutrality: it favours neither of two or more coexisting varieties, being no more aligned to Malaysian than Filipino English, say. Unfortunately, they are not neutral in relation to the Inner Circle Englishes such as British or American Englishes. Even more unfortunately, there is a long tradition, in FL teaching, applied and pure linguistics, of respect – bordering on reverence – for the native speaker (NS). This reverence for the NS is well documented and evaluated in Alan Davies's (1991b) book: in chapters 8 and 9 we see enumerated 12 defining characteristics of the NS, all positive. The reason for this reverence is the NSs' purported infallibility in their 'native' language, which rings circular however – they might be making up their own rules! For Mey (1981: 69) 'The Native Speaker is always right', like a king or pope. Similarly, 'We believe, as do most linguists, that native speakers do not make mistakes. Native speakers for the most part speak their native language perfectly' (Andersson and Trudgill, 1990: 111). By 'mistake' here they mean 'error', of course, a distinction we explore in Chapter 3. NSs obviously do make mistakes or slips. They are the subject of intense psycholinguistic research (Baars, 1992a), and the source of some humour, whether it be in the form of malapropisms in literature, or on television.

Mey goes on to suggest that there is a natural scale reflecting the NSs' authority: NSs are at their most authoritative on matters of phonology, less so on morphology, less still on syntax, and least on semantics. Moreover, this scale corresponds to a scale of the NSs' tolerance of linguistic deviance: they instinctively abhor phonological deviance, hate the morphological sort, merely dislike the syntactic, and can live with semantic deviance. This, as NSs' love of poetic licence and punning shows, is an amusing toy that can be played with. Phonetic waywardness, by contrast, is seen as a sign of helpless incompetence and just cause for derision.

Alongside this reverence for the NS we meet at times an irreverence towards the learner or nonnative speaker (NNS). The NNS is often the butt of humour, as is the case with the earnest but bungling 1930s immigrant to the USA desperate to learn English, the (anti?)-hero in Leo Rosten's hilarious (or is it?) *The Education of Hymen Kaplan* (1937). Here is an excerpt:

> One night Mrs. Moskowitz read a sentence from 'English for Beginners' in which 'the vast deserts of America' were referred to. Mr. Parkhill [Teacher] soon discovered that poor Mrs. Moskowitz did not know the meaning of 'vast'. 'Who can tell us the meaning of "vast"?' asked Mr. Parkhill lightly.
> Mr. Kaplan's hand shot up, volunteering wisdom. He was all proud grins.
> Mr. Parkhill, in the rashness of the moment, nodded to him.
> Mr. Kaplan rose, radiant with joy. '"Vast"! It's commink fromm *diraction.* Ve have four diractions: de naut, de sot, de heast, and de vast.'   (Rosten, 1937: 6–7)

Mr Kaplan has contemporary counterparts: the bullied Spanish waiter Manuel in the BBC TV comedy serial *Fawlty Towers* comes to mind.

Such intolerance of the linguistic limitations of NNSs and the associated celebration of the NS has come to be called **native speakerism**. It is an attitude on a par with sexism, racism, ageism and other such nefarious social malpractices, all of which invite the disapproval of the 'politically correct'. Native speakerism crops up in the most unexpected places. A leader in *The Times* (29 October 1992), entitled '*Exit, pursued by Nikon*', reprimands, on the grounds of its blatant native speakerism, the decision announced by the celebrated British actor Sir Alec Guiness never again to appear on the London stage because he can no longer tolerate the blank faces of the uncomprehending (largely Japanese) tourist audiences. The newspaper's leader writer reminds Sir Alec that foreign tourists packed the theatre in Ancient Greece in 423 BC when Aristophanes first staged *The Clouds*. Moreover, British audiences themselves flock to see performances on the London stage in languages they hardly know. So we Brits have no right to deny the same pleasure to our Japanese (and other) tourist guests. Nor is incomprehension unique to the foreigner: NSs can be uncomprehending too, as was shown a century ago in an elderly British lady theatregoer's loud reaction to Sarah Bernhardt's portrayal of Cleopatra. This theatregoer stood up and proclaimed: 'How different, how very different from the home life of our own dear Queen.'

In linguistics and FL teaching, native speakerism has been challenged on three fronts, perhaps too vigorously. The pendulum has swung fully to the other extreme now, however. Any reference, no matter how objective or constructive, to a defect in the learners' language is taken to be disparaging and is roundly condemned. First, the claim has been made that the NSs hold an excess of **power** over the NNSs by virtue of their native-speaker status. Nayar (1991) calls this the **ethoglossia** of the NSs, which he defines as 'the power of the NS as the controller of the language and the gatekeeper of the communication' (Nayar, 1991: 247). It is power won by virtue of the NSs' superiority in knowledge and command of the language. This power advantage must apply to the NSs of any language in an encounter with a learner. The second line of criticism of this NS-worship applies in cases where the power advantage derives rather from the superior status of the language, not of the speakers' superior command of it. It applies particularly to the NSs of *English*, and is a consequence of English being a world language. Phillipson (1992) sees the phenomenon in the broader context of '**linguistic imperialism**'. Gee (1990: 155) uses a concept close to 'imperialism' when he speaks of '**colonization**'. Intellectual and social colonization takes place whenever NNSs attempt to learn a FL. They are generally only partially successful in their learning, and in their efforts to speak the FL they 'keep signalling that others [the NSs] are their "betters" and become "complicit with their own subordination"' (Gee, ibid.). But, as observed above, we should note that when external norms are replaced by internal ones, it is just another, indigenous, elite that takes over from the colonial masters.

This view of NS status – native **speakerhood** – bestowing pure advantage should not go unchallenged, however. As Michael Howard points out in *The Lessons of History* (1991), NSs of English can be disadvantaged by the fact that English is a *lingua franca*. This may enable NNSs to understand the rest of the world – which includes each other and us – more clearly than the NSs understand them. Lord Jenkins, reviewing Howard's book in *The Observer* (31 March 1991), recalls his own impression of the French and German statesmen Giscard d'Estaing and Helmut Schmidt understanding one another better than they understood the NSs Mrs Thatcher or Mr Callaghan. The contrast between the **idiomatic** English of NSs and the **accurate** English of the foreigner, suggests Jenkins, 'constituted an opaque curtain between Britain and the rest of Europe'. It is the NNSs' mastery of accuracy but not of idiomaticity that Graham Greene had in mind when he wrote:

> The young man spoke excellent English; only a certain caution and precision marked him as a foreigner. It was as if he had come from an old-fashioned family, among whom it was important to speak clearly and use the correct words.
>
> (G. Greene, *The Ministry of Fear*. London: William Heinemann, 1973, p. 42)

And, had she not been describing 'looks' but 'sounds', Agatha Christie would have been paraphrasing Greene:

> Nobody, I thought, could be more English. . . . I suddenly wondered if, in fact, she was, or indeed could be, as English as she looked. Does the real thing ever have the perfection of a stage-performance?'
>
> (A. Christie, *Crooked House*)

The NS teachers of English are people who benefit doubly from their NS status, which bestows on them a 'superior' command of English and enjoyment of privileges emanating from the colonial power of English. These advantages seem particularly unfair when the individuals are otherwise poorly qualified as teachers, sometimes to the extent of being quite unfamiliar with linguistic descriptions of English and quite incompetent when it comes to providing 'explanations' of the TL for the benefit of learners. Andrews (1996), in a study of NS and NNS ESL teachers' meta-linguistic awareness, has data that show NS trainee teachers to be too ignorant of grammatical categories of English, such as the present perfect, to be able to plan a lesson to teach it to foreigners: a sad reflection on British education! Even more irresponsible are the untrained NS teachers who make no effort even to serve as a standard model to their learners. I have come across such 'teachers' who continue to use, in class as well as in private, nonstandard forms like *He don't know. We didn't say nothing.* Some resist even the natural accommodative forces to modify their strong regional pronunciation, and continue to teach in Scouse, Geordie, Cockney.

Even experimental research has revealed that there are NSs, people who must qualify as being 'educated', who would not be fit to teach their language to foreigners. Garrett and Austin (1993) investigated three groups' knowledge of the English genitive apostrophe 's'. The three groups were: (A) 15 NNSs, first- and second-year English majors at the University of Bielefeld, Germany; (B) 15 English NSs, first- and second-year undergraduates in a range of disciplines at a British university; and (C) 15 English NSs, PGCE students on a one-year TEFL course at the same British university. Group C had some slight TEFL experience. The researchers assessed the subjects' knowledge of the structure in question by asking them to respond to 33 sentences containing 29 attested genitive apostrophe errors. They were asked to do three things: identify any errors; grade them on a 5-point scale of gravity; and correct each error. The errors were of three kinds:

(a) Omission of the 's in genitive contexts: *Mother*s Day gifts. Today*s best buy* . . . .
(b) Using the apostrophe as a plural marker: *Tea*'s and coffee*'s. Jaguar*'s wanted.*
(c) Misuse on possessive pronouns: *He took their*'s. His and Her*'s towels.*

There were significant differences between the groups' abilities to recognize errors and in their gravity assignments. Groups A and C recognized respectively 30 and 29 of the 33 errors, while the younger NSs of group B recognized only 24. Gravity assignments ran parallel to recognition scores: the Germans and the TEFL teachers were the least lenient, the NS undergraduates most lenient. Similarly, Groups A and C had an explicit knowledge of the rules, which Group B lacked. It is possible that Group C learned the rules from NNS colleagues during their brief teaching experience. What is clear is that to be 'educated' (in Britain) does not guarantee any explicit knowledge of English grammar, which an EFL teacher must have.

I am not claiming that the linguistically naive NS teachers have no role to play, They certainly do. But it is a different role from that of the NNS 'local' teachers. What we do not need, however, is a 'mums' army' or even a 'dads' army' of NS 'teachers' whose sole qualification is being a NS of one nonstandard dialect of Inner Circle English. We shall explore the most appropriate roles of NS teachers in Chapter 8, when considering **reformulation** as an aspect of error correction.

The third reaction to native speakerism comes from applied linguists who subscribe to the theory of Universal Grammar, finding in that theory relevance to issues in FL learning and teaching, the IL hypothesis in particular. Their suggestion, as we have seen, is to reject as illegitimate setting the NS norm as the learners' goal. According to this view, as we saw above, the learners' and the NSs' versions should not even be compared, and doing so is a 'fallacy'. They would object strongly to a statement like the following: 'Relative to native speakers' linguistic competence, learners' *interlanguage* is deficient by definition' (Kasper and Kellerman, 1997: 5).

Chomsky makes his own position perfectly clear in a statement in his *Knowledge of Language* (1986) that rejects what he calls the 'commonsense', prescientific and in his view naive approach to describing the language of a learner, be it a child or a foreigner. The approach Chomsky attacks involves the following claim: 'that the child or foreigner has a "partial knowledge of English", or is "on his or her way" toward acquiring knowledge of English, and if they reach the goal, they will then know English' (Chomsky, 1986: 16). His principal objection to this approach is that it has 'sociopolitical' and 'normative teleological' implications. 'Normative' because the learners are assumed to need to conform to standards, and 'teleological' because they are assumed to have learning goals. The alternative, 'scientific' approach he advocates would 'say that the person has a perfect knowledge of some language L, similar to English but still different from it' (ibid.: 16). This is obviously a formulation of the Interlanguage hypothesis, a framework which sees a learner's repertoire in the FL as an **idiosyncratic dialect**. And the speaker of such a dialect is its sole native speaker, who knows it perfectly, as do any native speakers their native language.

Cook insists that it is not the aim of FL teaching to produce 'imitation native speakers' and 'not . . . to manufacture *ersatz* native speakers' (1991: 114). Cook is not alone in his conviction. Byram refers to 'the unattainable and insidious ideal of imitating and evaluating communicative performance by comparison with the native speaker' (1988: 11). He urges us 'to stop striving after the unattainable ideal of the native speaker' (ibid.: 17). This stance of course calls into question the whole EA enterprise, and must be addressed.

What, though, is Cook's alternative? It is the 'Interlanguage' solution: 'The model for language teaching should be the fluent L2 user, not the native speaker' (Cook, 1991: 114). Such a fluent L2 user possesses what Cook (1992) calls **multicompetence**, which he defines as 'the compound state of a mind with two grammars' (1992: 558) and 'people with multicompetence are not simply equivalent to two monolinguals but a combination *sui generis*' (ibid.: 565). If comparisons must be made, he insists that 'at best L2 learners should be compared with the fluent bilingual, not the monolingual' (ibid.: 558).

The first part of this definition refers to a 'compound' state. I take this to mean that such learners have one single unified language system serving both languages. 'Compound bilinguals' are usually defined as those bilinguals who have **one** mental lexicon and grammar serving the two languages. But Cook specifies multicompetence as implying **two** grammars, then talks of 'a combination *sui generis*'. The idea resembles Ferguson's (1978) suggestion that it would be preferable not to write a separate grammar for each language of a bi- or multilingual community, but rather to 'try to write a unified grammar in which all this variation fits somewhere' (Ferguson, 1978: 1). These are interesting theoretical speculations, but they fail to address the L2 learner's and user's overriding wish to interact with NSs on equal terms and not to be categorized by NSs as 'the foreigners'. If it is legitimate to decry native speakerism as discriminatory, it must be just as legitimate to object on the same grounds to **foreignerism**, the view that learner language merits special consideration.

The Incompleteness hypothesis

Recall Byram's phrase: 'the unattainable ideal of the native speaker' (1988: 17). He thus subscribes to the **Incompleteness hypothesis**, elsewhere also referred to as the issue of **ultimate attainment**. This is the issue of whether adult FL learners can ever achieve NS competence in the core aspects of the target language grammar. The issue seems to occur in a strong version and a weak version, reflecting the distinction drawn by Chomsky (1965) between **weakly equivalent** and **strongly equivalent** grammars. If the learners' grammar and the NSs' grammar generate the same set of sentences, the two are weakly equivalent. If they do that and additionally assign the same meanings to these sentences, then they are strongly equivalent. For example, suppose both a NS of English and a learner each produce the sentence *One man walked along the road.* They are only weakly equivalent, however, if the learner meant *one* as an indefinite specifier, while the NS meant it as a quantifier (meaning 'not two', etc.). There is ample evidence that learners' IL grammars and NSs' grammars do contrast extensively in both weak and strong (non)equivalence. There are errors of weak nonequivalence and errors of strong nonequivalence. The former are known as **covert** errors and the latter as **overt** errors.

To return to the broad question of **ultimate attainment**. First, we might ask why it is an important issue. If we establish that NS-equivalence *is*, in principle, attainable by learners, then there is some point in attempting to help as many learners as possible to attain it. The very least we could do is to increase the success rate for FL learning beyond the present abysmal 5 per cent that Selinker (1969) estimated to be the case. I would like to suggest two approaches to increasing FL learning success rates. The first is by discovering what it is that those who *are* successful do and those who are unsuccessful do not, that is, studying successful learners' strategies and teaching them to less successful learners, as Reiss (1981) and Oxford (1990) have advocated we might. I call this the **positive strategy** approach, in line with Chomsky's notion of the 'positive evidence' that learners receive, informing them that such-and-such *is* possible in the language. Positive strategies lead to Completeness.

The other approach is the **negative strategy** approach, again in line with Chomsky's insight that learners can benefit from finding out, directly or indirectly, what is *not* possible in the language. And what do we call these entities that are *not* possible in the language? Ill-formed sentences. Malformations. Why not **errors**? Now, since the number and types of non-sentence 'in' a language is infinite, there would be no point in trying to list them all for the learners to avoid. To make the screening manageable we disregard all but those malformations that the learners themselves – or learners like them – do make. How do we know they do? By doing Error Analysis. That is what this book is about.

We have identified two sorts of **equivalence**: strong and weak. I believe there is a third. In James (1980: 24) I suggested that two learners with different native languages (NLs) can be wrong (commit two errors) in the FL in ways that look the same, but have different causes. Both a Spanish L1 speaker and a Russian L1 speaker could produce the covertly erroneous **One man walked along the road*. The Spaniard has transferred or overgeneralized his L1 *un(o)* – 'a' or 'one'. But the Russian has not transferred any indefinite article from L1, since Russian has no articles: it must be a quantifier he has used. In this case the two learners' grammars and the English NSs' grammar are weakly but not strongly equivalent. The important point, however, is that equivalence does not imply sameness: it is possible for two grammars to generate the same forms with the same meanings but to use different procedures in doing so. This is the question that Coppieters poses: 'Does a language impose a grammar on its speakers?' (1987: 544) – native and learners alike.

Research has not solved the Completeness question. Three studies have yielded conflicting evidence. Coppieters (1987) compared the grammatical intuitions for French of 21 NSs and 21 near-native speakers (NrNSs). The latter, who had lived an average of 17.4 years in France, spoke a French barely distinguishable from that of the NSs. They were all asked to comment on 107 sentences using a selected range of French grammar: *il/elle* versus *ce* as subjects; prenominal versus postnominal adjective order; Imparfait versus Passé composé; *de* versus *à* in verb complements, and more. Those constructions on which the NSs registered 80 per cent agreement were adopted as the 'prototypical native norm', and the NrNSs' responses were compared with this norm. There was considerable agreement about the **forms**, so much so that Coppieters concluded that his data 'do not . . . prove the existence of qualitative differences between native and near-native grammars' (ibid.: 553). There was, in other words, ample weak equivalence between the NSs' and the NrNSs' grammars. But there was no strong equivalence, since the NSs and NNSs often gave 'radically different interpretations of the meaning of those forms.' (ibid.: 554) The NrNSs often interpreted the French structures 'in terms of the native language' (ibid.: 555). And some of their interpretations were bizarre rationalizations, for example 'I say *une histoire triste* before telling the story, *une triste histoire* after telling the story' (ibid.: 559). The overall conclusion is that the NrNSs had developed significantly different grammars.

Schachter (1990) studied the judgements about English Subjacency (how far and across which categories of **bounding nodes** certain elements can be shifted in sentences) by learners with Dutch, Chinese, Indonesian and Korean L1s, which are listed here on a scale of decreasing similarity to English in their Subjacency rules. Learners will only achieve Completeness, which will be demonstrated by having intuitions about these processes identical to those of NSs of English, either if they have kept open access to Universal Grammar (UG), or if their L1 is identical in this regard to the FL. Schachter found that the learners with L1 Dutch got closest, and those with L1 Korean had least success. Since access to UG has atrophied and no two languages that might be L1 and FL pairs are ever completely identical, Schachter concludes soberly that: 'Incompleteness will turn out to be an essential feature of any adult second language grammar' (1990: 119). Not only does Schachter's work establish that learners will fall short of NSs, but it also refutes the hypothesis of the integrity and essential incomparability of Interlanguage. If IL and TL differ along certain specifiable parameters rather than randomly, then they become eminent candidates for comparison, and to refuse to compare them would be perverse. Her work also refutes the claim that IL is one of the set of natural human languages and as such it is to be described *sui generis*: having no access to UG, it cannot be a natural language.

Birdsong (1992) also studied Incompleteness, which he sees as 'the centrepoint for arguments that L1 acquisition and L2 acquisition are profoundly different epistemological phenomena' (1992: 707). If they are, it does not logically follow that IL and the FL are incomparable of course. *How* you built your boat may be different from how I built mine, but in assessing their seaworthiness we need refer to neither design. Birdsong submitted 76 grammatical and ungrammatical French sentences to 20 NSs of French and 20 near native speakers (NrNSs) who had come to France as adults and had lived on average 12 years in France. It was found that the two groups differed significantly in their judgements on 17 of the 76 items (22 per cent). One is surprised, therefore, to see Birdsong conclude that his data constitute 'only modest evidence for differences in ultimate attainment . . . little support for the notion of generalized competence differences between natives and near-natives' (ibid.: 721).

There was, however, one important difference between the NSs and the NrNSs: the think-aloud data revealed that the NrNSs tended to refer to **grammar** in justifying their judgements while the NSs tended to refer to use, pragmatics, style and aesthetics of use – all of which fall under the rubric of **acceptability**. This led Birdsong to ask 'Does this mean that NSs are relatively insensitive to "grammar"?' (ibid.: 726). I suggest that this is not necessarily the case: think-aloud protocols call for a command of metalanguage, and NSs (who have learned their language by exposure rather than by using reference books) are less likely than non-NSs to have been exposed to metalanguage. So NSs may be not 'insensitive' to grammar and may have clear intuitions about it, but nonetheless be unable to talk about it.

Birdsong suggests that the success of the NrNSs amounts to FL learning **expertise** or 'skill at attending to and organising target language input and an ability to overcome biases imposed by one's native language' (ibid.: 742). It would obviously be interesting to study this expertise, with a view to imparting it to those learners (alas the majority) who lack it: this is what I called earlier the 'positive strategy' approach. However, success tends not to reveal its own secrets, whereas breakdown (error) does. If you want to learn about motor mechanics, do not buy a trouble-free Rolls-Royce: it just runs forever. Buy an old banger, and every time it gives trouble it will reveal a further secret to you.

Other reference points for Error Analysis

There are several domains of EA that I shall not try to explore. For example, the whole area of language pathology and clinical linguistics (Crystal, 1982a) I shall merely touch upon. Some other areas will be mentioned in other chapters (e.g. profiling in Chapter 4, spelling errors in Chapter 5). But there are a few areas that had better be at least opened up to the newcomer, since their intellectual content is exciting, and rewards scrutiny.

Language change

Language change used to be thought of as a dull philological field of study, involving the parroting of sound changes and vowel shifts. Now interest is focused more on the *causes* of change as a socially driven phenomenon. Let us start by asking why change occurs: usually for no particular linguistic or structural reason. In other words, language change is not driven by the forces of structural efficiency, and language is not gradually improving with time. So we have to reject these 'teleological' attempts to explain change. Secondly, we tend to be conservative and to want to slow down change. The reason for this is, as Milroy points out, 'linguistic changes in progress are commonly perceived as "errors"' (1992: 3). The connection with EA is obvious: society (the elite it may be) appoints Academies or academics to keep a watchful eye with a view to monitoring changes that seem unwarranted. And some in fact are. Milroy cites several cases of loss of intelligibility between speakers of different dialects, for example the Ulster dialect speaker who, in reply to the question *Do you think he's going to die?* replied *I doubt so*, which in that dialect means *I'm afraid so*. It seems, however, that the watchdogs are not always successful and many minor changes do succeed, with the consequence that the language changes. When it does, new canons and standards emerge. What was an error a generation ago might no longer be; and conversely, what was acceptable to our parents might not be to us.

Language loss

We know that languages can die: Cornish did, with its last monolingual adult NS, in 1777. Similarly, individuals can lose their languages, NL, FL or both. The cause can be pathological, as is the case when stroke victims lose their language (usually suddenly), or natural. The usual cause of natural loss is non-use, and so it makes sense to speak of 'forgetting' a language.

Most people who learned an FL to a reasonable standard in school but who have had no opportunity to use it much since leaving school claim to have forgotten most of it. This is serious, both educationally and economically, and makes FL teaching in school seem an unwise investment in time and resources. Should FL teaching therefore be abandoned in schools and postponed till such a time as adults have found jobs and know what FLs they need to learn? It depends on whether the loss can be made good.

Irrespective of these practical concerns there are questions of theoretical interest about FL loss that interest the Error Analyst, and these have been listed by van Els (1989). I shall repeat only the central questions: Can loss be minimized if a high proficiency level is attained prior to cessation of contact with the FL? How fast does loss happen? How powerful are the forces leading to loss? For example, can loss be averted by a weekly hour immersion in the FL? In what order are elements of the FL lost? Does their loss spread in the inverse order to the one they were acquired in, in which case there is operation of the 'last in-first out' principle, seen in Jakobson's theory (1971) of the aphasic's loss being the mirror image of the child's acquisition? What is lost first? Phonology? Lexis? Grammar? There is evidence suggesting that idioms and formulae are more resistant than other more formal features. If total loss has occurred, is relearning faster than if no initial learning had taken place? And finally, what types of error show up in the process of loss? Are they the same as the ones attested during initial learning?

A special aspect of language loss, ripe for research, is of FL teachers' language attrition, both NSs and NNSs. Most complain that they lose contact with the TL, and even backslide when they incorporate into their own repertoires their own students' errors. NS teachers overseas not only miss the latest current slang invented by their compatriots at home, but even find their judgements of grammaticality blurred with the passage of time. At least teachers' ability to report their language loss is a positive sign of their **awareness** of this hazard. What we need, though, are ideas on how to arrest and reverse such loss when it occurs among key personnel in this way.

Deviance in literature

We know that writers, especially poets, but also novelists like James Joyce, experiment with their medium, often to the point of licence. Dylan Thomas delighted in breaking the rules of English. Consider the two following 'original' adverbial time phrases: *'Once below a time . . .'*, *'On the first of each hardship'*. These are intentionally deviant, and their special effect resides in the way in which their deviance is manipulated, in the sense that novel combinations are forged. One gains the impression of the poet as iconoclast. Leech (1969: 42f.) offers a useful typology of poetic deviance.

Eirlys Davies (1985) questions two assumptions concerning literary English: first, that there is a 'normal' English which is in essence different from literary language; and secondly, that it is this normal or everyday language that should be taught as an FL. She shows that there are thousands of everyday texts, spoken as well as written, that have the properties we assume, wrongly, to be unique to the language of literature, even specifically poetic language. Such mundane texts are forms to be filled in, public notices, newspaper headlines, directions given by a passer-by to a lost stranger. These abound with **ellipsis** – *Leave blank*; **metaphor** – *It cost the earth!*; **archaism** – *Manners maketh the man*; and **poetic licence** – *Be a smileaholic!*. Davies rejects claims about the advisability of avoiding literary texts in EL2 teaching, on the grounds that the same features and the problems of recognizing their communicative force crop up equally in the reading of many everyday texts. However, she advocates for advanced learners explicit and systematic awareness-raising of the characteristic stylistic markers in a wide range of text types.

Lott (1988) also discusses the implications of literary deviance for the teaching of literature, and for the teaching of language *through* literature, to foreign learners. There is a common belief that learners are more disposed to learn deviant language than correct language. This claim is part of the broader question of whether it does any harm (or any good for that matter) to expose learners to deviant forms of the FL and will concern us in Chapter 8, where we discuss error treatments.

Error Analysis in instructional science

It was Harlow (1959) whose research launched the general study of what he called **error factors** (EFs), defined as 'orderly but inappropriate responses to problem solving' (ibid.: 524). EFs became the focus of thought on the general nature of learning, and learning was conceived as 'nothing but suppression or inhibition of error factors' (ibid.: 526). Subsequently, other labels were introduced: **miscues** designate errors in reading, while in mathematics one talks of **procedural bugs**. Pickthorne (1983) gives examples of these 'bugs' made by leaners of maths from elementary to college level. One example, according to Pickthorne, surfaces when learners do decimal multiplication. They follow the teacher doing: $0.3 \times 0.5 = 0.15$; $0.7 \times 0.8 = 0.56$, etc., and infer the rule '$0.a \times 0.b = 0.ab$'. The rule inferred is right for the examples given, but unfortunately cannot be generalized to cover $0.3 \times 0.3 = {}^*0.9$, since it does not! Nor does 0.11×0.12 yield 0.132. The fact is that the rule inferred only works provided the products are two-, four-, six-, etc., that is, even-figured. The last two give correct even-figure products: 0.09 and 0.0132 respectively.

Troutman and Lichtenberg (1982: 137) discuss errors in tabular addition such as:

$$\begin{array}{cc} 25 & 27 \\ \underline{27}\ + & \underline{18}\ + \\ = {}^*412 & = {}^*315 \end{array}$$

and

They point both to the complexity and also the ambiguity of such operations, since they might be caused by the children's failure to regroup, or by the fact that the children are computing from left to right. The study of such miscomputations is fascinating in itself. Furthermore, they seem to have many unmistakable affinities with the misformations that occur in FL learning. Accounts of such errors in doing mathematics and suggestions for their avoidance and remediation are to be found in Bitter, Hatfield and Edwards (1993) and are regularly discussed in the journal *For the Teaching of Mathematics*.

Forensic EA

Forensic EA is a small part of the larger field of **Forensic Linguistics** (Kniffka, 1990), which includes forensic phonetics (Baldwin and French, 1990) and forensic stylistics (McMenamin, 1993). Whenever linguistic evidence is utilized in criminal investigation or presented in a court of law, by defence or prosecution, we have forensic linguistics. Kniffka (1990) distinguishes two broad types of forensic linguistic evidence: that relating to **interpretation** (how is such and such an utterance to be understood?), and that relating to **identity** (who said or wrote this?). It is under the latter that forensic EA plays its main role, for the simple reason that at least some of the characteristics and idiosyncrasies of speech and writing that allow us to recognize (identify) an individual involve linguistic deviance. Spillner (1990) refers to the main character in Alfred Hitchcock's film *The Wrong Man* who is mistakenly convicted of robbery on the basis of his having made a spelling error identical to that which the real bank robber had made on his demand note. This miscarriage of justice, Spillner argues, would never have been perpetrated if the prosecution had engaged a linguist with sound training in EA, who would have been able to distinguish these two errors, so acquitting the suspect.

Hubbard (1994) is a personal account of how one linguist with sound training in EA went about proving that a man arrested on suspicion of having written ten extortion letters to a South African chain store was indeed the perpetrator. Hubbard proceeded on the basis of two assumptions. First, that the frequencies, types and patterns of language error made by such a person will be reasonably consistent from one occasion to the next, possibly over a period of years. Secondly, that the L1 of the subject, if he is writing in an FL, will be a significant source of forensically pertinent clues. The accused was indeed convicted of attempted extortion, largely on the basis of Hubbard's evidence from spelling errors and article errors. The accused's L1 was Polish, a language having no articles whatsoever, and Poles have tremendous problems with the English articles, which showed up in the demand notes.

Of course, we must not harbour unrealistic expectations of forensic EA. Popular press reporting of 'linguistic fingerprinting' is sensationalist, and the techniques have been used for years as ways of investigating disputed authorship, for example the question of whether it really was Shakespeare and not Bacon who wrote the plays attributed to Shakespeare.

Recall the aim of this chapter: to indicate the scope of Error Analysis. Its scope is, as we have begun to see, virtually endless. Lewis expressed the point eloquently:

> The message . . . is that if error is at the root of all our problems, then it is high time that theorists started to look at the nature and genesis of error more carefully. They might even discover that, in the final analysis, the problem of error is the only problem there is.
>
> (Lewis, 1981; 256)

3

Defining 'Error'

'The errors of a wise man make your rule,
Rather than the perfections of a fool'
(William Blake, *Poems*, ed. W.H. Stevenson,
text by David V. Erdman. London:
Longman, 1971, p. 600)

The purpose of this chapter is to define key terms, since we shall
only be able to think clearly about EA if we understand precisely
what these terms mean, how they differ from each other, and how
they are mutually defining.

Ignorance

The study of knowledge is called **epistemology**. Specialists in the
theoretical fields of language acquisition and syntactic theory are
epistemologists, more specifically language epistemologists. They
study the nature and development of people's (tacit, not explicit)
knowledge of language. They then write accounts of that knowledge, which are called 'grammars'. EA is on the other side of the
equation, being the study of linguistic **ignorance**, the investigation
of what people do not know and how they attempt to cope with
their ignorance. This latter, coping, dimension establishes a link
between EA and the study of **learner strategies** (Færch and Kasper,
1983), since strategies are devices learners only resort to when
either their learning or communication in the L2 are not going
smoothly but have become problematic – perhaps critically so.
Learner strategies are for this reason generally seen as comprising
two kinds: **learning strategies** (Oxford, 1990) and **communication
strategies** (Tarone, Cohen and Dumas, 1983).

The Error Analyst's object of enquiry, then, is the FL learner's ignorance of the TL. This ignorance can be manifest in two ways. First, in silence, when the learner makes no response, that is, says or writes nothing. We need to distinguish two sorts of silence: on the one hand, we sometimes witness **cultural silence** on the part of EL2 learners from 'silent cultures' such as Finns or Japanese. This is different from the silence induced by ignorance, for which we need a special term perhaps. In the terminology of strategy use, this is **avoidance**. Now, if silence of this sort were the only way of signalling one's ignorance, we would learn very little, and would be forced to give up EA. But learners usually prefer to try to express themselves in the TL by alternative means: they 'beg, steal or borrow'. This is the second way they compensate for their ignorance. The study of this **substitutive** language (called IL) is EA. Second language acquisition (SLA) theoreticians study this IL *sui generis*, as if its speakers were a newly discovered lost tribe in Amazonia. Error Analysts study it in relation to the TL.

Ignorance is not synonymous with **Incompleteness**, but as long as there is Incompleteness or failure to attain full NS-like knowledge of the TL, there will be EA. First, let us distinguish it from **ignorance**. Incompleteness is a global concept that refers to an overall insufficiency (compared with NS competence) across all areas of the TL, while ignorance is specific in the sense that one is normally said to be ignorant of such-and-such a structure, irrespective of one's overall proficiency in the TL. Notice that we are defining error in terms of the discrepancy between IL and the NS's version, the TL. We have already (in Chapter 1) defended this approach and rejected the Interlanguage hypothesis of incomparability. There is, however, an apparent exception to the rule of learner Incompleteness which should be settled before proceeding: I refer to those occasions where it seems that the learners (the NNS) know the FL better than the NS they are talking to. This frequently happens, and the NSs are usually the ones who assert (unashamedly too) that the foreigners' English is 'better', and that the Incompleteness lies with the NSs, not with the learners. What does this mean, and how does it affect our definition of error? What the NSs usually mean is that the foreigner is using a more standard version of the language than the NSs. This should come as no surprise, since foreigners learn languages in school from teachers with access to standard forms, whereas NSs acquire it informally from their parents or in the streets, and nonstandard forms may predominate in these settings. So yes, the foreigner is less likely than some (but not all) NSs to say *It *were *him *what *done it*. On other occasions it is not a matter of who uses standard forms but of whose language is 'richer', in terms of utilizing a bigger vocabulary and exploiting syntactic devices more adventurously. Again, it is just as likely to be the foreigner, for similar reasons to those just cited, plus the fact that when a language has been learnt from written texts it tends to be more 'literary', in the sense of using forms in speech that would normally be reserved for writing. In that case, it would be reasonable to point out to the NS that the NNS's language is insensitive to the medium.

So when we define errors with reference to NSs, which implies comparison between NNSs' and NSs' utterances, we must make sure not to idealize the entities compared. It must not be a comparison between real learners and an ideal NS of the sort that Chomsky envisages: 'a person presented with uniform experience in an ideal Bloomfieldian speech community with no dialect diversity and no variation among speakers' (1968: 17). The comparison should rather be between two real individuals, or at least two categories of person. It is for this reason that I endorse Lennon's concrete definition of error as 'a linguistic form . . . which, in the same context . . . would in all likelihood not be produced by the learner's *native speaker counterparts*' (1991: 182). One of the strengths of this definition is the way it sidesteps the problem of semantic intention and formal intention: what the learners wanted to communicate, and the means they deployed to achieve that end. Lennon's 'in the same context' makes the meaning intention a constant, so we are left with but one variable – linguistic form. Lennon's idea of associating the learners with their social counterpart is also ingenious. The counterparts will be individuals with a similar level of education, of the same age-group, socioeconomic class, sex, and perhaps even profession.

Measures of deviance

Learners' ignorance of TL can be expressed in terms of four categories:

- Grammaticality.
- Acceptability.

■ Correctness.
■ Strangeness and infelicity.

Grammaticality

This is synonymous with 'well-formedness'. It is the grammar (not you or I) who decides whether something said by a learner is grammatical. The grammar bases decisions about the grammaticality of contentious cases on principles extracted from observing clear cases. Appeal to grammaticality is an attempt to be objective, to take decisions such as whether some bit of language is erroneous or not out of the orbit of human whim. So, if we can point to a bit of language and say that there are no circumstances where this could ever be said in this way, we are dealing with ungrammaticality. The reason for this is that ungrammaticality is context-free. Thus a judgement of the grammaticality of a sentence does not appeal to context. As we have seen, there is *no* context where an ungrammatical bit of language could be right. If, on the other hand, we can agree that it might be said in some context, it is well-formed. A high ideal, but with limited scope. The main problem with using grammaticality as a reference point is that different grammars will register different decisions concerning borderline cases. On the clear-cut cases there will be no such inconsistencies. These clear-cut cases we can confidently refer to as the 'code' or the 'core' grammar, and agree with Corder that ungrammaticality involves 'breaches of rules of the code' (1971: 101).

For Lyons, 'the best indicator of grammatical unacceptability' is **corrigibility** (1977: 379). But this test runs into difficulties. First, there is the fact that some ungrammatical sentences exist that are so disjointed (we might say 'agrammatical') that they are incorrigible, for example: *Butted to when in did sorry he town.* Lyons decides nevertheless to treat 'such grossly incorrigible sequences as ungrammatical' (ibid.: 380). Then there are problems with phonological rather than grammatical unacceptability, in other words, mispronunciation. We can certainly correct them, but can we call mispronunciations 'ungrammatical'? If we broaden our definition of grammar to embrace all levels, and equate it with **ill-formedness**, the problem goes away.

Lyons's third misgiving about his corrigibility test concerns semantic and collocational anomalies as in *The milk turned *rotten* or *A *flock of elephants*. These are not, for Lyons, cases of ungrammaticality, since the rules they violate are not the general rules of grammar, but 'local' and sometimes even unique rules (as in *court martial*) determining what word combinations are natural. They are in Lyons's view (1977: 381) readily corrigible, however: substitute √*sour* and √*herd* respectively. If these sentences are not ungrammatical but are still corrigible, the test is invalid: since they are undeniably corrigible, they must be ungrammatical. Again, it would be possible to escape this dilemma if we broadened the scope of the term 'grammar' to include **semantic** well-formedness, as we have already done to include **phonological** well-formedness. Lyons himself seems inclined to take this step when he concedes that an infringement like **rotten milk* 'falls outside the scope of syntax' (ibid.: 383). It does, but stays within the orbit of grammar, broadly defined.

There is a problem though: the speaker might fully have intended *rotten milk* (stressing hereby its solidity in putrefaction) and have intended *flock of elephants*, intending to activate a metaphor, suggesting that these elephants were as pacific as a flock of sheep. In this case we would have to concede that the utterances were not corrigible after all, at least not automatically so. It would depend on whether the speaker intended *rotten* or *sour*, *flock* or *herd*. The probability of a NS having intended the doubtful *rotten* and *flock* is, of course, higher than would be the case if a NNS learning English had spoken these utterances. So, it appears that it is not the grammar which is going to decide, but the speaker's intention and the hearer's judgement. Radford discusses an analogous case, *An *honest geranium*, concluding that this is not syntactically ill-formed, as the word order is accurate, but that 'the oddity of such a phrase seems to be essentially **pragmatic**' (1988: 14). In this case we are dealing with the user's viewpoint, with **acceptability**.

Acceptability

This is not a theoretical but a practical notion, being determined by the use or usability of the form in question, or, as Beaugrande and Dressler put it, it is to do with 'actualization procedures' (1981: 130). In other words, when non-linguistic factors militate against the use of a form, we attribute this to unacceptability. While it is the knower (NS) of a language who decides whether an utterance is grammatical, it is the user who decides whether it is acceptable.

For some there can be no acceptability without grammaticality. In other words, grammaticality is a prerequisite for acceptability: 'An acceptable utterance is one that has been, or might be, produced by a native speaker in some appropriate context and is, or would be, accepted by other native speakers as belonging to the language in question' (Lyons, 1968: 137). The part of Lyons's definition that refers to the utterance 'belonging to the language in question' appeals to grammaticality. This relationship between acceptability and grammaticality recurs in his later work: 'an ungrammatical utterance is one that a native speaker can not only recognise as unacceptable, but can also correct' (Lyons, 1977: 380). As shown in the previous paragraph, corrigibility is the criterion for grammaticality, whereas *de facto* use and unproblematicity are the tests for establishing acceptability.

To decide on the acceptability of a piece of language we refer not to rules, but to contexts, trying to contextualize the utterance in question. Try it for yourself. Can you think of a context where the following could be said?: *Pele (the Brazilian footballer) wore a green dress.* Yes, if he were taking part in the Rio carnival celebrations. But the learner who said this was referring to the context where Pele was playing football, and by 'dress' meant 'shirt' or 'strip'. So this is an error of acceptability. Or can you think of contexts where *I came to London last summer to study the English* would be acceptable? The first question is whether the speaker was an anthropologist studying the English people or a linguist. The second problem is one of **location deixis**. It is acceptable if spoken when the speaker is back in London, on a subsequent visit, or (strangely) if the speaker is outside London but speaking on the phone or writing to someone who is now in London. It would be quite unacceptable if spoken to a listener outside London, and even more so if the addressee was not from London or Britain. Real and imagined contexts raise the degree of acceptability of doubtful sentences, but judgements about the grammaticality of a sentence have to be made in the face of the sentence in isolation, not in a context. For this reason, to decide whether something is acceptable, even when it satisfies the grammaticality test, is seldom clear-cut and takes some thought, even imagination. Professor Willy Haas (p.c.) told of the time when the ungrammatical and thitherto unacceptable *Quadruplicity drinks procrastination* suddenly became acceptable when he saw in a newspaper a photograph of the 'Big Four' statesmen – Stalin, Churchill, Roosevelt and De

Gaulle – assembled to drink a victory toast at the end of World War II.

We shall return to the criterion of corrigibility below (p. 77). First, though, there is a point that needs to be questioned. The idea that one refers to 'the grammar' when deciding on grammaticality whereas one refers to context in deciding matters of acceptability cannot be quite right. Lennon makes the valid and perceptive point that 'Most "erroneous forms" are, in fact, in themselves not erroneous at all, but become erroneous only in the context of the larger linguistic units in which they occur' (1991: 189). And this is true: there is nothing intrinsically wrong with *I* or *me*, but they are wrong in the contexts *Come with* – and – *did it*, respectively. Wider context, in the sense of 'setting' or even 'speaker intention', also determines whether a form is erroneous. Thus, *She decided to answer the telephone call* is acceptable if it means 'to return a call, perhaps recorded on an answer-phone', but is not acceptable if the meaning is 'pick up the receiver while it is ringing'. Lennon's point refers to the accompanying linguistic context or **cotext** of a possible error, while I have hitherto been referring to situational context: we are not in dispute therefore.

When the error is only revealed by reference to the larger context of discourse, that is the real world, in this way, we can also speak of the error being a **covert** (not **overt**) error, a distinction introduced into EA by Corder (1973: 272). A covert error is superficially well-formed, but does not match intentions: it is **right by chance**. For example: *... and I therefore bought him a ticket* is well-formed but unacceptable, since the speaker intended 'bought a ticket FROM him'. It would seem that we have a terminological option: either to distinguish acceptability from grammaticality or to distinguish between ungrammatical (**overtly erroneous**) and **covertly erroneous** (unacceptable) language. This usually results from the learners making a L1 transfer which is successful or 'positive': 'bought HIM a ticket' above originates in L1 Portuguese 'comprei-lhe um bilhete'. Yet the positive transfer does not lead to total success, because the learner is not saying what he means, even though what he is saying is in impeccable English. It is a half-successful transfer and we might call it **semi-positive** transfer, distinguishing it from **fully positive** transfer such as the following:

(i)   *... and therefore more important now is the attempt to express it precisely* based on L1 Portuguese [... e por isso mais importante agora é a tentative de a exprimir com precisão].

(ii) *I feel myself the happiest person* based on L1 German [Ich fühle mich den glücklichsten Menschen].

(iii) *Once we have decided ourselves* based on L1 French [Une fois que nous nous sommes décidés].

Medgyes (1989) attempts to make a connection between overt and covert errors and the two types of learner strategy: **achievement** strategies and **reduction** strategies. The former involve the learners finding alternative ways to express their meanings in the face of discovering that they lack the most natural means to do so, while the latter involve deciding to say less than originally intended, since one lacks the means to say all one wishes to. Medgyes contends that the errors resulting from learners deploying achievement strategies will be 'easily detectable and palpably present', since the learners just won't bother, preferring to risk all on getting their message across by whatever means. By contrast, the learners deploying reduction strategies will, Medgyes contends, seem to commit few errors. But only 'seem', he insists. It depends what the learners are choosing to avoid – certain forms or certain intended meanings. If they avoid certain forms and nevertheless succeed in putting across their message in paraphrase, there will be little overt error. But if they deliberately sacrifice part of their desired meaning then they will be committing *covert* errors, Medgyes contends. It is an interesting suggestion that touches on the distinction between errors and mistakes, which we address below.

The relationship between acceptability and grammaticality is worth examining more closely: can they cooccur, or are they mutually exclusive categories? Lyons (1977) offers a discussion of the degree to which grammaticality determines acceptability. It would be reasonable to assume that the notions of grammaticality and acceptability cross-classify, giving **four** possible combinations, the first two of which are uncontentious enough to pass over.

(i) There are sentences that are [**+Grammatical (GR) +Acceptable (ACC)**]. Most of the sentences in this book (even a book about errors!) are of this type.

(ii) There are sentences that are both ungrammatical and unacceptable, [**−Grammatical −Acceptable**]. Indeed, they are unacceptable precisely because of their ungrammaticality, since ungrammaticality is one of several grounds for unacceptability. EA is concerned principally with this category.

(iii) There are sentences that are [**+Grammatical −Acceptable**]. Borsley (1991: 4) gives *The horse raced past the barn fell* as an example of this type, arguing that despite its grammaticality, it 'leads the perceptual mechanisms astray' (indeed, it leads the reader 'up the garden path'!) and is consequently unacceptable. By contrast *The horse ridden past the barn fell* is of type (i), being both grammatical and acceptable, since it does not mislead the reader.

(iv) Finally, there is the fourth pairing, sentences that are [**−Grammatical +Acceptable**]. This type ought to be impossible, if it is indeed the case that ungrammaticality is one of the grounds for unacceptability, or what Lyons calls 'grammatical unacceptability' (1977: 379). Borsley (1991) therefore considers it 'questionable' that there are any examples of this type, but suggests as a possibility *He is a ?not unintelligent person.* People say this and do not object to others saying it, despite its breaking the grammar rule that '*not* cannot generally combine with a prenominal adjective' (ibid.: 5): *a *not grey sky, that *not rich man* are clearly ill-formed and, as is normal, thereby also unacceptable.

Milroy and Milroy (1985: 74ff.), however, claim that all four combinations occur, including the one rejected by Borsley: [−GR +ACC]. Their examples of [+GR −ACC] are *This is the house√whose/√of which the roof fell in.* Both versions are grammatical but tend to be avoided, especially in spoken English: *of which* is felt to be too pompous, while *whose,* by association with *who,* is (wrongly) felt to be illicitly indexing a human pronoun with a nonhuman noun antecedent *house* (see *Cobuild English Grammar,* 1990: 39). Little wonder that when used they tend to jar the nerves: they are [−ACC] therefore, but well-formed.

What, then, have these linguists to say about type (iv), [−GR +ACC] combinations? They suggest *This is the house *that its/*that's roof fell in.* Both versions are [−GR], the first in its use of a non-English resumptive pronoun **its,* the second in its coinage of the nonexisting neuter possessive relative pronoun **that's.* Nevertheless, both versions are widely used in informal speech and go unnoticed, in other words are acceptable. Notice the extent of the Milroys' reference to the **spoken** medium in their attempt to define acceptability. The general rule that ungrammaticality precipitates unacceptability is relaxed by saying that what is deemed ungrammatical in **written** English may nevertheless be acceptable in **spoken** English. At this point the reader might like to consider the pronoun '*who*' on the first line of the section headed (ironically?) *grammaticality* on page 65.

Pawley and Syder (1983: 215) draw attention to learners' errors that arise when they wrongly 'assume that an element in the expression may be varied according to a . . . rule of some generality' as for example *You are pulling my leg**s*. Generally speaking, what makes especially advanced FL learners' IL odd or strange or 'foreign' is its tendency to be unacceptable while being grammatical. Widdowson (1989: 133) refers to 'linguistically ill-formed' though syntactically 'grammatical' segments like *?Before you leap, look*. But 'ill-formed' is a misnomer here and Widdowson possibly means 'unacceptable'. It is unacceptable because it disappoints the hearer's expectation of **idiomaticity**. We shall say that language that has these sorts of characteristics exhibits a certain **strangeness** (Bridges, 1990). Such strangeness is one of the ways that an IL can be **infelicitous**.

Following on from Lyons's suggestion that ungrammaticality is one source of unacceptability, we might ask whether there are more sources. I would like to suggest that there are eight:

1. Failure to fit the intended context:

   Pele wore a green ?dress and ?made three goals.

   Pele was not in fancy or carnival 'dress' but was playing football wearing a green strip: the German for this garment is *Dress*. He did not just 'set up' (engineer) goals for other players to score, but scored them personally.

2. The unusual, bizarre nature of the idea expressed, or reference to an inconceivable situation. Borsley (1991) speaks of expressions which 'conflict with our views of how the world is' and gives as an example:

   My lawnmower ?thinks that I don't like it.

   People do not normally attribute thought processes to machines, not outside fairy stories and science fiction at least. Other examples are:

   Inside the cow she lost her handbag slowly.
   Quadruplicity drinks procrastination.

3. An unusual way of referring to a nonetheless conceivable situation:

> *Be underneath Cyril.* (Said by a photographer to athletes/ models striking a pose.)

4. Flouting customary collocations:

> *The ?white and black cat grinned like a ?Cornishman.*

It is not ungrammatical to say '*white and black*', but the inverse order '*black and white*' is more or less fixed, and known as an **irreversible coordinate**. 'More or less' since the order can be reversed if special effect is meant to be expressed, for example, to claim pointedly that the cat was mostly white with just a little black in colour. Likewise we normally eat *fish 'n' chips* and not *?chips 'n' fish*. Coordinated pairs of verbs, adverbs, prepositions can be subject to this constraint: *save and prosper* (*?prosper and save*); *slowly but surely* (*?surely but slowly*); *votes for and against* (*?votes against and for*). Interestingly, the corresponding cat in Spanish is *el gato blanco y negro*: in a language where adjectival phrases follow the head noun, the irreversible coordinates are inverted. And there is no convention for associating Cornishmen with grinning: cats, when they do grin, do so like a '*Cheshire cat*' – at least English cats do.

5. Producing unusual grammar or phonological configurations:

> *He was finishing doing computing approaching retiring.*

Lyons (1977) concentrates on grammar-induced unacceptabilities of this kind.

6. Producing hard-to-process syntactic or phonological complexity. We looked at the example of a 'garden path' construction earlier. Another sort is the multiple self-embedded construction, exemplified by:

> *The flea the rat the cat the dog chased killed carried bit me.*

This is indubitably grammatical, but intolerably hard to unravel, since there is a mounting pile-up of subject noun phrases (NPs) to store in memory while waiting for the structurally appropriate verb to which to pair each NP later in the sentence.

An everyday example of phonological complexity is the tongue-twister, such as:

She sells sea shells by the seashore.

7. Upsetting the balance of sentence parts, for example excessive end-weight being assigned to a sentence element of little import, as in:

Eat the porridge your sister has so carefully cooked for you **up**.

8. Breaking rules that are not so much natural rules 'of the language' but that have been superimposed on the language by purists. Some people consider violations of even these prescriptive rules unacceptable since they are '**incorrect**':

Just try to?always(√always to)say thank you (split infinitive).
What did he write such a long letter about? (stranded preposition).

Recall that we linked grammaticality to the grammar or the code. Note also that we have tended to speak of the (un)grammaticality of sentences but of the (un)acceptability of utterances. For Beaugrande and Dressler (1981) this distinction is crucial. Acceptability is a property of texts, and relates to whether the text is 'capable of utilization' and to the receiver's 'ability to extract operating instructions' from it (Beaugrande and Dressler, 1981: 129ff.). Acceptability thus becomes synonymous with processability. The problem with this definition is that some individuals are more skilled processors than others, so on this criterion the degree of acceptability of a text would be determined not by the text, nor by the context of its utterance, but at least in part by the processing skill of the receiver. This is an important issue – whether acceptability, like beauty, is in the eye of the beholder. Furthermore, it raises the question of whether it takes a native speaker to decide whether something is acceptable or not. And this seems to be the case: whether some text is acceptable will depend on its naturalness, its fluency, its idiomaticity, its appropriacy. All these are aspects of texts which apparently one has to be a native speaker to pass judgement about. Nor can a text be declared acceptable solely on the grounds that it is intelligible, because the sense that the receiver extracts from it might not correspond to that which its producer intended. However, we should not take a native speaker's word that something is unacceptable: he or she might reject an utterance like *Who did you meet at the zoo?* as unacceptable and yet use it themselves. In fact I have just done exactly that: I find 'themselves' used as a generic reflexive or emphatic pronoun (as here) with a 3rd. person singular antecedent unacceptable, but use it – under protest – just to be **politically correct**. Even Error Analysts, and even NS ones, sometimes produce forms that they would unhesitatingly reject. The late S.P. Corder took some time to notice the error in the title of one of his most celebrated papers: 'The significance of learner*'s errors'. And in a recent book about English, R. Bain writes *'During the course of their reading they have discussed a great deal *about language'* (Bain, 1991: 28). Does one discuss *about* as well as have discussions *about*?

Correctness

It is usual to distinguish grammaticality from acceptability in terms of Chomsky's competence:performance contrast. Radford, for example, calls unacceptability 'a performance notion' (1988: 11). As a grammarian, Radford gives priority to competence and grammaticality, and refers almost resentfully to extraneous factors 'interfering with the natural competence of the native speaker' (ibid.: 12). Examples of such sources of 'interference' are familiar: when the ideas expressed are distasteful to the speakers or in conflict with their personal beliefs, when they are tired, sedated or bored, or, more interesting for our purposes, if they are 'influenced by prescriptive notions inculcated at school' (ibid.: 12). In the latter case, the speakers might reject *Who did you meet at the zoo?* and insist on *Whom . . . ?*, even though they themselves always say *who* and never *whom*. The term reserved for referring to such recourse to prescriptive normative standards is **correctness**. An utterance can be accepted spontaneously, and used with conviction by the NS: it is thus **acceptable**. But reflection about explicitly learnt canons can induce a change of heart: it is then adjudged **incorrect** and rejected. But it was not spontaneously rejected by reference to NSs' intuitions of grammaticality or of acceptability. Its rejection was based on a **metalinguistic** decision. There are, as we shall see, many cases of learner language that are deemed erroneous by NSs, not because they do not say that, but because they have been told no one should. For example, the grammatical *They went with Tom and√me* is edited and replaced by . . . *with Tom and *I*. This is a case of acceptability being overruled by correctness.

Strangeness and infelicity

Allerton (1990) describes a number of types of 'linguistically strange' word combinations. There are four sorts, the first of which he calls 'inherently strange' giving *fax* and *glasnost* as examples. I fail to see what is strange in the first, given that *fox* is not strange (neither as noun nor verb) and, as to *glasnost*, it is simply not English – but what is inherently strange about that? There are English words with the same phonotactics as *glasnost*: *glisten, cost*. His second sort are semantically disharmonious combinations like *crooked year, down they forgot*, even *wet water*. They are tautological, contradictory or in some other way anomalous. They are not usual among learners. They are typical of poets, or of the poet in all of us. His third type involves simple ungrammaticality of the sort discussed above, for example *The man *which came enjoyed *to talk*. Allerton's fourth type is special, being instances of 'locutional deviance' of the sort we expect from foreigners: *He was listening *at me when I *put the statement*. They are the results of violating **cooccurrence restrictions** of English, which are not governed by fixed rules but are probabilistic or 'weighted' in unpredictable ways.

A type of strangeness not catered for by Allerton is that resulting from switching parts of speech: verb-ing nouns, for instance. Former United States Secretary of State Alexander Haig is parodied for his penchant for this sort of language in the following:

> Haig, in Congressional hearings before his confirmatory, paradoxed his auditioners by abnormalling his responds so that verbs were nouned, nouns verbed and adjectives adverbised. He techniqued a new way to vocabulary his thoughts so as to informationally uncertain anybody listening about what he had actually implicationed. . . . What Haig is doing, they concept, is to decouple the Russians from everything they are moded to . . .
>
> (Leader, *The Guardian*, 3 February 1981)

The point about this example is that it would have different status and a different level of acceptability as produced by a native speaker (General Haig) from its status if produced by a learner. From Haig, just the same as the poet's collocations, it is **strangeness**, while from the learner it would be viewed as **ungrammaticality**. For example, L1 French learners of English might produce *auditioners* for intented *audience* in an attempt to transfer French *auditeurs*. I cannot agree with Widdowson's (1987) claim that learner language and literary (poets') language are of a kind. It is true that the abnormality of poetry contributes to the creation of new meanings, but can one say the same for the learner language? Only in the sense that it is part of the meaning of a situation where one of the speakers is a nonnative speaker. And is it true of learner language, as it is indisputable for poetry, that 'we are meant to puzzle out what is said'? (Widdowson, 1987: 14). While it is true that we ought to be prepared to work at understanding IL, and not dismiss it out of hand, I doubt that the learner *means* the listener to ponder the meaning of what he says, in the quest for some extra level of subtle meaning that cannot be expressed in standard language and processed by the addressee with minimum effort.

Errors at the level of pragmatics are called infelicities by Austin in his seminal work on speech acts (1962). He identifies, in Lecture 3, four sorts of infelicity (he calls them **misfires**) that can vitiate the doing of the **performative** class of speech acts, for example *I declare you man and wife*. Though Austin limited his remarks to performatives, his infelicities are a good starting point for developing a fuller set to deal with a wider range of speech acts. In each case an infelicity will yield a different sort of sociolinguistic *faux pas*. I shall list them:

(i)   A **gap** arises when the speaker lacks in his L2 repertoire the linguistic means for performing the desired speech act. This might be the simple table manners formulae like *Guten Appetit!* or *Mahlzeit!*. Not conforming by omitting to use the required formula might be seen as foreign uncouthness by the NS host.

(ii)   A **misapplication** arises when the act performed is rightly executed – but by the wrong person, or to an inappropriate addressee, or under the wrong circumstances.

(iii) A **flaw** arises when the right language is used by the right person in the appropriate setting, but the linguistic execution is imperfect. This is the situation that arises when a purely formal error has unforeseen pragmatic consequences.

(iv)   We have a **hitch** when the execution of the speech act is cut short.

Other dimensions: errors and mistakes

We are now in a position where we can begin to construct a definition of 'error'. **Intentionality** plays a decisive role in this definition: an error arises only when there was no intention to commit one. One cannot spot so-called 'deliberate errors' because they do not exist. When any sort of deviance is intentionally incorporated into an instance of language, we do not say it is **erroneous**, but **deviant**, examples being poetic language or an advertizing jingle.

Taylor also suggests that 'The only way we can reasonably determine whether a mistake is a slip or a genuine error is by reference to the writer's semantic and structural intentions' (1986: 154). Notice the two sorts of 'intentions' identified here: what he wants to say, and how he expresses it. If the learner intends to be vague (a semantic intention) or sees it as a price worth paying for error avoidance, and consequently deploys an avoidance strategy, he or she is not committing an error of imprecision. Remember how Medgyes (see above) conceived of a learner who uses reduction (avoidance) strategies and so 'deliberately sacrifices part of his desired meaning' (1989: 74). The key word here is 'deliberately', which excludes the interpretation of the ensuing **covert** deviance as error.

We can extend the range of the concept 'intentionality' as it applies to error. Recall Lyons's suggestion above (p. 65) that the **corrigibility** of a sentence is an indication of its ungrammaticality. So corrigibility is a property of an instance of language. Moreover, the corrigibility of a sentence is up to the grammar to decide. I cannot know whether it is corrigible until I have consulted (consciously or not) the grammar. By contrast, we can test a learner's degree of commitment (another facet of 'intentionality') to an instance of language the learner has produced by inviting he or she to reconsider it. We are not now interested in whether the bit of language is corrigible in principle, but rather in whether the learner can correct it, without reference to an authority such as a grammar or dictionary. The focus has shifted from the utterance to its author. The same distinction applies to learning: a feature of language can, on the one hand, be **learnable** (in principle). This is a different question from the question of whether a given student *has learnt* it. In both examples we have shifted the focus on to the ability of the person who produced that sentence to correct it. The shift is from corrigibility to correction, and similarly from learnability to 'learntness'. We can now see how crucial the intentionality criterion is: if the learner has produced a questionable sentence, one starts to determine its status by asking him or her whether he or she intended to. We ask the learner to register his or her strength of commitment, whether he or she wishes to let it stand, or harbours doubts about it. This procedure has become the standard adopted to ascertain intentionality – after the fact. If the learner is inclined and able to correct a fault in his or her output, it is assumed that the form he or she selected was not the one intended, and we shall say that the fault is a **mistake**. If, on the other hand, the learner is unable or in any way disinclined to make the correction, we assume that the form the learner used was the one intended, and that it is an **error**.

We can now refine the definition of **error** as being an instance of language that is unintentionally deviant and is not self-corrigible by its author. A **mistake** is either intentionally or unintentionally deviant and self-corrigible. The **error:mistake** distinction was introduced into modern debate by Corder (1967, 1971) although the distinction, which is marked in other languages too (*Fehler/Irrtum* in German), had been made before. Bertrand (1987) suggests that French has the doublet *faute/erreur*, but that the former has associations of culpable inattention. Corder associates errors with failures in competence and mistakes with failures in performance, making use of Chomsky's distinction. We referred above to Radford's (1988) claim that competence determines grammaticality, while performance determines acceptability. Does it follow then that deviance in grammaticality produces errors, while deviance attributed to unacceptability produces mistakes? There is a sense in which this is true. Where the deviance is the product of the learners' own IL grammar, and is well-formed in terms of that grammar, we have **error**; and where the utterances are at odds with their authors' own grammar, leading them to reject the utterances on reflection, since they were not as intended, we have a **mistake**. If the learners reject their own utterances on the grounds of their ungrammaticality (in terms of the learners' IL grammar), it is **grammatically** unacceptable. As we have seen, there are perhaps eight sources of unacceptability, and there must logically be eight subtypes of **mistake**. The reader might care to identify these.

There is some inconsistency between Corder's two papers, suggesting he was reconstructing his EA theory over this five-year period. Corder (1967: 167) upholds the competence *versus* performance distinction, insisting that **mistakes** are of no significance to the process of language learning since they 'do not reflect a defect in our knowledge' (are not caused by incompetence) but are traceable to performance failure. The learner is 'normally immediately aware of them' (ibid.: 166) and 'can correct them with more or less complete assurance' (ibid.: 166). They can occur in L1 as well as L2, that is, native speakers as well as learners make them. **Errors**, one must assume, are everything that mistakes are not: they are of significance; they do reflect knowledge; they are not self-correctable; and only learners of an L2 make them.

By 1971, however, Corder seems to have shifted ground, for now he states that **errors** are 'the result of some failure of perform-ance' (Corder, 1971: 152). Moreover, the 'noticeable thing about **erroneous** sentences is that they can readily be corrected by the speaker himself' [sic] since they are 'cases of failure to follow a known rule' (ibid.: 152). The mistakes of the 1967 paper are the errors of the 1971 paper. What were originally competence-based errors are now features of the learner's **idiosyncratic dialect** (ID). ID forms cannot be self-corrected, and moreover need not be, since they are 'grammatical in terms of the learner's language' (ibid.: 153) and in no way erroneous, deviant or ill-formed.

In fact, plausible though it may look in theory, the test of auto-correctability (by their author) of **mistakes** is a problematic criterion to apply in practice. Their author may be able to sense intuitively that something is wrong, while being unable to put it right. It is well known that people who compose in a FL, in an exam for instance, can be given ample time to review and monitor their text, be quite convinced that there are no more ungram-maticalities in it, but still overlook ungrammaticalities that they would be immediately and effortlessly able to self-correct if only the fact that such and such a form is wrong were pointed out to them. In that case the question of whether the learners were able to auto-correct is 'yes' and 'no'. They were unable to spot the howler unaided (so it was not a mere mistake) but, once pointed out, had no trouble correcting it (so it was a mistake). Then time tells: something I said or wrote a month ago or even an hour ago and could not self-correct then, I can now correct confidently, without having done any learning of the item in the meantime. Where is the change, in me or in the defect? Is what was originally an error now a mistake?

Nor is the link between knowledge and error much less prob-lematic. As Johnson (1988) points out, if learners say or write a form that is wrong, it could be for either of two reasons: either they **lack** the requisite knowledge (this is a case of ignorance) or they deploy knowledge that they do have, but it happens to be wrong knowledge. Are these both cases of error? Do they have equal status? We could add to this question that concerning **partial** knowledge. It is becoming more and more obvious that language is learnt and used in lexical phrases of varying sizes (Nattinger and DeCarrico, 1992). Is it a question of either knowing or not knowing the unit, or can one partially know something? Shaughnessy is clearly uncomfortable with the notion of students 'not knowing' a word say, since that would imply they do not even know of its existence, whereas errors 'already attest to the student's knowledge, at some level, of the words he [sic] is using (or misusing)' (1977: 190). An advantage in distinguishing not knowing from knowing wrong is that it allows us to identify progression in FL learning, rather than the dichotomous 'on:off' idea of knowing versus not knowing. This idea of progression through a series of modes of knowing is attractive, and Snow makes a case for seeing the process in this way: 'in the first stage you are doing something completely wrong without knowing it, in the second stage you know you are doing it wrong but do not know how to do it right' (1977: 49). These would be two stages of error, following which would come the stage of mistake: getting it wrong but knowing how to put it right.

Edge (1989) is one writer who has attempted to enrich and to humanize our view of learners' errors. For him **'mistakes'** is the cover term for all ways of being wrong as an FL learner, corresponding to my own neutral term **deviance(s)**. He divides these into three types: **slips, errors** and **attempts**, the division being made 'according to the teacher's knowledge of his or her learners' (Edge, 1989: 11). Let's take these in turn:

(i) **Slips** for him are caused by processing problems or carelessness. The learner could auto-correct them 'if pointed out' and 'if given the chance'. An example is: *He had been *their for several days.*

(ii) **Errors** are, for Edge, wrong forms that the pupil could not correct even if their wrongness were to be pointed out. However, 'we can recognise what the student wanted to produce' (ibid.: 10) and the 'class is familiar with that form' (ibid.: 10). For example: *It is unfortunate the fact that he left her.* Edge's definition of 'error' seems to depend mainly on whether the target structure has been taught or not, a line also taken by

Hammerly (1991: 72). Error status is in part dependent too on whether it is idiosyncratic or is shared by other members of the same class. We see here Edge wishing to replace Corder's idea of idiosyncratic dialect with learners' social dialect, spoken by a community of learners. Such a community needs to be defined, but it will comprise pupils with a common L1, who have been exposed to the same syllabus, materials, method, and taught by the same teachers at least.

(iii) Edge's third category are **attempts**, an example of which is: *This, no really, for always my time, and then I happy.* This is almost incomprehensible, and the learner obviously has no idea how to use the right form. Yet Edge applauds the learner since they are 'trying to mean something', that is, the learner is activating their compensatory **communication strategies**.

Let us consider Hammerly's classifications. For Hammerly (1991: 72), like Edge, the status of learner deviance must be determined in terms of the classroom: 'I propose that we refer to classroom errors as they relate to systematic instruction' (ibid.: 85). In the classroom or formal learning context, then, he identifies two main categories of deviance. First, we have **distortions** (sometimes also labelled 'mistakes' but without the specificity of Corder's label). Distortions, Hammerly believes, are unavoidable and necessary, occur even with known TL forms, and should be ignored by the teacher. No appeal is made to self-correctability in defining them, but Hammerly does claim that they 'occur as **known** structures begin to be used meaningfully' (ibid.: 72), that is, presumably, at the P3 or **production** stage of the typical FL lesson, after the P1 (presentation) and P2 (practice) stages.

Distortions are of two types, reflecting whether or not the item in question has or has not been taught. If the item has been 'adequately taught . . . clearly understood and sufficiently practised' (ibid.: 85), Hammerly seems to want to blame the learners, so we shall call this **learner distortion**. He insists that 'Errors that students make with what has been taught are essentially different from . . . errors they make with structures they have no reason to know because they have not yet been taught' (ibid.: 85). Hammerly suggests that when the TL item has not been 'adequately taught' the blame for the resultant deviance should be placed at the teacher's door, since he or she 'has failed to clearly illustrate or explain, or provide sufficient practice': hence the term **mismanagement distortion**.

But Hammerly is on dangerous ground here and spinning in a vicious circle. Why does he assume that *teach* is a telic verb? How do we know that something has been 'adequately taught' apart from seeing whether it causes problems and resultant error? If a teacher has spent 20 minutes 'teaching' contractions like *can't, won't* to a class and one minute later one student gets it wrong, does that mean the teacher has not taught that form? As Kamimoto, Shimura and Kellerman so aptly observe: 'If only there were such a simple equation between the contents of the textbook and the ultimate contents in the learner's head. Then we would never need to set exams at all' (1992: 258).

Hammerly's second category are **faults**, which occur when learners 'venture beyond what they have learnt' (1991: 86) and 'attempt to express freely ideas that require the use of structures they haven't yet learnt (ibid.: 72) – the economics analogy to living beyond one's means. Again, someone has to be blamed, so there are two sorts of fault: **learner faults** occur when the students overextend themselves without being encouraged to do so by the teacher, and **mismanagement faults** signify the teacher's connivance in the overextension.

One sees the ideological divide between Edge and Hammerly clearly in their attitudes to faults. Edge applauds learners who, finding themselves ignorant of the TL form, keep trying and taking a risk rather than playing safe or avoiding error (Kamimoto *et al.*, 1992). Hammerly takes the opposite line. He is looking for someone to blame. Usually it is the learners who are to blame for 'engaging in linguistic adventurism' (1991: 74). One feels that Edge would applaud the teacher who encourages this 'adventurism' and helps learners to mobilize compensatory communication strategies, while Hammerly finds them guilty of a **mismanagement fault**.

Edge and Hammerly represent extreme views, Edge's nonchalant, Hammerly's censorious: the truth, as always, lies in the less sensational centre ground. The label used by Burt and Kiparsky (1972: 1), **goof**, strikes a neutral tone, its association with the Walt Disney character making the very notion reasonably endearing in fact. Their dictionary definition of goof is: 'An error students tend to make in learning English as a second language, for which no blame is implied' (ibid.: 1). Compare this attitude with that of Hammerly.

Hammerly, like Corder, considers the relationship between native speakers' and L2 learners' deviances. The strict Chomskian line on this issue is that native speakers (NSs) do not and cannot commit errors (of competence) since they know their language perfectly and comprehensively: they can only make mistakes, when they are distracted and tired. Hammerly claims that 'almost all the errors of SL students are markedly different from those of mono-lingual native speakers' (1991: 89). The sorts of NSs' 'errors' he proceeds to enumerate 'involve style', are 'nonstandard', concern 'spelling' and are all norm infringements. They reflect not so much competence as Chomsky conceives this, but level of education, lit-eracy and compliance with the standard. They are failures of **incor-rectness** in fact, for which we shall use the traditional term **solecism**.

It must be stressed that Error Analysis is in no way concerned with apportioning 'blame'. When we say that a piece of learner language is 'wrong', we are merely using the label as shorthand to refer to a **discrepancy** between what this particular learner (or some typical population of learners) tends to say and what the collective entity of NSs (or the ideal NS) tend to say. The 'sanctity of Interlanguage' lobby, which we discussed in Chapter 2, is based on a misconception that error identification has to be censorious.

The clearest and most practical classification of deviance is a four-way one:

(i) **Slips**, or alternatively **lapses** of the tongue or pen, or even fingers on a keyboard, can quickly be detected and self-corrected by their author unaided.

(ii) **Mistakes** can only be corrected by their agent if their devi-ance is pointed out to him or her. If a simple indication that there is some deviance is a sufficient prompt for self-correction, then we have a **first-order mistake**. If additional information is needed, in the form of the exact location and some hint as to the nature of the deviance, then we have a **second-order mistake**.

(iii) **Errors** cannot be self-corrected until further relevant (to that error) input (implicit or explicit) has been provided and converted into intake by the learner. In other words, errors require further relevant learning to take place before they can be self-corrected.

(iv) **Solecisms** are breaches of the rules of correctness as laid down by purists and usually taught in schools: 'split infinitives' and

'dangling participles', for example. They often conflict with
NSs' intuitions – and hence also with their own usage –
although at times they manage to adapt their usage to conform with the rules of correctness they have been taught. It
is probably the case that FL learners taught in formal classrooms, by NS as well as NNS teachers, get heavy exposure to
correctness-based instruction, and as a result tend to offend
against purism **less** than their NS counterparts. This might
be one of the factors that give NSs the impression at times
that foreign learners speak their language 'better' than they,
its NSs, do.

The error/mistake dichotomy exists in many alternative formulations. Let us quickly call these to mind. We have discussed **incompleteness** at length: it is a notion linked to error. It corresponds
to **imperfection** on the mistake side of the coin. The philosopher
Ryle distinguished between 'knowing that' and 'knowing how'.
The same distinction is maintained in the pair **declarative** knowledge and **procedural** knowledge (Bialystok, 1982; Anderson, 1983).
It has been suggested (Færch and Kasper, 1983) that defects due
to L1 **transfer** are errors, whereas those caused by **interference**
from the L1 are mistakes. This means that transfers are reflections
of L2 competence limitations while interference testifies to performance weakness. Bialystok and Sharwood Smith (1985: 115)
argue similarly that while transfer errors occur when the learners
are forced to fill a gap in L2 knowledge with an L1 equivalent,
interference is 'an aspect of control', in this case a lack of adept-
ness on the learners' part in retrieving a unit of knowledge they
need to access. However, to sustain Kasper and Færch's distinction requires us to view transfer as a systematic process, but interference as unsystematic, perhaps even random. I believe this is a
distinction that cannot be convincingly argued for. And finally,
there is the idea that the error/mistake dichotomy corresponds
to the NS/NNS distinction. Hammerly claims that 'almost all the
errors of SL students are markedly different from those of monolingual native speakers of the language' (1991: 89). While the
simplest response to this claim would be that NSs do not make
errors, since they, by definition, know their language perfectly, a
more interesting answer comes from considering the sorts of errors
that Hammerly ascribes to NSs. They are 'intralingual', 'involve
style', 'spelling' and so on. All are norm-infringements that are

indicative of low educational achievement or **solecisms**. Indeed they
are the sorts of problem that Davies sees as being typical of NSs:
'lack of correctness in writing . . . a lack of precision . . . an incoherence and non-clarity . . . a failure to take the reader with you'
(1991a: 56). It is also interesting to compare NSs and NNSs according to the types of **malapropism** they produce (see Chapter 5).

Error:mistake and acquisition:learning – an equation?

It is illuminating at least to enquire about the extent to which the
error/mistake dichotomy cross-associates with Krashen's (1982)
acquisition/learning distinction. There are four possible states of
knowing (see James, 1994b: 190):

- *–ACQUIRED –LEARNT*: If one has neither acquired nor learnt
  a TL form that one must now process, the result will be **error**.
  You are ignorant of the TL form, and have not the surrogate
  explicit knowledge of the TL form that would allow you to construct the target form from the rules. You are wrong and cannot
  convincingly put it right.
- *+ACQUIRED –LEARNT*: You have acquired the TL rules, and so
  you are not in a state of ignorance. You will not make **errors**, but
  you might still make **mistakes** (if you are distracted, for example).
  You will have no explicit knowledge with which to correct these
  mistakes, but might do so 'by feel', that is, by reference to your
  implicit acquired knowledge – your 'Sprachgefühl' as it is called
  in German.
- *–ACQUIRED +LEARNT*: You will make **errors**, but may be able
  to correct or avoid these by invoking learnt explicit knowledge.
  You may not actually commit the error: you may anticipate and
  avoid it by synthesizing utterances out of learnt TL knowledge.
  In this case you might be said to seize a 'hollow victory' (Krashen,
  1983: 142) over your TL ignorance. You will also possess **consciousness** of language, as defined by James: 'Consciousness gives
  the learner insight into what it is he does not know and therefore needs to learn' (1992: 184). The more often the learners
  have to correct an error, the more heightened will be their consciousness and inclination to notice input.
- *+ACQUIRED +LEARNT*: If one has both acquired and also learnt
  (about) a particular TL form that one is now called upon to

produce, the outcome will probably be right, though there may be mistakes, which one can correct. More important, however, is the fact that you have Language Awareness: 'an ability to contemplate metacognitively a language over which one already has a degree of skilled control and about which one will therefore have developed a coherent set of intuitions' (James, 1992: 184). In other words, you know the language well and know something about the language too.

We should, however, return to our definition of error. It remains for us to decide whether **mistakes** really are 'of no significance to the process of language learning' as Corder (1967: 167) claims, or is it the case, as Ellis (1985: 68) claims, that the distinction between errors and mistakes is unobservable in practice? Johnson (1988, 1996) challenges both these assumptions and pointedly gives his 1988 paper the title 'Mistake correction', arguing that too much attention has been given to errors, while the more viable prospect of mistake eradication has been relatively neglected. In other words, learners know more than we credit them with knowing. We seize upon every deviance, assuming it to be an error, whereas it is more likely to be a mistake. He is right, especially since when you have established that such and such a defect in the IL is an **error**, there is no cure but acquisition. There is no point arguing, like Hammerly, that the form 'has been taught': the teachers might have gone through the motions, and might sincerely believe they have taught this construction, but if the learners did not come out of the lesson with the targeted knowledge, the teachers did *not* teach it. The only interesting conclusion is that there has to be a new approach (not a 'reteach', because there was no first teach) that stands a better chance of success. Mistakes, by contrast, can be attended to: feedback can be given, the learners can learn how to monitor, and opportunities for further practice can be provided. It therefore follows that mistakes are of interest, at least to teachers and learners. Whether or not they are of interest to the researcher is irrelevant, like much of the research itself.

Lapsology

The study of **slips** (or lapsology) has been until recently wholly directed to native speakers' slips, and has been the research preserve of psychologists interested in how language is stored and processed in the brains of normal people, and the clinical consequences when these mechanisms go wrong. Some have tended to trivialize these phenomena as incidental, nonsystematic and superficial disturbances in verbal executions which could be repaired by the speakers if they were given the opportunity. In fact, there is ample evidence from slips made by native speakers that they are in fact systematic and for this reason alone should not be viewed as superficial. Reason insists that slips are 'not a sign of incompetence but of misplaced competence' (1984: 515). Slips are the price we pay for expertise, since they arise out of people's ability to perform thousands of highly complex mental and physical operations in short time spans. This is achieved by the **automatization** of these behaviours beyond the level of consciousness. It is this relaxation of conscious control over behaviour that, at the same time as allowing consummate versatility, renders the speaker vulnerable to slips. When these occur, it takes a restoration of consciousness, which incurs a temporary loss of fluency, to repair the fault.

Baars (1992b: 9–10) points out that there are 'good' and 'bad' slips and that the ones that make sense (intended *barn door* coming out as √*darn* √*bore*) greatly outnumber nonsensical ones like *dart board* ⇒ *bart *doard. Moreover, they tend to conform to the phonological, morphological and syntactic rules of the language. So, for instance, phonotactic constraints are obeyed in **spoonerisms**: *fried soup* becomes *side froop* (as 'good' slip) and almost never the 'bad' *sride foop or *ried fsoup, both of which break the phonotactic rules of English. In other words, 'The form of errors is lawful: the erroneous components of actions tend to conform to the constraints of the immediate context within which the error appears' (Sellen and Norman, 1992: 320). MacKay (1992) identifies what he calls the 'three puzzles' in connection with slips. First, there is the **awareness puzzle**, which asks how the speaker manages to make fine context-sensitive adjustments unconsciously. For example, when spoonerizing *cow tracks* as *track cows,* the speaker miraculously manages to convert the voiceless noun plural [s] suffix on *tracks* to the voiced variant [z] on *cows*. The second is the **practice puzzle**: why is there a higher incidence of slips on the most thoroughly practised level of language (the phonology) and fewest slips on the least practised (the grammar)? One would expect the opposite. The third is the **detection puzzle** which asks why it is that we are most able to perceive slips on the level of language (pronunciation) we are the least aware of? Again, one would expect the opposite: to be able to spot slips in our grammar, since our awareness of grammar is greater than that of the other levels of language.

It would be interesting to compare natives' and learners' slips. A first question is whether FL learners' slips conform to L1 or to TL constraints, or whether this depends on the proficiency level of the learners, that is, their degree of near-nativeness. A second question would be whether the characteristics of FL learners' lexical substitutions resemble those of natives' malapropisms, as outlined by Fay and Cutler (1977). Let us suggest the following answers to their five questions, as they relate to FL errors:

	NL	FL
1. Is the erroneous substitute a real word?	Yes	Yes
2. Are target and substitute related in meaning?	Yes	Sometimes
3. Are the pronunciations of target and substitute close?	Yes	Yes
4. Are target and substitute the same part of speech?	Yes	Yes
5. Do they have the same stress pattern and syllables?	Yes	Sometimes

The only study of FL slips I know is Poulisse (1997). She analysed 2,000 spoken slips made by 45 EFL learners at three proficiency levels. She made the following findings: (i)   L2 learners self-correct more of their own slips than L1 speakers do; (ii)   Less proficient learners produce more slips and correct fewer of these slips than more proficient learners; (iii)   People are selective about what they correct: slips affecting meaning are corrected more than slips of form; (iv)   the type of speaking task (retelling a story/ describing an abstract shape/describing a real-world scene) had no effect on the rate of slips and their correction. She looked at two types of slips closely: the third person singular -*s* ending, and the interdental fricatives /ð/ and /θ/, which do not occur in the L1. A difference between the slips in these forms made by the less and the more proficient L2 learners is of special interest: the least proficient learners failed to supply these target forms and also supplied them when it was unnecessary to do so. Poulisse's interpretation of these data is that learners who are on the threshold of acquisition of a particular feature of the TL pay extra attention to it, but this extra attention leads to oversuppliance. Furthermore, when the learners are developing fluency ('automatization'), they lose control and fall headlong into dysfluency, which leads to slips. These explanations are plausible, and very suggestive. What they clearly show is that slips (or mistakes) are far from insignificant in L2 learner language.

We are in search of learners' errors and in this chapter we have begun to define our quarry. In the next we shall come face to face with real-life errors.

4

The Description of Errors

In the end it came down to just two letters. Black or chalk. I didn't believe, I still don't believe that any sensible person, whatever his colour, objects to the word blackboard. It's black and it's a board, the word black in itself cannot be offensive. I'd called it that all my life so should they try to force me to change the way I speak my own language?

(P.D. James, *Devices and Desires.* London, Faber and Faber, 1989, p.88)

In the preceding chapters we have been concerned with the rationales for doing Error Analysis. We now move on, in this and the following chapters, from the *why* to the *how*. We hope to identify a number of key procedures that are followed, either partially or wholly, consciously or routinely, when undertaking an EA. We shall also assume that these procedures are to be executed in the order in which they are discussed here. We assume that the procedures are discrete, but concede that this assumption is an idealization, and that they tend, in practice, to merge one into the other.

I would maintain, moreover, that the 'analysis' in EA is not restricted to one relatively late procedure. That is, there is not a step in doing EA which we could properly call the 'analytical' step, a step which might, say, coincide with the collation or interpretation of one's data. One is engaged in error **analysis** right from the time that one decides systematically to assemble relevant data, using the appropriate **error elicitation** procedures. In this chapter we move to the **identification** of errors.

Error detection

Let us draw an analogy between identifying learner error and identifying, say, a suspect in a criminal investigation, but without suggesting that error-making is a culpable act. One procedure used for the latter purpose is the identity parade, which involves assembling a line-up of individuals (including the suspect) who all resemble the suspect, and asking an eyewitness to pick out the perpetrator of the crime. In EA we assemble a line-up of utterances produced or processed by a learner and ask the 'witness' or knower to pick out the one or ones that look suspicious, that is, those which are potentially erroneous.

At the identity-parade stage of criminal investigation, the police are only interested in the ability of the witness to identify the suspect. Was any one of the persons in the line-up at the scene of the crime or not? It is a yes or no decision that is made, nothing more. The term I shall reserve for this stage of identification is **detection**: if you detect an error, you become aware of its presence, nothing more. You have spotted the error. Now error detection is not as simple as you might think. People find it harder to spot error in spoken, informal language than in written, formal texts. But error detection in written texts is not always easy either: strangely, people who use word-processors find it harder to spot errors 'on screen' than in a print-out, even though both of these modes are written. Spotting one's own errors is more difficult than spotting other people's errors, which again is surprising.

Another interesting question concerns the differences between the error-detection capacities of native-speaking teachers compared with nonnative-speaking teachers on the one hand, and between teachers and non-teachers (ordinary humans!) on the other. Hughes and Lascaratou (1982) submitted 32 sentences containing an error and four without error to 30 judges, ten Greek native-speaking teachers of English, ten English native-speaking teachers of English, and ten native-speaking non-teachers. One of the error-free test sentences was *Neither of us feels happy.* It was judged to be erroneous by two of the Greek teachers, by three of the English NS teachers, and by no less than five of the ten non-teachers. Note the wide variation in detection rates. The opposite can also happen: people can overlook errors where they should be obvious. Another of Hughes and Lascaratou's test sentences was *The boy went off in a faint* (which is licensed by no less an authority

than the *Oxford Advanced Learner's Dictionary of Current English*).
Notwithstanding, two of the Greek teachers, and nine each of the
English NS teacher and non-teacher groups declared this sen-
tence erroneous. They sent an innocent man to the gallows!

Another relevant study is Lennon (1991). After having transcribed the L2 English speech of four German advanced learners
of English, he was able to identify 568 clear errors; but there were
also 208 doubtful ones. These he submitted to a panel of six educated NSs of English, and found little agreement, for all six rejected
as ungrammatical 103 of the 208, five rejected 53, and four rejected
22. Here is a sample of those 14 sentences over which the six subjects' opinions were divided equally. What do you think?

(a) *She makes ?some? gestures when she calls.*
(b) *You can see a gentlemen ringing ?at? the doorbell.*
(c) *The bank manager was told not to hold him back, so this man
?could? escape.*

As for (a), it was thought that the quantifier 'some' created oddity, but that this was corrected if an adjective was supplied before
the noun, for example *some √frantic gestures*. As for (b), it was
pointed out that you could 'ring the bell' or ' knock at the door',
but that these two constructions could not be joined. The problem with (c) for many judges was the past tense form *could*, which
was ungrammatical with the one-off (semelfactive) meaning while
being good with the 'habitually in the past' meaning. It would also
be unobjectionable if negative: *couldn't* is fine with the semelfactive
meaning.

In error detection, as we pointed out earlier, no more than a
reasonably firm yes/no decision is called for. We use the sentence
as our unit of analysis and ask our informants to report their intuition. Error analysis has to be more demanding than this, however,
as additional questions are asked about the putative 'detected'
error.

Locating errors

First, we can ask the informant to do what the police ask an eyewitness to do: to identify the suspect in some other way, such as
saying he is the third from the left, or simply pointing him out.
This is **error location**. In the three error-containing sentences above

we can point to the quantifier '*some*' in (a), to the preposition *at* in (b) and to the past tense modal *could* in (c), and say 'The error is right here'. However, error location is not always so straightforward. Not all errors are easily localizable in this way: some are diffused throughout the sentence or larger unit of text that contains them: they are what are known as **global** errors (Burt and Kiparsky, 1972). The sentence does not simply contain an error: it is erroneous or flawed as a sentence. Secondly, it is often difficult consistently to locate the error in what the learners have said or written, or in what they should have written. Take the error in *We *have visited London last weekend*. We have a tense error here, but does it consist in the learners having said *have visited* or in their having not said *visited*, that is, in having failed to select the simple past tense? Is it an error of commission or an error of omission? Or consider *Her *wet lips gently kissed the sleeping child*. Does the error lie in the misselection of *wet*, or derive from a failure to select *moist*? Turton (1989) lists the following error involving the quantifier: *Mrs. Moss said that this was the *biggest (√largest) number of dogs that she had ever come across in a Housing Board flat*. He explains that 'With "*amount*" and "*number*" use "*large/small*" (not "*big/little*")' (1989: 19). This raises the question of whether the error should be listed under *big/little* (what the learners said) or under *large/small* (what they should have said).

Burt and Kiparsky are quite clear on this point, suggesting that we should identify errors by reference to the TL, 'according to what the person who says them has to learn about English', that is according to 'a rule which he has been violating' (1972: 8). Likewise, Dulay, Burt and Krashen attribute the error in *Then the man *shooting (√shot) with a gun* to 'use of the progressive tense' (1982: 149). But is it really? Does it not, as the suggested correction indicates, reside in a failure to use the simple past? The distinction is not a specious one. People have criticized EA for wishing to censure failure (that is, what the learners have not said) rather than credit them with success. If we locate error in what the learners did say, we are at least acknowledging something that the learners do say.

This is a reasonable suggestion: the learners first need to stop making the error, and to start producing the TL form. And this, it has been suggested, is how learners do proceed. Gatbonton (1983) adopts the **gradual diffusion** model of language change developed by the creolist Bickerton and applies it to the FL learning process. This model suggests that learning involves two stages: the first is the learning stage, where the learners accumulate, in a fixed order, good (TL-like) repertoires that they did not have before. But they do not immediately reject the wrong forms they have been using prior to learning the right ones. The wrong and the right forms coexist side by side for a while, and we say that their IL is **variable**. Stage two involves not learning more good and new responses but extirpating all the old and wrong ones, so the learners are left with only the good ones. Interestingly, the order of learning and the order of rejecting are determined by the same factors.

Describing errors

Instead of asking the eyewitness to indicate the miscreant by pointing him or her out, the police might ask the witness to describe him or her. In fact this seems to be the logical thing to do. Now that the witness's memory has been jogged, he or she ought to be able to make the switch from identification by location to identification by description. And it is also the case that error description is the next step in the analytical procedure.

We made reference above (see Chapter 1) to the Interlanguage hypothesis, the essence of which is that learner language is a language in its own right and should therefore be described *sui generis* rather than in terms of the target. After all, we are all aware nowadays of the absurdity of describing English in terms of Latin, or Swahili in terms of English. To do so would imply making use of the descriptive categories that have been developed for a particular language in order to describe another language. So is it ever justifiable to describe learners' errors in terms appropriate to, or even derived from, the TL? It would be if the two codes were closely related, or 'cognate', if they were two dialects of the same language for example. Now Corder (1971) called the learner's version of the TL their 'idiosyncratic dialect'. This must imply that the learner's and the NSs' codes are dialects of the same language, the first 'idiosyncratic' and incomplete, the NSs', by contrast, a complete and a social rather than an idiosyncratic, private one. Being co-dialects of the same language, they should be describable in terms of the same grammar. Bruneian children are expected to learn standard Malay (Bahasa Melayu) in primary school (James,

1996). They tend to transfer forms from their nonstandard home dialect, Brunei Malay, to the target dialect. Since, as Nothover (1991) claims, the two dialects are 85 per cent cognate (overlapping), there would be no problem in describing the Bruneian child's errors in terms of Bahasa Melayu. A second reason for the standard EA practice of describing the learners' errors in terms of the TL is that EA is, by its very purpose, TL-oriented: this presumably is the reason why Burt and Kiparsky (1972: 8) categorize learners' errors 'according to what the person who says them has to learn about English'. The ideal would be to describe learner errors in terms of some language-neutral system, what is referred to in translation theory as an **étalon** language: texts are translated into and out of this étalon, not directly from one language to the other.

It is worth bearing in mind that Corder (1973) considered description to be the first-order application of linguistics, whether the language described was the TL, the L1 of the learner, or, in our case, the learner's errors. The system used for the description of learners' errors must be one having two essential characteristics. First, the system must be well-developed and highly elaborated, since many errors made by even beginners are remarkably complex: it is not the case, as one might expect, that only advanced learners make 'advanced' errors, since even beginning learners are very adventurous, as Hammerly (1991) reminds us. The grammar used for describing them must be the most comprehensive we have, and the one capable of maximum 'delicacy' of descriptive detail. The second essential characteristic of the system in terms of which the learners' errors are described is that it should be as simple, self-explanatory and easily learnable as possible. To borrow a term from computers, it has to be 'user-friendly'. The reason for this is that its users are teachers and learners, and it ought not to be necessary to learn theoretical linguistics before one can involve oneself in the analysis of one's pupils' or one's own errors. For this reason I can see little hope of using Chomsky's Government and Binding (GB) model of Universal Grammar (UG) for describing learner error. Descriptions of error couched in terms like C-command and barriers to proper government are just too esoteric and unlikely to be helpful to the teacher or learner. It could be argued that the system of Universal Grammar is an ideal language-neutral étalon in terms of which one could describe IL, and theory-oriented students of language acquisition, for example

Towell and Hawkins (1994) or Cook (1988), do strive to describe Interlanguage in terms of universal principles and parameters. They seem, however, not to have discovered ways of describing errors that are useful to learners wishing to improve.

A distinction is commonly drawn between 'scientific' and 'pedagogic' grammars (Bygate *et al.*, 1994). The former are of the type we have labelled in terms of UG and GB theory. They are highly technical systems that can only be understood and appreciated and used by the few people who study them full-time. Their purpose is to explain languages. Pedagogic grammars lie at the opposite end of the scale. They do not describe but exemplify, and give practice opportunities. Pedagogic grammars do not aim to be comprehensive in their coverage, but prefer to focus on those aspects of an L2 that give trouble – and trouble is usually manifest in errors. So pedagogic grammars are grammars aimed at preventing or repairing errors. They focus on difficult areas of the TL, areas where learners are known to experience problems. They are thus focused on those areas where **learnability** has been shown by EA to be problematic.

Halfway between the two extremes of scientific and pedagogic grammars we have **descriptive** grammars. The most informative, compendious and accessible of these are the theory-neutral grammars of English (see Quirk *et al.*, 1985). They are eclectic and they seem prepared to incorporate insights gained in any kind of linguistic research, at the same time wisely eschewing the apparatus and metalanguage of such research. They recycle and often reconcile adversarial insights provided by more theory-based grammarians like Chomsky and Halliday. They cover the grammar from the morpheme to the thematic organization of discourse. They succeed well in keeping things simple, and offer the best framework for practical error description. Most successful and usable applied linguistic research, including Crystal's (1982a) GRARSP (see page 118 below), has been cast in this framework.

Next, we need to ask ourselves a question: what purposes does description serve? I believe there are three main purposes. The first is to make explicit what otherwise would be tacit and on the level of intuition, so as to justify one's intuitions. Perhaps it is as basic as the human instinct to apply labels to entities and by so doing to give them substance: in a word, to reify them. Labelling a structure such as *I once saw Pele *to play football* as an 'Accusative with Infinitive containing redundant *to*' somehow captures that item. Without the label it would be difficult to talk about the item in question, so as to compare one's intuitions with those of another person. A second purpose of description is that it is a prerequisite for **counting** errors: in order to ascertain how many instances of this or that type you have, it is necessary to gather tokens into types. We shall return to this question of error quantification presently. The third function of description and labelling is to create **categories**. Labelling the Pele error in the way suggested above does two things: first, it signals that it is a different sort of error from *I once saw W.G. Grace* *to playing cricket*, since the latter requires a different sort of label. The reverse also applies: labelling *You will now hear Ashkenasy* *to play Chopin* in the same terms as the sentence about Pele indicates that they are members of the same **class** of errors. Intuitions about error do not tell us which errors belong in the same class: when it comes to raw intuitions, all errors 'feel' the same, though some might feel more serious than others. The fourth major step in the EA procedure then, after error detection, error location and error description, is error classification – or its synonym, error categorization. We turn to this now.

Error classification

We pointed out earlier that one of the prime purposes of describing errors was that this procedure reveals which errors are the same and which are different, and this was a necessary step in putting them into categories. We shall here describe a number of classificatory systems that have been used in EA, and even risk recommending the 'best'. First we shall consider what must be the simplest way of organizing a collection of errors into categories: the **dictionary** of errors.

Dictionaries of errors

Dictionaries are generally organized according to the alphabetic principle, and dictionaries of error are no exception. But there is an important difference: general dictionaries have tended to target information on the lexical system of the language, and are in this respect distinct from grammars. This is an unfortunate state of affairs, since they should complement one another. Dictionaries of error do combine these two functions, and contain lexical information alongside grammatical information. We shall look at some recent examples.

The title of Turton's (1995) *ABC of Common Grammatical Errors* conceals the fact that this book contains not only entries on grammatical errors, in the domains of subject-verb agreement, tense, passives, interrogatives, etc., but also what Turton calls 'word grammar errors'. Word grammar errors, as distinct from the other 'system Grammar errors', arise when learners violate 'rules that control the use of particular words' (Turton, 1995: vii). For example, *allow* and *let* are **synonymous**, despite which they require different complement structures: *She allowed her son to smoke* and *She let her son smoke* are both grammatical, while both *She let her son *to smoke* and *She allowed her son *smoke* are not.

Each entry in the dictionary contains the right form alongside the erroneous form, the error being asterisked in the conventional way. But a new sort of flagging symbol is used with some entries: the warning sign '!', which I feel could have been more visible and effective had it been enclosed in a triangle so as to resemble the international road sign for 'Danger': △. The symbol would be best located immediately adjacent to and to the left of the nucleus of the 'local' error, which is where we locate the asterisk in this book, so as to pinpoint the relevant direct negative evidence for the learner. Turton uses it to indicate three sorts of problem item: those where British and American usage differ, for example !*Call us during office hours at 622123* (American) versus !*Call us during office hours on 622123* (British). This is a useful category, allowing the teacher to be non-judgemental on coexisting forms in different standard dialects of English. Its second use is to flag stylistic problems connected to levels of formality, such as !*If the country's economy was (were) to improve.* And its third use is to indicate forms that people might condemn as erroneous if they followed somewhat dubious old-fashioned prescriptive rules of the sort that forbid speakers of English to end a sentence with a preposition. Examples are: using a conjunction to open a sentence as in !*And the band played on,* or use of 'their' as a possessive pronoun coindexed with *everyone* as in !*Everyone has to leave their bags outside the library,* for which purists would demand *his or her.* In the terminology developed in Chapter 3 these are errors of **incorrectness**.

What we are beginning to see therefore is a second system of error classification operating in parallel with the first, the conventional alphabetic system. There are in fact a third and a fourth system operating alongside these two, one addressing form, the other use or meaning. These correspond to [−Grammatical] and [−Acceptable], as in Chapter 3. Consider the very first entry in the *ABC*: *a/an*. First, the question is posed about the **forms** and which to select under what circumstances: *a* before spoken consonants and *an* before spoken vowels and 'silent' *h*. Next, questions of **use** are addressed: how *a/an* contrasts with *one*, with *some*, with *the* and with ∅ (zero), and how ignorance of these systematic contrasts precipitates errors such as:

Only **a person attended the meeting.*
He gave me **a good advice.*
*A number six is my lucky number.
My brother is **electrical engineer.*

Another dictionary of errors is Alexander (1994), which he intends as a compendium of 'particular words and structures which are a well-known source of error' (1994: viii). Note the division drawn between 'words' (lexical) and 'structures' (grammar). Like Turton, Alexander does not target learners from a particular part of the world, but aims for a more general coverage, as indicated by the fact that the original database of error (Alexander's private collection, assembled over years of ELT work) was checked against *The Longman Learner Corpus*, which was drawn from 70 countries. The resulting collection runs to over 5,000 items. Alexander's classification is also multidimensional, like Turton's, with the alphabetical dimension being the most superficial, again providing the main key to access. The organization is in terms of **topics** (e.g. health), **functions** (e.g. *Doing things for people*), and **grammar** (e.g. phrasal verbs). What we see here is an attempt to produce a reference book on errors that is (or at least appears to be) in harmony with the current fashion in ELT textbook organization: an attempt to produce a **notional-functional** (see Wilkins, 1976) error dictionary to use alongside EL2 notional-functional teaching materials and syllabuses. Surprisingly, in view of the avowed universality of the database, one category of error is that caused when the students' native language interferes with English. An example is the German learners' tendency to say **benzine* for √*petrol*. Here 'universal' does not mean that every error contained in the database is equally likely to be committed by all students, irrespective of their L1. It means that all the major learners' L1s are represented in the database.

Turton (1989) by contrast is not for world-wide consumption but targets learners of EL2 in South-East Asia and Hong Kong wishing to improve the accuracy of their written English. The restriction to *written* English was dictated by the sources of his data: examination scripts, and readers' letters to the English-language press in the region. The *Guide* lists 'in alphabetical order, all the common words and phrases which writers in the region find troublesome' (Turton, 1989: vii). However, even a superficial examination of the book shows that the alphabetical dimension is not by itself the operative criterion for error categorization. Its main purpose is to facilitate rapid look-up. The alphabetic organization is little more than a key to give access to the store-room of errors. Turton uses three other criteria, all more informative than the alphabetic. First, **incorrectness** regardless of the situation in which it occurs. Secondly, **casual** versus **careful**, which is a matter of the style or appropriacy of a particular form: for example the verb *nab* as in *The police nabbed the arsonist at the scene of the crime* would be designated as casual, or even as slang in British English, but has no such overtone in South-East Asian English. Likewise *kids* (for 'children') is considered over-casual if not offensive in written British English, but not so in South-East Asia. His third criterion is whether certain forms and expressions (with their associated meanings), while being unacceptable in British English, might be quite **acceptable** in South-East Asian English. An example is *bungalow*, which in British English refers to a single-storey house, while in South-East Asian English it simply means 'dwelling house' irrespective of the number of floors. Other examples are *cheeky*, meaning 'impertinent' in British English but 'flirtatious' in South-East Asian English; *chop* ('cut of meat' versus 'rubber stamp'); *compound* ('large enclosed open space' versus 'yard'). Other slightly different examples are expressions such as *airflown*, as in *airflown carrots from New Zealand*, or *heaty* in *This fruit is very heaty*, which are non-existent in British English but widely used in South-East Asian English.

Even the prototype of error dictionaries, Fitikides's *Common Mistakes in English* (1936), is only organized alphabetically at a superficial level. Its more informative and system-oriented organization divides the collection of errors into five sections, as follows:

1. Misused forms: wrong preposition, misuse of tense, and miscellaneous 'un-English expressions'. Examples are: *instead of *to wait/√waiting*; *a poem to learn *from out/√by heart*.

2. Incorrect omission: of prepositions, etc. For example, *He ran lest he *Ø miss/√should miss the train.*
3. Unnecessary words: prepositions, articles, *to*, etc. For example, *Please answer *to/√Ø my letter.*
4. Misplaced words: adverbs, etc. For example, *He worked *yesterday at home/√at home yesterday.*
5. Confused words: **to/at, *to/till, *lie/lay, *borrow/lend, made *of/from, *less/fewer, *cost/price.*

While Fitikides's classificatory system is what concerns us primarily here, it is evident that many of his entries and examples are dated (hardly surprising, given that the year of publication was 1936), pedantic or debatable. For example, on page 32 he rejects **Whom do you think will be chosen,* claiming the pronoun should be √*who* on the grounds that *who* is the subject of *will be chosen* and *do you think* 'is a mere parenthesis'. This is a misanalysis: there would have to be commas in writing or pause in speech if *do you think* were an aside, but it is not. *Who* is right, not for the reasons Fitikides adduces, but because it is the subject of the embedded passive clause *N will be chosen* and because this entire clause is the object of the transitive verb *think* and not its subject *who*. Or to take another example of misanalysis from dozens: **He was disappeared from the house* is deemed by Fitikides to be wrong on the grounds that 'intransitive verbs . . . cannot be used in the passive voice' (1936: 35). Yet it is unlikely that the learner was intending in this instance to form a passive: it is more likely a case of over-indulging the frequent past tense marking Auxiliary *was* and consequently double-marking. One last example: **I and my brother* is rated deviant, the suggested correction being √*My brother and I . . . ,* with one exception 'when confessing a fault' (ibid.: 87) as in *I and my brother broke the window.* This is ingeniously imaginative – but a purely chimerical bit of grammaticizing on Fitikides's part.

Dictionaries of 'false friends'

The most specialized kind of alphabetically organized listing of errors is the dictionary of 'false friends'. It is relevant to learners of a specific L2 who speak a particular mother tongue (MT): so there can be no **universal** dictionary of false friends. In fact the danger of false friends increases in proportion to the degree to which MT and L2 are related, that is, to the degree of their cognateness. Helliwell (1989) is intended to help German learners of English and has the amusing title *Can I become a beefsteak?* The German verb *bekommen* is a false friend to the English *become*, but its translation is *get, receive*. Similarly, German *Tablett* does not correspond to English *tablet*, but to *tray*. Helliwell lists small digestible-at-a-glance sets of true and false friends, and gives useful contextualized examples of the pitfalls, with clear explanations. She recommends use of the book as a way to 'avoid many misunderstandings' and 'embarrassing' (*peinlich* does not mean 'painful') errors. She also lists good reliable friends as well as words that can be good or false, for example *Fieber* can reliably mean 'fever' as in 'yellow fever' but it also falsely often means 'temperature' (Helliwell, 1989: 29). Working on false friends is an effective if simple form of consciousness-raising, and learners seem to be able to avoid these errors once they have been warned. But why are false-friend listings limited to lexical items? There are false friends on other levels of language too, most pervasively in grammar, for example the English *that-clause* misleads many French or Spanish learners to produce errors like: *I want *that you pay the bill.* Listing of these could be effective aids to error avoidance.

Error taxonomies

We shall now move on to consider how errors are categorized in collections other than dictionaries of error. We shall call these collections error taxonomies. Taxonomy is defined in the *New Shorter Oxford English Dictionary* (1993) as 'the branch of science that deals with classification'.

A mere listing of errors, including alphabetic ones, is not a taxonomy. A taxonomy must be organized according to certain constitutive criteria. These criteria should as far as possible reflect observable objective facts about the entities to be classified. Many criteria are in principle available for use in error taxonomies: the sex, age, or nationality of the learner, type of school attended, type of activity which gave rise to the errors, such as translation, dictation, free speech, guided composition, dictogloss, and so on. Some of these criteria will be more revealing than others, and more informative for some sorts of decision-making than others.

Note also that the criteria I gave as an illustration are not mutually exclusive. It is not the case that you can only choose one of them to classify a particular error. In other words, it is possible to classify errors simultaneously according to a number of criteria. Besides indicating that such and such an error was made by an adult, we can also indicate that this adult was male, Japanese, extrovert, intermediate, and that the error was committed in a free (not controlled) writing task. So it will be possible to specify an error in terms of a large number of features relevantly associated with it, its author, and its context of use.

The third thing to note is that the criteria listed may be binary or may allow more than two grades of the attribute in question: a learner is either male or female (binary) but could have any one of a score of nationalities. Specifying errors in terms of a set of criteria in this way yields a sort of taxonomy which we shall call a **feature taxonomy**. Legenhausen (1975: 22ff.) makes use of such a taxonomy, pointing out that the idea of feature-specification originated in phonology, but can be applied to other levels of language too. He suggests that feature-specifying an error is especially revealing when the error is **ambiguous**, since this technique enumerates the set of TL targets it might be related to. Thus, the error in *I want *her to show (the necklace)* could be reconstructed in terms of the learner having intended any one of (a), (b), or (c):

(a) *I want her to see . . .*   with features: *want* + *NP [+Raise]* + *see*

(b) *I want her to be shown . . .*   with features: *want* + *NP* [+Raise] + show [Passive]

(c) *I want to show her . . .*   with features: *want* + *show* + *NP [−Raise]*

This is very technical, but it is an attempt to make sense of the syntax of NP-raising. But surely, the learner's target in this case was (c), since her L1 is German and the verb *show*, which is cognate with the German *schauen* ('look at'), has been selected as a false friend on account of its phonetic similarity, and verb and object misordered. The learner cannot plausibly be said to have got confused over NP-raising.

Error taxonomies are usually done with paper and pencil, and the maximum number of dimensions of error that one can show on a plane surface is three: usually two dimensions are reflected in the taxonomy. The decision as to which two these shall be is a crucial one, since some are more revealing than others.

When I introduced the idea of error taxonomy above, I listed a number of theoretically possible criteria. It would be useful to look at the types of criteria people use for describing and classifying errors. We attempt to teach people how to talk and write correct, standard language, but pay little attention to their metalanguage for talking about deviant language. Not only do we need collections of errors, but as a preliminary we also need collections of error types. It is therefore worth mentioning again *DENG* or the *Dictionary of English Normative Grammar* (see Sundby, 1987) to which we alluded briefly in Chapter 1. This is a dictionary of the classes of terms used by a number of eminent eighteenth-century **proscriptive** English grammarians for stigmatizing what they considered erroneous usage of the period. *DENG* 'starts from the arguments with which these grammarians support their views on correctness' (Sundby and Bjørge, 1983: 748). Seven recurrent categories for specifying types of linguistic deviance are identified: **ambivalence**, **dissonance**, **ellipsis**, **idiom**, **incoherence**, **incongruence** and **redundancy**. Most of these labels refer to defects in the message organization, rather than in form, and are oriented towards the amelioration of style and rhetoric. They were also intended to guide English native speakers rather than learners of English as a second or foreign language. They are still valid categories today, all the more so since they were derived not from speculation but from observation of language judgements being made by experts. They are therefore empirical categories. It would make sense to replicate this approach to error categories experimentally with contemporary subjects. We need to know what criteria and what metalanguage are used by people in the present century and in L2 and FL contexts when making observations about deviant language.

Dulay, Burt and Krashen (1982, Ch. 7) suggest that there are four kinds of error taxonomy, but two of these – the *Comparative Taxonomy* and the *Communicative Effect Taxonomy* – deal with error causes and error gravities respectively, and we shall consider these issues later in Chapters 6 and 7. For the moment we are concerned only with *descriptive* taxonomies. They suggest that there are two kinds of descriptive taxonomy of the sort we are concerned with. Let's consider each of these.

Linguistic category classification

This type of taxonomy carries out specification of errors in terms of linguistic categories, in terms of where the error is located in the overall system of the TL 'based on the linguistic item which is affected by the error' (Dulay *et al.*, 1982: 146). First, it indicates on what **level** (or in which 'component') of language the error is located: in phonology, graphology, grammar, lexis, text or discourse. Next, there is a specification of the 'category' of linguistic unit where the error occurs. If it is a grammar level, what particular grammatical construction does it involve? Some possibilities they list are: the auxiliary system, passives, sentence complements – in fact, the sorts of categories conventionally used for constructing structural syllabuses for TEFL and the related teaching texts. I suggest some refinement of this system. Having established the level of the error, one next asks about its **class**. Given that it is a grammar error, does it involve the class of a noun, verb, adjective, adverb, preposition, conjunction, determiner, etc? Then we need to assign a **rank** to the error, in terms of where it lies on the hierarchy of **units** that constitute its level. Finally, we need to specify the grammatical **system** that the error affects: tense, number, voice, countability, transitivity, etc. So, if it is a grammar level error, and involves the class noun, we want to know if it is located at the 'rank' of, for example, (noun) morpheme, word, phrase, clause, or sentence and what grammatical system is affected. The taxonomy is rigorous in that these categories of level, class and rank are mutually defining. For example, the class 'noun' is manifest at different ranks: as word noun, as noun phrase, as noun clause. As an example, consider the following error:

We *use to/√∅ go swimming every morning

The learner is attempting to use *used to* (indicating habitual behaviour) in the present tense. So, it is a grammar **level** error involving the word **class** verb, and the **system** of tense.

This framework is certainly useful, and can handle the errors of relatively advanced learners. One problem with the scheme is that while we have a reasonably well-understood set of units on the level of grammar, what the corresponding units are on the levels of phonology, lexis and text/discourse is not so clear. For analysing lexical errors, the categories of **sense relations** (synonymy, hyperonymy, opposite, etc.) and of **collocation** will be appropriate. There are also emerging at the present time useful categories for describing discourse errors, such as coherence, cohesion, signalling, and so on.

The Surface Structure Taxonomy

This is the second type of descriptive taxonomy proposed by Dulay, Burt and Krashen (1982). It is not a very satisfactory label. Why make reference at all to 'surface' structure, when the deep versus surface structure distinction is immaterial anyway, there being no 'deep structure taxonomy'? A more acceptable descriptive label for this would be the **Target Modification Taxonomy** since it is based on the ways in which the learner's erroneous version is different from the presumed target version. Are we steering dangerously close to the 'comparative fallacy' again? Dulay, Burt and Krashen themselves describe this taxonomy as being based on 'the ways surface structures are altered' (1982: 150). We must not lose sight of the fact that we are speaking metaphorically, however. It would be quite misleading to say that the learner 'alters' or 'distorts' the correct form so as to produce an error. This formulation would imply that he or she knew the correct form all along, in which case he or she would not have produced an error in the first place. Nor are the four main kinds of 'alteration' in any way suggestive of the behavioural or cognitive processes involved in learning L2 forms: it is merely a vivid, albeit loose, useful metaphor.

Dulay, Burt and Krashen suggest that there are four principal ways in which learners 'modify' target forms, in other words, four ways in which IL and TL forms diverge 'in specific and systematic ways' (1982: 150). In addition there are four further subtypes, yielding eight in all. I shall discuss these, and conclude that viable taxonomy can operate with four of their categories plus a fifth (**blends**) of my own.

1.   Omission (Ø)

This is to be distinguished from **ellipsis** (E), and from **zero** (Z), elements which are allowed by the grammar (indeed are powerful grammatical resources), whereas omission is ungrammatical. Compare:

> *He'll pass his exam but I won't* [*pass my exam*]. Ellipsis
> *He'll pass his exam and I'll* [Ø] *too.* Omission

A high omission rate leads to a truncated IL with features similar to those found in pidgin languages, and is typical of untutored learners or learners in the early stages of learning. It tends to affect **function** words rather than **content** words at least in the early stages. More advanced learners tend to be aware of their ignorance of content words, and rather than omit one, they resort to **compensatory strategies** (Kasper and Kellerman, 1997) to express their idea. Dulay, Burt and Krashen do appear here to equate omission with non-acquisition, which is disturbing. It does not seem reasonable to describe non-use of 3rd. person -*s* and progressive -*ing* in early second-language English as omission.

2.   Addition

This manifestation of error, Dulay, Burt and Krashen suggest, is the 'result of all-too-faithful use of certain rules' (1982: 156), and they suggest there are subtypes. First, **regularization**, which involves overlooking exceptions and spreading rules to domains where they do not apply, for example producing the regular *buyed for *bought*. As one might expect, omission, being the mirror image of over-inclusion, tends to result from the converse, **irregularization**. This occurs when a productive process such as affixation is not applied, but instead the form is wrongly assumed to be an exception to the general rule: *dove for the preterite form √dived. A second subtype of oversuppliance is **double marking**, defined as 'failure to delete certain items which are required in some linguistic constructions but not in others' (ibid.: 156). A typical result is an English sentence having two negators or two tense markers instead of one. Here is an example: *He doesn't know*s me* contains a redundant third person -*s* on the main verb *know*, redundant because the auxiliary *do* already carries that marker. One presumes that the learner has intuitively formulated a rule 'the lexical verb must carry any required third person inflection', overlooking the exception to (or overregularizing) this rule and applying it in contexts where there is an auxiliary that carries the -*s* already. A very similar account could be rendered of the double past tense markings in: **I didn't went there yesterday*. However, some of their examples of regularisation, such as *sheeps and *putted could just as well be seen as double marking, suggesting that the distinction is not clear-cut. Regularization and double marking seem to be two ways of referring to the same phenomenon. They might be distinguished by saying that while regularization is the process or the cause, the second is the product or effect. We shall presently suggest that double marking is an error type that can be better accommodated under the heading of **blend**. The third category of addition error is **simple addition**, which caters for all additions not describable as double markings or regularizations.

3. Misformation

This is Dulay, Burt and Krashen's third category, and again they identify three subtypes. They define **misformation** as use of the wrong form of a structure or morpheme, and give examples like:

I *seen her yesterday.
He hurt *himself.
I read that book*s.

It is indeed clear that *seen* for *saw* is use of the wrong form, but why call it 'misformation'? It is not, no more than *that* is a 'misformation' of *this*. What the learner who produced this error has done is not misform but misselect, and these should be called **misselection** errors. Dulay, Burt and Krashen do in fact use this term, when defining another subtype, **archiform**, which they define as 'The selection [sic] of one member of a class of forms to represent others in the class' (1982: 160). For example, out of the set *this/ that/those/these* the learner might use only one: *that*. This is clearly misselection of a special kind, what Levenston (1971) referred to as **overrepresentation**. While it is probably not the case that these four demonstratives occur with equal frequency of use by native speakers of the TL, it would be very unlikely that NSs use only *that*. But learners do, and **overrepresent** this one form and at the same time, as a consequence, **underrepresent** the other three.

It is strange that Dulay, Burt and Krashen designate **regularization** as one of the three subtypes of misformation. The examples they give – **runned, *gooses* – seem to have exactly the same origin as **hitted, *womans*, which were given to exemplify regularization as a subtype of overinclusion.

Another of the subtypes that Dulay *et al.* assign to the category of misformation is what they call **alternating forms**, which they define as 'fairly free alternation of various members of a class with each other'. Let's simplify by considering cases where just two 'members' are involved. There are three possible pairings: [right +

wrong], [right + right], and [wrong + wrong]. We can disregard the second of these as being irrelevant in EA. Consider then the first case, using the wrong and the right forms of a particular construction at the same stage in learning. An example is early EL2 negation, where *I √don't play* and *I *no play* alternate in the IL of a learner. Now, if one of two forms used by a learner alternately is well-formed, it is not an error, and only the other, deviant, form is of interest to the error analyst. On the other hand, being right in some linguistic contexts and wrong in others does suggest that the learner is not in a state of total ignorance of the rule concerned: would it be legitimate to say that the learner 'half-knows' the rule? Can one half-know anything? These are indeed pedagogically relevant phenomena, since teachers are often frustrated by such inconsistency in learners, and are tempted to see the pupil as culpably careless. Even more irritating for teachers are alternations of the [wrong + wrong] type, such as *I *seen her yesterday* occurring alongside *I have just *saw her*. This learner seems to have totally reversed the two rules in question, and some radical intervention seems to be urgently called for.

Such variation in IL can have the status of either **free variation** or of **conditioned variation**, both familiar concepts in basic linguistics. If two or more forms that are thought to be instances of the *same* entity occur in random alternation, that is, without there being any apparent principle differentiating them, such as formality or their linguistic environments, we say the forms are in **free** variation. If there is a principle such as the sex of the addressee, one form being used when speaking to boys and the other when speaking to girls, determining the choice of variants, we say they are **conditioned**. Now, it may be the case that one of the variants is right, the other wrong. Or both might be wrong. Or both might be right. Whatever the combination, it is the erroneous one or ones that are of interest to Error Analysts. Therefore 'alternating forms' is not *per se* an error category or even a subtype: the erroneous form is the concern of EA. This is not to say that the coexistence of right with wrong forms in learner repertoires is not an interesting fact, since it raises the question of whether it is sensible in this case to talk in terms of learners 'half-knowing' a TL form, or whether it is indeed the case that 'nothing is "fully" learned until everything is "fully" learned' (Corder, 1973: 283). A second question arising is whether the learner knows the **form** but not the **distribution** of L2 items. We usually specify rules of language on two dimensions: in terms of the forms involved, and in terms of their location. So, in transformational grammar, some specified form gets moved from location x to location y. We might wish to specify linguistic knowledge in the same terms. The Surface Strategy Taxonomy divorces these two properties, dealing separately with formation and with placement. 'Alternating forms' is therefore not a discrete type of error, since the relationship between the deviant and the targeted form can be adequately described in terms of the other categories. We now turn to the last of these.

4. Misordering

This category is relatively uncontroversial. Part of linguistical competence, in addition to selecting the right forms to use in the right context, is to arrange them in the right order. Some languages have stricter word-order regulation than others. Russian is freer than English. Modern English is less free in its word order than Old English. In English certain word classes seem to be especially sensitive to misordering, for instance adverbials, interrogatives and adjectives, yielding errors as in: *He every time comes late home, *Tell me where did you go, *The words little.

Just as important as syntactic ordering is rhetorical ordering: different linguistic-cultural groups develop conventions determining what each considers consensually to be the 'right' way to order one's arguments or reasons in writing for example. Getting these rhetorical orderings wrong is part of contrastive rhetoric (Connor, 1996).

Slightly different from misordering is what I call **misplacement**. For example (see Chapter 9), letter-writing conventions in different cultures specify whether the date on a letter shall be at the top left or top right of the page. Failing to conform to such conventions is misplacement.

As Dulay, Burt and Krashen observe, misordering is often the result of learners relying on carrying out 'word-for-word translations of native language surface structures' (1982: 163) when producing written or spoken utterances in the TL. An insightful account of the use learners make of 'mental translation' when producing and processing a FL or L2 is to be found in Cohen (forthcoming).

To summarise so far, Dulay, Burt and Krashen (1982) offer a useful descriptive error taxonomy which I suggest we call a *Target Modification Taxonomy*, so acknowledging the fact that it is based on a comparison of the forms the learner used with the forms that a native speaker (or 'knower') would have used in the same situation. Dulay, Burt and Krashen's system comprises four main categories plus four subcategories. Some of these I reject. Others I coalesce or relabel, and so retain the following categories: **omission**, **overinclusion**, **misselection**, and **misordering**. However, to these I shall want to add a fifth not considered by Dulay, Burt and Krashen.

5. Blends

There is one category that complements the **Target Modification Taxonomy**. It is typical of situations where there is not just one well-defined target, but two. The learner is undecided about which of these two targets he has 'in mind'. In such situations the type of error that materializes is the **blend error**, sometimes called the **contamination** or **cross-association** or **hybridization** error. There are subtle differences implied by these different labels waiting to be teased out. Blending is exemplified in *according to Erica's opinion which arises when two alternative grammatical forms are combined to produce an ungrammatical **blend**. In this example according to Erica and in Erica's opinion seem to have been blended.

There are also contentious cases: for example, Dechert and Lennon (1989) suggest that the blend in (*The punishment consists of*) *a sentence to prison results from a combination of the two following noun phrases: *a prison sentence* and *being sent to prison*. It might also be the case that the near-homophony of *send* and *sent(ence)* reinforces the confusion.

Blending has been widely studied in speech error ('slips') research, and Hockett (1967) and later Baars (1992a) explain it in terms of the **competing plans hypothesis**. As Dechert and Lennon put it: 'The blending errors we have found in written composition may derive from the co-temporal availability of two alternate syntagmas' (1989: 134). This means that the speaker or writer has activated two structures that are semantically related, either of which could serve his present purpose. But they fail to make a clear choice, and instead combine a part of each to produce a structure with characteristics of both. In fact, as Stemberger (1982: 319) suggests, three types of outcome are possible:

(i)   There is total mutual inhibition of each potential target, so the result is a **deletion**. Torn between the options *ask* and *raise*, the speaker articulates neither and so produces *I just wanted to ∅ that.* This is not a case of avoidance, however.

(ii) The conflict of choice is not resolved: the speaker selects both options, and the result looks like an **addition** or **overinclusion**:

(a) *The only thing I want*
(b) *The one thing I want*
> (c) *The √only one/*one only thing I want*

(iii) This is the standard blend. Part of each target is inhibited, and part is used, resulting in 'a blend of the intended and unintended'. So, at word-rank, a simultaneous accessing of *stops* and of *starts* results in **starps*. Or, to use one of Dechert and Lennon's VP-rank examples, (a) and (b) are simultaneously accessed, and the blend (c) results:

(a) *The question is easy to answer.*
(b) *The question is easily answered.*
> (c) *The question is *easy to be answered.*

Francis (1994) gives an interesting example of a blend involving the verb *comprise*:

(a) *a typical Indian meal comprises rice, dhal . . .*
(b) *a typical Indian meal is comprised of . . .*
> (c) *a typical Indian meal *comprises of . . .*

Her explanation is suggestive: 'It seems that language users are unable to cope with having interchangeable active and passive forms, and systematically mix them up to get a hybrid' (Francis, 1994: 23). It is possible that the near-homophonous and near-synonymous verb *composed* was involved here.

Three questions of interest to the Error Analyst arise here: first, is there any consistency in what the learner 'decides' to keep and what he or she decides to jettison? Consider the blend error in

(a) *This will facilitate *learning of a second language.* I assume this originates from the co-accessing of (b) *. . . facilitate the learning of*

a second language and (c)   . . . *facilitate learning a second language.*
Why did the learner keep the preposition *of* and jettison the article *the*? He or she could just as well have done the opposite, keep
the *the* and jettison the *of*, producing the equally erroneous *This
will facilitate *the learning a second language.* The second question is
whether the two co-available options must be from the same language, that is: can MT and L2 elements get blended? Nemser (1991:
359) suggests they can, giving as an example a hybrid German +
English preposition created by a learner combining *bis* with *until*
to give **untis.* Another example (Gomes da Torre, 1985) is the
sentence written by a Portuguese learner of English: **Tobacco is
very nocent to the health,* the adjective being a blend of Portuguese
nocivo ('harmful') with the English *innocent* ('not harmful').

The third question about blends is their **status**: are they errors,
that is, signs of ignorant incompetence? Yes and no. No, because
the learner knows the two co-available inputs. Yes, because the
outcome certainly has the appearance of a **syntactic malapropism**,
originating as it does in the simultaneous availability of two options
and resulting as it does in a solecism. The speaker does not know
that the two parts cannot be combined, at least not in the way he
combines them. Ignorance is the problem.

Learning strategies

Readers familiar with the literature on learner strategies (see Kasper
and Kellerman, 1997 for an up-to-date discussion), which postdates
the heyday of EA by at least a decade, will perhaps have noticed
affinities between some of the categories used there and those of
our Target Modification Taxonomy for errors. So Selinker (1972)
mentions '**overgeneralization** of TL rules' and '**system simplification**' as pervasive learning strategies. Richards (1974b), for his
part, draws up a fuller but similar list, including '**overgeneralization**', '**ignorance of rule restriction**', '**incomplete rule application**'
and '**hypothesizing false concepts**' as learning strategies. Some of
these strategy types are very dubious; how, for instance, can being
ignorant of a rule's restriction be a 'learning strategy'? Ignorance
might lead one to devise a strategy, either for learning what one
was ignorant of, or something that will serve the same purpose.
But ignorance is not itself a strategy. 'Generalization' is a strategy, involving the search for parallels and grounds for analogy;
but overgeneralization is an unwanted consequence of applying

generalization indiscriminately. Finally, 'system simplification' surely is not a strategy for learning the TL, but one for learning a related but simpler system: one might call it a learning avoidance strategy rather than a learning strategy. These behaviours on the part of learners fail the test as learning strategies. Fortunately, they do rather better as descriptive categories within the metaphor of **Target Modification**.

Combined taxonomies

Recall that Dulay, Burt and Krashen (1982) propose the two taxonomies we have just described as if they were *two* alternative taxonomies. This, however, is to overlook the considerable advantages of multidimensional taxonomies. Rather than using these two taxonomies in succession, why not combine them into a single bidimensional one? Each would provide one of the two axes for the new taxonomy, which we illustrate in Figure 9.2 on page 274.

But why do we have to stop at a two-dimensional taxonomy? A three-dimensional one would be feasible (using a graphic cube) and the increase in information provided by the third dimension would be invaluable. What would be a useful third dimension? I suggest some quantitative information. The problem of error counting is worth considering further.

Counting errors

A further reason why we classify errors is to allow us to count tokens of each type. Stemberger (1982), whose data are of native speakers' slips, recognizes the four categories of error we have just outlined in the Target Modification. He adds some quantitative information as a bonus: that the order of relative frequency of the four types of error, from most to least frequent, is as follows:

MOST: Misselections > Blends > Deletions > Additions :LEAST

It would obviously be useful to know whether this order of frequency is also reflected in L2 learners' errors.

One study which made good use of quantitative aspects of errors is the *Good Language Learner* study conducted at the Ontario Institute for Studies in Education (Naiman *et al.*, 1978). The aim of this project was to identify the cognitive styles and personality types of successful anglophone learners of French as a second language in Canada. A necessary preliminary was therefore to separate learners who made many errors from those who made few on a spoken imitation test. Additional information was inferred from the types of error that were made, and their relative proportions. There are two definite articles in French, masculine LE and feminine LA. Let's look at the scores from one group of students for their use of the target article form LA. First, a count was made (1978: 70) of the number of **occurrences** or 'occasions of use' of LA: 24. The number right was 12 (50 per cent). The number of **substitutions** was 6, which is 25 per cent of occurrences. Next, the percentage of substitutions of LA by LE was 4 (66 per cent). Finally, LE replaced LA on 4 out of 24 (16.7 per cent) occasions. Similar details are calculated for **substitutions** (or better **misselections**) involving UNE, MON, UN for LA. As the scope of enquiry widens to cover the complex system of determiners, substitutions for LE, UN, UNE and DES are noted and can be counted and converted to percentage scores or segments on pie charts.

Given that the French determiner system comprises the forms LE, LA, UN, UNE, it would be interesting to know what preferences for substitutions are exhibited by 'good' and not-so-good language learners, and by language learners at different stages, from beginner through intermediate to advanced. Naiman, Frohlich, Stern and Todesco discovered an increasing general tendency to prefer LE, that is to overgeneralize LE, up to and including Grade 10, with LE/LA being successfully differentiated by Grade 12. These findings are consistent with Stemberger (1982), who, in a very insightful study of speech errors ('slips' in our terminology), points out that there is 'an asymmetry between substitutions, with one direction being far more common than another' (1982: 323). His diagnosis is in terms of **markedness**: relatively infrequent, more complex structures tend to be replaced by structures that are more frequent, less complex and have 'fewer restrictions'. These are categories we have met before, expressed in the more familiar terms of '**overgeneralization**', '**system-simplification**' and '**ignorance of rule restrictions**'. Stemberger gives as an example the distinction between full and pronominal noun phrases (NP): the latter are marked relative to the former, which means that pronouns are subject to more constraints on movement than full NPs. Consequently, while (a) is as acceptable as (b), (d) is not so while (c) is:

(a) *Write down your name* ⇒ (b) *Write your name down*
(c) *Write it down*   ⇒ (d) **Write down it*

Stemberger makes a second observation that is relevant to the question of counting errors, and which, incidentally, is also relevant to the issue of error gravity (see 1982: Ch. 7). This is what he calls the 'snowballing effect'. It occurs when the learner's use of one erroneous form opens up the floodgates for a whole series of contingent errors to surface. These would not be errors if the structures they occur in had been themselves correct choices. But in relation to the original target structure they are errors compounded upon error. Stemberger's example (1982: 326) is in the sentence **It was all told me about* for √*I was told all about it*. Its genesis is as follows: first the noun phrase *it . . . all* has been made subject of the sentence. The obvious sentential function left for the remaining NP pronoun *I* is to become object of the transitive verb *tell*: this is the first **concomitant** error. We now have **It all was told me about*. Now 'quantifier float' takes place, moving *all* to the left. One wrong move has invited two further ones. Here is a simpler example of concomitance: *People *has the right, but *he has also *his duty*. This was produced by a learner of English with MT Portuguese. In Portuguese, *o povo* ('the people') is a masculine singular noun. This leads to the first error, the third person singular verb *has*. At this point the snowball begins to roll, causing first the selection of *he* as the subject of the second clause. This subject pronoun in its turn precipitates the selection of the third person possessive pronoun *his* in the object NP position of the same clause. These last two are **concomitant errors**. It is arguable that they are not errors at all, since they reflect not ignorance but poor control, and would be better classified as performance mistakes. In other words, one might argue that the only error in this sentence is the misselection of the first (wrong) finite verb *has*, and in the context of that selection, the subsequent *he* and *his* are non-errors, but are well-formed. Some would even wish to point out that they are at least consistent, and show that the learner is treating the L2 systematically.

Lennon (1991) makes some useful proposals for counting error. The first issue is whether we should count **types** or **tokens**. In other words should we count repeat occurrences of the same error? He suggests that if the repeat is a **lexical replica** of a prior error, it is not to be counted as a distinct further error. There is thus one error in *He *play¹ tennis very well but football he *play² badly*, since *play²* is a lexical replica of *play¹*. The one exception is where the two lexical replicas (homonyms) represent distinct targets, as was the case when one of Lennon's German subjects used **lucky* in one place to mean '*happy*' and elsewhere to mean '*ugly*'. In all other cases, that is, if the two tokens are not replicas but are distinct in lexical representation, they are counted as two errors, as in *She *play tennis very well and also she *swim very well*. These proposals are sound, but they do not address the more complex and contentious cases involving grammar error repeats. Consider *Yesterday he *steal my book and *accuse my friend*. One or two errors? They are not lexical replicas but different verbs, having distinct past tense morphology, the first involving internal vowel change, the second suffixation. They are wrong in different ways, despite both being tense errors, which argues for them being treated as two distinct errors, not repeats of one and the same error.

Profiling and Error Analysis

A technique for describing and categorizing features of pathologically deviant language developed in the field of language therapy is **linguistic profiling**. It is a technique that ought to be exploited in FL teaching, specifically in EA. Crystal defines a profile as 'a chart which describes an aspect of a person's spoken or written language in such a way that distinctive patterns of achievement readily emerge' (1982b: 314). He suggests that if profiling is expertly executed and the relevant facts are displayed in a meaningful way, quantification of the data will not be necessary. The relevant tendencies will be clear for all to see on the profile. We also see in Crystal's definition an attempt to stress positively the 'patterns of achievement' that emerge, and thereby to disassociate himself from the alleged morbidity of EA. But of course where these 'normal' patterns are not clear-cut or fail to emerge uniformly, there will be patterns of under-achievement, and the enterprise again takes on interest for the Error Analyst.

Crystal (1982a) gives detailed accounts of linguistic profiling of English children and adults referred for remedial intervention by a language therapist. Outlines are given for producing and interpreting profiles of several types, each of these types reflecting a **level** of language. Unlike the schemes for error classification we have seen, which try to reflect a global picture of competence on all levels of language, the profiles we shall now consider are each restricted to one level. There are four such instruments in use:

- GRARSP is the Grammar Assessment Remediation and Sampling Procedure.
- PROPH is the Profile in Phonology, which categorizes the segmental features of phonetically pathological speech.
- PROP is the Prosody Profile, whereby suprasegmental features of speech – especially intonation – are analysed.
- PRISM is the Profile in Semantics, and shows how a child's system of meanings is developing, or an adult's is disturbed.

We shall consider only GRARSP and PROPH, to see to what extent they resemble those taxonomies discussed above, and to see whether these sorts of profile could be used for the analysis of FL learners' errors.

GRARSP for grammar profiling

Notice, first, that the data sampled for the purposes of profiling 'must be graded in terms of its degree of approximation to adult norms' (Crystal, 1982a: 7). Crystal realizes that a profiling operation that has remedial goals must be normed. Just as in EA we orientate learner data to NS norms, so in therapy adults' language provides the norm. Both have a teleological bias. What NSs and normal adults have in common is that they are both 'knowers', as we have argued elsewhere in this book. Notice also that Crystal 'would like all profiles to have an acquisitional dimension' (1982a: 7). This means that the patient's language development, apart from being compared to adult norms, that is to what we might call **attainment** norms, is also compared to the norms of language **development**. This is to endorse the 'natural order hypothesis'. For this reason, one of the axes of the GRARSP chart reflects the seven stages of grammatical acquisition that all normal MT-English-acquiring children go through, between the ages of nine months and four and a half years.

'Normal' (in both senses of the word) developmental sequences are referred to in other profiling enterprises developed for MT teaching. The British National Curriculum makes reference to **attainment targets**, which are assumed norms of development. The Australian primary school materials for teaching oracy, reading, writing and spelling (the language arts), *First Steps* (1994), refer to **developmental continua**. Children are supposed to proceed through from five to eight **phases** in developing each of these skills. In learning to spell, for example, there are five phases: preliminary spelling, semi-phonetic spelling, phonetic spelling, transitional spelling and independent spelling. Detailed accounts are given of the characteristic behaviours of children at each stage, and a matching set of resource books is available to ensure that each child takes each phase in its stride, so that the 'national profiles' are achieved. There is here, as with Crystal, a strong assumption of the existence of an invariant 'natural' order of learning.

The question arises as to whether a taxonomy of FL learners' errors could likewise refer to the invariant order hypothesis. Now, as Crystal admits, the said hypothesis is not very safe, even for plotting MT **acquisition**, 'because research findings are unclear' (1982a: 7). It is even less safe for FL **learning**, where orders seem to vary a great deal, according to the type and quality of teaching and the learner's MT. In foreign language EA, therefore, we are left with but one norming reference, the NS, and it seems sensible, in the absence of reliable alternatives, to retain the Target Modification Taxonomy which we explored earlier.

To return to our account of GRARSP, stages I to IV are the stages of one, two, three and four-element utterances respectively. This is a useful mnemonic: at stage III the normally-developing child is forming mainly 3-element utterances, together with some 2-element and some 4-element utterances. It is at stage VI that GRARSP opens its first '**error box**', where errors at the rank of word, phrase, clause and **connectivity** are to be entered. One axis for the GRARSP taxonomy is thus the rank of the unit of grammar at which the error was committed. The other axis is one likewise familiar from our account above: it is articulated in terms of Target Modification. The symbols ∅, =, and 'category' (**N**, **V**, etc.) are used to indicate how the child's form differs from the presumed target: ∅ indicates **omission**, so the annotation D∅ for the form *I see *man* indicates that the determiner has been omitted. D= for **Man a there* indicates the **misordering** of the determiner. Pr. tagging **On my photo* indicates a **misselected** preposition. The category which appears not to be catered for is that of **overinclusion** or addition.

What is particularly strange is that the notion of 'error' does not arise until stage VI, which children normally reach between ages three and a half and four and a half. Let us look at the reasons for this late recognition of errors. There seem to be three. The first is that the GRARSP approach takes a 'positive' view of errors 'as indications of progress . . . logical extensions of principles previously learned' (Crystal, 1982a: 38). The second reason is that 'errors should be tabulated only when there is an indication of correct learning elsewhere in the sample' (ibid.: 40). This means a deviance in use, say of a determiner, would only be entered as an error if the same child was using that determiner correctly elsewhere in the sample. This would constitute evidence that the child can 'cope with the construction' (ibid.: 41). The third argument is that the child should not be 'penalized for not doing something which is only to be expected at some later stage of linguistic development' (ibid.: 40).

One's first reaction is that Crystal seems not to be dealing with errors (of ignorance) but with mistakes in performance. If children are capable of producing the target form accurately at one point in the sample it is assumed that they know it and that any failure to produce that form at some other appropriate point is irrelevant, 'positively' viewed not as an error but as a mere slip. There are two problems with this argument: first, reference to the natural order of acquisition suggests that the procedure **is** concerned with knowledge rather than with performance, with errors rather than slips. Secondly, the significance of a child's inconsistency in first producing, and then failing to produce, a target form is overlooked. Variability theory in SLA research (Tarone, 1983) suggests that such inconsistency is not random and trivial, but is systematic and explicable, for example by reference to context. To **know** a TL form is to be able to process it in all the relevant contexts where it occurs, not just in a subset of those contexts. Moreover, as Gatbonton (1983) has shown, it is a characteristic of language learning that there is a **gradual diffusion** of correct TL forms that occur alongside deviant forms for a transitional period. Eventually, if learning continues, the non-target-like forms are suppressed by the TL forms.

The idea that children cannot be expected to 'beat the clock' and produce forms that they are not yet ready to produce is plausible. FL learners, however, might well be able to beat the clock, since they benefit from instruction and are often exposed to syllabuses that present features of the target language in an order that is different from the order in which they would be naturalistically assimilated. The FL learners' MT is also likely to influence the order of acquisition, speakers of an MT having articles being less overwhelmed than speakers of article-less MTs when it comes to learning an L2 that uses them (Oller and Redding, 1971). These reservations do not apply, however, to child MT acquisition. Comparative constructions do not occur regularly in children's speech before stage V, at the age of three. The reason is that the very notion of comparison is beyond the cognitive capacity of younger children, who cannot be expected to encode it. Consequently, we would not classify the non-use of comparatives at age 2.0 as errors of omission.

PROPH for phonology profiling

While PROPH uses adult norms as its matrix, it has no developmental axis, because the case for an invariant order of phonological acquisition is weaker than that for the development of grammar. As Crystal writes: 'It is therefore not possible, as yet, to construct a profile chart in which [m], say, was singled out as an early-learned segment, [ʃ] as a late-learned segment, and so on' (1982a: 73). What is slightly surprising is the decision to norm the child's emergent phonology to Received Pronunciation (RP), a decision which Crystal himself seems to be slightly uncomfortable with (ibid.: 58). After all, only about 3 per cent of British native speakers use RP, though the percentage is probably higher among speech therapists. However, there ought to be no valid objection to RP norming when the PROPH instrument is used in EL2 settings, where, provided British English is the target, RP is likely to be favoured also. Crystal realizes, of course, that not all children referred to a therapist are incipient RP speakers and he suggests that each child's 'accent conventions' should be annotated on the PROPH chart. He also suggests (ibid.: 65) that the vowel section of PROPH should be altered if the patient is targeting a 'regional' that is, a nonstandard variety of English. In an L2 setting these 'accent conventions' would be the phonological interference coming from the learners' MT, that is their 'foreign accent'. Though these are not the sole sources of problematicity in L2 phonology learning, they are a major source, and should not be marginalized as they might when PROPH is being used for clinical purposes. It will suffice to specify the L2 learners' MT, at this stage, enter their phones in the chart, and postpone further reference to the MT until a later stage of the EA, when one's concerns are diagnosis and remediation.

The first step in PROPH is to elicit and record 100 words of spontaneous speech and to transcribe these. In FL phonological profiling the literate L2 learner can be asked to articulate a standard text. 'Articulate' can mean either read aloud or repeat in chunks. It is true that this way of eliciting speech samples is unnatural, and that monitoring will take place to an extent that would be impossible in the production of spontaneous speech. Unmonitored spontaneity is at this time less important than control and comparability, which can be achieved if the sample is read or repeated. If all subjects produce the same text, we shall be able to compare each L2 learner with a native-speaker model, not an abstract or ideal model but an individual whose speech has been subjected to exactly the same analytical procedures as the speech of each learner. We shall also be able to compare the pronunciation profiles of different learners from different backgrounds and at different stages in their learning. I have found the text '*Arthur the Rat*' (Abercrombie, 1964: 65) useful for eliciting speech samples from different subjects whose pronunciations I have wanted to compare. It is a text that elicits all the phonemes of RP, and Abercrombie supplies an RP transcription which makes a useful and authoritative basis for comparison.

The second step in PROPH is when the phones transcribed are transferred to a **segment classification** chart where each vowel and consonant is entered according to the position it occupies in the syllable in the patient's speech: the positions are: initial consonants (C-), vowels, which are syllable nuclei, hence -V-, final consonants (-C), and consonant clusters (CC/CCC) in initial, medial or final positions. In addition to their syllable positions, the patient's phones are also classified conventionally according to place and manner of articulation (for consonants) and as short, long, monophthong/diphthong, open/close, front/mid/back for vowels. The third step involves extracting from the data quantitative and qualitative information about the patient's performance, for example, the proportions of phones of each category pronounced well or mispronounced in the three syllable positions. There are three kinds of analysis undertaken in PROPH:

(i) *Inventory.* This section displays which phones actually occur in the speech sample. One can read off which consonants, classified by place and manner of articulation, were used in C-, -C-, and -C positions. Similarly one can read from a vowel chart how many vowels of which length and complexity were produced on the front/back and the open/close axes of vowel classification. One can calculate the overall vowel-to-consonant ratio, and determine whether the patient's speech makes abnormally high use of vowels, thus producing an excessively 'open syllabled' English. This is a tendency that one would predict to occur among learners of EL2 whose MT has high incidence of open syllables, for example Spanish. There is also an inventory of consonant clusters, organized according to whether they are initial, medial or final, and according to their place and manner of articulation.

(ii) *Target analysis.* At this stage, sound segments and clusters elicited from the patient are compared to the pronunciation that the 'normal' adult speaker would have used. For each 'target' phone and for each cluster there are three columns, one each for correct, omitted and substituted realizations. This is close to our **Target Modification** chart, except that there is no space for 'oversuppliance' of a phone. Presumably, this is because a phoneme is the minimal phonological segment, and the set of them is inventorized. If one pronounces an extra segment, one creates a cluster. Whether it is a legitimate cluster or not is a matter to be determined by looking at the target inventory. So, if the patient says [pn-], this is a case of a non-target-like cluster, not a case of a redundant [p] or [n].

The Target Analysis is claimed to be 'an initial representation in terms of phones and phonemes' (Crystal, 1982a: 94), but in fact the consonant TA is in terms of degree of fit between the patient's version and the target in terms of manner and place of articulation features such as **bilabiality**, which involves not one but a whole class of phones [p, b, m] or **plosion**, which affects [p, t, k, b, d, g]. These are very informative classifiers. The Target Analysis also contains a set of parameters to cater for other kinds of phonological error. In each case the patient's pronunciations are compared with the target: for example, the patient monophthongizes where the target diphthongizes, or vice versa: *[kold] for √[kould]. There are matrices for dealing with nasalizations, a common problem in Brazilian English; word stress misplacements, as when Germans say '*free time* for *free 'time*; vowel rounding or unrounding, as when French speakers articulate English like Inspector Clouseau in *The Pink Panther* film; excessive or over-reduced vowel length; and voicing/devoicing.

(iii) *Phonological Process Analysis.* PROPH has so far dealt with 'phones', idealizations of speech segments. However, the speech chain does not use discrete segments in this way: minimal segments are combined and fused into more fluent stretches of speech. How this happens is explained by reference to phonological processes. PROPH makes reference to several sorts. First, the **syllable structure processes**, which lead to simplifications, deletions or additions: saying *[na:na] for 'banana', *[ka:] or *[kaka] for 'cat'. Then there is **assimilation**, when two sounds in a word are made the same, converting [dog] into *[gog]. In PROPH, these processes are pathological and the focus is on the **deviance** these forms represent from 'normal' speech. In L2 teaching we take a **positive** view of these processes, since they are keys to fluency. For example, while it is right to say [sekreteri] on four syllables, in casual speech one simplifies and deletes and in fact says [sekətri] on three. We would therefore modify the PROPH in the direction of making special note of the emergence of any tendency for the L2 learners to employ these processes in a native-like manner.

Profiling L2 learners along the lines that have been developed by Crystal and others in clinical linguistics has the potential to make a big impact on EA and L2 pedagogy. GRARSP and PROPH obviously cannot be imported into L2 EA unadapted, but they do provide a solid basis for developing FL profiling. The greatest value of a profile is that it displays, at a glance and without the need for complex calculation, the 'state' of the learners' language in terms of features like C:V ratio, numbers of substitutions and omissions.

Computerized corpora of errors

Computerized corpus linguistics continues to have a profound effect on language studies, both descriptive and applied. The Birmingham University corpus, known as the 'Bank of English', has yielded the *COBUILD Dictionary* and *COBUILD Grammar.* The corpus is constituted of texts collected from native speakers of English. A complementary corpus is the *International Corpus of English* (or *ICE*) being assembled at University College in London (Greenbaum, 1991). It contains samples of English from all over the world, the so-called 'New Englishes' of India, The Caribbean, Malaysia, and so on. These New Englishes (Kachru, 1985) have their own native speakers of course and are not learner varieties (Interlanguages). It is natural that there should also be interest in carrying out the computational analysis of **learner corpora**, of English, to which we now turn. We shall consider two projects on the computer analysis of learner language, with particular attention being paid to their potential relevance to error description and classification.

The International Corpus of Learner English

ICLE is being assembled at Louvain University, Belgium, by a research group headed by Granger (Granger, 1993). It involves English as the TL and nine (at the latest count) learner varieties of English, the learners having the mother tongues: French, German, Dutch, Chinese, Swedish, Spanish, Finnish, Czech and Japanese. Two essays written by advanced learners of English from each of these nine MT groups were collected, as well as 'models' from English native speakers, the latter 'to act as a control for the learner corpus' (ibid.: 63). Ultimately, the ICLE will contain a minimum of 200,000 words for each learner variety, representing around 400 essays of 500 words each.

Note, then, the comparative dimension, which we have defended throughout this book as being essential to EA. Yet Granger denies that errors as such are to be the focus of the study. It is rather the stylistic and quantificational **differences** between authentic NS English and learner English that she intends to identify. This is exactly the sort of undertaking to which computer analysis is especially well-suited. Granger refers to this quality of learner language which she wants to describe as 'foreign-soundingness . . . which cannot be attributed to real errors' (ibid.: 63). She seems to have '**linguistic strangeness**' in mind, of the sort we discussed in Chapter 3. An example is the tendency for MT French learners of EL2 to overuse *can* and to underuse *could* in comparison with NSs. She also refers to collocational oddities, similar to the kinds we discussed above under the concept of 'strangeness'. One could also classify these as **covert** errors. She will probably also include for analysis the rhetorical and discoursal infelicities that are discussed in the emerging field of contrastive rhetoric (see Connor, 1996).

There are four stages in processing the data: **encoding**, **markup**, **tagging** and **parsing**. The first, encoding, involves entering the text into the computer. Typing up is very time-consuming, but a scanner can be used to machine-read typed text straight into the computer. Markup means identifying errors and indicating their nature. Tagging means assigning part-of-speech labels to structures in the corpus, while parsing means identifying and specifying syntactic structures. The question that arises here is whether the categories used for parsing should be TL categories or should be any categories that suggest themselves by an objective and independent analysis of the IL itself, *sui generis*. ICLE tags the head noun *progresses* in [*the progress*es in nuclear physics . . .*] as [third-person singular verb], that is, with the only possible descriptor for that form in the TL. But it parses the whole as a noun phrase. The error lies in the learner using a finite verb in such an NP, and the error will be automatically registered. In other words, the error supposedly lies in the discrepancy between intended structure and selected part-of-speech. This is convenient, but asks us to believe that the learner, in producing this NP, intended *progresses* as a verb. This is difficult to justify.

COALA or Computer-Aided Linguistic Analysis

This project, described in Pienemann (1992), has been developed over the last ten years at Sydney and Canberra Universities in Australia, and is designed to handle a corpus of learner language or IL. After transcription, there follows the procedures of tagging and parsing. First, a sentence is selected and its lexical constituents are checked against a COALA lexicon. Now phrases in the sentence are assigned functions such as subject, object, adverbial, etc. Next the structure of each phrase is analysed. Take the learner sentence *work in restaurant* as an example. First, *work, in,* and *restaurant* are checked off against the lexicon, then *in restaurant* is assigned the function 'Prepositional Phrase' in the IL, and finally the structure [PP [P in] [NP[N restaurant]]] is assigned to the utterance.

The user-interface of COALA is called the **Report Generator**, and this displays on-screen or in printouts sets of relevant information 'on demand'. As would be expected, it gives access to a concordancing facility called KWIC (Key Words in Context): this will allow the researcher to see in what contexts and collocations the learners use a specified word. The Report Generator has other functions too. For example, it will collect and display all recorded tokens of a specified structure type. It will thus display morphological types such as [VERB PAST Participle *equals*: -ED], or syntactic types such as [Word Order *equals* WH-word + Aux + NP Subject], or [NP Subject *is a* Pronoun]. It would be interesting for example to make this last structural specification for a subcorpus of EL2 recorded from learners whose MT is a PRO-Drop language, in order to see if avoidance is taking place.

COALA raises again the issue of the *comparative* dimension of EA. Pienemann (1992) shows some ambivalence on this issue. On the one hand, he claims that a learner's IL is essentially an unknown language that has to be analysed *sui generis*. As a consequence of this, the parser must '*discover* the rule system . . . rather than *recognise* the instantiations of a given rule system' (ibid.: 61). He goes on to argue that a parser based on the English TL would tell us little about the IL. His example is the learner utterance *German plenty work* which is assigned the parsing [[N] NP1 + [det + N] NP2]S, where the det(erminer) is '*plenty*'. This would be 'blocked' on purely distributional grounds by an English-based parser, since proper nouns do not precede determiners in English. That is precisely what the Error Analyst wants though, an automatic error-detection device of this sort. Every formula blocked would be entered into the error corpus, while all formulae not filtered out would pass as being well-formed and therefore not relevant to the EA. But that would not be sufficient: as well as detection we want to build in mechanisms to describe and categorize errors. COALA seems to offer good prospects for these ambitions. In fact, the comparative dimension that we view as essential to EA is well catered for by COALA, particularly by the Lexicon. This ensures that structures are marked not once, but twice; first in the sentence analysis of the actual IL data, and then, secondly, in the Lexicon itself, but this time in terms of the TL (English). And, crucially, 'Information stored in the Lexicon represents the Target Language' (ibid.: 88). So in the IL utterance *him go work*, '*him*' is marked {Subject} at the sentence analysis stage, but the

Lexicon specifies for '*him*' that it must be {+Object}. This is sufficient dissonance to turn on the error-detection bell. At this point we are beginning to specify the nature of the error, in terms of the IL-to-TL discrepancy that is the hallmark of EA.

In this chapter we first addressed some basic problems that arise when one starts to identify, describe and classify language errors. We saw the approach taken by those who compile dictionaries and similar such collections of errors, and evaluated some proposed schemes for classifying errors according to linguistic (where does the error locate in the system?) and behavioural (what did the learner do wrong?) dimensions. We proposed the **profiling** techniques that have been developed for language therapists as having much potential for profiling foreign language learning achievement and its shortfall. Finally, we briefly introduced readers to some ongoing work on the computer analysis of corpora of learner language, stressing its relevance to EA.

5

Levels of Error

Mrs Malaprop: An aspersion on my parts of speech! Was ever
such a brute! Sure, if I reprehend anything in this world, it is the
use of my oracular tongue and a nice derangement of epitaphs.
(Richard Sheridan, *The Rivals*, 1775, Act 3 Scene 3)

In the preceding chapter we looked at ways to describe errors. In
this chapter we focus on the classification of those errors. We do
so by reference to three criteria: **modality**, **medium** and **level**.
Modality refers to whether the learners' behaviour was receptive
or productive. Notice that we prefer 'receptive' as a label to 'passive' since language processing is never passive: on the contrary,
'passive' processing calls for considerable mental activity and interpretive involvement on the receiver's part. **Medium** indicates
whether the language produced or received was spoken or written.
Was the learner operating, when the error was made, with speech
sounds or with written symbols? Taking modality and medium
together, we are able to specify which of the 'four skills' the learner
was operating at the time of the error: speaking, writing, listening
or reading. In addition to this we want to specify on what **level** of
language the learner was operating at the time he or she erred.
We recognize just three levels of language: the levels of **substance**,
text and **discourse**. If the learner was operating the phonological
or the graphological substance systems, that is spelling or pronouncing (or their receptive equivalents), we say he or she has produced an **encoding** or **decoding** error. If he or she was operating
the lexico-grammatical systems of the TL to produce or process
text, we refer to any errors on this level as **composing** or **understanding** errors. If he or she was operating on the discourse level,
we label the errors occurring **misformulation** or **misprocessing**

1	Errors in encoding in speaking (Mispronunciations)	
2	Errors in encoding in writing (Misspellings)	SUBSTANCE
3	Errors in decoding in hearing (Misperceptions)	ERRORS
4	Errors in decoding in reading (Miscues)	
5	Errors in composing spoken text (Misspeaking)	
6	Errors in composing written text (Miswriting)	TEXT ERRORS
7	Errors in understanding spoken text (Mishearing)	
8	Errors in understanding written text (Misreading)	
9	Errors in formulating spoken discourse (Misrepresenting)	
10	Errors in formulating written discourse (Miscomposing)	DISCOURSE
11	Errors in processing spoken discourse (Misconstrual)	ERRORS
12	Errors in processing written discourse (Misinterpretation)	

Figure 5.1   Levels of error

errors. These six types are then differentiated further according to the **medium** of each. The result is the classificatory system of errors with TWELVE categories shown in Figure 5.1.

This simplified classification reflects standard views of linguistics: while 'medium' relates to **substance**, 'text' can be equated with **usage** and 'discourse' equates with **use**. Following a suggestion by Connor (1996: 83–4), text will take **cohesion** into account, while **coherence** is treated as a feature of discourse organization. Each of the twelve types allows further classification, in terms of the five categories we identified in Chapter 4: *omission, redundancy, misselection, misordering* and *blends*. The grid is now capable of differentiating 12×5, that is 60 error types, which we consider to be powerful enough. The rest of this chapter discusses only some of these, since space does not allow an extended account of all.

Substance errors

Misspellings

A misspelling (MS) is a substance level production error. It is one of the four types of substance error and one of the three subtypes of writing error – the other two being text level and discourse level **writing** errors. Textual and discoursal writing errors involve violations of connectivity and incoherence, which we shall discuss presently. However, there are other sorts of substance errors besides

MSs that involve writing. They are referred to as 'mechanical' errors. There are four kinds:

1. Punctuation errors

The most frequent are overuse of the exclamation (!) by some writers; misordering of closing inverted commas; underuse of apostrophe<s>; under- or overuse of capitals; overinclusion of a comma between an antecedent and a restrictive relative clause: *I know a man**, *who fought in the Boer War*; and misselection of the colon instead of the comma after the salutation in letters: *Dear Mrs. Merton**: for *Dear Mrs. Merton*√,. There is one sort of error that could be seen either as a spelling or a punctuation error: overuse or underuse of the space between parts of compound words. Carney (1994: 84) calls this a **split**, examples being <*to#*gether*>, <*out#* side*>, <*in#*tact*>. The inverse type – lets call it **fusion** – is seen in *<*takeaway*>, *<*cashpoint*> and involves failure to separate the constituent words. However, there is considerable indecision and apparent normlessness surrounding this phenomenon in English education, some forms appearing with three variants: split <*cash point*>, fused <*cashpoint*>, and hyphenated <*cash-point*>.

2. Typographic errors

People who are normally (when using a pen) good spellers might be poor typists and their writing be full of '**typos**'. Their problem is in automatizing the required temporal and spatial mechanisms that underlie skilled fingering on the typewriter, or keystrokes on the word-processor. In fact, we are dealing here with mistakes (of manual execution) rather than errors (of linguistic competence), and this probably explains why psychologists interested in skill learning have paid more attention to typing errors than applied linguists have. An excellent study is MacNeilage (1964), in which he analysed 623 typing errors committed by five typists: note that 'nothing that could have been a simple spelling error was included in the sample' (1964: 147). He found that 33.4 per cent of the typos could be best described as **spatial errors**, since a key was struck adjacent to the intended one on the keyboard, while 28.7 per cent were **temporal errors**, involving the misordered typing of letters. The spatial errors fell into three subtypes – **horizontal**, **vertical** and **diagonal** – according to positions of the intended and typed keys relative to each other. Thus *<e> for intended <w>

or <r> is a horizontal error, *<r> for <f> a vertical error, and *<x> for <d> a diagonal error. The temporal errors included **reversals** (*<ht> for <th>), **omissions** (<len*th> for <length>), and **anticipations** (<ex*texted> where the <-t-> anticipates the sixth letter in <expected>). Note that the reversals are anticipations, since they result from premature selection of a later-occurring letter in the word. There are fewer examples of **delayed** reversals, that is, of selecting a letter after it is required, as in <explana*nion> for <explanation>. The following general findings emerged from MacNeilage's study:

- Errors made with the left hand significantly outnumber right-hand errors for both horizontal and vertical types of spatial error, but handedness has no effect on temporal errors.
- Columns of letters typed with the left index finger (<r,f,v,t,g,b>) were the most susceptible to error.
- With reference to the three rows of letter keys on the **QWERTY** keyboard, horizontal errors are most frequent on the bottom row and least so on the top row. The tendency is to omit letters on the bottom row and to type to excess letters on the middle or 'home' rows.
- The less frequently used (in English at least) letters are the most error-prone; but this is to be expected, since these keys are inconveniently situated on the QWERTY keyboard, in order to maximize its efficiency.
- Spatial errors tend to occur more on shorter words, temporal errors more on longer words.
- Spatial errors tend to occur on the first three letters of a word, as do temporal errors, except that the latter do not often affect the first letter.

These findings are even more significant today than when they were first published, owing to the widespread adoption of the word-processor. The mechanical problems of jamming at high typing speeds that dictated to some extent the QWERTY keyboard layout are no longer operative in the non-mechanical (electronic) word-processor. It would therefore now be possible to design a new key-board that is more efficient than the QWERTY. It is also absurd that speakers of other languages (Welsh for example) should be forced to use the QWERTY, which was designed to optimally exploit the letter frequencies and transitional probabilities across adjacent letters of English. It is inevitable that these frequencies are different in other languages. For reasons that must be commercial, or inertial, the manufacturers of keyboards refuse to listen to such objections and continue to market QWERTY. There is scope for research into typos, looking specifically at the obstacles created by QWERTY, and comparing English typing efficiency with that of typing in other languages that use QWERTY or other keyboards.

3. Dyslexic errors

Some of the errors dyslexics make are MSs: *<parc> for <park> is a misselection from two letters that can represent the same sound [k] in English, and *<tow> for <two> is a misordering. Dyslexics also produce errors that are not MSs. One such is *<deb> for <bed> and *<adowt> for <about>, involving the reversal of the letter <b> into <d> or **strephosymbolia**. Even *<sat> for *asked* (perhaps originating in the allegro pronunciation [ast], is pathological, not the sort of simple inversion a child might make in the course of learning to spell.

4. Confusibles

Carney gives the amusing example '*to marry a *devoiced woman*' and observes that 'These are *lexical* errors involving confusion between similar sounding morphemes and words' (1994: 82). What Carney calls 'phonetic near-misses' belong there too, examples being *<choix> for <schwa> and *<anus> for <onus> as in *the onus of proof.* These look like **malapropisms**, which we shall discuss in the section on lexical errors. However, Mrs Malaprop's solecisms were all spoken; we do not know whether she produced written ones as well. Perhaps literacy raises people's awareness of differences to the point where they can avoid such confusions in their writing at least. There are further complications. First, there are occasions where two lexically different words are 'pure homophones in the speaker's accent': *<course> for <coarse> as in *the *course/√coarse [kɔːs] fishing season,* *<chords> for <cords> as in *vocal *chords/√cords.* These are not lexical confusions: the speaker knows two words in each case, but has failed to differentiate between them in spelling. Even less likely candidates as lexical errors are those showing confusion in word parts such as an affix: <conson*ent> for <conson√ant>, <d*escriminate> for <d√iscriminate>. In this case the writer is not confusing two words but the graphemic representation of a syllable or morpheme forming part of a word. This has much in common with the misselection of a grapheme where more than one candidate is available, for example selecting <ff> instead of <gh> to represent the phoneme /f/ in the word <draught>. All this suggests that the line of demarcation between lexical and spelling errors is vague.

Misspellings proper

Misspellings (MSs) as such violate certain conventions for representing phonemes by means of graphemes. A **grapheme** (the term was coined by Boudouin de Courtenay in 1901) is 'a feature of written expression that cannot be analyzed into smaller meaningful units' (*Concise Oxford Dictionary* (Sykes), 1989). So <f>, <ff>, <ph> and <gh> are graphemes which represent the phoneme /f/ in English; <x> represents the sound sequence [-ks] as in <box>. The error:mistake dichotomy is in force with regard to spelling also: *<shoos> for <shoes> is a MS, but writing double <mm> in *<ommission> in anticipation of the double <ss> is a performance slip (of the pen) or mistake.

As to the similarities and differences in the spelling strategies (and resultant MSs) of MT and L2 spellers, there is surprisingly little clear evidence. James and Klein (1994) analysed the MSs of German learners of English and found that the L2 spellers have at their disposal four 'routes' to spelling an L2 word: the routes via L1 phonology, via L2 phonology, and via L1 and L2 graphology. Moreover, these different resources may influence L2 spelling, either separately or in combination. L1 transfer was found to be operative in spelling, but not in proofreading. Lester (1964: 749) compared the spelling success of EL1 and EL2 spellers on four categories of words:

A: High frequency and high regularity, such as <cat, paper>
B: Low frequency and low regularity, such as <tsetse, ghoul>
C: Low frequency and high regularity, such as <fen, yak>
D: High frequency and low regularity, such as <of, one>

The ascending order of difficulty for the EL1 spellers was found to be: A<C<D<B, suggesting that their strategy is to rely on regularity and learn rules. The EL2 spellers had a different difficulty order: A<D<C<B, indicating that they rely slightly more on frequent exposure and learn by rote rather than by rule. Brown (1970) replicated the Lester study and found the opposite: that 'both

ENL and ESL speakers perform better on words of high frequency than on words of low frequency' (1970: 235).

There are two other noteworthy studies of L2 spelling. Ziahosseiny and Oller (1970) showed that learning to spell an L2 that has a Roman script is harder if one's L1 also uses a Roman script: the learners expect the script to have the same spelling conventions in L2 as in L1, so they transfer from L1. Ibrahim (1978) analysed the spelling of learners with L1 Arabic. His analysis is aimed principally at diagnosis, although, as he claims, one common diagnosis of MSs, L1 interference, is ruled out in this instance since Arabic uses a different alphabet from English. Some of the MSs were, however, caused by the contrasts between Arabic and English phonology: Arabic has no /p/:/b/ contrast, only /b/, which leads to the MSs <*blaying>, <Ja*ban>. Arabic has no consonant clusters, so vowels are inserted in the spelling to split up English clusters, giving MSs like <communis*em> or <s*ecool> 'school'. The majority of Arabs' MSs, however, arise from the 'nonphonetic' and arbitrary nature of English spelling, and are therefore similar to those committed by native speakers.

James, Scholfield, Garrett and Griffiths (1993) analysed the MSs in the EL2 writing of a group of 33 Welsh-dominant primary school children of average age 10:7. This study was part of an investigation of the claim made by Plann (1977) that children who acquire a second language in an immersion classroom develop a classroom dialect of that language. We wondered whether it might be the case that such children also develop an idiosyncratic system of spelling the L2. We did indeed find evidence of massive transfer of L1 Welsh phonographic (PG) or sound-to-spelling rules to L2 English spelling. Here is an example of Welsh children's English spelling:

> There has been a pyst paip in the tawn all of the tawn has had a flyd. Water was rysing awt the siop has flydod saw badli that the poles has to get them awt thrw the wyndow. The water has gyst and browcan the tow frynt window. Wen the wotermen ceim they said: 'We are sow sori that there is a pit mising and we cannot finis of the pit has too cym from America it will teick 2 or 3 weeks to araifd.'[1]

We identified several types of phonetically motivated MSs. These and the children's route to them are displayed in a flow chart (Figure 5.2).

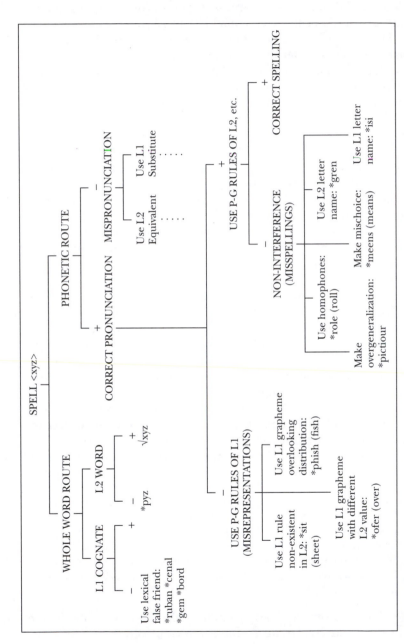

Figure 5.2 Phonetic route spelling strategies

It is immediately obvious that there are two broad categories of MSs here:

1. Mispronunciation errors

First, there were those MSs that were in a sense committed before pen met paper. They are the result of the mispronunciation of the EL2 target sound. We therefore call them **mispronunciations**. They are of two types, reflecting whether the bilingual used an L1 substitute phoneme or substituted a phonetically close EL2 sound. We carried out a Contrastive Analysis (see James, 1980: Ch. 4.3) of the Welsh and English phonologies and identified a dozen contrasts, in the form of sounds present in English but absent from Welsh, that would lead to mispronunciation of English by Welsh-dominant children: English [æ], [aː], [ɜː], [ʌ], [ɪə] , [ɛə], [uə], [z], [ʒ] and [ʧ]. Now, as a result of mispronouncing the target sound, the children access a grapheme which they wrongly think represents the 'target' sound. But of course it does not; it represents the sound they have substituted for the real target. So, for example, the [ʌ] in 'blood' gets phonetically substituted by Welsh [ə], which is normally spelt <y>: the resultant MS is *<blyd>. Another example is [uə] in 'poor' which is pronounced [uː] in Welsh and accordingly spelt <w> to yield *<pwr>. English [z] is pronounced [s], so 'zoo' is spelt *<soo> or *<sw>.

2. Written misencodings

Clearly not all MSs originate in mispronunciations. Assuming the pronunciation is correct, the spellers now have to access and activate TL phonographic (PG) or sound-to-symbol rules to represent the pronunciation of each phoneme. Many good spellings result. But there will also be MSs. Since they do not reflect mispronunciation we call these **misencodings**. Again there are two sources of misencodings: bilinguals might err in applying a Welsh mother tongue PG rule, or they might use an inappropriate PG rule of the EL2 itself. Accordingly, we call the first type **interlingual** and the second type **intralingual** misencodings:

Interlingual.   There are three subtypes:

- Use of an L1 PG rule non-existent in the L2. Welsh has a rule [ʃ] ⇒ <si>, as in <*siarad*> [ʃarad] *speak* or in <*siop*> [ʃɒp] *shop*.

When misapplied to English, where this rule does not exist, the result is the misspelling *<sit>* for intended *sheet* [ʃiːt].

- Use of an L1 grapheme that does exist in the L2, but with a different sound value. For example, in Welsh but not English <f> has the value (can represent the sound) [v], as in <ofn> [ɒvn] *fear*. In English <f> ⇒ [f] only. Applying the Welsh rule to English yields the MS *<ofer> for *over*. The digraphs <ll> and <dd> fall into this class: in Welsh these graphemes represent the sounds [ɬ] and [ð] respectively, while in English they are geminates representing [l] and [d]. These are therefore graphemic 'false friends', similar in appearance, but different in the sounds they signal.

- Use of an L1 grapheme that also exists in the L2, but has different distributional constraints in each language. For example, there is a PG rule in Welsh and English alike whereby [f] ⇒ <ph>. In Welsh we have <ei phen> 'her head' and in English <phone>. However, while in English <ph> ⇒ [f] can occur word-initially, medially and finally, as in *phone, nephew, graph* respectively, in Welsh it can occur only word-initially. We do not therefore expect from Welsh speakers George Bernard Shaw's notorious MS *<phish> for *fish*, but do predict a tendency for them to 'underrepresent' (Levenston, 1971) English [f] ⇒ <ph> and to favour instead the <ff> spelling, producing MSs like *<neffew>, *<graff> in mid and final positions in the word. This is exactly what happens.

Intralingual.   These are MSs that cannot be attributed to the L1 PG rule system and are thus non-interference MSs. James, Scholfield, Garrett and Griffiths (1993) identified four subtypes:

- Overgeneralization of a productive L2 PG rule. For example, the rule [jə] ⇒ <iour> works well for words like *saviour, behaviour*, but cannot be generalized to serve for *picture* since the result is *<pictiour>. Likewise [tj] ⇒ <tu> works for *tune* and [dj] for *dune*, but not for *<duse> *deuce*.

- Homophone confusion. This is the result of failing to differentiate between two existing words that sound the same but are differently spelt. Examples are: *<tern> for *turn*, *<role> for *roll*, *<there> for *their*, and *<through> for *threw*.

- Mischoice. An example is the misspelling *<meens> for *means*. This is different from the homophone type, since there is no

English word *meens*. There is no reason why there should not be however. In a sense, the speller is unlucky.

■ Letter naming. This is a spelling strategy that consists of using a letter to represent a sound which is identical to the sound of the name of that letter. An extreme example is *<mt>* [emti] for *empty*. Examples in the Welsh data are: *<ether>* [iːðə] for *either*, *<shak>* [ʃeik] for the vowel of *shake*. The preceding examples involve the English name for the letter; the following use the Welsh letter-name: *<rich>* [riːtʃ] for *reach*, *<a>* and *<ant>* for *are, aunt*, the Welsh name for the letter *<a>* being [aː].

Mispronunciations

Mispronunciations, as we have seen, can trigger misspellings, but they are a category of medium errors in their own right. They are errors in encoding at the productive phonological level when speaking an FL. Here 'speaking' means speaking spontaneously or from memory, and not reading aloud from a written text. Errors arising in this second situation, defined as 'oral reading errors made when reading a passage of prose', are **miscues** (Potter, 1980: 116). They result from using the wrong GP correspondences. However, though mindful of its legitimacy, this is a distinction I shall ignore here for practical reasons: in order to make a systematic study of the EL2 mispronunciations of learners from a wide range of L1 backgrounds it has been convenient to elicit from subjects renderings of the same set of articulation problems. To this end I have asked them to read aloud and record the same prose passage, a text entitled *Arthur the Rat* (Abercrombie, 1964). Whenever possible I supplement the reading aloud data with some of spontaneous speech elicited under interview conditions. As Dickerson (1977) showed, IL pronunciation accuracy reflects the degree of formality of the situation in which it is elicited. Since the reading aloud situation is more formal, and allows more opportunity for monitoring than the interview, we expect accuracy to be higher in the former condition.

Where the text read aloud has a representative sample of the sounds of the TL (in this case English), it offers excellent opportunities for **profiling** the pronunciation skills and shortfalls of either individuals or groups of learners with shared characteristics, notably a shared native language. The profiling procedure PROPH was described in some detail in the previous chapter. Here it will suffice to demonstrate how to start a phonetic profile of an FL learner.

Pronunciation errors are of three broad types: **segmental, combinatorial** and **suprasegmental**. We look at each in turn, illustrations coming from a reading aloud of the first paragraph of the *Arthur the Rat* passage by a Thai advanced learner of English, transcribed below:

[də stɔri ɒv atɜ də ræt].

[deə wɒz wɒn eɪ jʌŋ ræt neɪm atə, hu wʊd nɛvə teɪk də trʌbu tu meɪk ʌp hiz maɪn. wɛnɛvə hɪz fren æsk hɪm if hi wʊd laɪk tu goʊ aʊt wis dɛm, hi wu oʊnli ænsə ai doʊ noʊ. hi wʊdn̩ sei jɛs ænd hi wʊdn̩ sei noʊ aidə. hi kud nɛvə lɜn tu meɪk ə ʧɔɪs]

Segmental

First, we identfy problems with segmental consonants. Note the problem with the interdental fricatives [θ] and [ð]: [θ] in *Arthur* becomes [t], while in *with* it becomes [s]. [ð] in *the* is [d], as it is in *there, them* and *either*.

As for segmental vowels, we see success and failure with the [ʌ] vowel, which becomes [ɒ] in *once* but is on target in *trouble* and *up*.

Combinatorial

The learner is finding it difficult to pronounce consonant **clusters**, especially in the word-final position, and tends to omit (∅) the second of two consonants, so that [wɒns] *once* ⇒ *[wɒn∅]* and [neɪmd] *named* ⇒ *[neɪm∅]*. Similar simplifications are seen in *mind, friends*.

Note the mispronunciation of the final syllabic /l/ in *trouble* as [trʌb*u] instead of [trʌb‌l]. The student seems not to have problems with pronouncing [l] as such, since she does so accurately in *like, only* and *learn*. Nor does she appear to have problems pronouncing other word-final syllabic consonants: [n] in *wouldn't* is accurate. We assume that the root of the problem is the position of the [l], being word-final and following [b].

Another aspect of the pronunciation of combinations of sounds, one which contributes to fluency rather than accuracy, is **linkage**. The best-known example of this is 'linking [r]': we see our Thai subject missing an opportunity to link two words with an [r] – *whenever[r]his* which she pronounces [wɛnɛv#[2] hiz]. But [r] is not the only linking sound used in English (Kenworthy, 1987: 82). In fluent English speech the utterance *do it and see it!* would be said [duwɪtnsɪjɪt] while a foreign learner would tend to say [du:ɪt ænd si:ɪt], perhaps even inserting glottal stops [ʔ] to yield [du:ʔitændsi:ʔɪt]. Our subject misses one [w]-linkage in *go out* [gɒwaʊt] and another in *no either* [noʊwaɪðə]. She also misses the consonant linkage with [d] in [wʊ(d)oʊnli] *would only*.

Also contributing to fluency in English is the systematic use of reduced or **weak forms**, increasing with the casualness of the speech. Our subject uses a good number of schwas, the commonest weak form. Her definite article is usually [də] and not the stressed [ðij]. But some full forms are used where a weak form would be more fluent: [eɪ] for [ə] in *a (young)*, [tu] for [tə] *to*, and [ænd] for [ən] *and*. Aitch-dropping is another source of weak forms: our subject avoids it, producing [hɪz] for *his*, [hɪm] for *him*, [hi] for *he*. Such **hypercorrection** – or what Bailey (1978) prefers to label 'phoney-correctness' – is not uncommon, and is, I believe, one of the sources of the conviction held by many linguistically unsophisticated native speakers (of English) that foreigners speak English 'better' than they themselves do.

Suprasegmental

This domain of pronunciation comprises the phenomena of **stress** (word stress and sentence stress), **rhythm** and **intonation**. Our Thai learner data yields two examples of wrong sentence stress, since the wrong word in the sentence is given stress: *go out with* ***them*** *(go√out with them)* and **I** *don't know (I don't √know)*.

We shall now move on to consider text errors, reminding the reader that we have dealt with only two of the four types of substance errors: we have not discussed **misperceptions** nor **miscues** at any length.

Text errors

The term **text** is sometimes used to refer exclusively to a unit of *written* language larger than the sentence – for which **paragraph** might be a suitable term. In that case, one wonders what its spoken counterpart might be.

We shall use 'text' in a much broader sense to designate any instance (or instantiation) of language that results from applying the rules of encoding and of lexico-grammar. Text is **usage**. The concept of text does not have to be restricted to grammar 'above the sentence', as once was customary in linguistics. As Widdowson puts it: 'Texts can come in all shapes and sizes: they can correspond in extent with any linguistic unit: letter, sound, word, sentence, combination of sentences' (1995: 164). Halliday and Hasan make it clear that text may be spoken or written and is not limited to the larger units: 'The word *text* is used in linguistics to refer to any passage, spoken or written, of whatever length, that does form a unified whole' (1976: 1). When it does form a unified whole, it is said to have the formal property of **texture**. In smaller texts this texture is supplied by their patterns of lexis, morphology and syntax. Larger texts, in addition to using these devices, resort to sentence-linking or **cohesive** ties. These, on a par with grammar, are 'part of the system of a language'. Across sentence boundaries, these ties are 'the only source of texture, whereas within the sentence there are the structural relations as well' (Halliday and Hasan, 1976: 9).

Text errors arise from ignorance and misapplication of the 'lexico-grammatical' rules of the language, including how these rules are exploited to achieve texture. It would be convenient to be able to make general and valid statements about how a unified system called lexico-grammar operates in language, but no such accounts are yet available; all we can do in the next section is suggest what directions such a system could take. For the present we must be content to account for lexical and grammatical (sub)systems separately.

Lexical errors

Chomsky has made this the Golden Age of syntax, and until recently the description of vocabulary was relatively neglected by linguists. Lexis has been sharply differentiated from grammar. Grammar is said to be organized in 'closed' systems, to be systematic and regular. Grammar is 'that part of a language which can be described in terms of generalizations or rules' while lexis appertains to 'all the particular facts about language . . . those which cannot be generalized into rules' (Leech, 1981: 179). Lexis is, by contrast, said to consist of 'open' systems, to be irregular and unsystematic. For Sinclair lexis involves 'the vagaries of individual words' (1987:). Cruttenden (1981) draws a distinction in MT acquisition between 'item learning' (of lexis) and 'rule learning' (of grammar).

Latterly, lexis has begun to take a central role in language study. There are a number of reasons for this. First, the boundaries between lexis and grammar are now seen to be less clear-cut than was assumed. Morphological aspects of words, which used to be treated as part of grammar, can just as well be viewed as part of the word: this is particularly true of derivational morphology, whereby words of different form classes can be derived from the same root: adjective *bright* ⇒ noun *brightness* ⇒ adverb *brightly*. Also, many lexical items consist of more than one word, and have a structure of their own. This is the case with idioms like *pull my leg* or *kick the bucket*, the integrity of which is easily shown by the impossibility of pluralizing the noun in each. But the expression does not have to be idiomatic: Becker (1975), Pawley and Syder (1983) and Nattinger and DeCarrico (1992) have shown how productive **lexical phrases** (LPs) are and how central they are to native-speaker fluency. Becker suggests that typical speakers have a store of about 25,000 such LPs, which is roughly equal to the number of one-word lexical items they know. Finally, Schmidt (1992) has even questioned the distinction drawn between item-learning and rule-learning, pointing out that 'Even errors, normally considered the best evidence for rule-based productivity, may be stored and retrieved as wholes by learners rather than being committed each time as a creative act' (1992: 378). Some apparently syntactic errors may thus be produced as wholes, and be no different on this criterion from lexical errors.

Secondly, learners themselves believe that vocabulary is very important in language learning, sometimes equating a language with its vocabulary. Wrong as this view may be, it has to be taken into account, since such learner-belief is likely to influence learning.

Thirdly, for some learner groups, lexical errors are the most frequent category of error. Grauberg (1971) analysed the errors of a group of advanced learners of German with MT English and commented on 'the preponderance of lexical errors': 102 out of 193 (53 per cent) recorded errors were lexical. Meara (1984) suggests that lexical errors outnumber other types by three or four to one.

Fourthly, native speakers consider the lexical errors in learners' IL to be more disruptive and irritating than other types – a question we shall discuss in the context of **error gravities** in Chapter 7.

Finally, vocabulary carries a particularly heavy functional load, especially in early IL. There is little grammar in such IL, and the message often has to be inferred, mainly from the lexical terms assembled for its representation.

There are therefore good reasons to undertake lexical EA. How though are lexical errors to be described? And how do these descriptions pave the way to their classification?

Classifying lexical errors

One convenient way to classify lexical errors is in terms of the sorts of knowledge of words that people have. Richards (1976) suggested that there are seven things to know about a word: (i) its morphology: knowing not to say *val*ious* but *val√iant.* Knowledge of a word's spelling and pronunciation would be included here also; (ii) its syntactic behaviour: not to say **Explain me this*; (iii) its functional or situational restrictions: not to say (electrical) **tension* but *√current*; (iv) its semantic value(s), or denotations: not to say *I broke my *foot* for intended *√leg*; (v) its secondary meanings or connotations: not to say *a *gang of policemen* when you mean *squad*, or *contingent*, since *gang* is pejoratively associated with trouble-makers; (vi) what other words it is associated with: that *sofa* belongs to the semantic field of 'furniture' and associates with *bed, stool,* etc.; (vii) roughly, how likely the word is to be used, that is, its frequency. This is a useful start, but it leaves out many details and subclasses, while obscuring certain broader tendencies. For example, it is possible to divide the seven categories between **formal** and **semantic** features: features (i), (ii), (iii), (vii) are formal while the remaining three are semantic.

The formal:semantic distinction is justified empirically. Henning (1973) conducted a vocabulary-learning experiment which involved FL learners spotting, in texts read aloud to them, lexical items that they could see printed on a card before them. The words to be spotted on the card were in the company of other, equally familiar words, which however were not used in the texts. Results showed two things: (a) that FL learners store (and access) their FL vocabulary according to the two criteria of form and meaning;

and (b) that less proficient learners prefer form-based (phonological) storage while more proficient learners demonstrate a preference for semantic storage: 'semantic encoding showed a positive correlation with language proficiency' (Henning, 1973: 191). This suggests that the learners studied by Meara (1984) must have been low-proficiency, since their lexical errors revealed 'some sort of phonological or orthographic confusion' (1984: 232). For example, when asked to respond to French *beton* (concrete), Meara's learners produced **animal,* a response triggered by confusing *beton* with *bête* meaning 'beast'. Other errors of formal misassociation of the stimulus *beton* were: *stupide (related to 'silly'), *conducteur (via *bâton,* a conductor's stick), and *Normandie (a French region, by misassociation with *bréton,* meaning 'from Britanny'). We shall accordingly set up a classification in which the formal:semantic dichotomy is central. An example of this approach to lexis error classification is Legenhausen (1975).

Formal errors of lexis

1.   Formal misselection

In this category we include errors of the malapropism type, what Laufer (1992) calls **synforms**, Room (1979) calls **confusibles**, and Phythian (1989) **confusables**. These are pairs (or triples) of words that look and sound similar: *parricide/patricide, accessory/accessary*. Laufer (1992) identifies six ways in which pairs of synforms can be similar: they can (i) have the same number of syllables; (ii) have the same stress pattern; (iii) be of the same word class; (iv) have the same initial part; (v) have some phonemes in common; and (vi) have phonemes with shared features. She proceeds to identify ten categories of synforms, which she then collapses into four main types: the **suffix** type (e.g. *consider<able>/consider<ate>*); the **prefixing** type (e.g. *<com>press/<sup>press*); the **vowel-based** type (e.g. *seat/set, manual/menial*); and the **consonant-based** type (e.g. *prize/price, ledge/pledge*). Grauberg (1971) found that 16 out of 21 such TL-based errors in FL German involved the selection of a wrong verbal prefix: **beirrt (√geirrt),* **entgegnen (√begegnen).*

There are affinities between the lexical problems met by learners and native speakers, affinities absent from other (grammar and phonology) errors. Take Mrs Malaprop, a character in Sheridan's play *The Rivals* (1775), and her pronouncement (not pronunciation, please!) that someone is *as headstrong as an *allego-ry (√alligator) on the Nile*. She produces many such **malapropisms**. The question is: why? Is it the case that she knows both words, but is experiencing a performance (control) problem of accessing the target item? Are these therefore mistakes? They could be, but apparently are not, for she is speaking confidently, assured that she does know the word she is using. In fact she is ignorant, not only of the word she needs, but also of the substitute: she is doubly ignorant. Ignorance leads to error. Now recall that the claim has been made that NSs cannot make errors, since they know their language perfectly. This seems to be true for syntax, but is not true for lexis. NSs can be ignorant of some of the lexical stock of their native language (NL), which they continue to accumulate throughout their lives. Doing a crossword puzzle, for example, usually results in NSs adding to their word stock, but I am un-aware of any grammar-expanding activity or game NSs indulge in. Shaughnessy makes it clear that Mrs Malaprop's problem is no eccentricity, but is common in 'students' – by which she means NSs:

> When we say that a student does not know a word, we do not generally mean that he has never heard or seen it. . . . At the deep-est level of 'not knowing' a student would not know of a word's existence or even perhaps of the existence of what it names. But errors in vocabulary already attest to the student's knowledge, at some level, of the words he is using (or misusing).
>
> (Shaughnessy, 1977: 190)

What makes Mrs Malaprop comical, verbally maladroit and *mal à propos* is that she thinks she knows these words, but her belief is contradicted by her behaviour. A more modest or cautious person would play safe, and use a word he or she is more sure about. Learners face a similar choice. Either they think they know and – if they are mistaken in this belief – blithely produce a lexical error, or they assume that they do not know the right word (in which belief they may be justified or mistaken) and use a lexical **communication strategy** – perhaps avoiding the concept or alter-natively resorting to paraphrase or language switch.

The crucial feature of the synform error type is that a real existent word is used. This substitute resembles the target word in form but not necessarily in meaning, though it might do so accidentally. The bigger the gap between the semantics of the substitute and the target, the more absurd the malapropism. This substitute can be either a TL word or an MT word. In the first case we have true (MT) malapropism, as in these examples:

(a) *He wanted to *cancel (√conceal) his guilt.*
(b) *It was a *genius (√genuine) diamond.*

Notice a further incidental difference between these two lexical errors: in (a) the substitute is lexically wrong, but is of the required part of speech – it is a verb. In (b) however, a noun is substituted for an adjective, so that there is a **concomitant** grammar error also. Another example of this is:

(c) *She listened to his *speak (speech).*

Where the misselection is motivated by the formal resemblance between the TL word and an MT word (an interlingual misequation), we talk of **false friends** or **deceptive cognates**:

(d) *Can I *become (√get ⇐ German 'bekommen') a beefsteak?*
(e) *I think Senhor is *constipated (√caught a cold ⇐ Portuguese 'constipado')*

This type of error is common where the MT and the TL are cognate, which is paradoxical: a difficulty is created by interlingual similarity, where one might well expect facilitation to result. Perhaps the similarity is insufficient to be helpful, or is of the wrong type. Another possible key to this enigma might lie in the facilitative effects of such cognates in **receptive** language use, where context will neutralize any potential semantic misassociations. In fact, a cottage industry has grown up in FL teaching based on false friends and how to avoid them. Too often overlooked in FL learning circles are the benefits bestowed by trusty friends, as Ringbom (1987) has shown. He demonstrates that Swedish-MT Finns learning EL2 have a headstart in their receptive competence over their Finnish-MT compatriots, on account of the facilitation coming from the cognateness of MT Swedish and the English TL, two Germanic languages.

Laufer (1992) shows how the L1 can influence synform difficulty. She compared the synform errors committed by 136 L1 Semitic, 58 L1 Germanic and 69 L1 Romance learners of English as an L2. Her first finding was that these three groups of learners, different only in their L1, showed different frequencies of synform errors overall: Semitic 70 per cent; Germanic 20 per cent; and

Romance 10 per cent. In other words, the Romance L1 group was less troubled by synforms in English than the Germanic, which in turn was less confused by synforms than the Semitic. Why should this be? Laufer offers four perceptive explanations:

(i)   Many of the English confusibles involved Latinate words, which Romance L1 speakers would already have distinguished in L1 use: the French *imaginative/imaginary* = *imaginatif/ imaginaire.*

(ii) German has in common with English a 'catenative' morphology, while Semitic is noncatenative. In other words, roots in Germanic tend to be continuous while their counterparts in Semitic are discontinuous: Arabic *k-t-b* = English *book.*

(iii) The Semitic speakers did worse on the vocalic synforms but better on the consonantal ones because Semitic script has practically no vowels in it.

(iv) Germanic learners did worse than their Romance and Semitic counterparts on the consonantal synforms because in German word-finally the opposition between voiced and voiceless consonants is neutralized – devoicing takes place. So the pair *extend/extent* were both heard as [ekstent] by the Germanic group.

Not all false friends are totally unrelated in their meanings. For example, the English learners of French who equate French *monnaie* ('small change') with MT *money* will not be totally incomprehensible to the French taxi driver, and the would-be book purchasers looking for a *library* and asking for a *libraria* in Spain might still find something to read if they land up outside a bookshop. There is partial semantic overlap between English *control* and French *contrôler* ('check', 'control'), as between English *push* and Portuguese *puxar* ('pull', pronounced [puʃar]). Granger (1996) draws a distinction between **totally deceptive** and **partially deceptive** cognates. The former are historically related words in L1 and L2 that used to be synonymous but which now have totally divergent meanings. An example is French *fabrique* (*'factory'*) and English *fabric* meaning '*cloth/material'*. Another such pair are French *expertise* ('expert's assessment') and English *expertise* ('skilfulness'). In the case of partially deceptive cognates, a single word in L1 corresponds to two (or even more) words in L2, only one of the latter corresponding in form and meaning with the L1 word. Granger gives the French/English pair *fatal/fatal* 'where the French word is more polysemous than its English equivalent' (1996: 109). The technical term for this is **divergent polysemy**, the popular term being **split** as in:

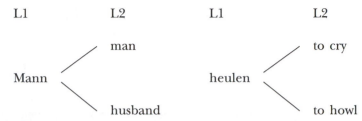

L1   L2   L1   L2

Mann   man / husband   heulen   to cry / to howl

Granger (1996) reports a study that made use of the *International Corpus of Learner English* (ICLE, see Chapter 4) to test two hypotheses about learners' use of L1:L2 cognates. First, she addressed the plausible question of whether L1 French learners tend to overuse the Romance vocabulary stock in English and to underuse the Germanic stock. She found, surprisingly, that they did the opposite, tending to make more use of the 'basic' Germanic vocabulary – such verbs as *think, take, put, find*, for example – than native speakers did on an equivalent writing task. The second hypothesis she tested was whether lexical false-friend errors are persistent errors. This was indeed found to be the case, since one-third of all lexical errors (260 out of a total of 750) were the result of partially deceptive cognateness. Granger draws an important pedagogical conclusion from her study: that we need more 'bilingualized learner dictionaries', by which she means dictionaries that cater specifically for learners with a particular L1, dictionaries that will serve to draw their attention to the pitfalls of false friends. There seems to be only one such bilingualized dictionary in existence: the Canadian *Password English Dictionary for Speakers of French*. As Gomes da Torre (1986) pointed out, publishers are guilty of promoting reference and teaching materials (for EFL in particular) that are claimed to be universally useful: this reduces their production costs and increases their profits, at the expense, however, of efficient teaching. He calls for more **locally oriented** language courses which take into account the learners' MT.

2. Misformations

These are errors that produce 'words' that are non-existent in the FL. Again, they can originate either in the MT or be created by the learner from the resources of the TL itself. We shall consider first those created for the TL from MT resources, known as **interlingual** misformation errors. There are three types:

(i)   If the MT word is used in the TL with no perception of any need to tailor it to its new 'host' code, we speak of **borrowing**: *I shoot him with gun in* **kopf* ('head' ⇐ German L1 *Kopf*).

(ii)   If the new word (derived from L1) is tailored to the structure of the TL, presumably because the learners think there is a trusty friend, we have **coinage**: to **massacrate* (massacre) the victims; . . . who* *preconizes* ('defends' ⇐ L1 Spanish *preconizar*); smoking can be very **nocive* to health ('harmful' ⇐ L1 Portuguese *nocivo*); one is here **insered* ('included' ⇐ L1 Portuguese *inserido*); these **mortific* wars ('bringing death' ⇐ L1 Portuguese *mortiferas*).

(iii) If the L2 word created is the result of literal translation of an L1 word, we have a **calque**: **baby car* ('pram' ⇐ L1 Spanish *cochecito de niño*); **sleep suit* ('pyjamas' ⇐ L1 German *Schlafanzug*); **goldworthy* ('precious' ⇐ L1 German *goldwert*); **cooking recipe* ('recipe' ⇐ L1 German *Kochrezept*). Calquing can be applied to a whole lexical phrase, and this is common, giving such forms as: *They have *made the same experience* ('had the same experience' ⇐ L1 German *dieselbe Erfahrung machen*); *America has *made profit* ('benefited' ⇐ L1 German *Profit machen*); *Ich *fand meinen Weg zum Speisewagen* ('begab mich' ⇐ L1 English *find one's way*).

The following formal lexical errors do not originate in the MT.

3.   Distortions

These are the **intralingual** errors of form created without recourse to L1 resources. The outcomes are forms non-existent in the TL. They result from the misapplication of one or more of the processing operations introduced in Chapter 4: **omission, overinclusion, misselection, misordering**, and **blending**. We give just two examples of each: (a) omission: e.g. *int(e)resting*, (b) overinclusion: e.g. *fresh(er)men, din(n)ing room*; (c) misselection: **delitouse*√*delicious*; (d) misordering: e.g. *littel (little), ferporate (perforate)*; (e) blend: e.g. *the *deepths of the ocean* (depth + deeps). Blends occur as performance **slips** in the speech of NSs: Stemberger (1982: 319) speaks of 'a blend of the intended and unintended' and gives **starps* (*stops* + *starts*) as an example. However, blending is more typical of syntactic deviance than lexical.

So much for the **formal** lexical errors. We now turn our attention to the **semantic** or 'conceptual' errors in lexis, where learners use forms that exist in the TL but these forms do not represent the meanings they wish to express.

Semantic errors in lexis

There are two main types.

1. Confusion of sense relations

Lexicologists describe vocabulary in terms of lexical systems, reflecting the meaning relations existing between words. Lexico-semantic clusterings are referred to as **lexical fields**. There is considerable neurolinguistic evidence to suggest that humans store words in the mental lexicon in terms of such sense-relations. It is therefore reasonable to try to categorize lexis errors by reference to these systems. The major types of error are:

(a) Using a more general term where a more specific one is needed (**superonym** for **hyponym**). The result is an under-specification of the meaning:

> The flowers had a special *smell (√scent/√perfume).
> The village women *washed (√scrubbed) the steps.
> Capitalism . . . made America *big (√great/√powerful).

(b) Using too specific a term (hyponym for superonym):

> The *colonels (officers) live in the castle.

(c) Using the less apt of two co-hyponyms:

> . . . a decision to *exterminate (eradicate) dialects.
> She is my *nephew.

(d) Using the wrong one from a set of near-synonyms:

> . . . a *regretful (√penitent/√contrite) criminal or sinner . . .

Such near-synonyms or assumed synonyms are what Room (1981) calls '**distinguishables**'. They are pairs (or more) of words that are semantically germane but can be differentiated. They are not true synonyms like *serviette/napkin*, *lift/elevator*, or *harmonica/mouth organ*, which are distinct in their respective contexts of use, but are distinguishable. Examples are: *malice/spite, border/frontier, coat/jacket, chemist/apothecary/pharmacist.* Obviously, the set of indistinguishables is smaller in proportion to one's proficiency in the language, and educated native speakers can make more lexical distinctions than FL learners, whose lexicon is suffused with synonymy.

2. Collocational errors

Collocations are the other words any particular word normally keeps company with. The psychologist's word-association tests rely on collocational knowledge, specifically when syntagmatic (not paradigmatic) associates are in focus. The question is not which word could substitute for this word, but which words typically precede and follow it. There are three degrees of collocation. First, semantically determined word selection: it is right to say *crooked stick* but not **crooked year* because in the world as we know it years cannot literally 'be' crooked. Next there are combinations with statistically weighted preferences. We can say that an army has suffered *big losses* but *heavy losses* is preferred. Finally, there are arbitrary combinations: we *make an attempt* and *have a try* but can neither **make a try* nor **have an attempt*, despite the synonymy of *attempt/try*. **Irreversible binomials** like *fish and chips* (not **chips and fish*) and *strawberries and cream* probably belong here too. Adherence to the collocational conventions of an FL contributes greatly to one's idiomaticity and nativelikeness, and not doing so announces one's foreignness or, as Bridges (1990) calls it, one's 'strangeness'. One could argue that this matters only to spies and prigs and that these are mere 'infelicities' rather than full-blown errors. But since collocationally idiosyncratic language can lead to hilarity and embarrassment, as well as to exam failure, it is worth understanding and minimizing. Consider some of the adverse reactions the following infelicitous collocations would provoke:

> There is much turmoil in the Middle **Orient/√East.*
> My wife did some **lavish/√extravagant* shopping in London.
> The **late/r√recent* dispute between France and Australia.
> A **vivacious/√lively* discussion in the House of Lords.

Collocation error can be intralingual or interlingual. In German, the adjective *hoch* collocates equally with nouns *Risiko* ('risk'), *Alter* ('age'), and *Summe* ('amount'), while by contrast in English only the combination *high risk* is idiomatic, and one would not say

?*a high sum/amount* or ?*a high age*. Transfer of L1 collocations leads to interlingual errors of this kind. Notice how cognateness of the adjectives *high/hoch* seduces the unsuspecting learners into assuming they collocate in the same way in both L1 and the FL. Also the learners' assumption of absolute one-to-one equivalence made on the basis of a perceived partial equivalence will induce such collocation violations: seeing that *hohes Gebäude = high building* invites the (over)generalization that **high age* is also possible.

An interesting comparative study of some collocations in English and French is Whitaker (1992). Here a comparison is made of the distributions of the verb pairs *come/go* and *aller/venir*, with the purpose of explaining why French learners of EL2 make errors in selecting *come* and/or *go* despite having a similar contrast in the L1. The reason is, of course, that students tend to assume there is a one-to-one correspondence, a belief sometimes encouraged by teaching. Whitaker proved this assumption false by getting high-proficiency French–English bilinguals to translate high-frequency uses of *come/go* into French. Only four of 24 instances of *come* were translated with *venir*, while only four of 64 sentences with *go* were translated with *aller*: a range of verbs other than *aller* and *venir* was used instead. Here is a selection of their translations of *come*: *come running>courir vers*; *to come a long way>faire des progrès*; *come to power>prendre le pouvoir*; *Christmas is coming>le Noël arrive*. There are even some surprises, where French uses the 'opposite' verb to the English one: thus *Come on. Let's go!* is in French *Allez, viens!*, while *Come on, Everton!* is *Allez, Everton!* How topsy-turvy!

I believe that we can categorize a whole range of error types mentioned in the EA literature as collocational. All sorts of errors involving what Leech (1981: Chapter 2) calls **associative meaning** fit the category: errors of affective meaning, of social meaning, of connotative meaning, collocative meaning, and of stylistic meaning. 'Style' is, of course, a notoriously broad concept, but still one that we can sometimes exploit. One type of error I would label 'stylistic' is the error of **verbosity**, otherwise referred to as pomposity and **babu**. Here are some examples:

> I informed my girlfriend of the party ?*through* the ?*medium* of telephone.
> I pretended to be ?*under* an ?*attack* of ?*fit*.

This is from a PhD thesis written by a student with L1 Arabic:

> *The contemporary trends of users and publishers alike are demanding*
> *that lexicography advance towards providing varieties of information*
> *within dictionaries' volumes that require less time to check or read.*

However, what Shaw (1975: vii) calls 'wordiness' is not a monopoly
of FL learners but is also a failing of the native speaker. It seems
to reflect insecurity on the user's part: an overcompensation for
the sense of linguistic inadequacy they harbour. Granger (1994)
invokes the 'style' dimension when suggesting that the computer
analysis of IL will be able to identify 'statistically significant overuse and underuse' (1994: 5) of certain lexical items by learners.
She found, for example, that the lexical phrases *a kind of, as far
as, on the contrary, a lot of* were used eight times more frequently
in the written English of French learners than by NSs of English.
Such **over-indulgence** of one set of lexical options is likely to be
matched by **under-representation** in the learners' language of
other options, as Levenston (1971) predicted before computerized learner corpora became available.

Grammar errors

Morphology errors

Grammar has traditionally been discussed in terms of **morphology**
and **syntax**, the former handling word structure, the latter handling structures 'larger' than the word. It is therefore not surprising
that we touched on some aspects of morphology when discussing
lexis errors. There are five lexical word types in English: noun,
verb, adjective, adverb and preposition. We can therefore define
as a morphology error one which involves a failure to comply with
the norm in supplying any part of any instance of these word
classes: *six book**, *aboli**shment (√*-tion*) are noun morphology errors;
bringed, was drinken (√*-ing*) are verb morphology errors; *visit me
soon**ly is an adverb morphology error; and *a colourfull**er scene,
an adjective morphology error. Prepositions happen to have no
morphology.

Shaughnessy (1977: 90) calls morphological errors 'small' errors,
as does Zoila, a Guatemalan migrant worker in the USA (Shapira,
1978, see Chapter 1), who admits that when she speaks English she
tends not to bother about *'the esses and little words'*. By 'esses' Zoila
means morphological markers of plurality, genitive, third-person

singular. By 'little words' she means the **function words** of English, which, according to Fries (1952) number 154.

These errors are basic but persistent, regularly resurfacing even in the EFL writing of PhD students. The most important are third singular -*s*, plural -*s*, past tense -*ed*, and progressive -*ing*. One might have included apostrophe -*s* in this list were it not for the fact that its use is so rare among English native speakers, even educated ones (Garrett and Austin, 1993), that it is no longer legitimate to claim that it˜is part of the canon.

Third-person singular -*s* is a facet of **concord** and is suffixed to lexical verbs (*drinks*) and to auxiliaries (*has, is, does*). It has been argued (Bickerton, 1971; Weinreich, 1953: 39) that for English L2 learners with Spanish MT the problem is not so much grammatical as phonological, since suffixing -*s* to a verb stem ending in a consonant creates a final consonant cluster. Shaughnessy (1977) makes a more general observation not involving MT influence: learners have more success with third-person singular -*s* when it is syllabic, and therefore salient, which would explain why the -*es* is right on *pleases* but omitted on **make* in *They do what √pleases them which *make life great.* I would say that the error is then phonological in cause but grammatical in effect. Moreover, the first observation by Weinreich applies only to -*s* **omission**. It does not explain the -*s* **misplacement** by Maslena, a nine-year-old L1 Malay speaker who suffixes it to the subject pronoun as in *He*s open the hot water. He*s get up and open it.*

Plural -*s* is less troublesome than third-person singular -*s*. It appears redundant when preceded by numerals and other quantifiers, so that **six book* and **several tree* result. We also encounter **overinclusions**, as in **every teachers*. A very plausible omission is in *One of my friend*∅*: how does one explain the need to mark plural on a noun governed by the quantifier *one*?

It seems though that these two rules of English (third-person singular -*s* and plural -*s*) strike the learners as incompatible: they are confused by what appears to them to be the same marker being used to signal noun plurality and verb singularity. The confusion (shown by the ?) is compounded when they meet apparent exceptions – cases where a singular subject is followed by a verb without -*s*: *Does the CAT WANT? a drink of water?* or *The teacher made this STUDENT WORK?*.

Past tense -*ed* is both omitted and overused. It is multifunctional, and error incidence probably varies according to whether it is Past:

He cooked it; Perfect: *He has cooked it*; Passive: *It was cooked by Fred*; or Adjectival: *a cooked dinner*. There is evidence that the redundancy principle operates, so that when there is a past time adverb in the sentence, there is greater likelihood of the *-ed* being omitted. Shaughnessy (1977) suggests that learners make 'false analogies'. Noticing that Auxiliary (*have*) + verb stem (*walk*) + *-ed* can be combined to give *Have walked*, it is assumed that *can + walk + -ed* can similarly be combined. The result is the error **Can walked*.

Syntax errors

These are errors that affect texts larger than the word, namely phrase, clause, sentence and ultimately paragraphs.

1. Phrase structure errors

Until recently linguists assumed there were as many phrase types as there were lexical word types: Noun Phrases (NP), Verb Phrases (VP), Adjective Phrases (AjP), Adverb Phrases (AvP) and Preposition Phrases (PP). This ought to yield five syntactic classes of error, but there are problems. First, the fact that these five phrase types are not discrete entities, since one finds NPs inside PPs and these inside NPs. For example, is **Some immatured teenagers* an NP with an error in its AjP *some immatured*, or is it an erroneous NP? Likewise, is the complement NP in (*There is*) *a vacancy *Ø/∧for a ledger clerk* wrong, or is its PP wrong? The second problem is that every phrase contains an eponymous nucleus or **head**, a noun heads an NP, a verb a VP, an adjective an AjP. Now, what if there is an error on this head? An example is *We have no firewood*S*. Heads being words, a head-located error will be morphological by definition. But also, by definition, a head-located error must render the whole phrase erroneous, so we have a syntax error. This is paradoxical. The third problem is modern syntactic theory's tendency to multiply the number of phrase-types. In addition to the original five we now have a growing number of '**functional**' ones: Determiner Phrases, Inflectional Phrases, Quantifier Phrases and Complementizer Phrases, to name only the more plausible. As a result, it is now possible to say that the error of article omission in *This is against *Ø law* involves the (head of the) Determiner Phrase, which is part of the 'bigger' NP.

For practical purposes of doing EA at phrase level, I suggest using the tripartite structure: modifier + head + qualifier (MHQ) where M and Q can be refined in terms of positional subclasses m1, m2, m3 . . . and q1, q2, q3, etc. Apart from its simplicity in use, this scheme has the advantage of consensus: syntacticians seem to agree that heads have Ms and Qs, or, if you prefer, Specifiers and Complements. So let us illustrate by analysing a few phrasal errors:

- *(He is)* **a cleverest boy in the class.* Misselection of the article at position m1 in NP. Note that m2 *cleverest,* Head *boy,* and Q *in the class* are unproblematic.
- *(He)* **no can swim.* A double error. Misselection and misordering of negator in VP. *Not* is an allomorph of *no* that belongs at m2 position, not m1: *can* *no/√*not swim.*
- *That* **fat big fish (is the mama fish).* An error of misordering m2 and m3 in the AjP inside the NP.

2.   Clause errors

These involve the ways in which phrases – themselves well-formed – operate in clauses. While phrase errors involve violations in the internal (or 'textual') relations between parts of phrases, clause errors involve whole phrases entering into the structure of clauses. Once again, deviance will arise where any one of five conditions holds:

(i)   The [phrase] in question is superfluous: *He shaved himself [*the beard]; New articles were invented, like 'chiclets' which nobody calls [*THEM] anything else.*

(ii)   It is omitted: *Give *[NP] to the dog.*

(iii)   It is misordered: *Watson sent [to him] the letter; In 1820 [were] many villages near Berlin* (Zydatiß, 1974).

(iv)   It is misselected: *He seems *[crying* /√ *to cry].*

(v)   It is a **blend** or hybrid: **You would be most likely get (first prize)* which is an amalgam of √*You would be likely to get* and √*You would most likely get.* Here is another example, taken from Dechert and Lennon (1989): *Today motoring offences are punished *[along similar laws] in most countries.* The two competing phrases simultaneously selected are plausibly *along similar lines* and *according to similar laws.* Note however that, as Stemberger (1982) suggests, certain omissions can also be described as blends. For example, a speaker's indecision about whether to use *ask* or *raise* in the following can result in total mutual inhibition of both verb options, with resulting zero: *I just wanted to *∅ that.*

3.   Sentence errors

These involve the selection and combination of clauses into larger units. Whole clauses can be blended, as in the following sentence from a PhD student's essay: *Lightfoot for example argues that it is only in terms of a hierarchical analysis like (26) *can we account for the ungrammaticality of the construction in (25).* The two candidate complement clauses that have become one are plausibly (argues) *that it is only . . . that we can . . .* and *that only . . . can we.* Other sentence errors are what Shaughnessy (1977: 55) calls **consolidation** errors, comprising the two subtypes coordination and subordination errors. The golden rule about **coordination** is that only syntactic equals can be joined, and attempts to conjoin unequals lead to 'broken coordination'. Consider *They believe [they can become leaders in their field₁] and [a good secure job₂].* The two conjuncts are not equals: in fact the first is a clause and the second an NP. What they have in common is that both are objects of the verb *believe.*

A tricky sort of **subordination** in English is relative clause formation. In the next chapter we shall be looking at some relativization errors found in the writing of Malay-speaking students of English. Probably the most common sort of relativization error is that involving the mischoice of (a) for (b) or vice versa:

(a)   *Gandhi, who led the independence movement in India, was a politician.*
(b)   *Gandhi, who was a politician, led the independence movement in India.*

They contain the same information, but it is differently packaged and differently valued in each. In (a) Gandhi's being *a politician* is what matters, and that he *led the independence movement* is an extra, an aside. In (b) just the converse weighting of information is achieved. So which is right? It depends on the context, and on what point the writer is attempting to make. If the next sentence is about Gandhi as a politician, for example *He had learnt politics from the British*, then (a) is the right formulation. If, on the other hand, the next sentence is about the independence movement, for example *The movement had become powerful ten years earlier*, then

(b) is right. We are now on the **discourse** level (McCarthy and Carter, 1994: 125).

4.   Intersentence errors (cohesion)

In their classic work on cohesion in English, Halliday and Hasan (1976) identify five types of cohesive link operating in the upper reaches of text structure: **reference, substitution, ellipsis, conjunction** and **lexical** cohesion. It is worth stressing that the use of cohesive markers, either by the speaker-writer in composing text or by the reader-listener in understanding them, is not compulsory. Their use is discretionary, and at times even undesirable. This is the case when the logical relations between sentences of a text are not obscure *per se*, or when the reader is able to make bridging inferences. Using explicit cohesion markers will at times be a courtesy to the readers, reducing their uncertainty and often their processing effort. At other times, depending on who the readers are, they may seem to be patronizing, taken as a sign of the writer-speaker not trusting them to see the logical relations without all this unnecessary signposting. Since their use is optional, it would be contradictory to talk of errors of omission of such markers: omission might be a case of discourtesy towards the reader, but hardly a case of text error.

The research to date on errors in cohesion marking in student EFL writing has concentrated on these. Leinonen-Davies (1984) undertook an analysis of 38 Finnish teenagers' EL2 compositions of around 150 words each in length. She found these writers to be parsimonious in their use of the **conjunctive** type of marker, a type elsewhere referred to as **logical connectors**. To a lesser degree they tended also to underexploit the **ellipsis** and **substitution** types. In short, her claim is that most of the cohesion errors are those of omission: as we have just suggested, this is a debatable point. On the other hand, the Finns made extensive – at times excessive – use of **lexical** cohesion. In one eight-sentence essay entitled '*Why I would like to live in a big city*' the writer used the word *city* no fewer than 13 times. Apart from over- and underuse of certain types, there was also some misselection of unsuitable markers, the effect being to render the text 'unstable, inefficient and ineffective' (Leinonen-Davies, 1984: 97).

Hubbard (1989) reports his study of the cohesion errors in the academic writing of EL2 students in South Africa. **Ellipsis** errors were very rare, and most of the cohesion errors in the corpus involved the **reference** and **conjunctive** types. Here are examples of errors in **reference** cohesion marking:

> *Samneric insist that there is a beast. Jack being controlled by *[this fear] he . . .*

There is no obvious referent of 'this fear'.

> *Simon is also a Christlike figure. We see *[it] in the way he gave his food to Piggy.*

The 'it' is a misselection, where 'this' is called for.

A more focused study, of Hong Kong EL2 writers' errors in using logical connectors (**conjunctives**) in their academic writing, is Tang and Ng (1995). They define conjunctives as words or phrases which signal some semantic relationship between or within sentences. They identify seven functional subtypes:

(i)   Listing: *first, next, then, to start with, last of all, likewise, further-more, . . .*
(ii) Summative: *in short, thus, therefore, overall, then . . .*
(iii) Appositive: *such as, for example, that is (to say), specifically . . .*
(iv) Resultative: *because, accordingly, as a consequence, since, . . .*
(v)   Inferential: *otherwise, in that case, then . . .*
(vi) Contrastive: *in other words, better still, on the other hand, anyhow, besides, . . .*
(vii) Transitional: *incidentally, meanwhile, finally, at first . . .*

These devices were highly exploited in the students' writing, compared with other genres. On average there were 2.56 occurrences per 100 words of text. The most frequently used subtypes were listing, summative and contrastive. This amounts to **overuse**, especially of *and*, the coordinating function of which gets generalized. Learners tend to use the connectors to 'support' logical relationships between propositions that just do not exist: in other words, they are superimposed. There was some **underuse**, of the inferential, transitional and summative subtypes, where the reader was abandoned by the writer and expected to spot logical relationships unaided. There was some **misselection**, especially of *however*, which was apparently assumed to be merely an alternative to *but*. Also, *besides* was misused in this way. Some **misplacement** occurred also: a few conjunctives were placed sentence-initially, when the more natural position would have been between the two clauses.

This resulted in forms like: *By the same token if you are too old I am too old also* (√*If you are too old, by the same token I am too old also.*)

Discourse errors

Coherence

Two early EAs of student EL2 writing are Bhatia (1974) and Das (1978). Bhatia evaluated the free compositions of Indian undergraduates, both in terms of 'mechanics' and also in terms of organization or 'paragraph development' they deployed. She attempted to analyse such desirable qualities in writing as relevance, clarity, development, and even originality. In fact, she was attempting to specify the **coherence** of student writing. Das (1978) clearly differentiates between 'value-as-text' (**cohesion**) and 'value-as-message' (**coherence**). The latter is defined in terms of communicative function, involving the writer's intention and the reader's interpretation. Such communicative events are related to those described in the speech-act theories of Austin (1962) and Grice (1975). Emphasis has now shifted away from text and the linguistic meanings of its propositions to speaker-meanings. We have moved to the realm of **discourse** and **pragmatics**.

We are now able to distinguish text from discourse, and therefore also to classify errors under these two types. Widdowson (1995) attempts to distinguish them in terms, first, of discourse being a process and text its product, and secondly in terms of meaning versus interpretation. 'It is your discourse you read into my text' (Widdowson, 1995: 165). This echoes Carrell, for whom coherence is 'what the reader or listener does with the text' (1982: 482). The problem with this definition is that it makes text the concern of the speaker-writer and discourse the activity of the listener-speaker: surely this neat division of labour cuts out the text-producer from participation in discourse and the text-receiver from engagement with text. The alternative is to relate coherence to text, defining it as 'the ways in which the components of the textual world i.e. the configuration of concepts and relations . . . are mutually accessible and connected' (Beaugrande and Dressler, 1981: 4). Hinds (1987) sensibly suggests there are two sorts of writer, and therefore also of texts: those who are speaker (self)-oriented, and the others who are reader (other)-oriented. These may be individual idiosyncrasies, but Hinds suggests that some cultures produce a preponderance of one or other of these sorts of writing.

Coherence is related primarily to content, to the conceptual relatedness of propositions. We are no longer looking at 'markers' on the surface: we are looking for underlying 'conceptual' relationships. That is what we do as analysts, and that is what we do as readers: the analyst steps into the reader's boots, so to speak. So what sorts of underlying relationships are there? Our first task must be to identify these, as only then shall we be in a position to see where the writer has failed to conform or adhere to the optimum relationships. There are three sorts of coherence in fact:

1. Topical coherence

Topical coherence refers to the need for the components of a discourse to be relevant to its general topic or goal. Where a discourse contains irrelevant propositions or moves, it loses coherence.

2. Relational coherence

Relational coherence refers to the requirement for the propositions constituting a discourse to be related to each other. One workable framework for annotating the kinds of relationship that are possible between pairs of propositions is Sorensen (1981). He distinguishes the following 'coherence types' as he calls them:

> an aspect of (A); some concretization of (C); a proof of (CF); some elaboration of (E); an effect of (E); an instance of (I); an exception to (EX); an identification of some entity within (ID); an implication (IM); something opposed to or contrasting with (OP); something parallel to (P); a reservation concerning (RE); a summary of (SM) . . .   (Sorensen, 1981: 681)

3. Sequential coherence

Sequential coherence refers to the need for constitutive propositions to be arranged in some effective order. Now the notion of 'effectiveness' introduces the concept of discourse **rhetoric**, which has been at the centre of interest for some time now among writing specialists. There is growing evidence that different cultures and language communities have different conventions for and expectations about maximizing rhetorical effectiveness. The observation that L2 users unconsciously transfer their L1 conventions has led to the development of a research paradigm known as **contrastive rhetoric** (Leki, 1991a: Connor, 1996). Kaplan's (1966) identification of a number of culturally distinctive 'paragraph movements', such as 'Semitic', 'oriental', 'romance', 'Slavic', has been most provocative. Purves (1988: 9) refers to 'international students' who 'did not write in the way that we expected' since they 'had learned ways of organizing and presenting what they wrote that did not match the standards of the target language'. What they wrote was not necessarily wrong, but it was different' (ibid.: 9). One does hesitate to label such 'differences' as errors: a preferable term, from Austin's (1962) speech-act theory, is **infelicity**.

We should subsume under this dimension of coherence the **informativity** of the discourse. This has two dimensions. First, the simple question of information load. A text will forfeit coherence if its writer has miscalculated the readers-hearers' knowledge. If this knowledge is overestimated, the text will be inaccessible, and will tell the readers too much, overwhelming them with information; if it is underestimated, it will be banal, telling them too little. To maximize its **communicative dynamism** a text should unveil its information in a stepwise manner: new information should be unpacked in the context of what is already familiar, the result being a chain of given ⇒ new ⇒ given ⇒ new, and so on. Here (Deyes, 1978: 26) is an example of EL2 discourse that fails to package information in this progressive given ⇒ new sequence:

> [*In the midst of a city street full of high buildings*][Given] *we found [a little house.]*[New]
> [*It had the appearance*][Given] *[of a fairy-tale house.]*[New]

Notice how the first sentence ends with new information (what it was that they found – *a little house*). This becomes 'known' information that the reader carries forward with us into the second sentence (legitimizing the use of the pronoun '*it*'). But now look what happens: the second '*house*' is wrongly put into the 'new' position at the end of the sentence. What is really new now is '*fairy tale*' and it is this element that should be final. To maintain the rhythm of given:new delivery of information, the end of this sentence should be rewritten as '*house in a fairy tale*'.

The following example is different in that it involves the use of a rhetorical convention that some languages, including French but not English, favour: **topic + comment structure** (Trévise, 1986).

What you do is first state what you are going to comment on, then you comment on it. When this rhetorical device is used indiscriminately in English, infelicitous utterances may result, such as:

> ?*The monkeys they live in the forests.*
> ?*Portugal it's very pleasant to live there.*

Compare the oddity of these with the normality of their French counterparts:

> √*Les singes ça vit dans les forêts.*
> √*Le Portugal c'est très agréable d'y vivre.*

Besides information load there is the question of **information structure** or what is otherwise called **rhetorical structure**. This refers to the 'architecture' of the discourse, the arrangement of its ideas and moves. 'Architecture' is an apt label, since one can usually draw a sketch to represent this structure. It is common practice in writing classes to show students how to 'design' their essays before they start to write: Buzan (1974) calls such sketches 'brain patterns'.

It is when text producers develop an architecture that is contradicted by their explicit plan that we notice infelicities of this sort. Boyle (1996) quotes a passage from an economics textbook in which the rhetorical structure is at odds with the way in which this structure is signposted:

> Assets fall into two broad categories, financial assets and tangible assets. A further subdivision [of what? of 'assets' in general, of 'financial' or of 'tangible' assets? CJ] identifies four main asset categories in the economy: money and other deposits (credit market instruments or bonds for short); equities, or stocks; and tangible, or real, assets. [It seems that only three – not the promised four – asset categories are listed, CJ.]   (Boyle, 1996: 123)

Pragmatic errors

All of the discourse error types identified so far reflect limitations not in linguistic competence but in one's deployment of that competence. We used the label 'pragmatic' error (or infelicity) to refer to these: since they involve putting linguistic knowledge into practice we call them **pragmalinguistic** deviations. Unlike text errors, they arise whenever speakers misencode (or hearers misdecode) a message, not to the detriment of its **meaning** but to the detriment of its pragmatic **force**, that is, what speech act it is intended to perform or what rhetorical force it should carry. For example, if a German says to an English waiter *Bring me a beer*! his utterance will be taken as a COMMAND rather than as a REQUEST, and this will give offence. On the other hand, as Janicki (1980) and Thomas (1983) rightly stress, there are discoursal or interactional gaffes that arise not out of linguistic incompetence but out of sociocultural incompetence: uncouth native speakers make them, perhaps more so than cultured foreign learners. Janicki talks of 'socio-interactional rule encroachment' and Thomas of **socio-pragmatic failure**.

Sociopragmatic failures result from culture-clashes, from cultural differences of view concerning what is appropriate social (and sociolinguistic) behaviour in certain settings. Thomas (1983) identifies a number of sources of such infelicities.

1. Taboos

These are topics that are 'off limits' in some cultures but not (or to a different degree) in others. Familiar examples are unmentionables like sex, defecation, food, cancer and AIDS. A less familiar one is mentioned by Malcolm, who claims that Australian Aborigines observe a principle of communicative **parsimony** which demands that 'one should use as few words as possible to get one's meaning across' (1994: 299). To be glib and verbose in this culture would be to commit sociopragmatic error.

2. Size of the imposition

Twenty years ago in Moscow a cigarette was of such little value that you could casually ask any passer by in the street to give you one. In the West, by contrast, you would have to be ultra-polite if you ventured to beg one, even from a colleague.

3. Values

Ask a Brazilian how far away a landmark is and he will assure you it is *pertinho, Senhor* ('very close by'). Ask a Spaniard when your parcel will be delivered and you get the assurance *mañana*. That neither answer is true is immaterial to the speaker, whose social priority is not to tell you the truth but to make you feel good and confident. The American 'cooperative' lie is similar: when

Americans declare *We really must get together some time,* they do not necessarily mean that literally. The intended force of this utterance is to tell you they like your company and, possibly to spare you embarrassment, they have chosen to communicate that sentiment indirectly.

4.   Power and social distance

The socially appropriate use of forms of address and pronouns of solidarity or inferiority (such as German *du* and French *tu*) is a skill that takes years to acquire in some communities, and the newcomer had better watch his Ps and Qs. In Portugal, all teachers, from primary to university, are addressed in speech with [dotur], but when it comes to writing the title, the fully-fledged doctorate holder must get the full '*Doutor*', and even the abbreviation *dr* will give offence. Interestingly, Thomas (1984) sees cross-cultural discourse as entailing an inherently 'unequal encounter' in which one participant might well, on account of differences in cultural convention, behave differently from the other. The inequality resides in three facts: the fact that the native speakers are usually the 'gatekeepers' that is, they decide whether or not the nonnative speakers (immigrant workers, for instance) are going to be allowed to get certain benefits or 'rights'; the second fact is that the NSs have a superior command of the language; and the third fact is that the NSs are often also the teachers, which enhances their status even more. Is it any wonder, then, that it is usually the learners who have to do most of the work to be understood, while the NSs make little or no effort?

A landmark study of miscommunication in English NS:NNS discourse is Gass and Varonis (1991). They adopt Milroy's definition of miscommunication as being a 'simple disparity between the speaker's and hearer's semantic analysis of a given message' (1984: 15). They also distinguish between **misunderstanding** proper, which refers to the addressee getting a message different from that which the speaker intended, and **incomplete** understanding (which may be total or partial). Notice, however, that their focus is on the 'semantic' aspect of message, not the pragmatic, and that the misunderstandings they describe are instances of text error, not discourse error. We shall now address this distinction.

Receptive errors

It is tempting to describe exclusively text and discourse **production** processes while neglecting the more elusive 'receptive' errors. The temptation is greater on the levels of text and discourse than that of substance, where failure is visible and leads to an immediate breakdown of communication. The former we call **misunderstandings**, the latter **misprocessing** (see Figure 5.1) which reflects the text:discourse distinction drawn by Widdowson (1995). An alternative formulation of the same distinction is to say that misunderstandings involve retrieving non-intended **references** (or failing to pick up intended ones) from texts, while misprocessing arises when unintended **forces** of discourse are identified – or intended forces are not identified. We should also distinguish misunderstanding and nonunderstanding, and between misinterpretation and non-interpretation, noting that the difference between these two pairs is something more than just quantitative. These would be parallel to nonspeaking (silence) and nonwriting (block) on the production plane of language. But let us look at some examples.

Children often misunderstand the texts of (often archaic) hymns and poems they have to learn by heart at school. The opening line of the Christmas carol *Good King Wenceslas* (with three syllables on the proper name) is re-analysed by young English children hearing the carol for the first time as *Good King *Wenses* last*. The hymn about *all creatures great and small* is recontextualized into the school scenario and so becomes *all teachers great and small*. At a conference in France, I talked to a delegate who told me (I thought) that she worked for *Le Courrier du Sud*. I took her to be a journalist on the *Southern Mail*, until she subsequently mentioned Seoul in *La Corée du Sud*. On another occasion I listened to a lecture in French about foreign language teaching (FLT) methodology and wondered why the speaker had so much use for *jeux drôles* (funny games): of course, it was *jeux de rôle* (role plays) he was advocating. These were misunderstandings, reflecting failures to process linguistic (phonological, lexical and grammatical) features of the respective texts. George (1972: 118) points out that such misunderstandings arise in the FL class, with dire consequences and error. He points out that when a teacher typically models the comparative construction with *Ahmed is taller than Ali*, this is not what the students hear. To them it sounds plausibly like

Ahmed is tall than Ali, and this is how they analyse its grammar. A misinterpretation of mixed provenance originated in the following item in *The Borneo Bulletin* of 10 August 1994:

> Diplomat to leave after 'touching' incident.
> Manila, Aug 9, Reuter
> An Iraqi diplomat accused of touching a Filipino shop assistant's breast and thing while he was buying shoes is being reassigned, foreign office officials said on Tuesday.

Most readers understood *thing* all right, but misinterpreted it as a euphemism for another part of the female anatomy. In fact it was a simple misprint for *thigh*. Now it could be claimed that the misinterpretation originated in the readers' prurience, but I suggest a different account: that NS readers were willing to believe that the EL2 journalist was here making creative use of his limited English. There was an assumption that this was an error (of ignorance) whereas it was merely a compositional slip. This reaction endorses Schegloff's claim that the gatekeeper NSs are all too ready to conclude that the learners are 'slow, witless, truculent, lazy, uncaring, unmotivated' (1987: 202). However, we should focus our attention on the receptive errors of learners rather than those of NSs, although they have a great deal in common. Of relevance here is the fact that learners as text and discourse recipients are by no means 'lazy' or 'unmotivated'. On the contrary, they are very energetic indeed at trying to achieve an understanding and an interpretation of what they read or hear. There is little non-understanding and non-interpretation, though there may be a great deal of misunderstanding and misinterpretation. Evidence of the receivers' strong work-ethic in trying to understand and interpret comes from research on **communication strategies** (CSs).

Tarone, Cohen and Dumas (1983: 11) define a CS as 'a systematic attempt by the learner to express or **decode** meaning in the target language' (1983: 11, my emphasis). Ciliberti (1991) goes further, suggesting that the four recurrent production strategies of addition, deletion, misselection and misordering are also receptive strategies. So, when part of the message is not clear, the recipient may 'try to make transpositions, substitutions or additions in an attempt to attribute some sort of meaning to what she has heard' (Ciliberti, 1991: 99). The effect of making this link between learners' errors and their CSs is far-reaching: it links two major research traditions in applied linguistics. In what follows we shall highlight some of this research, looking first at work in reading and then moving on to work in listening. It must be stressed that communication involves both production and reception of language. It follows that communication strategies are neutral between these two modalities.

Laufer and Sim (1985) studied students' use and misuse of clues in EFL reading. Each student was asked to read in English short passages from Margaret Mead's *Male and Female* (1950). At the same time they were asked and required to answer (in their L1, Hebrew) oral comprehension questions on these passages. These oral protocols were found to provide insights into their processing strategies. In actual fact, misunderstandings and misinterpretations were both investigated, though the authors blur the distinction between the two. They tried to establish how incorrect answers had been arrived at, first, 'in terms of the textual clues' (**misunderstandings**) and, secondly, in terms of 'the extratextual knowledge he brought to the text' (**misprocessing**). For an example of the former, the Mead passage about modern marriage has a phrase *He outgrew her*, which was misunderstood as **They grew together*. When asked to justify this reading, the student said (in Hebrew): *'I don't know exactly what "outgrow" means. I know what "grow" means. So I fitted "outgrow" into the general idea of equal rights, equal education – all kinds of positive things; so "outgrow" implies probably "mutual growth"'* (Laufer and Sim, 1985: 8). In fact, 'outgrow' means quite the opposite to what this student takes it to mean, not mutual but unequal growth.

As an example of **misinterpretation**, take the original sentence *'marriages have been endangered by the possible development or failure to develop of husbands and wives'*. The question arises why the reader refused to interpret 'endangered' as 'made dangerous' – even though he was able to access this meaning. His explanation is lucid: *'I've always assumed that equality and emancipation contribute to happiness, better human relations. Therefore I associate women's education with better marriage.'* In other words, he had a 'mind set' or 'schema' of marriage (possibly culturally determined), which disposed him towards an optimistic view of the effects of education on marriage, at the same time blinding him to the converse interpretation. As Laufer and Sim put it: 'the information in the text may be distorted into a false construct to suit the reader's conviction' (ibid.: 9). This is a clear warning to those who believe that schema-activation is the key to successful reading.

Another study of the on-line deployment of CSs in FL reading (and translating) which has illuminating spin-offs for receptive EA is Hosenfeld (1977). It compares, by recording their protocols, the reading strategies of a good and a weak student processing the same French FL text. The pupil and the researcher interact in the former's attempts to extract meanings from the text. One of the stumbling blocks for the weaker student is the sentence *Pourquoi a-t-il choisi la Martinique?* He knows *pourquoi*, but does not know *choisir* and so looks it up in a dictionary. At this point therefore we have a case of nonunderstanding, but the question arises as to how much he does not understand: the whole sentence (as he claims), or just the verb *choisir*? By contrast, he misunderstands *a-t-il*, translating it as **Why did you . . .* and as **Why are you?* Subsequently, having realized that *il a* is a form of the verb *avoir* ('to have'), he concludes (again erroneously) that it must mean **Why did you have to choose Martinique?* The source of his two problems is his inability to process the **text**: these are therefore **misunderstandings**.

Neither student shows a **misinterpretation**, but the stronger student arrives at a valid interpretation of an unknown element, namely the noun *vol* (flight). He does this by the process (or CS) of **inferencing**, that is he makes use of contextual information and his real-world 'encyclopaedic' knowledge of the schema for AIRPORTS. *Vol* is an entity that takes place at airports (Orly), has a number (*vol numero 250*) and is connected with a *départ* and a *destination* (*pour la Martinique*): it just *has* to mean 'flight'. Had it not, there would have been misinterpretation.

The processing can also be a group effort. Jacquet and Palermo (1990) give an example where three students are working collaboratively on a French FL text. Look what happens when they come to the following passage: '*Depuis 1983, les Français ont droit à un minimum de cinq semaines pour vacances par an*' (1990: 23–6). One group recall that *droit* means either 'left' or 'right', but are unable to decide which. We capture their cognitive state at the point where they favour 'left': '*If it was "left", they have left a minimum of five weeks.*' Note that this reading requires them to ignore evidence to the contrary, in this case the preposition *à*: such insensitivity to the linguistic signal (text) constitutes misunderstanding.

We see another group struggling with the same item *droit à*. They submit to two successive misunderstandings: first, one of the group has heard (perhaps from another nearby group) [rait], and assumes this is the verb 'write'. The others in the group quickly reject his information, and one of them recalls *'to the right of' like droite and gauche*, a suggestion supported by another student: *Right. What was 'straight ahead'? Wasn't it droit?*. The group's judgement on this however is *But it doesn't make sense*. This group have not reached the interpretation stage of their reading. They have formulated a few tentative hunches about the meaning. We might call these temporary misunderstandings, but the important thing is that all were rejected and none of them retained. We have a case, therefore, of conscious **nonunderstanding**, as the disavowal *It doesn't make sense* shows.

Let us now return to receptive errors in listening. Recall that I cited some of my own above. Bremer, Broeder, Roberts, Simonot and Vasseur (1993) is a report of studies, undertaken in a European Science Foundation project, of adult untutored immigrants' communication problems, the FLs being English, Dutch, German and French. The report focuses on two problems: what causes misunderstandings, and how the immigrants behave when they arise. From this information it is possible to glean something about the nature of their mistakes. The distinction is made, albeit implicitly, between **misunderstanding** – when the immigrants 'cannot process the linguistic feature' (Bremer *et al.*, 1993: 159) – and **misinterpretation** – when reliance shifts to contextual clues. Misunderstanding results primarily when there is mishearing, that is 'a lexical element is not heard as intended' (ibid.: 159). An example cited is when an immigrant in France misheard *formation* ('training') as *information*:

NS: *Quelle formation vous aimeriez faire? (What sort of training would you like?)*

Immigrant: *J'aime que le dit moi . . . une information pour chercher du travail.*

(I'd like you to give me some information on finding a job.)

The obvious question to pose here is: what features in messages uttered by NSs tend to render them likely to be misunderstood? We can list some of these: excessive syntactic or informational complexity; highly elliptic and colloquial utterances; hypothetical statements (which are often understood as factual ones); and **indirectness** – if the NSs resort to indirectness in order to mitigate a taboo or face-threat to the listener, they will run the risk of being misunderstood or even misconstrued.

The third source of 'misunderstanding' identified in Bremer, Broeder, Roberts, Simonot and Vasseur (ibid.: 164ff.), namely 'pragmatic and situational problems', is really a source of misinterpretation. For example, an immigrant being interviewed by a British social worker was asked *Where do you live?*, which, as the one-word reply *Walsall* shows, was misinterpreted (misconstrued) as a curious enquiry about the immigrant's local affiliation, whereas it was intended as a formal enquiry about his address. A second example is where the social worker asks an Arab mother how many children sleep in each room (possibly to see whether she is being forced to breach regulations). Fatima misinterprets this question as a trespass on her private, domestic and thus nonpublic space, and takes offence. Here Fatima's culturally conditioned schemata are distorting her perception of the official enquiry.

It is significant that the examples we have been examining of receptive error fall into two categories, misreadings and mishearings, and that the former have been investigated in the 'formal' classroom while the latter have been recorded in real-life settings. I doubt that it is the case that mishearings are less frequent in classrooms than in streets and social security offices. Clearly, we need more research in both types of setting.

Notes

1. 'There has been a burst pipe in the town. All of the town has had a flood. Water was rising out the shop. (The shop) has (been) flooded so badly that the police have to get them out through the window. The water has gushed and broken the two front windows. When the watermen came they said: "We are so sorry that there is a bit missing and we cannot finish off. The bit has to come from America. It will take 2 or 3 weeks to arrive."'
2. The # symbol indicates a hiatus, momentary pause or 'checking' in speech.

6

Diagnosing Errors

It seems to me that too many doctors treat disease empirically, that is to say, they treat the symptoms individually. They don't bother to combine the symptoms in their own mind and puzzle out the diagnosis.

(A.J. Cronin, *The Citadel*. London: Victor Gollancz, 1939)

Description and diagnosis

In the previous chapter we commented on the desirability of distinguishing between error **description** and error **diagnosis**. There is widespread acceptance of this principle: Dulay, Burt and Krashen clearly state that 'the accurate description of errors is a separate activity from the task of inferring the sources of those errors' (1982: 145). Abbott makes the same point: 'One may at least *describe* errors without recourse to causal considerations' (1980: 133, my emphasis).

However, we might ask what motivates this insistence on keeping description and diagnosis separate. Is there a danger in allowing one's concerns with causes to influence the description? Who might wish to conduct description and ignore diagnosis? Well, a linguist with leanings towards purely structural explanations of learning problems (that is, with a strong interest in **learnability**) might wish to exclude all 'extraneous' factors, since these might distort the picture of learning as a purely formal process. For example, some might claim that such factors affecting language learning as motivation or attitude are irrelevant to accounts of leaning *per se* whereas the practical teacher would wish to exclude nothing that might shed light on the mysteries of learning, be they structural or whatever else.

173

The medical analogy does not completely hold. Sick patients visiting the doctor show visible signs of their illnesses, which the doctor 'describes' in order to reach a diagnosis. In addition, the patients are usually asked to describe their sensations to the doctor, who interprets this account in terms of a diagnosis. The Error Analyst has traditionally had nothing but the learners' output (analogous to a rash) as evidence, though there has been a move towards asking the learners to give an account (or **protocol**) as a source of supplementary information. Such introspective data has contributed a great deal to our understanding of the mentality of FL learners.

The diagnosis question is therefore one that transcends description and invokes **ascription** or explanation, tracing errors to their causes, sometimes called error **etiology**. Now, what causes error can be a general question or a specific one. We can ask: what causes learners to commit errors? The answer to this first question is the systematicity of language. If a language had no systematicity, no rules, then it would not be learnable in the first place. Paradoxically, it would, as a result, be impossible to make an error with it, since there would be no criterion against which to measure success of the learners' attempts. A second consequence of language being systematic, that is, in Bally's (1937) famous words '*un système où tout se tient*', is that it is in principle impossible for the learning of it to be gradual or cumulative. Since a system is an integration of its terms or parts, and these are mutually defining, you only know a system when you know it all, and only 'know each part' when you know the whole system. As Corder put it: 'In a sense, nothing is "fully" learnt until everything is "fully" learnt' (1973: 283). System learning is thus very different from item learning, as Cruttenden (1981) and Ringbom (1987) have shown.

You don't have to be a linguist to know that a language is systematically organized: learners, even the most linguistically naive of learners, seem to know this too. Proof of their assumption of systematicity is the systematicity or 'logicality' of most if not all of their errors. They fall into patterns (as we saw in the previous chapter) and have **concomitances**. For instance, if there is overuse of one article *the,* there is likely to be corresponding underuse of a co-term in the determiner system, so we see underuse of *a.* Similarly, many errors are plausible, and could be instances of the TL but are not: *flaind* is non-existent but could be an English word. This is how 'exceptions' and **gaps** arise.

I suspect that learners left to their own devices know that they cannot really instantaneously or part-know a system, and wait until they feel they know quite a bit of the system before they try it out actively: this explains the so-called **silent period** that naturalistic learners go through and which proponents of incidental learning (Asher, 1986) try to replicate in the FL classroom. In this phase learners will minimize people's perception of their production errors, but it is very likely that they will be committing many **receptive errors**, living in a world of half-understanding and feeling somehow sidelined out of the action. MacWhinney (1987: 232) refers to 'a kind of comprehension analogue to foreign accent' and quotes research that shows English L1 learners of Japanese trying desperately but in vain to make sense of the Subject–Object–Verb constituent order of Japanese.

The first two questions we have raised then concern what causes error in **principle**. A more concrete question is one that concerns the Error Analyst: what causes errors to have the forms they do, and not other forms they might have had? We therefore see our concern as being the mirror image of that which linguists have. They are concerned with the formal cause of error, whereas we are concerned with the cause of such and such form of error. This difference reflects the theoretician's concern for understanding of language phenomena, and the practitioner's concern for action: in this case, appropriate remedial action.

Ignorance and avoidance

The ultimate cause of **error** is, as we have made clear, **ignorance** of the TL item aimed at, or, in Johnson's (1996) system, lack of **declarative** knowledge. Similarly formed **mistakes** testify to uncertainty over the corresponding procedural knowledge or automatization. It is worth noting here that any formal deviance can have either declarative or procedural causes. So, when the required TL item is unknown and the learner **borrows** an L1 substitute, the consequence is an L1 **transfer error**, but when the learner knows the TL item but fails to access it, and instead accesses an L1 substitute, we have a case of an L1 **interference mistake**. Poulisse and Bongaerts (1994), discussing the origins of unintended L1 lexical intrusions, suggest that interference mistakes of this sort are signs of 'spreading activation'. This takes place when the semantic feature [+L1] somehow gets switched on together with a set of other essential features such as [+male], [+bovine], and [+adult], and L1 English *bull* emerges instead of the intended L2 Welsh *tarw*. The cause is no different in kind from selecting, in monolingual performance, [−male] for [+male] and retrieving *cow* for intended *bull*. The effect of activating the unintended feature [−male] or [+L1] spreads to the whole lexical item.

We can also explain (diagnose) the phenomenon of **avoidance** by reference to ignorance. Through negative feedback the learners find that they are ignorant of a TL item, and so turn to their L1 for a surrogate resource. But they find that the L1 cannot help: either they are ignorant of the L1 equivalent, or the L1 simply lacks an equivalent (it has a lexical or syntactic gap in this domain). Either way, the learners are in a state of double ignorance – ignorant of the TL item and ignorant of a possible L1 substitute – and have no alternative recourse than to 'avoid' the item affected. The choice facing them now is either to keep silent – to **topic-avoid** – or to find in the L2 some alternative or approximative way of expressing their meaning. They might resort to the communication strategy of paraphrase and circumlocution. The first strategy will be manifest in the covert error of **underrepresentation**, the second in the overt error of either **verbosity** or **vagueness**. In either case the learners are not using the form that a knower would use.

Of course, avoidance can be misapplied. There are situations where the learners believe something to be wrong in their IL system and so decide not to access it but instead either to stay silent or to use an alternative. They might, for example, believe something to be a false friend, and choose to avoid that item. But their self-assessment of their ignorance is wrong, and they are overmonitoring: the result is error, since they have, in effect, avoided using the right form that they know. An example is the L1 Portuguese EL2 *I would be extremely pleased to ?earn a scholarship*. Native speakers would probably prefer *win* here, but in fact *gain* is acceptable. The learners were aware that L1 *ganhar* corresponds to *gain*, *win* or *earn*, and also knew that *gain* is a false friend. In turning their back on the false friend, they put their accuracy in greater jeopardy.

It has been argued that errors of avoidance ought not to be committed in a carefully controlled learning environment, and they are a result of the learners being forced into premature production of TL forms they have not yet learnt – since it has not been taught. This argument has some logic to it, and it is not inconceivable that with computerized delivery, input could be so tightly controlled that no learner need be required to perform a bit of language not yet input(ted?). Still, as we saw in connection with Hammerly's (1991) suggestion about whom we should blame for errors (see Chapter 3), it is impossible to reconcile the teacher's conviction of having taught something with the learners' demonstration that it has not been learnt. Moreover, in naturalistic acquisition outside the classroom, such control will never be feasible, and TL knowers cannot be forbidden to broach topics that might involve the learners having to use language they do not know.

While it is true that ignorance is the ultimate cause of error, explaining the actual forms which ignorance-induced errors take on (and description of forms is the business of EA, as we showed in the previous chapter), diagnosis proper has to refer to a number of secondary reasons why errors take on the forms they do with a particular learner or category of learner. **Primary diagnosis** simply 'explains' why error occurs. **Secondary diagnosis** 'explains' the forms that errors assume. As pointed out in James (1980: 24), it is not unusual in mixed classes to find two or more learners who are all equally (totally) ignorant of some feature of the TL, for instance the pattern used to enquire after a person's name in English: *What is his name?* [wh- be – possNP]. Their ignorances are equal, but the equally wrong solutions they find, if based on their L1 patterns, are all wrong in different ways:

L1 Spanish:	*Como se llama?*	leading to	**How him(self) calls?*
L1 Russian:	*Kak evo zovut?*	leading to	**How they call him?*
L1 German:	*Wie heißt er?*	leading to	**How he calls?*

For this reason alone it is necessary to attempt error diagnosis that goes beyond the simple ascription that the learners were ignorant of the TL form. At the same time it is essential to try to maintain the primary diagnosis of ignorance, which, as we have seen, is necessary to distinguish error from mistake. Mistakes, remember, are performance phenomena. Corder (1981, 1983) took the distinction a little further by distinguishing between **borrowing** 'for immediate purposes' (1981: 104) an item from L1 for use in IL communication (as a communication strategy), and **incorporation,** which is what happens when that borrowed item is 'accepted by the interlocutor as well-formed in the L2' (ibid.) and consequently is integrated into the learners' IL. What originated as a communication strategy has reaped a rich reward, and has become learnt knowledge. Corder had in mind borrowing from the L1 or any other previously known language that comes into contact with the TL. We could, however, extend the scope of this borrowing-then-learning move to the TL itself. I want to ask your name in Spanish, and have heard *Como se llama?* used in such a context, so I borrow (or imitate) this. It has the intended effect, and I receive positive cognitive and affective feedback from you: as a result I add this form to my TL knowledge. FL learning is indeed a process of 'borrowing' something that belongs to someone else – native speakers and other knowers. They do not begrudge your wanting it, and readily share, but they expect you to take good care of what you have borrowed, as if it were their lawn mower, and to return it intact – not mutilated and disfigured with errors. When the loan becomes permanent, and the lender does not expect redemption, then the borrowers can take some liberties with the loaned language, giving it the stamp of their own personality. We see this happening with the New Englishes (Kachru, 1985) overseas.

While we have tried throughout this book to distinguish competence from performance-based, or declarative from procedural, deviance, at least one writer (Littlewood, 1992: 44–6) makes a plausible case for including all under the proceduralization rubric. In an attempt to answer the question *What goes wrong in performance?* he rephrases the issue in terms of **lower-level** and **higher-level** plans. Three predicaments are conceivable: (i)   When learners aim at a communicative act in L2 but lack the requisite low-level plans, they must either abandon (cf. avoid), or resort to alternative plans; (ii)   When they possess these low-level plans but they are not automatized, they face the defects of dysfluency and interference from related plans; (iii)   When they have the needed low-level plans but cannot combine these and cannot activate them in unfamiliar contexts. There seems to be some loss of precision here concerning the scope of 'plan': surely, the only 'plans' in operation are the lower-level ones, and the higher-level ones have been left out of the picture. Perhaps these are the communicative intent, the intended illocutionary forces. I would suggest that failures of type (i) in Littlewood's scheme are examples of ignorance of the TL items, and are errors proper. By contrast, the situations described in (ii) and (iii) will yield mistakes.

There is general agreement over the main diagnosis-based categories of error. There are four major categories.

- Interlingual
- Intralingual
- Communication-strategy
- Induced

Mother-tongue influence: interlingual errors

In Chapter 1 we mentioned Contrastive Analysis (CA) as an early paradigm for FL learning research. Detailed accounts of CA (James, 1980) are numerous and I do not intend to repeat them here. The crux of the CA hypothesis is that elements that are 'similar' in the L1 and the FL will be easier to learn than those that are different: in the first case, the learners benefit from positive L1 transfer, in the second they are encumbered by negative transfer or **interference**. Now it is common to hear the layperson explain errors originating in L1 transfer in terms of 'translation' from the L1. The Guatemalan immigrant Zoila described by Shapira (1978, see Chapter 1) says: 'I know the house is "casa" for me.' This is to misconstrue translation however, because the good translator does not allow the L1 (or the source language text) to distort the output, but edits out unwanted transfers and carries out the adjustments necessary to make the final text natural. It would be acceptable though to talk of learners indulging in over-**literal** or word-for- word translation, by which is meant precisely the sort of translation that overlooks these sorts of adjustments made in 'real' translation.

Lado (1957: 2) states the relationship between difference and difficulty in its simplistic form, suggesting the relationship to be proportional: the greater the difference, the greater the difficulty. Closer observation has prompted a refinement of the equation, and Jackson gets it right when he states that interference happens 'when an item or structure in the second language manifests some degree of difference from, and some degree of similarity with the equivalent item or structure in the learner's first language' (1987: 101). Clearly, Jackson is equating the probability of L1 interference not with difference, but with contrast. This is why we do **contrastive** analysis and not '**difference**' analysis. Contrast is defined as difference in the context of similarity.

The clearest proof of L1 interference is where L1 nonstandard dialect features get transferred to L2. Gomes da Torre (1985) gives some examples of this process at work with L1 Portuguese learners of EL2. Interestingly, he chooses to account for this in terms of these learners' *ignorance* of standard Portuguese, and if this is the case, it would justify doing some Language Awareness work as error remediation of the kind that I shall outline in Chapter 8. Note the erroneous overinclusion of the resumptive pronoun in: *New articles were invented like 'Chiclets' which nobody calls *them anything*. This, Gomes da Torre argues, reflects the learners' non-standard Portuguese: ... *'Chiclets' a que ninguem *lhes chama outra coisa*. The learners need not be totally ignorant of a (positively) transferable L1 form to commit such an error: that form may simply be unusual in their repertoire, though they recognize it when they see it and on special occasions even use it themselves. An example would be the fronted preposition in *With who(m) did he come?* Ninety-nine per cent of the time the learners might prefer: *Who did he come with?* Now when they come to learn French or German, they will have a problem, since in these languages the preposition must be fronted. Failure to do so results in errors like *Qui est-il venu*avec?* and *Wem ist er gekommen *mit?*

There are also occasions where learners have L1 patterns that could be advantageously transferred to the L2 but they do not exploit this potential, and the explanation has nothing to do with infrequency. Take the noun pluralization overinclusion error in the following: *I am a seventeen year*s old girl from Györ*. Now, this learner's L1 is Hungarian, which has a rule that nouns do not pluralize after a numeral, so one says in Hungarian the equivalent of *five √horse* and not *five *horses*. One wonders what might have blocked this potential positive transfer: suffice it to say at this point that the learner made this error not out of ignorance of English, but because she knew too much English!

As was pointed out by Wardhaugh (1970), the CA hypothesis existed (and still does) in two versions, a strong version and a weak version. Both versions are equally based on the assumption of L1 interference in L2 learning. They differ in that the first 'strong' version claims to be able to **predict** learners' errors before they ever commit them, on the basis of identifying in advance the contrasts between the two language systems. The less ambitious (hence 'weak') version of CA claims no more than the power to **diagnose** those errors that have been committed as a result of L1 interference. I personally have never shared Wardhaugh's view: for me, CA is not CA unless it is predictive and so-called 'diagnostic' CA is not CA but part of Error Analysis, or of Transfer Analysis (see Chapter 1).

I do mean *part of* EA, since errors triggered by L1 interference are not the only errors, as we shall presently see. But they are a significant subset of all errors, though estimates and counts vary between 3 per cent and 25 per cent of all errors. The remaining 75 per cent of errors are what Richards (1974a) aptly called 'non-contrastive' errors, which we shall discuss presently. It must, however, be stressed that no responsible Contrastive Analyst ever claimed that *all* FL errors were due to L1 interference, and to go to the opposite extreme of claiming that virtually *no* errors are caused by L1 transfer is to throw out the baby with the bath water. Nickel (1989, 1992) refers to the controversy over the relative importance of 'contrastive versus noncontrastive' errors, and shows clearly that both types exist in sufficient numbers and persistence to make the inclusion of both inevitable in any diagnostic EA framework. He also shows that L1 transfer, the psychological basis of CA, is enjoying renewed acceptance as a crucial component in modern L2 learning theories.

The main value of L1 transfer-based diagnosis is that it can lead to the compilation of compact and practical **profiles**, not of individual learners' ILs, but of the shared characteristics of the ILs of a group of learners, a group having the same L1 or L2. They may be as compact as a single volume or a chapter in a book – a cameo profile. Examples of book-length accounts are Fisiak, Lipinska-Grzegorek and Zabrocki (1978), *An Introductory English–Polish Contrastive Grammar* and Krzeszowski's (1970) *Teaching English to Polish Learners*. It is not surprising that these Polish applied linguists, who have led the world in CA research for decades, should have produced national learner profiles. The best collection of shorter sketches of L1-defined types of English is Swan and Smith (1987).

Ongoing developments in the specification of L1-homogenous learner populations are in **contrastive rhetoric** (Connor, 1996). Here we see an accumulating documentation of how the rhetorical-discoursal conventions are carried over from writing in the L1 to EL2 writing done by Japanese, Arabs and other language and cultural groups.

Markedness and L1 transfer

Other developments reflect refinements in language transfer theory, refinements motivated by linguistic research into Universal

Grammar (Cook, 1988) and first-language acquisition. The most researched area is that of **parameter setting** (or more appropriately *re*setting) in L2 learning. 'Parameter' is a notion in Universal Grammar theory which sees L1 acquisition as involving children being on the lookout for clues as to the nature of the language being used around them. They know innately that the world's languages either retain or drop subject pronouns. Portuguese is a PRO-Drop language, allowing *quiero (I want)*, while English is not: the pronoun must be used, hence **want* is ungrammatical in English. Learning a language involves setting hundreds of parameters, like so many switches, to the 'on' or 'off' positions on the mental switchboard. The computer analogy will be obvious, although not all parameters have to be binary: some might have three or four possible settings. Now it is equally obvious that the CA hypothesis can be formulated in terms of the transfer to L2 of the parameter settings of one's L1. Nothing is gained over classical formulations of the CA hypothesis, except that the metaphor is more graphic. The prediction would be that the Portuguese will tend to err in English by saying: **want* and the EL1 learner of Portuguese by saying **Eu quiero,* which has the (here unintended) force of an emphatic '*I* want'. The prediction for English learners of Portuguese is true, but for Portuguese learners of English it is not. Another parameter is final obstruent devoicing: some languages, such as German and Polish, devoice final voiced obstruents while other languages (like English) do not. In German *die Hand* is pronounced [hant], while in English one says [hænd]. The CA prediction is that Germans will say [teik mai han*t] and English speakers will mispronounce German *Hand* as [hæn*d]. Again, the first prediction is valid but the second not. Why?

The answer lies in the concept of **markedness**. This refers to the tendency for linguistic phenomena to occur in binary oppositions, marked versus unmarked member. The **marked** member of each pair is the more uncommon, more specialized, more complex, more focused and more constrained than the unmarked. The indications are that the marked option will be harder to learn, since it is more complex, rare, special and constrained. The question that arises now is: which setting (marked or not) for each parameter is assumed by the FL learners (as a default setting) until they hear evidence for the actual setting? There are two options:

(i)   To refer back to some UG principle that determines a priori assumptions, and this principle seems to be that parameters should be set as *unmarked* until evidence suggests otherwise. This explains the pidgin features of early child language and other **simple codes**: all those deletions or empty categories constitute evidence for an unmarked setting over all parameters.

(ii) To assume that the FL structure has the same setting as their L1, irrespective of its markedness polarity. If the learners know this TL feature already, by virtue of using it in their L1, it does not matter whether it is intrinsically more complex: complexity gets neutralized when it has been mastered.

The interaction between classical Contrastive Analysis L1 transfer theory and markedness is brilliantly captured in Eckman's (1977) **markedness differential hypothesis**. This says that a TL form will be difficult to learn if it is different from the corresponding L1 form, *and* if the TL form is marked (or more marked) while the L1 form is unmarked (or less marked). When Eckman says an L2 form will be 'difficult', this means that making the L1 transfer will be unsuccessful, and will result in error. He also means that learners will nevertheless be inclined to make these negative transfers. Now to look at the other side of the coin: learners whose L1 and TL forms are different but whose L1 form is marked will not make the negative transfer to an L2 where that feature is unmarked. As a result they will not commit this sort of interference error – though they may of course commit other sorts of error. They will still find the TL form 'difficult', and possibly their sense of its difficulty will be more acute, since they have no easy solution for their difficulty in the form of L1 transfer. This means two things: (i) An unmarked L1 form will be transferred to the L2 with resulting error if the L2 has a different (that is, marked) parameter setting; (ii) A marked L1 form will not get transferred, so the interference error predicted by classical CA does not materialize. This explains why our CA predictions of errors involving the PRO-Drop and the final obstruent devoicing parameters were valid for one directionality but not the other. Pronoun dropping is the marked setting, so learners are not disposed to transfer it to an L2. Consequently, the Portuguese do *not* say *$\emptyset$ (√*I*) *arrived at six* whereas English students of Portuguese do assume transferability of their unmarked PRO. They retain overt PRO, and say *Eu cheguei às seis.*

Explaining why Germans do have difficulties with the voicing of the final stop consonant in English *hand* requires us to invoke a slightly different definition of the concept of markedness. This is closely associated with linguistic infrequency. The maintenance of a voiced:voiceless obstruent contrast in word-final position as in the English minimal pair *bold:bolt* is relatively rare and therefore highly 'marked' among the world's languages, that is, 'typologically'. Making the contrast word-medially is somewhat less marked and making it word-initially is the least marked. Now the German does make the contrast initially and medially but not finally, whereas English makes it in all three positions: German makes it in less-marked positions than English, so the German is disposed to transfer – and, the transfer being negative, the learners get it wrong and say [*mai han*t*]. English speakers will not be disposed to transfer their more marked L1 setting to the less marked German, which would lead to the mispronunciation [*main hæn*d*]. One could say, with Kellerman (1983) that the learners have applied their **psychotypology** to block the transfer of the L1 rule to L2, perceiving maintenance of the final obstruent voice contrast as 'infrequent, irregular, semantically or structurally opaque, or in any other way exceptional' (Kellerman, 1983: 114).

Let us emphasize the options open to the learners faced with L2 ignorance. If they judge an L1 form to be sufficiently unmarked to be transferable, they will transfer it. Whether the transfer is successful ('positive') or calamitous ('negative') is in the lap of the Gods, depending on the chance isomorphism of L1 and L2 at the structure in question, or on their historical cognateness or their areal affinities. If they do attempt transfer, but without success, the result is what Hammerly (1991) calls **intrusive** interference. If the learners decide not to transfer from L1, but to keep quiet instead, the outcome is Hammerly's **inhibitive** interference. These are two interlingual strategies. In addition to these there is a range of intralingual strategies, which we shall now consider as causes of error – and at times also, like interlingual transfer, causes of success. We must be careful not to perpetuate the myth that transfer is a morbid activity, leading only and inevitably to failure and never to success.

Target language causes: intralingual errors

Apart from recourse to L1 transfer, the learners in ignorance of a TL form on any level and of any class can do either of two things: *either* they can set about learning the needed item, engaging their learning strategies *or* they can try to fill the gap by resorting to communication strategies. Learning strategies are used for code-breaking while communication strategies are encoding and decoding strategies. Both types of strategy can be the source of error. It is possible to multiply these causal categories, but then some duplication creeps in. I shall try to keep the number as small as possible.

Learning strategy-based errors

1. False analogy

The learner wrongly assumes that the new item B behaves like A: she knows that *boy* (A) has its plural *boys* and assumes that *child* (B) behaves likewise, so pluralizes to **childs*. This strategy corresponds to George's (1972) **cross-association**.

2. Misanalysis

The learners have formed a hunch or hypothesis concerning an L2 item, which they are now putting into practice. The hypothesis is not based on L1 knowledge at all. Unfortunately, the hypothesis is unfounded. An example of this strategy occurs in: *They are carnivorous plants and *its (√ their) name comes from.* . . . The false concept in operation here is that *its* is the *s*-pluralized form of *it*, a hypothesis plausible on the basis of TL evidence alone, but possibly reinforced by the learners' L1 (Portuguese) having the third person singular personal pronoun *ele* which is pluralized to *eles* ('them'). A false concept is the result of the learners misanalysing the TL. This is not to deny, however, that some of these misanalyses are quite ingenious. Take the following: *'Tinker, Tailor', as every story *who tells about spies.* . . . The learner has hypothesized that since the book's title refers to humans, therefore the [+human] relative pronoun should be selected.

3. Incomplete rule application

This is the converse of overgeneralization. One might call it *under*generalization. An example is seen in the deviant order of subject and verb 'be' in: *Nobody knew where *was Barbie (√ Barbie was)*. Here the learners have applied only two components of the interrogative formation rule: they have selected and fronted a wh-element (rule components 1 and 2), but have omitted to invert subject and verb. The strategy at work here is aimed at simplification: rather than attempt to get the whole of the complex interrogative structure right at one go, the learners have decomposed it into smaller operations, one of which they perfect at a time.

4.   Exploiting redundancy

Human languages carry considerable redundancy. This is manifest throughout the system in the form of unnecessary morphology and double signalling, for example signalling subjecthood both by word order and by inflection. Intelligent learners, George (1972) clearly showed, can sense this redundancy and try to dispense with some of it to lighten their learning task. We referred to this pidginization in simple codes above. Here we might also mention the late and opposite tendency on the part of some more advanced learners: to **overelaborate** the TL and to lapse into verbosity and **babu**. We illustrated this in Chapter 3 with the text lampooning a speech by General Alexander Haig. Here is an example, from the letter of an advanced learner: *Every day with great expectation I looked for the mail but am very sorely disappointed. . . . Unless all formalities are finished noone will deem my completing the course.*

5.   Overlooking cooccurrence restrictions

An example of this is *I would enjoy *to learn (√learning) about America*, caused by ignorance of the fact that the verb *enjoy* selects a gerundial complement. Another example is *People in America live more *quick than we do*. We have a double error here: first, *quick* is wrongly assumed to be synonymous with *fast* and to have the same distribution. This is not the case: we talk of √*fast food* but not of **quick food*. Secondly, it is wrongly assumed that *quick* can serve as either adjective or adverb, as *fast* can, without suffixing *-ly* to the adverb: a system over-simplification.

6.   Hypercorrection (monitor overuse)

This results from the learners over-monitoring their L2 output, and attempting to be consistent, so it is akin to system simplification: *Il √est descendu et *est (√a) attendu.* The learner seems to have learnt that the marked auxiliary *être* is used with *descendre* but wrongly assumes that it should also be used with *attendre*. We saw a more complex case above of an L1 Portuguese learner of EL2 monitoring out the assumed false friend *gain: ganhar,* and using the wrong *earn.* One might claim that the learners' deliberate suppression of a potential L1 transfer for fear (born of experience of failure) of being wrong is another form of hypercorrection: we saw a case of this with the *seventeen year*s old girl* above.

7. Overgeneralization, or system-simplification

An example is the generalization of the relative pronoun *that* as in:

> Bill, **that had a great sense of unconventional morality* . . .
> The observing qualities of Roach, **that was a great observer* . . .

Note that this strategy leads to the overindulgence of one member of a set of forms and the underuse of others in the set: these learners use *that* to the exclusion of *who.* Similar overgeneralization to one of two TL alternatives happens with *other/another, much/many, none/neither, some/any* and many more such 'confusibles'. It is not restricted to lexical pairs of course. System options such as tense-marking are also susceptible. The learners of French who write *J'*ai (√suis) parti* are basing their selection of auxiliary *avoir* on the fact that the majoriy of French verbs do indeed form the perfect with this auxiliary.

Communication strategy-based errors

1. *Holistic strategies*

The term 'holistic' refers to the learners' assumption that if you can say X in the L2, then you must be able to say Y. Lacking the required form, it must be all right to use another near-equivalent L2 item which they have learnt. The most general term for this is **approximation**. It takes on a number of forms, the first of which is to use a near synonym. An example is the L1 French learner of English who substitutes the cognate **credibility* for the intended √*truth.* Alternatively, one can use a superordinate term: **fruits* for √*blackberries.* A third option is to use an antonym or opposite: **not* *happy* for √*sad.* A fourth option is to **coin** a word: *Until you be unconscious to lose your *sensities (√senses).*

The four Communication strategies (CSs) exemplified so far are TL-based. There are L1-based CSs also, which have already been mentioned above. Some examples from Greek L1 learners of English are:

■ **Language switch**: *I go to my . . . room, inside to *cambina (√cabin).* Here the Greek word καμπινα has been transferred.
■ **Calque**: This is a literal translation into L2 of the L1: *to find . . . *rest (√change) for the ticket.* Here the Greek false friend ρεστα has been substituted.

2. *Analytic strategies*

Analytic strategies express the concept indirectly, by allusion rather than by direct reference: this is **circumlocution**. The learners identify one or more criterial attributes of the referent and mention these in an attempt to refer to the entity in question. Here is an example of an extended circumlocution representing a Greek learner's attempt to express the concept of *decompression chamber* in EL2:

> *the big . . . medical . . . thing . . . you go inside and they put air, press air . . . Yes . . . you go down for your ears, they test.*

James and Persidou (1993), in their study of the CSs used by Greek learners of English, showed that different learning experiences determine strategy preferences. They compared the CSs used in describing in EL2 the game of backgammon by two types of learner: those who had picked up English informally by interacting with tourists at the popular resort of Halkidiki (**Acquirers**), and a group with about the same EL2 proficiency who had studied English in British Council courses in the city of Thessaloniki (**Learners**). The data showed that:

■ The Learners used the L1 transfer strategy much more than the Acquirers, probably because they had been taught English in settings where fellow learners and teachers all knew Greek, so would not be confounded by recourse to Greek. The Acquirers by contrast had learnt English by interacting with tourists from a variety of L1 backgrounds, who knew no Greek and therefore would not allow the Acquirers to fall back on Greek when they encountered a problem with English.

■ The two groups did not differ in their overall preference for holistic strategies over analytic strategies.

■ The Acquirers were much more verbose, but also more resourceful, than the Learners, and the Learners' frequency of recourse to the avoidance strategy was 'quite alarming'.

Induced errors

This term was first used by Stenson (1983) to refer to learner errors 'that result more from the classroom situation than from either the students' incomplete competence in English grammar (intralingual errors) or first language interference' (interlingual errors) (Stenson, 1983: 256). They are the result of being misled by the ways in which the teachers give definitions, examples, explanations and arrange practice opportunities. They can be distinguished on the one hand from **spontaneous** errors, for which the learners are 'responsible', and, on the other hand, from **elicited** errors, which are prompted from learners in research settings where data need to be gathered. Note that we have again stumbled on to the issue of who is to blame, which we discussed in Chapter 3.

Some of what Stenson calls induced errors could be explained in terms of the diagnostic categories we have outlined above. For example, she reports the teacher who introduced the verb *worship* 'as a general word for *pray*', which the students already knew. They also knew that *pray* selects the preposition *to*, which they assumed also applied to *worship*. The result was *worshipping *to God*. This is a clear case of **cross-association** or **overgeneralization**. It was the learners who did the mental work to draw this false analogy, but the teacher should perhaps have tried to separate these two near-synonyms in the learners' minds, either by embedding them in distinctive contexts or by doing some language awareness work to isolate them cognitively one from the other.

Similarly, there are those errors that Stenson suggests are induced by imprecise **teacher explanations**. One such is the pedagogical 'explanation' which distinguishes the modals *should* and *must* on the grounds that the former is 'stronger' than the second. The error precipitated was *We *should have worked in order to buy clothes, but we *must have worked in order to eat*. The learners are attempting to convey the idea that it is less important to spend money on clothes than on food – which they see as conforming to the teacher's rule of thumb. In fact the learners have hypothesized a false concept (a common intralingual error), not, however, on the basis of their own analysis of input but on that of their teacher's mediation of the lexical opposition. The same could be said of other induced errors cited by Stenson, for example, the use of *any* as a negative marker, or the equation of *like* with *as if*: these both testify to false conceptualization of the TL structure. The learners would have done it anyway. Stenson's point, however, is that the teacher's attempt to forestall these errors probably made their commission more likely.

Even errors induced by the drill-type of exercises have affinities in their etiology with some of the intralingual types listed earlier. Stenson talks of errors caused by learners 'failing to make some secondary change which goes along with the transformation being drilled' (Stenson, 1983: 264). This could refer to the learners' tendency to attend to one thing at a time, which is best achieved if complex structures (we gave the example of interrogatives) are broken down into their simple constituents. Attending to one is the first step, and this implies ignoring the others.

Then there is oral practice that elicits erroneous forms. The most notorious of these is the **directed question**, which involves the teacher (T) directing student A to put a question (use an interrogative) to student B. Here is how it goes:

> T: Where do you live?
> A: I *do live in New Street.
> T: Yes, you live in New Street. Where does Laura live? Ali, ask her where she lives.
> A: Where *you lives?
> B: I *lives in King Street.

There is no denying that **induction** is a widespread source of learner error. It can never be fully eradicated. This is not only because so many teachers know the TL imperfectly (this applies to native speakers and nonnative speakers); but because even textbook writers include language that is inaccurate (no matter how 'authentic' it may be). We shall only be able to engineer perfect intake when we fully understand the human mind as an information-processor, as yet a distant goal. I would like to suggest the following sources of induced errors:

1.   Materials-induced error

I pick up a recent European coursebook for beginners of EL2 (which I shall not name) and notice the following:

> *By my watch it's five past eleven, but I *think it isn't right/√don't think it's right.*
> *My birthday is on the *tewlfth[1] /√twelfth of March*
> *He is *a/√∅ Chinese . . . *a Portuguese . . . *a Swiss*
> *What's the weather like in autumn? Many people *are wearing/√wear raincoats and *are carrying/√carry umbrellas*

In one dialogue a son is asking his mother for suggestions for what to buy his sister Betty as a birthday present. He has no idea what to buy:

> Mother: *I suggest you give her a record.*
> Son: *Oh, that's a good idea mum! That's what I *am going to/√'ll give Betty.*

I'm going to implies that he had made up his mind what to give some time ago, which clearly is not the case in the dialogue. A sudden snap decision, as here, requires the use of *will.*

2.   Teacher-talk induced error

One of the roles of teachers is to provide models of the standard TL in class. They have other roles too, one of which might be to expose advanced learners to nonstandard and dialect forms of the TL for receptive control (Hughes and Trudgill, 1996). Modelling the standard of the TL is sometimes a problem even for NS teachers, if they happen not to speak it themselves, but instead are monodialectal speakers of a local nonstandard. As for NNS teachers of a language, their own command of the TL is often a cause for grave concern, and in many places young trainees' expertise in up-to-date methodology is far in excess of their command of the TL itself. The following error-inducing errors were noted in the EL2 of a group of Brazilian teachers:

> *Put them in the right *[orðə] /√[ordə].*
> *I will do this in order *to/√that my students perceive well the difference.*
> *In order *to become learning meaningful/√for learning to become meaningful . . .*

We shall study article*s/√Ø usage . . .
*Can be used just one determiner /\ Just one determiner can be used.

The following were written on the blackboard and left there till the end of the lesson, so allowing the class ample time to absorb (or 'notice') them: *commo*m noun; poten*cial problems.*

Note that we are not talking now about the teacher's ability to survive in the TL, or even to read some of its literary classics. FL teachers have their own **professional** TL needs, and need not only methodological teacher training but also language proficiency training in order to prepare them to meet the linguistic demands of the FL classroom. Moreira (1991) outlines an empirical study relevant to the question *What type(s) of language difficulty are encountered by trainee teachers in the course of their lessons?* As a first step she established that FL teachers need language skills adequate to the performance of four central roles. These are the roles of **classroom manager**, **instructor**, **spontaneous communicator** and **resource person**. Next, lessons given by trainees were observed and notes were taken of the teaching activities (associated with the above four roles) which most consistently led to language 'difficulties' on the part of the trainee teachers. The activities identified as being the most problem-causing were: setting out and changing tack in a lesson; dealing with the unexpected; using metalanguage; and directing the lesson. The final question to which an answer was sought was how the trainees' difficulties manifested themselves in the language they used. Four categories of 'deficiencies' were identified. The first and most widely found was **error**, comprising defects on any of the levels we mentioned in Chapter 4, these being particularly manifest in 'the production of incorrect explanations of meaning and grammar and non-existent rules' (Moreira, 1991: 44). Significantly, error occurred when the trainees were dealing with the unexpected and talking about language. The second sort of deficiency was '**Portuglish**' which leads to the use of forms that are not ungrammatical in the TL but 'are considered unnatural in English' (ibid.). Presumably these were forms originating in L1 transfers. They surfaced mainly when the teachers were operating in their organizer/communicator roles, concentrating on getting something done. Thirdly, there was the apparently conscious use of **Portuguese**, or language switch, which was taken as a sign of difficulty in expressing the same meaning in the EL2. Finally, there was what Moreira calls **confusion**, that is 'instances in which a trainee's language became confused and incoherent' (ibid.: 44). This is taken as a sign of low confidence, uncertainty and vagueness on the trainee's part.

Clearly, the deficiencies identified in this study are all either errors of inaccuracy, inauthenticity or dysfluency, and their enumeration adds nothing much to our understanding of learners' errors themselves. On the other hand, they do suggest some of the necessary ingredients to be included in a special-purpose syllabus for teaching EL2 teachers the English they need for them to be able to perform their professional functions.

3.   Exercise-based induced errors

There are times when the teachers' or textbook's input to the learners is not in itself deviant, but prompts error from the learners as a result of the learners being required to perform certain manipulations on bits of language. A case is the **combining** exercise, recently advocated anew by William Strong in his *Sentence Combining: A Composing Book* (1994). In order to elicit from learners a complex sentence, one involving embedding or subordination for example, the teacher feeds to the learners the raw ingredients: simple sentences that the learners must combine. Conditionals linked by *if* or *unless* are examples: *I can't afford a new car* combined with *I shall win the lottery* should yield *I can't afford a new car unless I win the lottery* but will also yield at times from at least one student forms like **Unless I can afford a new car I shall win the lottery.* The likelihood is especially great when the students have been told that *unless* is equivalent to *if . . . not,* which will suggest to them the possibility of replacing the negative element in *can't* with *unless.*

Another example of this process involves combining clauses to give practice at relative clause formation. Chapter 1 of *Write Ideas* by Glendinning and Mantell (1983) has a section called 'Linking Facts'. The learners are confronted with a set of six to eight simple sentences that describe historical figures like James Watt, Gandhi, Columbus and Shakespeare. Their task is to combine each pair of simple sentences by converting one of them into a relative clause using one of the three relative pronouns *who, which* and *where,* as appropriate.

It is a useful exercise of the sentence-combining type. I tried it out with a first-year university class in Brunei as a piece of action research. These students did not encounter major problems in combining successive pairs of contiguous sentences. The problem of misplacement of the relative clause, predicted by Glendinning and Mantell on page 8 did not in fact materialize in class, where students appeared to have a clear perception of the problem and so avoided it:

> *The Nile flows from Lake Victoria, *which is the longest river in Africa.*

This problem and the resultant error of displaced relative did materialize later, however, as anticipated by the textbook. Some students produced:

> *Alfred Hitchcock was born in 1888 in London and trained at St. Ignatius College as an engineer, *who became an American film director.*

This looks like **overgeneralization**. The students have hypothesized that the relative clause is always extraposed to become the final clause of the complex sentence. The hypothesis is derived from direct positive evidence contained in the textbook.

Three problems occurred which had not been anticipated. First, the problem of redundant retention of the personal pronoun and the place adverb, yielding errors like:

> *Watt, who he was an engineer, invented a steam engine which *it had a special part.*
> *Watt was born in Scotland, where he made his first experiments *there.*

This error of redundancy or overmarking looks as if it might have resulted from negative transfer from an L1 that has such **resumptive pronominal copies**. Our students' first language (Malay) does not have this feature[2] however, so the error is not due to transfer. According to Pavesi (1986), errors of pronoun copying are typical of formally instructed learners, while errors of full noun copying are more typical of acquirers, who would opt for . . . *invented a steam engine which *the engine had a special part.*

A second surprise problem sprang from total disregard in this coursebook of the distinction between defining and non-defining relative clauses. This oversight is surprising, in view of the fact that the section gives practice on writing about four famous (in fact unique) people: a proper noun is involved in every case. Errors occurred like:

> *Shakespeare* who was born in Stratford was a writer.*

The third problem is even more interesting. It emanates from indecision about what information is to be assumed as 'given' as opposed to 'new' in the complex sentence resulting from combination. In a word, it is a 'rhetorical' problem. The procedure modelled on page 8 of the textbook indicates clearly that the students are intended to relativize the **second** clause of each pair on the Subject Proper Noun NP in the first, main clause. In other words, the students are required to produce the following:

(a) *Gandhi was a politician who led the independence movement in India.*
(b) *Columbus was an explorer who crossed the Atlantic in 1492.*
(c) *Shakespeare was a writer who was born in Stratford in 1567.*
(d) *Einstein was a great physicist who was born in Germany in 1879.*

In these four examples the Subject Proper Noun is 'given' or 'known' information (since this same Proper Noun constitutes the paragraph title in each case). The 'new' information revealed about this person is carried not by the whole of the predicate but by the relative clause contained in that predicate: *who led the independence movement in India.* But this observation seems only to hold true for examples (a) and (b) but not for (c) and (d). After all, what characterizes Gandhi and Columbus is precisely that they respectively *led the independence movement* and *crossed the Atlantic in 1492.* Those were their signal achievements. But the same does not hold for (c) and (d): Shakespeare's claim to fame was not that he was *born in Stratford.* Nor did Einstein get his Nobel Prize for having been *born in Germany.*

One way out of the dilemma would be to specify the common noun *politician, explorer, writer, physicist* as the 'new' part of the predicate. After all, if it were 'given' it ought to be marked as such with the definite article *the.* Since this is not the case, we must regard it as 'new'. This works for (c) and (d):

(c) *Shakespeare, who was born in Stratford in 1567, was a writer.*
(d) *Einstein, who was born in Germany in 1879, was a great physicist.*

but it does not work for (a) and (b):

(a) ? *Gandhi, who led the independence movement in India, was a politician.*
(b) ? *Columbus, who crossed the Atlantic in 1492, was an explorer.*

These two are certainly not ungrammatical. They are pragmatically inappropriate to the communicative intent of the writer, as far as the reader can ascertain it. A nondefining relative provides information that is interesting but in no way crucial. However, the fact that Gandhi led an independence movement or that Columbus crossed the Atlantic should not be subordinated to the status of an incidental aside.

These errors are induced by the materials providing the learners with examples in the form of positive evidence that are not in sufficiently homogeneous sets. As we have seen, examples (a) to (d) are not four instances of the same grammatical selections: information in (a) and (b) is differently organized and linearized from that in (c) and (d).

At this point I set homework: students were asked to jot down ten facts about a famous personality 'living or dead', and then to combine these ten facts into one **megasentence**, using the relativizing devices we had been observing at work in our classroom texts. A wide range of errors and infelicities cropped up, most of which had not been anticipated.

The first common one resulted from assuming the title to be rhematic (or 'new'), so that the first in-text mention of the person named in the title was assumed (quite reasonably) to be thematic, familiar, and therefore pronominalizable:

> Title: *Elvis Presley.* First sentence: *He was an actor and singer who . . .*
>
> Title: *Marie Curie.* First sentence: *She was born in 1867 in Poland . . .*

There was one instance of a rhematic pronoun being immediately relativized, with bizarre consequences:

> Title: *King Mongkut.* First sentence: **He, who got many wives and children . . .*

The second problem was the result of taking advice (given by me the teacher) too literally: I had suggested using the present participle as a linking device, as in:

> *He studied to become a lawyer in London, √returning to South Africa in . . .*

I had omitted to mention that the voice of a participialized lexical verb used in this way has to be active voice. Participialization was consequently **overgeneralized** to passives, giving:

> . . . *became the first female lecturer at the Sorbonne,* *appointing as
> *professor in 1934.*
> . . . *was born in 1926,* **educating in the role of constitutional monarch
> by her father . . .*

Another overgeneralization is more tricky to specify. I had taught use of the *after which* relativization as an elegant linking device, as in:

> . . . *became the leader of the Indians (there), after which he returned to
> India.*

One student overextended this into:

> . . . *from 1857 till 1868, during* *which (√*time*) *he abolished slavery.*

For some unfathomable reason, the prepositional phrase must have a noun complement *time*, a requirement that does not hold for the corresponding prepositional phrases *after which* and *before which*.

Relative pronouns that are simultaneously complements of prepositions caused a lot of trouble:

(a)   . . . *six hundred paintings,* *where√/*among which many were of
      himself.*

(b)   . . . *has written books on marital law,* *where/√*on which he also
      gives lectures . . .*

There was an especially interesting case of the **resumptive pronoun** type of error:

> . . . *scores of brilliant films* **which most of them* /√*most of which were
> psychological thrillers.*

There were times when it was difficult to decide whether a learner's production was erroneous or not. I felt this to be true of the relative in:

> . . . *he was the first man who invented the telephone . . .*

One can criticize the 'style' here, and one can invoke logic to point to the redundancy of *first* in the context of *invented*: aren't all inventions by definition 'firsts'? But that is not my problem here: why does *first who invented* seem strange, and why do I want to suggest instead *first to invent*? After all, was not Sherpa Tensing both *the first* **to climb** *Everest* and *the first man* **who climbed** *Everest*? The problem, I suggest, lies in the lexical item *invent*, which is inherently semelfactive: you only do it once, and something once invented cannot (unless it be a wheel!) be reinvented, whereas a mountain that has once been climbed is sure to be climbed many times again.

There was one error that, to my initial surprise, was committed by the two best students.

> . . . *Elvis Presley (√,) who*, became a legend in his lifetime.*

Descriptively, this is a simple error of **misplacement** of the clause boundary (marked by the comma). One could hypothesize that the students' operating strategy is that a relative pronoun needs an accompanying comma. I had repeatedly urged the students to use 'more commas' with nondefining relatives. But these students knew better: they probably had a faint recollection of parenthetical adverbials that are typically inserted after the relative pronoun, set off by a comma:

> . . . *Elvis Presley, who, as everyone knows OR even before his death, was already a legend.*

A plausible diagnosis of this error is that it was caused by copying. The text copied contained such an adverbial, which the students decided to delete – but they forgot to delete the comma at the same time.

There was one culturally precipitated **sociopragmatic error** (Thomas, 1983) which is worth commenting on although relative clause structure is not involved. Describing a Hollywood star, the claim is made that:

> *One of his favourite wives was Ava Gardner.*

This sentence is probably acceptable in a polygamous society.

4.   *Errors induced by pedagogical priorities*

Students' achievement tends to match other teachers' expectations of what they will achieve. It is also the case that students quickly develop insights into what pleases the teachers, so much so that when nothing pleases them, the students give nothing that might. Some teachers are perceived by their pupils to prioritize one of the following: accuracy, fluency or idiomaticity. If fluency is seen as paramount, the students will feel justified in de-emphasizing accuracy, and vice versa. Fluency has been at a premium under the Communicative Approach, and learners have been rewarded for keeping communication moving by the liberal use of communication strategies. Accuracy has suffered. As for what happens when 'idiomaticity' (interpreted literally as using idioms) is at a premium, look at this composition from a Singaporean child after six years of English (overlooking other errors):

> Ann is a pupil who is unpopular with the other pupils. . . . Once Fatty was reckless and stepped her shoes. She scolded Fatty was [**as blind as a bat**]. And other pupils said that she ws [**as proud as a peacock**.] . . . I tried to be friendly to her. Firstly I assisted her in her Chinese, because she was [**as poor as a church mouse**] at it. . . . At first she remained [**as cool as a cucumber**] and later she became [**as good as gold**] . . .

These are certainly not **spontaneous** errors. They betoken the pupil doing what is expected of her. In a sense she is making use of what she has been taught – even though she might harbour some doubts about the appropriacy of this stilted style. Of course, the pupil's perception of the pedagogical priorities might be ill-founded: the teacher might be the victim of a misunderstanding, and the pupil is doubly wrong. Or the teacher may merely be following syllabus guidelines or examiners' biases, without any conviction as to their validity: but if this is what it takes to help pupils pass examinations, that is what the teacher will do, tongue in cheek nonetheless.

5. Look-up errors

There has been a proliferation of learners' dictionaries and grammars in recent years, and these publications usually come with useful guidelines on how to look up aspects of the L2 about which one is in doubt. Yet, strangely, learners seem reluctant to read such user-instructions, and as a result they frequently misuse these reference aids. These errors are so common that we learn to expect them and we even develop a blind spot for them (which is not the same thing as ignoring them). A common one is *dictionary* used to translate L1 items such as *slownik, slovar,* in contexts where √*word list* or √*glossary* is appropriate. Some are more 'original', and show learners attempting to be a little ambitious and use words from the dictionary that are novelties: so they try *circumlocution*, which stands in the dictionary alongside √*conversation* as a translation of *razgovor*. We tend to hear mainly of the preposterous examples of naive look-up skills, for example, the student who 'translated' the French *Rose émue répondit* as *The pink emu laid another egg*. He had analysed the verb into a prefix *re* ('again') and the root of the verb found in the dictionary *pondre* ('to lay an egg').

Compound and ambiguous errors

In the preceding sections we have listed four main diagnosis-based categories of learner errors: interlingual, intralingual, strategy-based and induced errors. These four were broken down into almost a score of subcategories. Now it is unusual to be able to ascribe with confidence a given error to a single cause. Generally, errors are either **compound** or **ambiguous**.

A **compound** error is ascribable to more than one cause, which operate either simultaneously or cumulatively. For example, consider the error in *My watch does not *walk well*. It is plausible to trace this to a lexical and a phonological cause, each reinforcing the other. The learner's L1 is French, and a back translation of the EL2 utterance is *Ma montre me marche pas bien*. 'To work' corresponds to *marcher*. But *marcher* also translates *march* as well as its synonym *walk*. Now for the phonological miscue: *work* [wɔːk] and *walk* [wɜk] are so close in English as to be phonological **confusibles** to a learner.

An **ambiguous** error is slightly different in that there are two competing diagnoses, whereas in the case of the compound error the two diagnoses were complementary. An example is: . . . *having explain*Ø∧ed my motives* . . . . Note first that there are not two competing reconstructions of the error, *having to explain* versus *having explained*. We know for sure that the learner intended the second of these: the ambiguity resides in the diagnosis, not the reconstruction. So what went wrong? Either the cause was phonological: this learner could neither produce in speech nor perceive the final consonant cluster [. . . nd#]. This was enough to drop or disregard the second consonant. Alternatively, the learner might believe that an infinitival form is required in this construction, which is not the case of course. This belief (hypothesis?) could have been prompted by analogy with the parallel construction (expressing obligation) *having to explain*. These two constructions could not have been simultaneously intended, so the source of the error is ambiguous.

There are times when a single learner's or a class of learners' errors, despite being descriptively identical, must be diagnosed differentially. That is, there may be one **descriptive** class of errors which are distributed over a number of **diagnostic** classes. Consider the following errors taken from the compositions of German learners of English (Oakeshott-Taylor, 1977). Descriptively, they all involve obstruent devoicing:

> 1.   *standart/√standard of living.   2.   can't *effort/√afford a holiday.   3.   The police *let/√led the man away.   4.   He hopes to *sent/√send it.   5.   He *graps/√grabs the newspaper.
> 6.   Here's a *scrab/√scrap of paper.   7.   There's a *cap/√gap in the fence.

Error 1 most plausibly results from L1 German interference of final voiced obstruent devoicing, lexically reinforced by there being a false friend (a real fiend!) cognate in the two languages as a result of borrowing. Error 2 has a partially similar diagnosis as far as obstruent devoicing goes. Yet there is no cognateness at work here. It is rather the existence of two intralingual **confusibles**. A simultaneous L1 interference reinforcing this confusion is the use of German [e], which the learner is wrongly trying to substitute for English [æ]: wrongly, because the sound in this unstressed position is properly schwa [ə].

Error 3 is attributable again to transfer of the L1 German obstruent devoicing rule. There is no cognateness at work here, but the phonological error does have lexical consequences in that there are two verbs *lead* (past *led*) and *let* (past *let*), each of which makes sense in this context, while being opposite in meaning! To *lead a convict away* is very different from *letting him (go) away*.

Error 4 again bears some similarity to 1, 2 and 3 as far as final obstruent devoicing is at work. Yet there is no L1:L2 cognateness, and these two verb forms are not what one would normally call confusibles. Yet confusion in a sense it must be, this time not confusion inherent in the forms and not the confusion to which even knowers are prone, but confusion created by the learner herself. The source of the confusion is misperception and mispronunciation of final obstruent devoicing, but the consequence of this overgeneralization is that morphological distinctions in the verb paradigm are lost.

Error 5 is just distinguishable from types 3 and 4. Not only in that another phonological voicing contrast /p/:/b/ is involved, but also in that the plosive is not the final but the penultimate consonant. But it is most interesting when compared to error 6, where we have the converse distortion: while in errors 1 to 5 we have seen devoicing where voice was required, in 6 we have voicing where voicelessness is required. What is happening? I suggest the learner is overgeneralizing. The learner has begun to notice that the [+V]:[−V] contrast is important in English, and that she herself is not conforming to the requirements of English in this respect – she has made the 'cognitive comparison' (see Chapter 8). She has decided to use more of the [+V] type obstruents, to compensate for her present underuse of these. This is a somewhat crude strategy, but it does indicate a realization of imperfection, so it is a first step in the right direction. One is reminded of Brecht's observation in *Die Maßnahme*:

> 'Klug ist nicht, der keine Fehler macht, sondern
> Klug ist, der sie schnell zu verbessern versteht.'
> > Brecht, B. *Die Maßnahme*, scene 4. P. 275 in *Stücke für das Theater am Schiffbauerdamm*, Vol. 4. Sufirkamp Verlag, Berlin, pp. 255–307.
>
> (Being smart doesn't mean never making mistakes, but knowing how to put them right at once.)

The trouble is, it is not a rule-based solution, but a statistical one: what we could call, adapting Corder's (1973: 272) idea of pre-systematic error, a **pre-systematic self-correction**.

Error 7 could be the reflex of interference from a German L1 dialect in which the voice contrast is lost in word-initial as well as final position, where *Grippe* ('flu') and *Krippe* ('crib') are homophones [krɪpə]. This would have made it difficult for such a dialect speaker aurally to distinguish *cap/gap*, both of which he would hear as *cap* – the commoner member of the pair. Another possibility is that there is some sort of **spreading** taking place in this learner's IL: the [+V]: [−V] neutralization is seeping from final to other positions. This might happen independently of the distribution of the neutralization in the L1.

In this chapter we have shown that error diagnosis is distinct from error description, although the former cannot be begun until the latter is available. We have also shown that there are major categories of error diagnosis, which however are not watertight, and which more often than not work in tandem or even in concert, and seldom simply in isolation. In short, error diagnosis is another dauntingly complex and difficult undertaking. Progress in understanding the causes of error will be slow, but the work is rewarding and there is no easy option to tackling it head-on.

Notes

1. This might well be a misprint.
2. *Dia (he) guru (teacher) yang (who) saya (I) sangat (much) sukai (like)* contains no echo (or resumptive) pronoun '*him*'.

7

Error Gravity and
Error Evaluation

Tangles like this still interrupted their intercourse. A pause in the
wrong place, an intonation misunderstood, and the whole conversation went awry. Fielding had been startled, not shocked, but how
convey the difference? There is always trouble [...] even when
the two people are of the same race
(E.M. Forster, *A Passage to India.* London: Dent, 1957, p. 238)

Evaluation

Humans are prone not only to commit language errors themselves but also to err in their judgements of those errors committed by others. The great concert pianist Artur Rubinstein used to
be asked to adjudicate at international pianoforte competitions.
On such occasions, he awarded to any contestant either zero or
twenty out of twenty, his reasoning being 'they either can play, or
they can't play'. Using such a crudely polarized system as this, the
probability of his making a misjudgement was very small. Once
you seek to refine this approach, as obviously we must in Error
Analysis, we have to start grading our judgements and specifying our criteria. This will place our activity within the science of
evaluation, which Scriven defines as 'the process whose duty is the
systematic and objective determination of merit, worth or value'
(1991: 4). Scriven proceeds to describe the science of evaluation,
pointing out that it must 'destroy the intellectual foundations of
the doctrine of value-free science' (1991: 2). As we pointed out in
Chapter 2, EA is an essential part of Applied Linguistics precisely
by virtue of its overarching concern with **value**.

There is also misunderstanding about the reasons why errors
have to be evaluated. The main reason for evaluation, and the

rationale for this chapter, is to get our priorities right. We do not seek to hone the analytical scalpel so as to lay bare the tiniest error, but the opposite: to prevent obsession with trivial errors and give priority to the ones that really matter. Passing judgement on error is not a matter of devaluation of learners and their language, but rather one of assigning relative values to errors. This may seem paradoxical: how can we give value to something that is undesirable? What it means is that this is an error which merits attention. As Williams puts it: 'Value becomes a consideration only when we address the matter of which errors we should notice' (1981: 64). Note the ethical imperative in 'should' here. Evaluation is indeed a matter of ethics, since society rewards those who get things right (what counts as right being decided upon consensually by each society, or at least by those who wield power in that society), and rewards must be seen to be given according to real attainment. Evaluation – of which EA is but a part – 'collects, clarifies and verifies relevant values and standards' (Scriven, 1991: 5). This reference to 'values' and 'standards' has affinities to the definition of **culture** (in the anthropological sense) formulated by Scollon and Scollon (1995: Ch. 7) in that it takes into account ideology, face-saving systems, history, world-view and the socialization rules of a community. How can concern with error be viewed as trivial while error has relevance to, and to a large extent determines, one's acceptability to a culture one seeks access to? Here is a recent example in the form of a confession by one (eminent) native speaker of English adjudging an EL2 learner not to be admissible to the culture which Mr Rong almost certainly would like to visit. The native speaker decides on grounds of linguistic inadequacy to gate the foreigner:

> Sir, Flying from Heathrow to Toronto last year I had a Mr Rong sitting on my right. Unfortunately his English was so rudimentary that I didn't even attempt to explain who was sitting on his left.
> Tom Wright, The Dean of Lichfield.
> (Letter to *The Times*, 7 December 1996)

There is no problem about deciding what should be treated as a trivial error: it is a form upon which native speakers cannot agree as to whether it is or is not erroneous. If it is so borderline as to split the ranks of NSs, we agree to disagree with them. Jones (1966) and Lennon (1991) gave us examples of such forms where NS opinion was split 'down the middle'. Although the study

of NSs' **acceptation** is interesting and valid as a form of sociolinguistics, it is not a part of EA, so we shall not dwell on this aspect.
We shall limit our attention to forms that are adjudged deviant,
and try to establish what degree of deviance or **gravity** they are
seen as representing. This chapter falls into two main parts: first,
we shall examine the main criteria that can be invoked when one
is called upon to decide on error gravities (EGs); secondly, under
the rubric **Viewpoint** we shall compare the views on EGs of native
speakers and of other parties to the FL learning and teaching process. Looking at criteria is a relatively theoretical enterprise, while
identifying the criteria actually invoked in assuming a viewpoint is
an empirical one.

Criteria for error gravity (EG)

Linguistic criteria

If, as we have claimed, EA is a cornerstone of applied linguistics,
the linguistic criteria for EG should be paramount. By 'linguistic' we
mean 'formal' features of language, the principal of these being
grammaticality, defined and discussed in Chapter 3. Judgements
of EG made on this basis are those based upon the criterion of
conformity (Quirk, 1968: 109).

Rule infringement

James (1974) attempted to show the relevance of linguistic criteria for EGs, using the then-current version of Chomskian syntax and exploiting an idea of Fowler's (1969) for accounting for
the deviance of the poetic line *he danced his did*. Chomsky (1965:
148ff.) had suggested that formal deviance could be explained
in terms of the breaking of two sorts of rule. First, there are the
subcategorization rules, which exist to specify what kinds of complement each verb in the language takes, whether it is transitive or
intransitive, mono- or ditransitive, preadjectival, presentential and
so on. Thus the following are deviant as specified:

> *John found *sad*: 'find' is not a preadjectival verb, but requires
> either a noun or a that-clause as complement.

John persuaded *great authority to Bill: 'persuade' is not a ditransitive verb (like 'send') but takes a single noun object, either
on its own or combined with a that-clause.

There are limitations to using this framework for specifying EG:
there is no immediate indication of which sorts of infringements
are more serious than others – which of our two examples is the
worse?

The second type of rule is the **selectional rule**. This rule specifies nouns as concrete, animate, human, count, etc., and the
infringement of such rules leads to errors such as **Golf plays John*
or the notorious **Colourless green ideas sleep furiously.* An advantage
this rule offers is that it gives some guidance on relative EGs
owing to the fact that the selectional features are ranged along a
dominance hierarchy: the higher the feature violated is on this
hierarchy, the more serious the error. Thus, use of a nonverb
[–V] where a verb [+V] is required is grave (*The teacher *virtued the
pupil*) while use of a subject that should be animate but is inan-
imate is a less serious error (**Sweaters admire he boy*). The framework is suggestive, but no more, and calls for extensive empirical
validation. A further limitation of both schemes is that such errors
tend not to be made by normal FL learners, but are more typical
of the sorts of linguistic deviances of aphasic and psychotic patients (Sacks, 1986).

Rule generality

Notice how these two rule-types of selection and subcategorization have the effect of focusing attention on individual lexical
items, making grammar decisions on the basis of word properties.
As we pointed out in Chapter 5 the traditional grammar versus
lexis divide is being narrowed. Or is this mere appearance, an
artifact of the move from the generalities of grammar to the idiosyncrasies of what is still lexis? And is the distinction one we can
use to help in EG specification? If grammar is more general and
predictable, and lexis more idiosyncratic and fine-grained, what
does that say about EGs? Surely it implies that grammar errors are
more serious *linguistically* than lexis errors. As Di Pietro so neatly
put it: 'the seriousness of error-making is a function of the generality of the rule' (1971: 163). Grammar rules are more general
than lexical ones in that the former apply to a larger number of

instances, while the latter apply only to a few: the **passive** rule, for instance, applies to all transitive clauses, while the oddity of *We fried some *milk* derives from the incompatibility of a particular verb with a particular noun object.

Unfortunately 'generality' can have different meanings. Di Pietro (1971) illustrated his point by reference to different-sized constituents, claiming that those errors leading to the misordering of major sentence parts like subject and predicate were more serious than those causing the misordering of smaller constituents such as adjective and noun. Let us call this a difference in **rule range**. It will predict a correlation between the EG and the proportion of the sentence that is distorted. This criterion is observed by teachers marking written work, who are more severe when they have to underline or strike out a whole clause rather than just a single word or morpheme. This reaction might be linked to a desire to quantify EG (in terms of the length of a red-ink line), but could more plausibly be related to the different degrees of processing effort needed on the part of the reader or listener to undo the error. The 'range' criterion underlies the distinction drawn by Burt and Kiparsky (1972) between **local** (low-level) and **global** (high-level) errors, the latter having a wider range than the former. Notice that the range dimension is not the same as the lexis versus grammar distinction: while *all* lexical errors are inherently local, grammar errors will be divisible into the local and the global. Moreover, where a particular lexical error is due to a collocational infringement, and where the miscollocated lexical items are not contiguous but at some remove from each other in the text, the resultant lexical error will at least have a 'global' feel to it.

A third sense of 'generality' is **scope**. This means that a rule applies not just in one context but in two or more different contexts: it has a wide scope. A consequence is that the learners who commit error in one context are very likely to do so in the other, related, context (or contexts) too. Thus the two errors in the following learner's attempt at producing two different German sentences, one involving a relative clause, the other interrogative form, spring from the same source:

(i) *Das Problem, *das Hans sprach über, ist schwer.*
     (*The problem that Jack spoke about is hard.*)
(ii) **Was sprach Hans über?*
     (*What spoke Jack about?*)

First, these are not lexical and not local errors There is a rule, known as the 'Pied Piper' rule, which requires prepositions to follow in the wake of either relative or interrogative pronouns that are fronted, that is, these pronouns have to get fronted too. The rule is obligatory in German, but optional in English. Since this rule has such scope, a single infringement of it indicates a second potential infringement, so carries a high EG.

A third sense of generality is **concomitance**: the learners who commit error (a) are likely *as a result* (concomitantly) to produce error (b) also:

(a)   **Er glaubt Hans ein kluger Kerl zu sein.*
   Lit.: (*He thinks Jack   a   clever chap to be*)
(b)   **Hans wird (von ihm) geglaubt ein kluger Kerl zu sein.*
   Lit.: (*Jack is   by   him believed   a   clever chap to be*)

Now (a) results from wrongly assuming that German grammar allows Accusative with Infinitive constructions like English: √*He believes Jack to be . . .* , and (b) results from the first assumption coupled with a second: that this can be passivized in German, which is not the case. The point is that the learner's plausible but false assumption about passivization originates from the prior naive assumption that German has Accusative + Infinitives: one thing leads to another, concomitantly.

Frequency

Another important and relevant formal feature of language is **frequency**, and this influences EG. Note that frequency is a **quantitative** measure, and its use presupposes that we know what and how to count relevant incidences of error. As we saw in Chapter 4, issues arise such as the type-token relationship, and what constitutes a repeated occurrence of an error.

Until recently, when computational methods became more widespread in linguistics, several word-frequency lists had been compiled 'by hand' for several major languages, but the relative frequencies of grammatical units were not so easily determinable. The relations between grammar and lexis we have explored above are inverse when it comes to frequency: so the two deviant utterances **I can to swim* and **He must to work* are lexically discrete while constituting tokens of the same grammatical pattern. We saw in Chapter 4 nevertheless how Levenston (1971) invoked nonnativelike frequencies of grammatical usages as error indices, distinguishing **overindulgence** and **underrepresentation**. We also saw how progress has been made in assembling corpora of learner language and invoking quantitative measures of grammatical forms.

When we say that frequency is a valid index of the gravity of an error, we can mean several things. We might have in mind the **correlation** identified by Olsson (1977: 31) between number and seriousness of errors in the least successful learners: it appears that the students who exercise no caution with respect to how many errors they commit are equally cavalier towards the enormity of some of those errors. Reckless learners are reckless on all fronts it seems. This is interesting, but we shall move on to explore some other senses of frequency in error-making. First, there is **production frequency**, by which is meant the number of times that a particular learner commits the error in question. The learner who produces **J'ai (√suis) arrivé* six times in a composition is awarded (or penalised with) an EG index of 6, whereas another learner who commits the same error only three times gets an EG of 3. To some extent – for example in free composition tasks – this is justifiable, since the first learner has created twice as many opportunities for making this error as the second, and is exhibiting a high degree of confidence in being so consistently wrong, and needs to be informed in no uncertain terms.

Now consider the case of three learners who all need to use the TL construction *I want you to drive* six times. Learner A gets it wrong six times, each time saying or writing **I want that you drive*. Learner B produces **I want that you drive* and **I want you drive* three times each. Learner C produces three times **I want that you drive* and three times *√I want you to drive*. The difference between the three lies in their **consistency**. Some judges might say that A is 'at least' consistent and give his error a low EG rating; that B is not only always wrong but shows versatility in his wrong-doing, which is very serious; and that C really knows the TL form, but makes **mistakes** 50 per cent of the time.

A second facet of frequency is linked to **frequency of use** by native speakers. If an NS frequency count reveals that, in formal written English, cleft sentences like *What we want is more money* are less frequent than *We want more money*, or the verb *drive* is less frequent than *go*, could it not be argued that errors involving misformation of clefts and of *drove* are less serious than errors on the more frequently used forms? One might counterargue that this stance is extreme native-speakerism and that we do not want to clone these creatures. I believe that having communicative competence in a language depends in part on 'knowing' (tacitly) the relative frequencies of use of its forms. One could also argue the validity of weighting the EGs on the grounds that the learner has had more exposure to the frequent forms, and therefore more opportunity to notice and acquire them, but something has gone wrong and an urgent signal is called for.

Yet another quantitative aspect of EG assignment is error **density**. This measure can easily be distinguished from production frequency (discussed above) as follows: 'density' is calculated by counting how many *different* errors occur per unit of text, while production frequency is a measure of how many times the *same* error is repeated over say one hundred words of text. High error density presents the listener-reader with a greater problem than production frequency, since when a particular error has been encountered once or twice, one has learnt to accommodate it, and to make adjustments in one's readings. After a fourth or fifth encounter with the error, one no longer notices it. Not so with text having a high error density, since each new error, coming in quick succession one after the previous one, presents a new problem, to which one cannot apply the same solution as the previous problem. One has to make a succession of different calculations. Though each particular error may *per se* be a straightforward one, the problem is the variety of errors. The overall effect or **cumulative effect** is dire. A few researchers have noticed the density factor. Zola (1984) observed that even minor spelling errors, provided they were of high incidence, often disrupted reading even when the misspelled words were highly predictable. Lennon (1991: 188) reports the case of an EL2 learner's sentence that a panel of NS judges were divided over: *There is a *dam wall which *should protect the village *from *flood.* Not one of the four errors in this sentence would merit a high EG rating, but the four co-occurring do. Gunterman (1978), in a study investigating the gravity effects of error frequency in L2 Spanish, found that multiply erroneous sentences were consistently less intelligible to El Salvadorian native speakers than sentences with one error. Note, however, that her main EG criterion was not conformity but intelligibility, a measure we shall now consider.

Comprehensibility

We saw in the previous section how EG relates to degrees of conformity. Quirk (1968) offered us a straight choice of criteria: 'conformity' or 'comprehensibility'. There has been an ideological shift in FL teaching methodology over the last 20 years away from form-focus towards a focus on functional-communicative proficiency (Littlewood, 1981). This swing has understandably impinged on EG ratings, suggesting that criteria of intelligibility, comprehensibility and communicativity ought to carry more weight. But what exactly do these three labels mean and how do they differ? We shall use 'comprehensibility' as a cover term to refer to all aspects of the accessibility of the content – as opposed to the form – of utterances. Of course, comprehensibility has its two sides: the success of the text producer and that of the text receiver.

Intelligibility

Let's reserve the term **intelligibility** to refer to the accessibility of the basic, literal meaning, the propositional content encoded in an utterance. Take the two utterances *Why you not speak like me?* and *Why you not like me?*. The first is ungrammatical through omission of the auxiliary *do*, but its meaning is relatively clear – if we disregard the interpretation *Why don't you say you love me?*. The same cannot be said of the second sentence, which, apart from also being ill-formed, is ambiguous between *Why are you not like (= similar to) me?* and *Why do you not like (= love) me?*. The second sentence is therefore unintelligible as well as ungrammatical. No definite reading can be assigned to it. The distinction drawn here coincides with that drawn by Page (1990: 104), who points out that 'Grammatical accuracy is not always essential for accurate communication'. In other words, where inaccuracy is transparent, as in our first example, it need not impede intelligibility. 'Communication' is perhaps a different matter, as we shall presently see.

Notice that we explained these instances of unintelligibility by using a paraphrase, that is a lexical substitute: *love/similar to*. Unintelligibility is thus closely related to the lexical level of errors. As Johansson (1978: 109) showed, the morphology errors **shelfs (√shelves)* and **have went/√gone* pose no intelligibility problem, whereas the use of **strings* for *shelves*, caused by transfer from L1 Swedish, does.

		No noise (%)	Noise (%)
Natives' understanding	NS SPEECH	98.26	91.00
	NNS SPEECH	93.00	75.80
Nonnatives' understanding	NS SPEECH	71.30	48.39
	NNS SPEECH	73.84	48.80

Figure 7.1 Natives' and nonnatives' perception of accented and distorted speech (adapted from S. Johansson, 1978: 82)

Foreign accent also can erect barriers to intelligibility, especially when there is background noise accompanying the accented speech. Lane (1963) calculated that foreign-accented speech loses 51 per cent in intelligibility when heard by native speakers and even more (54 per cent) when heard by nonnative speakers. However, under conditions of noise, the intelligibility loss is 55 per cent to NSs compared with 63 per cent loss when NNSs are at the receiving end. These are global measures. What is required is information concerning which phonological characteristics of particular ILs (especially those of the emergent New Englishes) precipitate most intelligibility loss when distorted by foreign accent.

Johansson (1978) asked both British English NS students and Swedish L2 English students to listen to tape recordings of NS and Swedish foreign-accented (FA) speech, each with and without superimposed distortions or 'noise'. They then did a partial dictation test with selected passages of the recordings, each passage having eight to ten gaps, each of three to nine words, that had to be reconstituted.

Several interesting facts are recorded here:

(i)   NNSs understand less than NS understand, as we would expect.
(ii) NSs understand FA and NS speech almost equally well under undistorted conditions, but the gap widens appreciably when there is background noise.
(iii) NNSs are more distracted by noise than NSs.
(iv) There is little difference between the NNS's understanding of NSs and of fellow NNSs with the same L1.

We need to establish, of course, whether NNSs with different L1s and therefore different FAs find each other difficult to understand.

Olsson (1972) submitted the erroneous EFL spoken utterances of 240 Swedish 14 year olds to native judges. The range of intelligibility was high, between 75 per cent and 90 per cent. She claimed to have established that formal (i.e. 'grammar') errors impair intelligibility to a lesser extent than semantic errors. This formulation appears circular, however: it is only to be expected that 'semantic' errors should impair access to meaning – and so be less intelligible. Thus it follows (Olsson, 1977: 75) that the morphological error *beated for √beaten is a minor error since it does not impair intelligibility because the receiver is more likely to recover the intended form *beaten* than an unintended one *baited*. By contrast *sought (by the police) is a major error because the receiver is likely to assume that that was what was intended, and harbour a misunderstanding: why after all, unless context strongly dictates, should the receiver make the lexical leap from *sought* to *caught*? Hence Olsson defines semantic errors as 'utterances which were contextually incorrect' (1977: 159). A syntactic example would be:

*The thief *catch (√was caught) by the policeman.*

Yet even this utterance was more intelligible than:

*The man *meet (√ was met by) his sweetheart.*

The reason for this, we are told, is that 'the presence of the preposition *by*' had rendered the former sentence the more intelligible. So it is context in the sense of 'cotext' that is the decisive factor now. But is not omission of this preposition a *formal* error? – In which case it is its formal deviance (omission of *by*) that makes the second sentence unintelligible, not the semantics. What we are suggesting then is that there is no such thing as a 'semantic error' (as opposed to a formal error) but that some formal errors affect intelligibility more than others, specifically when context so dictates.

There are empirical studies of the relative intelligibility of different kinds of English. A well-known study of the intelligibility of Indian English is Bansal (1976). Another is Tiffen's (1992) on the intelligibility of Nigerian English. He recorded 24 Nigerians speaking English, 12 having Hausa as their L1, and 12 with Yoruba. The recordings were played to 240 British listeners and intelligibility ratings elicited. The average intelligibility score was 64 per cent, and the range was from 93 per cent to 29 per cent). Four major causes of intelligibility reduction were identified, and their relative percentages calculated: faulty rhythm and stress (38 per cent), mispronounced phonetic segments (33 per cent), phonotactic errors (20 per cent), and lexico-grammatical errors (9 per cent).

These figures are interesting. First, note the importance of stress and rhythm – a point underlined by Taylor (1981), and more recently by Anderson-Hsieh, Johnson and Koehler (1992), who found from native speakers' overall rating of the deviance of the recorded speech of 11 L1 groups that **prosodies** consistently tended to be most correlated with poor accent. However, although unstressed schwa [ə] was underused by Tiffen's Nigerian learners, this did not impair intelligibility, suggesting that it might not be cost-effective to spend a great deal of teaching time on the weak forms. A better time investment would be teaching the diphthongs, which tend to be substituted by monophthongs: *[te:k] for √[teik] for example. In general, distorted vowels are more disruptive than mispronounced consonants, so teaching should focus on the former. Note, finally, how little intelligibility loss was attributed to the lexis and syntax, perhaps because these were spoken texts.

When discussing intelligibility, one must always ask 'intelligible to whom?'. The most obvious line to draw is that between intelligibility in class, and in the real world of communication. Consider the following classroom exchange.[1] The students' and the teacher's L1 is Malay.

> Teacher: *Now, class, give me examples of animals around you.*
> Student 1: *Dog.*
> T: *Yes, that's good: dog.*
> S2: *Cat, cat.*
> T: *Hartini, give me an example, please . . .*
> S3: *How about [gʊʔ] teacher?*
> T: *Pardon? [gʊd] oh that's . . . [gʊd] is our Creator.*
> S3: *No, no. I mean G-O-A-T.*

That such genuine, unfeigned, intelligibility-loss should occur in the English class is remarkable, especially where the teacher and students share a common L1. One expects a classroom dialect to develop which is easily accessible at least to the closed company of the class, but here we see this expectation confounded.

Smith and Rafiqzad (1979) is an explicit study of comparative intelligibility. They asked a representative sample of 30 EL2 speakers in each of 11 countries to listen to nine speech recordings, eight done by nonnative speakers and the other one by native-speaker Americans. The results, while only tentative, are suggestive and ought to be expanded into a larger research enterprise. First, a speaker of high intelligibility was deemed to be so by all listeners, irrespective of their own L1 background. Secondly, only two groups of listeners (the Japanese and the Koreans) found their fellow countrymen to be the most intelligible. Thirdly, perhaps the most surprising finding, 'the native speaker was always found to be among the least intelligible' (1979: 375) by all listeners. This contradicts not only popular expectation, but also long-standing experimental findings, for example Lane's finding that 'foreign-accented speech is approximately 40% less intelligible than native speech' (1963: 451). The scale of intelligibility of the nine groups of speakers was as follows (from most to least intelligible):

MOST: :LEAST
Sri Lankan > Indian > Japanese > Malaysian > Nepalese > Korean
> Philippino > American > Hong Kong

Bowen and Porter (1984) compared two native speaker 'models' of English for intelligibility. They played samples of British-accented and American-accented speech to 259 EL2 learners with a wide range of first languages. Scores on the American-English (AE) version of this listening test were higher than on the British-English (BE) version, suggesting that BE is more 'difficult' – even to subjects who have had primary exposure to that accent. Numerous explanations are offered, such as the fact that *been* in the utterance *What's been done?* is pronounced unambiguously as [bɪn] in AE but as [bin] in BE, the latter pronunciation inviting confusion with that in *being*.

The reader will have noted that our account of **intelligibility** has focused on learner-produced language. We ought not to overlook the other, receptive, dimension, which will involve looking at the misunderstandings and misinterpretations the learners make when processing perfectly well-formed language input. We exemplified this sort of problem at the end of Chapter 5, but data and research on this dimension are relatively sparse.

Communicativity

Communicativity is a more ambitious notion, involving access to pragmatic forces, implicatures and connotations. The distinction is related to that drawn between text and discourse outlined in Chapter 5. The distinction is not new and Smith and Nelson (1983), in a study of the international intelligibility of English, distinguish between the 'comprehensibility' of syntax and semantics and the 'interpretability' of discourse and pragmatics. This corresponds in our scheme to the 'intelligibility' of text as distinct from the 'communicativity' of discourse. It would be realistic, however, to have different expectations with respect to these two kinds of achievement. We are right to insist on the intelligibility of learners' language, in terms of its textual well-formedness, and we should always welcome communicativity when we see it, but we should realistically admit that we cannot demand it. It is a higher order achievement of language users, both native and nonnative. We must be vigilant about terminology. When in 1956 Einar Haugen observed that 'Mere *communication* may be satisfied by a relatively modest mastery of the second language; social *identification* with a dominant group may require something approaching native command' (1956: 73), he was using the term 'communication' to refer to our 'intelligibility' and his 'identification' corresponds to our 'communicativity'. Littlewood (1992) has the same distinction in mind when he distinguishes between failures to transmit propositional content (intelligibility failures) and failures to transmit the right social information, as when one invites a superior to *Take a pew* rather than *Please have a seat*. Haugen was right to point out that the failure is the one that is punished by social isolation and exclusion from the community of speakers. This may be native-speakerism again, but it is a viewpoint that many learners endorse.

The trouble with **miscommunication** (MCM) is that it is intelligible: if it were not, there would be **noncommunication**, that is, unintelligibility. When the reader-listener blithely assigns a meaning (and interpretation) to an utterance, but his reading is not what was intended, we have miscommunication. MCM is not easily detected, and so has aptly been labelled **covert error** by Corder (1973). A reader's letter to *The Guardian Weekly* (18 December 1994) addresses the contentious issue of whether Finland is in Scandinavia. The writer argues thus:

> *Historically, Finland *[has been]* part of Sweden for 700 years, i.e. for most of her historical time, and has inherited numerous institutions from Sweden.*

You have to know Scandinavian history to spot the covert error in the misuse of the present perfect tense of the first clause: for this to be acceptable, Finland would still have to be part of Sweden, by the semantics of 'current relevance'.

Another example comes from a scientific text written by an EL2 user:

> *The main property of vinyl, which distinguishes it from butyl, is that it expands.*

Here the parenthetical relative clause, while being perfectly grammatical, miscommunicates by saying that vinyl's main property is its expansibility. That is probably not true, and certainly not what was intended. The intended meaning was that of all the properties that distinguish vinyl from butyl, the expansibility of the former is the main one. This meaning would best be encoded as *The main property of vinyl distinguishing it from butyl is that it expands.*

Finally, a letter from an international alumnus to a university Registrar began:

> *I was a so-called nongraduating student in your university from 1982 to 1983.*

This is unintentionally pragmatically infelicitous and an example of MCM: to call someone a '*so-called*' student is to suggest the title is inappropriate or undeserved. Note that what is miscommunicated here is not so much content as attitude: the Registrar gets the impression that the alumnus is disparaging the status accorded to nongraduating students. These MCMs are serious, not only because they unintentionally misinform, but also because they tend to go unnoticed, by speaker and listener alike. They can become the basis for cumulative MCM and alienation in the 'communicative' process.

Noticeability

We have drawn a distinction between **overt** and **covert** errors. Covert errors are not simply those that go unnoticed, but are those that are by their nature unnoticeable. Overt errors are likely to be noticed, particularly by a listener or reader whose competence in the language is relatively high. Overt written errors are also more likely to be noticed than spoken ones, not only because what is written has some permanence while what is spoken is transient, but also because we have higher expectations of written performances than of spoken ones. We expect less error in written forms, because we can put right or pre-edit what we write, whereas speech cannot be unspoken once committed. The noticeability of an error (type or token) will also depend on its **frequency**, as we suggested above. We might argue that high frequency is an extreme case of the overtness of error.

Are we therefore to conclude that high noticeability of error implies high gravity? Paradoxically, such a conclusion would be unsound. Page (1990) tells the story of two EL2 messages being sent to two ladies walking in the forest, warning them of an approaching tiger. One formulation (textualization) of the message is ungrammatical, but the message is somehow conveyed and the first lady is saved. The other formulation is perfect in grammar but fails to communicate and that lady is mauled. The moral: you can achieve communication without grammar, so wrong grammar is not serious. Relating this to noticeability, we must conclude that in life-or-death situations we do not bother to notice grammar errors. Similarly, when the speaker is an eminent scientist or a skilled statesman like the former US Secretary of State Henry Kissinger, even the most precious or pedantic listeners will make an effort not to notice the linguistic imperfections, and frequently no effort on their part will be required because the import of the message automatically overrides those imperfections. This explains why it is the case that humble immigrants have to brush up their L2, while the Kissingers or Pavarottis of this world have all their imperfections overlooked. Page (1990: 105) seems to realize that this is the case: that explains his allusion to 'the sympathetic native speaker'. Sympathetic native speakers are people who are more interested in the message or its bearer than in its formulation, people who overlook imperfections of form. Notice, though, that we are not claiming that these sympathetic souls are not *noticing*, but that they are not reacting to what they have noticed. They notice but overlook.

This point has wider currency in the general context of anti-native-speakerism and the insistence that it is wrong to try to impose global norms on the many international varieties of English. So Smith (1987: xii) stresses that users of English in international contexts 'must be prepared to deal with diversity'. It depends on what Smith intends by 'deal with'. He certainly does not mean 'not notice' or 'be oblivious to' diversity, which would lead to communication débâcle. He means we must accept as inevitable (and perhaps even desirable) and learn to deal with potential miscommunication. For it is very important that any 'errors' be noticed and adjustments be made in the message to their presence in its textualization.

We know less about noticeability of aspects of language in objective terms than we know about people's ability and inclination to notice. Note how again our knowledge and awareness of the productive versus receptive dimensions of this problem are unbalanced. We know more about noticing than about noticeability. One person you would expect to notice error is the teacher, but Legenhausen's (1975) study of 24,000 EL2 errors in the marked written work of German *Abitur* level students revealed the teachers' **recognition** of error to be disturbingly low. Over 30 major error types, the recognition quotient was a mere 57 per cent, meaning that 43 per cent of their errors went undetected by their teachers. This figure should give pause to those critics of EA who claim that teachers are obsessed with error: not all are, since there are many whose capacity to spot errors is severely limited. If all teachers had approximately the same error recognition capacity, learners would know where they stand. But, as Legenhausen's study also revealed, this is not the case. He even discovered substantial regional differences, in the same German province, of teachers' ability to spot error. Such discrepancies are bound to influence learning outcomes, for not only are some learners less leniently assessed than others, depending on their teacher's capacity, but one presumes that the same pupils enjoy less corrective feedback from these same teachers.

We referred earlier (see Chapter 1) to the alleged morbidity of EA, the suggestion of critics being that we only notice error and overlook (or even ignore) achievement. Now, last year I found myself in a backstreet eating house in South-East Asia, and enquired of the young waitress, in English, whether her *laksa* was very spicy or not. I was amazed when she informed me quite precisely and unambiguously that her laksa was '*fierce, fierce*'. I had simply not expected her to know this lexical item, certainly not in the culinary context. We do notice achievement as well as error, a point that Williams (1981) argues cogently in a paper on the phenomenology of error. He suggests that one way to categorize language involves two steps. First, deciding whether or not there has been a rule-violation (+V or –V), that is, whether or not there is an instance of error or of **achievement** (such as our *fierce*). Next, whether or not the person receiving that language responds or not (+R or –R) to the presence *or the absence* of error. A third step, of course, would be to see if the response is positive or negative (approving or not), and a fourth step would be to measure the *strength* of that (dis)approval, which would be a measure of gravity. Staying with the first two steps, Williams (1981: 161) suggests there are four combinations of response:

1. +V, +R: this describes a reader, say, responding to a perceived violation (error).
2. −V, −R: the reader makes no response as there is no perception of error.

These two possibilities are where EA usually stops, or at least where it is assumed to stop: errors are condemned but non-errors are unnoticed. Our extended **noticing dimension** suggests we look at the other two options:

3. +V, −R: one overlooks the error, in the sense of not noticing it (like Legenhausen's teachers).
4. −V, +R: there is no error, and this is noteworthy, since we had expected error: the 'fierce laksa' was a case in point.

In terms of EG type 1 would be more serious than type 3, since the former is noticeable. But here is where the paradox thrusts itself into the picture: I can accommodate for the error that I have noticed, but not for the one that went unnoticed. We shall try to resolve the paradox later (see page 226ff.), when we show that **viewpoint** is what matters, that is, *who* does the noticing.

The irritation factor

As Sartre said: 'Hell is other people.' That includes people who speak our language in ways different from how we ourselves speak it. While it is true that a foreign accent – on all levels of language, not just the phonological – can be charming, alluring and socially advantageous, it can also elicit the opposite reactions from native speakers.

Giles (1970) used Lambert's Matched Guise Technique to study what he calls the 'aesthetic' aspect of accents, which he defines as 'the pleasantness–unpleasantness associated with listening to a particular accent' (1970: 212). An actor recorded the same spoken text in 13 different foreign and regional accents of English. These recordings were then played to native speakers, who were invited to indicate their assessment of the pleasantness of each on a 7-point scale. The average scale of approval of the accents was as follows starting with the most pleasant and ending with the least pleasant:

Received Pronunciation (RP) > French > Irish > South Walian > Northern England > Indian > Italian > Somerset > American > Cockney > German > Birmingham

Notice how RP is admired as the norm, and how German and 'Brummie' (as it is affectionately or patronizingly called) are not. In other words, accents become more **irritating** as they are positioned towards the end of the list.

The first to use the term 'irritation' to refer to one aspect of linguistic nonconformity (error) was Johansson, observing that errors can 'affect the relationship between the speaker and the listener (e.g. make the listener tired or irritated or draw away his attention from the contents of the message' (1975: 25). Another possible effect is to give the impression of the speaker as apathetic or even surly. His observations led Johansson to carry out research to identify which *types* of error are the most irritating. His results suggested that word-order (WO) errors are the least irritating, complementation (CP) errors the most irritating, with concord errors (CD) occupying the middle ground:

WO *Not a single mistake *they have/√have they made.*
    The golfer *frequently has//√has frequently received a prize.
CD *Your new boss want* you to resign.*
CP *The doctor suggested *Mrs Jones to take /√that Mrs Jones take a rest.*
    They prevented him *to receive//√from receiving the award.

The claim to be able to establish an irritation scale has, however, been challenged, notably by Albrechtsen, Henriksen and Færch (1980), who assert 'All errors are equally irritating . . . one should not expect to be able to establish a hierarchy of errors with respect to irritation' (1980: 395). I would argue, however, that the irritation potential of an error is a reflection of three factors: its **predictability,** the **social relationship** obtaining at the time between speaker and hearer, and the degree to which it infringes **social norms** (as well as linguistic ones). Let's look at these in turn.

1.   I used to lecture on the British Council's annual summer school for Soviet teachers of English, most of whom spoke Russian as their L1. Since Russian has no articles, these teachers spoke an article-less English: they predictably underused articles and within a few hours of contact this began to be irritating to the listener. The opposite – overindulgence – also occurred with dogged

predictability: in Russian there is a word *koneshna*, the dictionary equivalent of which is 'of course'. But Russian uses *koneshna* in contexts where '*of course*' does not fit. One day after lunch I tried to strike up a conversation with one Svetlana, asking if she was joining the afternoon excursion to Blenheim Palace, to which her reply was a curt, even censorious '*of course!*'. An enthusiastic '*you bet!*' or '*rather*' was no doubt her intent. One doesn't have to be a Contrastive Analyst to predict these errors, of course: a few hours exposure to any Interlanguage will reveal to the observant what the recurrent and predictable errors are likely to be.

2. The same examples illustrate also the second irritation potential that is triggered by a simple error. Every class has its obnoxious or disruptive member: I used to call her 'the Commissar' in Soviet summer school days. Now when she produced ?*To my mind* (from '*po moyemu mneniyu*') instead of simple *I think*, I was usually prepared to see Red! Where the relationship is sweet, however, irritation will have a hard time coming to the surface.

3. Santos (1988) reports that American professors found the double negative in overseas students' writing highly irritating. Why? A plausible explanation is that they were transferring a *social* criterion of linguistic evaluation, appropriate for categorizing NSs, to an outsider. The outsider is perceived as being of high status, and such a person's use of this low-class form contradicts that expectation – and is therefore irritating. An error, then, will tend to cause irritation (or embarrassment) when it has **sociopragmatic** consequences, that is, when it is not so much language rules as social norms that are violated by the error. We have already (see Chapter 5) referred to the distinction drawn between **pragmalinguistic** and **sociopragmatic** errors by Thomas (1983). She defines the latter thus:

> It is cross-cultural mismatches in the assessment of social distance, of what constitutes an imposition, of when an attempt at a face-threatening act should be abandoned, and in evaluating relative power, rights, and obligations etc., which cause sociopragmatic failure. (Thomas, 1983: 104)

In a series of studies, James, Scholfield and Ypsiladis (1992, 1994) investigated the strategies deployed by overseas (nonnative English) students in doing persuasive writing when called upon to compose a letter of application for a highly desirable study scholarship. Native-speaking 'judges' were asked to evaluate and rate the **rhetorical moves** deployed in these letters of application, and they were asked to give their reasons for deeming some good and some not so good. Two strategies in particular met with strong disapprobation from the NSs:

1.   '*Your scholarship is my only chance to make a study visit to the USA, since . . .*' Our English judges explained that the use of the phrases '*only chance*' and '*sole chance*' constituted 'emotion black-mail' since they imply that a refusal would have dire consequences for the applicant, and the donors would bear the blame. The applicant is therefore flouting Lakoff's **Maxim of Politeness** *Leave the hearer with options*. At the very least the hearer's options are being reduced by this arm-twisting.

2.   '*I speak four languages . . . do not have problems socialising with other people . . . also I hold one degree already in Social Policy*'. The English NSs saw this as an egotistic recital of the applicant's attainments, likely at least to bore and possibly to infuriate the reader. This move, then, constitutes an infringement of what Leech calls the **Modesty Maxim**, which requires the speaker/writer 'to minimise praise of self and maximise dispraise of self' (1983: 136ff.). This must be an Anglo-Saxon attitude, because when questioned, non-English judges expressed no such disapproval of this move, considering it a suitable way of 'presenting yourself in a positive manner'. It is interesting that You Sihai also found that 'application letters written by Chinese students read rather arrogant and unconvincing because of the frequent use of superlatives when they evaluated themselves' (1990: 84). This came as a surprise to her, since 'actually Chinese society advocates modesty' (ibid.).

Although we have chosen to classify these as **social** solecisms, it could be argued that the negative feelings they evoke even extend to the personal level: 'egotistic', 'immodest', 'blackmail' refer to personality defects and border on ethics. Albrechtsen, Henriksen and Færch (1980) assume the same, as is evident from their decision to use Osgood's **Semantic Differential** scales to measure the attitudinal effects on NSs of Danish learners' spoken English, that is, to decide whether they viewed the speaker to be 'eager' or 'hesitant', 'confident' or 'shy', and so on. We referred above, in the context of the letter of application studies, to the perceived quality of the **rhetorical** strategies (or 'moves') used by applicants. Albrechtsen, Henriksen and Færch looked at the **communication strategies** (CSs) of Danish learners. They found that English NSs positively evaluate language to the extent that it is both error-free

and does not make extensive use of CSs. Conversely, they negatively evaluate inaccurate language that also betrays extensive use
of CSs. Most interesting, though, is their finding that L2 learners
can expect positive evaluation of their language by NSs provided
they avoid the use of CSs, even if it contains errors. As it stands,
this constitutes a claim that formal errors do not affect attitude,
or, to use the authors' own words: 'Learners do not improve the
attitude they evoke towards themselves and the content of what
they say simply by improving their correctness' (Albrechtsen *et al.*,
1980: 395).

We could reinterpret their findings, however. While claiming
that accuracy does not affect the listener's attitude, Albrechtsen,
Henriksen and Færch also make two further claims: that texts with
many CSs are difficult to understand, and that learners who use
many CSs tend also to make many errors. Putting two and two
together, the implication is that some learners are difficult to
understand because they commit many errors (and use many CSs).
This is so obvious as to be a truism. It is also, to say the least,
highly probable that low intelligibility evinces low opinion of the
speaker.

There is also the question of the **visibility** of the CSs. All the
CSs counted in the Albrechtsen, Henriksen and Færch study must
have been visible to the researchers and to the native-speaking
subjects. As such they were *failed* CSs, since CSs that are successful not only serve to put the message over but also do so unobtrusively – without drawing attention to themselves. As James (1991a)
in his review of O'Malley and Chamot (1990) points out, there is
a paradox underlying the predilection of Communicative Language Teaching methodologists for CSs: that, while they may res-
cue the learners from their present communication crisis, they do
nothing to bring about the learning which would avoid a similar
crisis arising in the future. On the contrary, reliance on CSs will
give the learners a false sense of security and they won't bother
to make the effort to learn the language item they lack. Perhaps
knowers (NSs) somehow sense this and their disapproval of CSs
comes from this insight. Perhaps they also see resort to CSs as a
kind of deception: the learners are trying to hide their ignorance,
which is seen as morally reprehensible, downright duplicity. There
might also be an element of self-interest in the NSs' disapproval of
CSs. A favourite CS is **circumlocution**, as exemplified in the substitution of '*things that come every week*' for the unknown target '*TV*

serials'. The point is that such circumlocutions result in expansions, leading the speakers to hold the floor longer than they deserve to. All this, in addition to taxing their patience, imposes a heavier processing load on the listeners. This in itself is an imposition, and is understandably resented. A successful CS will therefore be one that not only solves the communication problem, but one that does so unobtrusively, without raising questions on the 'ethical' dimension.

We have again returned to focus on NSs' judgements. These are not the only ones, and we must consider the role of **viewpoint** in EG assessments.

Viewpoint

I have said a good deal about the **noticeability** of errors, perhaps giving the false impression that it is a constant, that is, that it is something that is fixed, a property of language. This is not the case, and noticeability, like beauty, is to some extent in the eye of the beholder. Some of us are more tolerant, less observant, more pedantic and less irritable than others. So noticeability is variable, depending not only on *what* is being observed but also on *who* is doing the observing. As we have seen, Legenhausen's (1975) work showed how German teachers of English in one province varied alarmingly in their error recognition quotients (ERQs). Since foreign teachers vary so widely in their ERQs, the question arises whether NSs are more consistent and whether the noticeability criterion can be referred to them. Page (1990: 106) after all insists that the right (or fair?) perspective to take on error is that of the 'sympathetic native speaker'. So NSs are useful after all, and need not all fall beyond the native-speakerist pale, provided they are 'sympathetic'. But what might this mean? I believe it is shorthand for a collection of epithets that characterize the *undesirable* stance (viewpoint) to take towards errors: pedantic, prescriptive, correct, norming, and so on. Note that these labels are all associated with the system of education and the role it plays in imposing standards, forcing conformity, or, as Gee (1990) claims, indoctrinating children into the 'Discourse' of the ruling classes. In other words there is a recurrent tendency to contrast the viewpoints on EG of people working in 'education' and those of ordinary humans, lay NSs. But there is a second dimension to take into account.

Author(s)	+NS +T	+NS −T Layperson	−NS +T	−NS −T
James, 1977	20 English		20 mixed	
Ervin, 1979	4 Russians	4 Russians	4 American	
Santos, 1988	Profs Sc/Hum		Profs Jp Sc/Hum	
Kobayashi, 1992	145 H/I/L		125 H. . . .	. . . . . I/L
Politzer, 1978		German adults		
Delisle, 1982		German children		
Hughes &				
Lascaratou, 1982	10 English	10 English	10 Greek	
Davies, 1983		43 English	43 Moroccan	
McCretton &				
Rider, 1993	10 English		10 mixed	
Garrett &				
Austin, 1993	P-grad English	U-grad English		U-grad German
Birdsong &				
Kassen 1988	10 French		10 American	L/I students
Schmitt, 1993	20 American		18 Japanese	

Sc − Science; Hum − Humanities; Jp − Japanese; H − high; I − intermediate; L − low;
P-grad − postgraduate; U-grad − undergraduate.

Figure 7.2   Empirical studies of viewpoint in EG (error gravity) ratings.

Since it is not the case that all NNSs are teachers and all NSs non-teachers, we have to add the two categories of teachers who are NSs of the target language and teachers who are not NSs.

Over the last 20 years there has been a succession of empirical studies comparing the viewpoints on foreign language EGs as registered by NSs and NNSs of the FL, teachers and non-teachers included. Just to summarize, the four viewpoints described are:

1. +NS +T (The native-speaker teacher)
2. +NS −T (The native-speaker layperson)
3. −NS +T (The teacher who has had to learn the language herself)
4. −NS −T (The foreign user of the language who is not a teacher.)

We might further distinguish 'learners' in the sense of those people who are undergoing language training at the moment, from 'non-learners', people who are making use of past learning but have ceased to learn, or are 'fossilized' in their learning of the FL. Thirteen studies that have investigated EG ratings with reference to these variables are summarized in Figure 7.2.

Six of these studies have compared ratings by NS and NNS teachers (+NS +T versus −NS +T): James (1977), Santos (1988), Kobayashi (1992), McCretton and Rider (1993), Birdsong and Kassen (1988) and Schmitt (1993).

James (1977) asked ten NSs and ten NNSs, all teachers of EL2, to rate on a 5-point scale 50 errors falling into ten error types. These types were: 'negation', 'tense', 'agreement', 'articles', 'transformation', 'order', 'noun', 'verb', 'adjective' and 'preposition selection'. The errors considered to be the most serious were given an EG score of five, while the non-errors were given a score of zero. The study yielded information. First, the NNS teachers tended to mark more severely overall than the NSs. This measure is referred to as the **rating**, which indicates in absolute terms how severely the judge penalises the error. Each NS deducted on average 123 out of 250 (5 × 50) points, compared to the NNSs' average of 138. A second finding was that individual assessors tended to assign EG ratings to each of the ten types consistently, which suggests that the categories have some psychological validity. Such consistency shows that teachers' EG ratings are not random but reflect their reliance on certain principles of evaluation. Without this consistency, teaching would of course become impossible.

A third finding of the study was that, against the background of consistency on the part of each individual judge, the two groups of NS and NNS teachers showed not only different **means** (123 versus 138), as we have seen, but also different **ranges** and different **distributions**. As to range, the highest total deducted in the NS group was 171, and the lowest total 91, giving a range of 80. The NNSs made deductions between 93 and 197, a range of 104. What this implies is that the NSs *as a group* were operating on an 8-point scale while the NNSs were using a 10-point scale. The NNSs were, so to speak, discriminating more finely than the NSs, quite the opposite of what we would expect. The distributions of marks deducted also distinguished NS from NNS judges. Almost all the NSs deducted marks totalling between 90 and 140: they were not only lenient individually, but consensually so. The NNSs, on the other hand, fell into two groups. one deducting marks totalling around 110, the other making deductions round the 160 total. One has to wonder why overseas EL2 teachers are 'split' into two camps. Does it reflect the EFL versus ESL division which we discussed in Chapter 1? Does it reflect inequalities in these overseas teachers' own command of EL2, or in their teacher education?

And finally, James's study carried suggestions concerning a **hierarchy** of EG attributions according to the ten error types identified. This involves giving the set of error types a **ranking**, that is, deciding how serious one type is relative to other types. The error types most stigmatized by the NNSs were those of **lexis** and **case**. By 'lexical' we mean misselections such as *Christ ascended into* *sky/ √*Heaven*. By 'case' we mean problems with prepositions, such as *He disapproved* *∅/√*of my idea, He laughed* *with/√*at my joke*.

Two other studies that, like James's, limited their enquiry to NS and NNS teachers' EG ratings, focused on these judges' perceptions of the relative EGs of types of error. Schmitt (1993) elicited in Japan data which supported 'the position that nonnative teachers are harsher on errors than native teachers' (1993: 186), observing further that these generalizations reflected mainly error types 'clustered at the "local" end of the hierarchy' while, by contrast, there was greater inconsistency in judging the discourse or global errors. McCretton and Rider (1993) asked 20 NS and 20-NNS teachers to evaluate on a 5-point scale 25 EL2 sentences containing seven types of error. They again confirmed James's claim that the NNSs were consistently more severe in their judgements, and also that the order in which both groups ranked the errors was remarkably similar to a statistically high significance of $p = 0.009$. They suggested there must be a 'universal hierarchy of errors', namely:

MOST SEVERE: :LEAST SEVERE
Lexis > spelling > negation > word order > prepositions > verb
forms > concord

Santos (1988) compared the ratings given by English NS and Japanese NNS professors (in the American sense of 'experienced tertiary level teacher') of two students' essays, one with L1 Japanese, the other Korean. Two new variables that Santos introduced are the rater's academic discipline (science versus humanities) and the professors' age (older versus younger). The focus is also different from previous studies reviewed here, being on student **compositions**, with the result that this study addressed more issues than EGs, for example the rating of content versus form, and the relative weightings for comprehensibility, irritation and acceptability of the two essays. The findings of relevance to our discussion were these: that the NNS professors were more severe in their judgement than the NS professors; the **lexical** errors were deemed the most serious since it is in lexis that 'language impinges with content'; older professors were less irritated than younger ones; and that professors of social science and humanities were more lenient than those of physical science. We shall return to this point presently, since it concerns the layperson's viewpoint.

Kobayashi (1992) compared, among other things, how NS and NNS raters assigned EGs, or, in her words, gave 'evaluative feedback'. She asked over 200 English NSs and Japanese EL2 speakers to read two EL2 compositions written by Japanese college students and rate them for grammaticality on a 10-point scale. At least one of her findings is at variance with those from previous studies: the NSs were stricter in their judgement of **grammaticality** than the NNSs, who, euphemistically, are stated to 'have rated both compositions more positively' (Kobayashi, 1992: 91). However, she proceeds to point out this result might be an artifact of the research design. The judges were asked *both* to detect errors and then to rate them, and the NNSs would, of course, be in no position to assign an EG to an error they had failed to spot. Recall the similar observation by Schmitt, mentioned above. It was for this reason that the James (1977) study had presented subjects with sentences to judge which contained errors, and common (therefore likely to be noticed) ones to boot. In fact, the Japanese NNSs, presumably assuming there must be error, in many instances provided **miscorrections** of well-formed sentences, as *Master always scold* me, so my self-respect √will be broken,* which was rephrased as *The master always scold* me, so my self-respect *will be achieved* (Kobayashi: 93).

Recall that James (1977) had identified the presence of a more and a less severely judging group (perhaps reflecting ESL versus EFL status) among his NNSs. Kobayashi addressed this interesting variable directly, in terms of the *relative* proficiency of her NNS judges. She identified three levels of EL2 proficiency, in Japanese professors, postgraduates and undergraduates. These categories are designated H (high), I (intermediate) and L (low) proficiency respectively in row 4 of Figure 7.2. She established a correlation between EL2 proficiency and error detection rates: 'the higher the academic status of the evaluating group, the more accurately it corrected errors' (Kobayashi, 1992: 81). What we see happening here is a refinement of the simple dichotomy NS versus NNS. There is a suggestion that we might be dealing with a **scale** rather than with a dichotomy, in that there are degrees of nonnativeness, and that H nonnatives can be quite close to NSs in their EG judgements.

A similar path of enquiry was that taken by Birdsong and Kassen (1988) but rather than enquire about the relative French L2 proficiency of *teachers* they looked at the differences between high and low proficiency *students* of French: −NS −T. Their concern was to establish first whether learners share judgements of EGs with their teachers. They assumed that this would be more likely if teachers and students had the same L1: they would be able to apply their **psychotypology** of transfer to EG judgements. The authors consider this to be a vital question for FL teaching, since learners are by definition in an 'error-intensive environment', where agreement between teacher and taught on priorities (as reflections of EG ratings) is likely to heighten cooperation and accelerate learning. Their study involved judgements by NS and NNS teachers of the L2 French, as well as two grade-levels of learners. Their data show the following hierarchy for EG rating by the four groups:

MOST SEVERE: :LEAST SEVERE
NS teachers > NNS teachers > more proficient learners > less proficient learners

Note the correlation between judges' own EL2 proficiency and EG severity. Note also how these data contradict all the other studies reviewed here, which showed NSs to be *less* severe raters than NNSs. All other studies, that is, except Ervin (1979). Ervin had studied the evaluations by American NNS teachers and NS Russian teachers of Russian of the communication strategies of American learners of that language. Like Birdsong and Kassen, he found the NS teachers to be more severe in their condemnation of errors than the American NNS teachers. The discrepancy between Ervin's findings and the others could be explained by the research design: subjects were asked to evaluate communication strategies for comprehensibility, rather than errors for unacceptability. But the same explanation would not apply to the Birdsong and Kassen study.

However, despite their finding about rating, Birdsong and Kassen also found that when it came to **ranking** of errors for relative EG, there were high levels of agreement with the French NSs on the seriousness of some errors relative to others. For example (Birdsong and Kassen, 1988: 17), all agreed on the order:

MOST SEVERE: :LEAST SEVERE
*Je *suis bois un cafe > J'ai *aime ce livre beaucoup > entr*[ei]/[Ne]*

One other study that has involved NNS non-teachers is Garrett and Austin (1993), a study which compared the abilities of three groups to spot errors in **apostrophe 's'** usage in English. The +NS +T group were experienced EFL teachers doing a postgraduate education course at a British university; the +NS −T group were undergraduates at the same university; and the −NS −T group were German undergraduate *Anglisten* at a German university. The three groups were again compared for error recognition (ERQs) and for EG rating. The German students had the highest and most consistent ERQs, as well as the highest EG ratings. The conclusion aptly drawn is that the great divide is not so much that of NS versus NNS as between those having explicit knowledge of the relevant linguistic features and those lacking such knowledge. There is also the suggestion that there may be areas of an FL (such as apostrophe 's' in English) which are so arbitrary as to require explicit teaching, something NNSs are more likely to receive than NSs.

This brings us to the last group of studies in EG ascription: those that add the '+NS −T' dimension, looking at the views of NS laypersons, people uncorrupted by the teacher's craft, and, as Garrett and Austin point out, people who are unlikely ever to have received explicit instruction on the language point in question. Politzer (1978), without making any comparisons with other groups, established the EG scaling by 146 German *teenagers* of the spoken errors in L2 German produced by American learners. The perceived hierarchy was:

MOST SEVERE: :LEAST SEVERE
Lexis > verb morphology > word order > gender > phonology >
                                                      case marking

Delisle (1982) was intended to complement Politzer's study, investigating the reactions of NS German *adults* (aged 13–17) to learners' written errors. Her six categories were the same as Politzer's, except for her **spelling**, which replaced his **phonology**. The problem is that there are not one but two different variables between the Delisle and the Politzer studies, so it is impossible to say whether the differences in EG rankings reflect the respondents' age differences or the spoken/written difference, or both.

Studies that did involve comparisons across groups, one of which comprised NS laypersons, include Garrett and Austin (1993), Ervin (1979), Hughes and Lascaratou (1982) and Davies (1983). Hughes and Lascaratou's study involved three groups of ten judges, one being NS non-teachers, the others +NS +T and +NNS +T. The two groups of NSs agreed in their overall rating of the sample of IL they were asked to judge, deducting 46 and 47 marks out of 160. They also agreed that rule-breaking was not serious *per se*, but set great store on intelligibility. Where they differed was in the degree of importance they gave to intelligibility: the NS non-teachers valued it three times as highly as their teacher compatriots. They objected most to the incomprehensibility caused by 'misspellings' of the type *He was *hightly/√lightly wounded* and *a*surious√curious crowd*. Yet these errors are more than misspellings; they are **confusibles** (see Chapter 5), since they could be misread (albeit in a different context) as intended *highly* and *serious*: they 'create lexical confusion' (Hughes and Lascaratou, 1982: 179). Hughes and Lascaratou interpret this as implying that with the NSs it is not a case of insisting on form for form's sake, but on making intelligibility the yardstick for gravity. One could argue the converse: that the NSs wish to decontextualize error, that is to take into consideration what might be the consequences of committing the same error in less benign contexts. One might see this as the NSs exercising their language awareness and extrapolating from context.

Davies (1983) made a direct comparison between the EG ratings of 43 Moroccan EL3 teachers and 43 'naive' non-teacher NSs of English. The latter were much more tolerant of errors, and Davies asks why. One interesting suggestion concerns those errors caused by L1 (Arabic) or L2 (French). These are familiar to the Moroccan teachers and easily explained, and easily compensated for, and so are judged non-serious. It is just the opposite case for the English NSs, for whom these interference errors appeared 'quite bizarre' (Davies, 1983: 308). A second explanation Davies offers is the English NSs' tolerance born of their familiarity with the many ungrammatical forms NSs do in fact use, forms like *He walks very *slow* or *There'*s lots of things to do*. Her third observation is similar to the one I used above to explain Hughes and Lascaratou's NSs' evaluations of confusibles: 'their greater readiness to think of contexts where such utterances would be perfectly natural' (ibid.: 305). We saw a case of this in Chapter 3, in Professor W. Haas's contextualization of the apparently uncontextualizable *Quadruplicity drinks procrastination*. Note though that while Davies sees the NSs as finding felicitous contexts for errors, and so upgrading them, we saw Hughes and Lascaratou's NSs as doing the opposite: downgrading errors on the grounds that in other contexts they would be highly infelicitous. Is this a difference in viewpoint among different groups of NSs – the pessimists and the optimists?

Among the 12 studies reviewed here we have identified three distinct designs: Type 1 studies compare NS and NNS teachers; Type 2 introduce non-teacher NSs into the picture; and Type 3 introduce non-teacher NNSs. The research done in this area is less voluminous than its importance should dictate. But one thing is clear: that it is the teacher who is at the centre of all these studies. This is rightly so, since error signals non-learning and the need for a teacher to help the learner put things right. How the teacher can contribute to achieving this end will be the subject of the next chapter.

Note

1. I am indebted to Jonathan and Ann Mossop for supplying this example.

8

Error Correction

What it should have been.
In our report yesterday 'State Mufti under Sultan' the State Mufti
was erroneously translated as religious council. It should have read
*as Religious Counsel.
Drawing attention to this report the Prime Minister's Dept. stated
that the news item was confusing as there was no mention of a
religious council in the press release issued by the *PMs Dept.
It did not *also make reference *that the religious council will
come under the direct order of His Majesty. The error is regretted.
(*The Borneo Bulletin*, 1 December 1994, p. 2)

One of the purposes of doing Error Analysis is to identify the
principles which should guide effective error correction (EC).
Principled EC is applied EA. As the above excerpt makes clear,
people's ideas about what is involved in correction are not always
clear, and as a result, neither are their purported corrections. In
this excerpt, 'what it should have been' never emerges clearly,
while, in the act of attempting to correct one error, several more
unrelated ones (those asterisked) creep in. The 'correction' move
fails to clarify. In this chapter we shall first try to say what is meant
by correction, then answer the question of whether and why it is
desirable, and if so, how one should go about it.

What is 'correction'?

The pragmatics of the speech act we call **correction** are complex,
but it is obviously a reactive second move of an **adjacency pair** to
a first speaker's or writer's utterance by someone who has made
the judgement that all or part of that utterance is linguistically

or factually wrong. EA limits its interest to linguistic deviance of course, and correction is form-focused rather than a reaction to truth-value. Correcting is a **metalinguistic** act, since it is a comment on language. In this it is more abstract than, say, a warning, which is a linguistic comment on non-language behaviour. The first speaker is usually a learner. The second speaker is a knower, usually a teacher, but not always: he or she may be a non-teacher, a helpful native speaker, a fellow learner, or even the learner him- or herself, in which case we speak of **self-correction**. Self-correction of a **slip** can be achieved without the benefit of feedback from another person, and, as we have been suggesting, feedback can be auto-generated. Self-correction is an intriguing phenomenon in that for some inexplicable reason we seem to be more capable of spotting other people's errors than our own, as anyone who has done some proofreading will testify. The reason probably is that self-editing a text one has composed oneself calls for an ability to clear one's mind of one's intended meaning at the time of writing and interpret one's own text with just the information actually available in the words. One needs to be scrupulously objective in reprocessing one's own textual creation, since there is some temptation to read meaning into it rather than out of it.

A question that arises is whether a 'correction' that is in fact no more correct or even less 'correct' than the original utterance still qualifies as being a correction: or is it a **miscorrection**? It may have the same effect – to prompt revision – as a good correction. More generally, do corrections, to qualify as such, have to present 'improved' versions of what it is assumed the first speaker was trying to say? Or does a statement *that* something is wrong, without mentioning *in what way* it is wrong, still constitute a correction? A second question is whether a correct utterance which anticipates – rather than follows in time – the incorrect one that was intended counts as a correction. Such a correction could be done by the second speaker or the first, in which case we would have an anticipatory self-correction.

The term 'correction' has been used in three senses:

1. Informing the learners that there is an error, and leaving them to discover it and repair it themselves. I would call this sort of intervention **feedback**, commonly defined as giving knowledge of 'results' – in the broadest sense, telling people whether their utterance or understanding is right or wrong.

2. Providing treatment or information that leads to the revision and correction of the specific instance of error (the error **token**) without aiming to prevent the same error from recurring later. In addition to indicating that the present attempt is wrong, the corrector can specify how and where, suggest an alternative, give a hint. This is like doing a temporary or 'running' repair on your car, just to get you home, but without getting to the root of the problem. It is aimed at **product enhancement**. This I would call **correction** proper.

3. Providing learners with information that allows them to revise or reject the wrong rule they were operating with when they produced the error token. The result will be to induce learners to revise their mental representation of the rule, so that this error **type** does not recur. This is like having a mechanic fit to your immobilized car a factory replacement part that carries a lifetime guarantee. Since its purpose is primarily to improve the processes for all future productions rather than merely 'cosmetically' to improve the present product, I would call this **remediation**.

You could say that feedback is an overture to correction, which in its turn is an overture to remediation, since having given feedback you can decide whether to stop there, or to enlarge your treatment by going on to correction and then remediation as well.

The distinction drawn between error-token and error-type correction is crucial for Prabhu (1987) who uses it to distinguish **incidental** from **systematic** correction: the former is 'confined to particular "tokens" (i.e. the error itself is corrected, but there is no generalization to the type of error it represents)' (1987: 62). Hammerly (1991: Ch. 9) has made the same distinction in terms of 'surface' and 'deep' correction of errors. 'Surface' correction is mere editing (putting right) but does not address the source of the problem. 'Deep' correction does, since it involves explaining *why* some bit of language is the way it is, so prompting leaners to 'reorganize their cognitive structures' (Hammerly, 1991: 93). We shall return to the function of explanation below.

We could further distinguish these types of intervention in terms of **diagnosis**. When we give **feedback**, we inform the learners that their attempt is wrong, but we do not tell them how, nor why it is wrong, that is, we do not carry out for the learners' benefit an Error Analysis between their IL form and the intended TL form, nor do we do a Contrastive Analysis between their L1 form and the corresponding TL form. In other words, we do not specify in what ways or for what reasons the form they have uttered or written is ill-formed: we merely say that it is wrong, no more. Now, when we do **correction**, we do more than say that it is wrong. We also indicate in what ways, describing the nature of the wrongness. And when we do **remediation**, we do indeed carry out the Contrastive and Error Analyses that explain why the error was committed. We might do this privately, without involving the learners in our deliberations, or we might do it collaboratively, taking the learners into our confidence, perhaps even leaving them to discover the diagnosis themselves. This is a methodological decision about consciousness-raising.

The distinction between feedback, correction and remediation parallels other distinctions in interesting ways. The first is the **slip** versus **mistake** versus **error** trichotomy that we have referred to frequently in this book. Corder (1981) said of mistakes (although I suggest he had **slips** in mind): 'We are normally immediately aware of them when they occur and can correct them with more or less complete assurance' (1981: 10). In other words, **slips** are self-correctable without benefit of feedback from another person. But feedback there must be, of some sort, from one's self. This is the sort of feedback that comes from one's intuitions: one just feels that what one has said or written is wrong. It is clear that when Mattson and Baars (1992) talk of native speakers' 'error minimising mechanisms' they have in mind the speakers' own treatment of slips, not of errors nor even of mistakes.

What I call **mistakes**, by contrast, are self-correctable only with the benefit of feedback: knowers have to tell the learners THAT they are wrong, but no more. They do not have to specify in what respect. In such cases, informing the learners that the present form is wrong, that is, doing no more than give feedback, will usually be enough to cause the learners to reject their current hypothesis and this will be a sufficient prompt to them to search for an alternative hypothesis with which to replace it. This is likely to be the case when the system is relatively simple and the learners have only two or three terms to choose from: for example, telling them that **speaked* is wrong triggers a shift of verb-morphology paradigm to √*spoke*; similarly, telling them that *I *am liking it* is wrong will normally be sufficient information to trigger selection of the only alternative, the present simple √*I like it*. The learners *knew* the correct form all along. It was simply insufficiently automatized as a part-repertoire, or as Johnson (1996) would say, has the status of **mistake**.

However, if self-correction is still impossible despite provision of simple factual feedback without specification of the nature of the deviance, then we have a case of **error** proper. The deviance springs from ignorance. The learners are not told simply that there is ill-formedness, but also the nature of this ill-formedness. In this case what is called for is **explanation** of the TL system. This explanation can be communicated explicitly to the learners, or can be implicit, merely determining the nature of the necessary instruction. It can take into account, again explicitly or implicitly, the respects in which the learners' erroneous IL version did not match the TL form. In each case we are giving **remediation**.

The hierarchy slip<mistake<error we have suggested exists raises the question of priority. Should the learners first aim for **accuracy** (error minimization), then go for enhancing access to their TL knowledge (mistake minimization) and finally aim for slip-free **fluency** – the icing on the cake? The converse prioritization might be preferable however. This would be the case if it were established by research that high levels of fluency and proceduralization enhance accuracy. Poulisse and Bongaerts (1994) take this view, arguing that once repertoires are automatized, producing them will make few demands on the speaker's attention, leaving spare attention for monitoring out any potential mistakes that would otherwise surface. If you are not making many mistakes, you have spare attention to correct the few you might make. Success breeds success, or, as they so aptly put it, 'you have to have money to make money' (Poulisse and Bongaerts, 1994). The more conventional view is that fluency and accuracy are somehow in competition (Hammerly, 1991), and the learners have to do a balancing act to achieve optimal fluency without sacrificing accuracy – and vice versa. This concept of a two-flanked attack on a problem of language is paralleled in ideas about engaging top-down versus bottom-up strategies in achieving reading comprehension.

The notions of feedback and correction are discussed extensively in the contemporary L1-acquisition and linguistics literature (Chomsky, 1986; Cook, 1988: 60; Radford, 1988: 44) in terms of **evidence**. Learners improve through receiving from knowers information or 'evidence' about the TL and about their own attempts at reproducing it. This evidence comes in four forms: positive or negative, direct or indirect. **Positive evidence** tells you which forms *are* used in the TL, while **negative evidence** tells you which are not. You get both these sorts of evidence 'indirectly', that is incidentally, just by observing the TL being produced: you notice **data**, that is, what the speakers of a language do and don't say or write. Noticing what they do and don't understand also mediates indirect evidence to learners: if natives or the teacher continue to appear happy with what I, the learner, say and how I say it, I take that as indirect positive evidence. I take it as negative evidence when they show signs of incomprehension or irritation without actually telling me I am unintelligible.

If, however, a knower (or informant) makes a point of telling you that such and such a form is or is not grammatical, correct or compehensible in the TL, we speak of the **direct** provision of evidence. Chomsky (1986: 55) proposes that children acquire their mother tongue from indirect evidence only: they notice usage (what is and is not said) and work out rules. FL learners are more opportunistic and rely on all four kinds of evidence. When new language is presented to them in class, they are getting **direct positive evidence**: the teacher is saying 'Look, this is how it is said in German'. They are being exhorted to **notice** this feature of German. When the teacher says 'Look, this can't be said in French. You will never hear a Frenchman say **J'ai arrivé hier*', they are getting direct negative evidence. A specific form of this is: 'Look, what you just said cannot be said in French.' No reasons are given, so this is correction. When the teacher says: 'Look, you can't say it that way in French because . . .', this is remediation, which can take a variety of forms, from simple to elaborate. Note the force of 'because' here: **explanation** has entered the picture.

Having established what correction is, and the three basic forms it takes – feedback, correction proper and remediation – and having made the link between correction and evidence, we shall proceed to the question of whether correction is an advisable strategy for promoting FL development.

Whether to correct: pros and cons

The question of whether or not to correct error is not as simple as it appears to be at first sight. There are two broader questions that it is bound up with. The first is whether prevention of error is better than cure; the second question is whether explicit formal instruction – in a word, 'teaching' – is effective.

Prevention or cure?

If prevention is better than cure, we ought to be researching ways of **preventing** errors from happening in the first place, rather than ways of correcting them once they have materialized. Our focus should be on teaching, not correcting. George (1972: 62ff.) makes a strong case and backs this up with practical guidelines for preventing errors. Paradoxically, he suggests that turning a blind eye to errors prevents them, since the learners will be less inclined to focus on them if they are ignored and no fuss is made. A second way is by 'orderliness of input': the teacher should make sure that newly taught items are repeated a lot, and are spaced away from other TL forms that are similar and which therefore might compete with the item being taught by **association**. Another teaching strategy calls for a willingness to reduce the syllabus, to teach a 'little language' (in the sense of a mini-version of the native speakers' TL), an example being a mini English that makes do with six vowels rather than the usual 20 something. Then learning will materialize rather than error if the learners can be induced to make a learning effort that is directed towards a search for meaning. Learners should not be required to produce the TL before they have had 'maximum receptive experience', which sounds like a plea for the recognition of the silent period. Error will be avoided in some instances by full contextualization of the TL form being taught. And recall or memory errors will be kept manageable if efficient ways are encouraged of storing and accessing TL forms when needed.

The main argument in favour of prevention was that if erroneous forms are learnt, these will first have to be unlearnt before the correct ones can be learnt. This is not true however. Gatbonton (1983) shows that right and wrong forms can coexist side by side in Interlanguage, giving it its characteristic **variability**. It is not the case that the learners use either the right or the wrong form, each exclusive of the other. It is more a case of helping the learners to retain the right while rejecting the co-occurring wrong form.

Error prevention by **overlearning** was the preferred strategy of the Behaviourists, whose ideas so influenced the audio-lingual approach to FL teaching, giving rise to the intensive use of structure drills. Drills provide intensive practice, and it was assumed that practice makes perfect and that perfect meant error-free. What is the contemporary view? It is that we learn from our mistakes, when we test our hypotheses about the TL, and when we receive direct negative evidence after making an error. This stance, taken to its logically absurd conclusion, would suggest that the more errors we make the faster we will learn, since we shall thereby be able to test out more of our hypotheses more quickly and get more of that valuable direct negative evidence. A more moderate assumption would be that we need not invest so much effort in error prevention, since error commission is not irreversible. Two recent studies have investigated this assumption that wrong learning has to be unlearnt.

Ehri, Gibbs and Underwood (1988) set up a series of learning experiments in which the experimental groups of EL1 children and adults were required to 'invent' spellings before being given a chance to study the correct spellings, while a matched control group were allowed to study correct spellings before being tested. A comparison of the test results showed that 'making spelling errors neither hindered nor helped subjects learn correct spellings' (Ehri *et al.*, 1988: 240). We conclude then that prevention is not better than cure. Nor is cure necessarily better than prevention, however. But when prevention has not worked, or not been attempted, and errors are being committed, then there must be cure, in the form of correction (as we have defined it). A second finding from the work of Ehri, Gibbs and Underwood is that delaying correction of misspelled words by even a day allows these 'inventions' to take a foothold in the learners' minds: correction must be *immediate*, certainly carried out before the erroneous forms can enter learners' long-term memory store. One of the 'explanations' for error offered in this paper is noteworthy: the idea that learners resorted to misspelling 'only when they could not remember correct spellings' (Ehri *et al.*, 1988: 244). This is a **strategic** concept of error-making based on the idea that when problems of language performance arise, the learners have to resort to alternative, secondary resources in order to cope.

The suggestion that we learn by making errors is the basis for the second study. In two papers by Tomasello and Herron (1988, 1989) the idea is explored that if we were to induce error-making by leading learners astray or 'up the garden path' into committing errors, we would be doing them a favour. These two papers report experiments in which L1 English learners were encouraged to make certain common types of French FL error so that they could be 'systematically' corrected by the teacher supplying the correct form immediately upon hearing the error. That was the experimental condition, which was contrasted with a control condition that involved the teacher trying to forestall the students' error-making: cure (experimental condition) is being compared with prevention (control condition). Two such experiments were conducted, the first (1988) one involving **intralingual** overgeneralization errors within French, the second involving L1 transfer (that is, **interlingual** overgeneralization) errors into the L2 French. In both studies the learners who had been led up the garden path, and who had consequently committed errors, and had then received immediate correction, performed significantly better than those whose potential errors the teacher had attempted to forestall. Prevention had not been as effective as cure therefore. A part explanation for this might be Reiss (1981: 122), who reported that learners whose cognitive style favours 'broad category width', which makes them tend towards generalization, are on the whole more successful FL learners: in the light of the 'garden path' studies it may be the case that the success of these learners depends not simply on their generalizing tendency, but on their being corrected on the spot. The reasons for the relative effectiveness of correction after commission compared with attempted prevention of error will be discussed presently, but first let us deal with the second broader issue related to that of error correction: that about the usefulness of teaching.

Is teaching effective?

For some years it has been fashionable to reject grammar teaching, or, as it is technically called, **Explicit Formal Instruction** (EFI), as being at best ineffectual and at worst an obstacle to L2 learning (Krashen, 1982; Prabhu, 1987). In fact, much of the research on the effectiveness of instruction makes reference to the relative persistence of error in learners' production, irrespective of whether they have or have not received instruction. Researchers like Dulay, Burt and Krashen (1982), who subscribe to the universal order of acquisition theory, claim that teaching cannot alter the **order** of acquisition of TL items, and so is a waste of effort. However, Pavesi (1986) for one has shown that even though the order of acquisition is not altered by teaching, the **rate** of learning is. In addition, instructed learners (adults especially) demonstrate higher ultimate achievement. These differences are surely desirable, and if correction is part of teaching (which it is) then correction is efficacious. Similarly, Pica (1984) compared the production – the errors in particular – of learners who had or had not received formal instruction, establishing that taught learners tend to produce errors of redundancy: they oversupply grammatical morphology. This is error, but it carries a bonus: this oversuppliance has the effect of inhibiting the development of pidginized forms of IL, pidginization being characterized precisely by its omission of morphology (Schumann, 1978). A second, related, positive effect according to Harley (1993: 245) of 'a code-focused L2 instruction', which must imply correction of error, is that it brings about **defossilization**. Now fossilization is desirable only when it is TL features (accurate forms) that have fossilized. Unfortunately, erroneous forms fossilize too, and improvement is blocked. Unblocking this route to improvement is essential for Harley, who emphasizes the importance of teaching that addresses seriously the 'barrier-breaking principle'. Error correction, surely, addresses this principle head-on.

Opposition to error correction seems to have been based mainly on evidence that it does not work with children acquiring the L1 (because they have too little language awareness to benefit), and does not work in untutored L2 acquisition contexts. The reason why it does not work in such contexts is probably that it does not occur there. But both of these contexts are irrelevant to the classroom practice of error correction, where the effect upon learning is considerable. Carroll, Roberge and Swain (1992) taught French nominals ending in -*age* (*le badinage*) and -*ment* (*le remerciment*) to two groups, one experimental and the other a control, and found that the group that had received corrections did considerably better, even in the long term, than the control group.

Views are now changing slowly and subtly. Long (1991: 44) claims that it was the teaching of **forms** that he was against, not the teaching of **form**, which he champions. It is now conceded that EFI does have an effect on production accuracy, though the effect is delayed: 'formal instruction appears to lead to acquisition only indirectly and after a delay' (Fotos, 1993: 387). It can be useful in the process of self-monitoring: 'Instruction can improve accuracy in careful, planned speech production' (Ellis, 1990: 151). Likewise, as we have seen, error correction (or direct negative feedback) is considered to be effective (Chaudron, 1988: 179).

In initial literacy teaching the concept of **reading readiness** is well established: each child reaches a maturational stage where he or she is ready to learn to read. Pienemann's (1985) **teachability hypothesis** proposes something analogous for TEFL. Grammatical structures are graded on a scale of processability. This may look like a replay of the natural order hypothesis, but Pienemann insists it is not: it differs from that hypothesis in that it does not 'predict that instruction has no influence on acquisition' (1985: 370). In fact, teaching a structure at the point of readiness has been shown (Doughty, 1991) to have positive effects on the speed of learning, the frequency with which the relevant rule is applied (and therefore the level of accuracy attained), and the range of linguistic contexts where the right rule is applied.

And finally, Ellis (1995a) has suggested that it is wrong to associate grammar teaching exclusively with the improvement of *active* production in the L2. He advocates 'interpretation-based grammar teaching'. He bases his arguments in the first instance on the success recorded in **receptive learning**, for example Total Physical Response (Asher, 1986) in which the emphasis is on perception rather than production. Production (in the form of practice) he contends, can encourage error by forcing premature production. Reception, on the other hand, allows scope for noticing.

Noticing seems to be getting rediscovered. Magnan (1979) describes her **Focus Approach** to FL teaching, an approach that closely links correction and 'receptive' noticing. Learners are exposed right from the outset of their course to fully formed sentences and are directed to 'focus on' [read 'notice' here] the part of the sentence that is to be learnt – receptively. The items to be noticed in this way are presented in a sequence corresponding to the order in which each is to be learnt for active use. This order corresponds also to the order in which they are to be corrected.

As Ellis (1995a) observes, grammar teaching can help develop **explicit** L2 knowledge or **learning**, which can be utilized in monitoring. It can also facilitate the **intake** of unknown features of the L2 grammar by bringing about **noticing**. Noticing is very important, so much so that Ellis categorically states: 'No noticing, no acquisition' (1995a: 89).

In addition to studies of the correcting behaviours of teachers, there have been studies of NSs in contact with second language learners in what we would call 'acquisition' contexts. Day, Chenoweth, Chun and Luppescu (1983) is one such study, for which 36 EL2 students in the USA were asked to tape-record the out-of-class conversations they had with their American NS friends. The corrective moves thus recorded in their informal encounters were counted and classified for the study. It was established that the NSs corrected barely 9 per cent of all the 189 errors committed, and the errors they most corrected were errors of fact and discourse, not of grammar. The ways NSs corrected their foreign friends was thus similarly motivated to those used with children by mothers. There is no reason to draw pedagogical conclusions from either sort of 'naturalistic' observations, however. Friends are friends, whose time together is meant to be enjoyed, not put to good use. The observation that friends do not correct learners' errors at leisure and play certainly does not imply that teachers likewise should desist from correcting pupils' errors in classrooms.

There is more clarity surrounding the arguments that favour correction. Let us list these:

First, correction works. Fathman and Whalley (1990) report the compared effects of correcting grammar, content, both grammar and content, and neither, in EL2 student compositions. Correcting **grammar errors** universally (for every student and every composition) brought about improvement of the grammar of rewrites and at the same time led to a 44 per cent improvement on content expression.

Secondly, learners want to be corrected, as several studies show. Cathcart and Olsen (1976) showed that students want their **oral** errors to be corrected. In a complementary study on EL2 student writers, Leki (1991b) likewise found that 100 per cent of these wanted all their written errors corrected. Now, learners may be wrong in their expectations that correction will bring about improvement, but why should we choose to ignore learners' feelings about correction when we are urged to take these into account in other domains of FL learning?

Thirdly, there is no evidence that correction adversely affects learning cognitively, that is, correction – provided it is not miscorrection – does not lead to misunderstanding and mislearning. There is a suggestion, associated with Krashen's (1982) **affective filter hypothesis**, that correction can raise learners' levels of anxiety, and that this impedes learning. But an alternative and equally plausible hypothesis might be that an optimal level of affect, in the form of 'arousal', is necessary for learning to take place. After all, consciousness, awareness, and any form of noticing of language is a sign of taking note, or arousal, and these are all thought to be beneficial.

Fourthly, a point related to the previous is that the type of risk-taking learners that Seliger (1977) called **high input generators** will readily self-correct, while the careful planners, the **low input generators**, will not. The latter, if Krashen is right, have higher affective filters, which will inhibit improvement. If they neither self-correct nor receive teacher correction, they could be doubly disadvantaged.

Fifthly, correction is essential in those cases where the language processing task is difficult, since in such cases the learners will be unable to self-correct. Task difficulty is determined by the distance between the learners' current level of comfortable processing capacity and the level required by the task they must now perform or the text they must process. If the distance is minimal, or if the procedures are routinized, the learners will have spare capacity for self-observation and self-correction. Where the distance is great, and the learners have insufficient proceduralized routines to draw upon, the teacher will need to offer corrective assistance.

Sixthly, the previous point relates again to the error:mistake distinction, that is, to the **status** of the deviance in the learners' production. The greater the amount of revision required of the learners to correct a deviance, the less rigorous should be the teacher's inclination to demand it – by eliciting correction. Thus, if the deviance has the status of a mere slip, nothing more than a raised eyebrow should be necessary to signal its existence to the learners; in the case of a mistake, the teacher has to prompt the learners to alter their hypothesis; in the case of an error, some remediation is necessary in the form of extra or new teaching, to induce the learners to restructure their knowledge of the point in question.

The previous point about the need for the teacher to weigh the cost of intervention in terms of the processing requirements for correction – Zipf's Law of Least Effort in Correction – could be rephrased in terms of the gravity of the error. If the error is grave – in any of the ways outlined in the previous chapter – then its claim for correction effort is stronger than if it were a minor error.

Finally, foreign language learners need more correction than second language learners. As we have shown, SL learners get surprisingly little in the way of direct or explicit correction from their NS friends: only about 9 per cent of their errors are corrected (Day *et al.*, 1983). On the other hand, SL learners have more access to indirect evidence, since the language they hear around them is contextualized and meaningful. FL learners have little exposure to indirect evidence, positive or negative, so need direct negative evidence in abundance to compensate.

Gee talks of people who 'choose to acquire a language just to carry out a limited array of tasks in a foreign setting, all the while accepting their status as an outsider' (1990: 171). These are *foreign* language learners, or perhaps even more specifically, learners of the language for 'special purposes'. He suggests that such learners will want only **functional** control of the TL and a degree of accuracy that makes that possible. Their output need only be corrected as far as it is unintelligible or bizarre. *Second* language learners, by contrast, who often want to be integrated into the TL community, will not settle for mere functional correction: they will want even 'sociolinguistic' correction, informing them of the infelicities in politeness, directness, or appropriacy of their output. Gee (1990) goes on to suggest that only NSs will be capable of giving the sorts of corrections that SL learners require, while FL learners will get adequate correction to their needs from teachers who are not NSs of the TL. As we saw in Chapter 7, NS and NNS teachers of FLs have different priorities for correcting, largely determined by their different perceptions of error gravity.

It would, however, be perverse to ignore the force of evidence against all forms of intervention, be they preemptive teaching, feedback, correction or remediation. Sheppard (1992) reviews the many studies, spanning some 25 years, of the options for teacher intervention on error, which lead him to conclude that 'the various types make little difference; indeed the use of any type at all may not be worth the effort' (1992: 104). Sheppard himself compared the effectiveness of giving coded error correction of student EL2 writing and merely asking for clarifications. The latter is not form-focused but meaning-focused and only the former constitutes correction. The resultant improvements in grammar were virtually the same for both groups, while, surprisingly, the group that only received clarification requests made more improvement on punctuation. We can only conclude that there is still uncertainty over the effectiveness of correction.

Having defined correction and identified a number of its subtypes, and having decided that on balance correction is not uniformly futile, we can proceed to the methodological question of **how** best to do correction.

How to do error correction: some options and principles

1. *Correct effectively*

This means two things: use correction techniques that bring about improvements in accuracy and use techniques that are efficient, in the sense of requiring the least effort to carry out by the teacher and to register by the learners. Robb, Ross and Shortreed (1986) compared four types of feedback on the EL2 writing of 134 Japanese students. The four types were ranged along a scale of **salience**, which corresponds both to 'explicit' (as in explicit formal instruction) and to ' form-focus'. Group A had their *formal* errors in their compositions corrected but not the errors of fact or content: this was the most 'salient' feedback. Group B received coded feedback that indicated *what* needed to be corrected but not *how*. Group C had uncoded feedback: a marker pen indicated *where* there was an error but without any indication of its nature. Group D had 'marginal' feedback, showing only *how many* errors there were on any one line, but indicating neither their precise location nor their nature. The effects of these four types of feedback on the students' writing over a two-year treatment period were not differentiated by their relative ' salience'. One must conclude that making feedback more overt, direct, salient, or explicit is not worth the effort and 'time may be more profitably spent responding to more important aspects of student writing' (Robb *et al.*, 1986: 91). However, this is too sweeping a statement, and I believe that the relative effectiveness of different feedback types will depend on individual differences and on some group factors such as the learners' level of attainment in the FL. This means correction must be subject-sensitive.

2.   Correction should be sensitive

Native speakers' spontaneous correction of learners is, as we have seen from the Day, Chenoweth, Chun and Luppescu (1983) study, parsimonious. But what little correcting is done by NS friends seems to be effective and, above all, sensitively executed. And they stay friends. Two sorts of correction dominate: **focused correction** and **confirmation checks**. Of all the 189 corrections, 125 were focused corrections, involving the NS supplying the correction in an utterance fragment with declarative (falling) intonation. Here is an example of a focused correction:

> Learner: *Then you say what *number it is.*
> NS friend: *What √letter . . .*

To do a confirmation check, the NS produces a corrected version of the learner's incorrect utterance with question (rising) intonation:

> Learner: **How do you do on weekends?*
> NS friend: *√What do I do on weekends?*

Both these corrections are form-focused, but the important point is that they are face-saving and do not embarrass the learner. The learner, or an eavesdropper, is free to interpret the correction as being incidental, and not likely to disrupt the message. They are treated as slips (as defined in Chapter 3), suggesting that the NS believes the learner knows these forms but was momentarily distracted. The Affective Filter is not raised, and the learner is in a position to note the error and avoid it at the next opportunity. The crucial point is that correction should be **non-threatening**. Now the most palatable non-threatening form of correction is self-correction or any sort of correction that appears to be self-initiated. In oral work, therefore, the teacher should try to extend the **wait-time** between hearing the pupils' erroneous utterances and they themselves correcting them. Given an extra second or two, accompanied by a slightly disapproving or puzzled gesture on the teacher's part, and the pupil will often be able to self-correct, with little or no loss of face. Walz (1982) claims that learners can self-correct between 50 per cent and 90 per cent of their own errors (read 'mistakes'), given time and encouragement. Extending wait-time is advocated by Holley and King (1971) and by Chaudron (1988). Of course, advocating a few seconds of wait-time does not contradict the principle that feedback should not be delayed, established by Ehri, Gibbs and Underwood (1988). An only slightly more obtrusive move by the teacher is **pinpointing** error, that is, repeating it with focused emphasis, lengthening a segment of the utterance or a questioning tone, as in *He is A (?) teacher.* Pinpointing in this way was found by Chaudron (1988: 145) often to trigger self-correction. The problem is that the low-proficiency learners might not spot the local lengthening and interrogative intonation and consequently might take this corrective repetition as accepting and confirming their own version.

Another way non-threatening correction can be achieved in class is for the correction to be aimed at the whole class rather than singling out individual students and making an example of them, as if they were a wrongdoer in the pillory. When the individuals are made an example of, it is likely that they will benefit less than the other pupils in the class, who hear the correction only incidentally. Raabe (1982) has coined the phrase **spectator hypothesis** to account for this phenomenon, which is part of a wide-ranging set of insights made over recent years into what has come to be called 'incidental learning'. For the same reason – to minimize threat to face – it is advisable whenever possible to engineer correction to be peer correction rather than teacher correction. To be corrected by one's classmates is relatively palatable, like being corrected by one's NS friends, as in the Day, Chenoweth, Chun and Luppescu (1983) study mentioned above. Edge (1989: 53–5) gives useful advice on organizing peer correction in groups, whole-class correction and even correction competitions.

As for the correction of spoken errors, the more sensitive the learner, the more gentle should be the correction. But there might be a price to pay for this gentleness. If we enquire why it should be the case that the relatively insensitive, extrovert risk-taker is the better FL learner, it may be because this is the sort of learner who can stomach correction, and that in the terms used by Vigil and Oller (1976), feedback is not effective unless it has palpable affective force, no matter what the strength of its cognitive impact.

There is a common but unwarranted assumption that feedback on writing must be written and that correction of spoken errors must itself be oral. It has been suggested that if one wishes to avoid oral feedback on oral error, one should resort to finger indications of error (Rixon, 1993: Unit 10). It is, however, possible to cross modalities, to give written feedback on spoken errors the pupil has been noticed making. This can take the form of a few well-chosen illustrations of the usage the pupil has been finding difficult: specific evidence to be perused at leisure. One can also give spoken feedback on written errors. Written feedback on written work is less traumatic, but many students ignore it anyway. **Conferencing** is one way to personalize feedback on writing: the students meet with the teacher to hear the teacher's reactions to their writing. More interesting still are the possibilities of giving oral (audio-taped) feedback (ATF) on students' written errors, a practice that developed organically with distance learning programmes as a way of personalizing correspondence with the student. Boswood, Dwyer, Hoffman and Lockhart (1993) report a year-long experiment involving four ESL teachers and 200 students at the City University of Hong Kong. The ATF given was of two sorts: **formative** (aimed at bringing about improvement) and **summative** (justifying award of a grade). Teachers' and students' attitudes to ATF were generally positive, particular value being seen in the personalization of the treatment, the wide range of comments recorded, and the chance to listen to them repeatedly. The more sensitive students found it less face-threatening than conferencing.

A fast-developing computer technology offers a further way to make correction less traumatic, by desocializing it, that is, delivering it in a private rather than a social context. This is the **text editor**. These are standard software appendages nowadays on PCs, in the form of spell-checkers, grammar-checkers, and style-checkers. Granger and Meunier (1994) assess these facilities in the light of ESL/EFL users' needs, taking two commonly used text editors – *Correct Grammar* and *Grammatik 5* – as prime examples. The first limitation they point out is that text editors are designed to correct NSs' errors, and learners' errors are very different, and are often passed over by the editor. However, as we saw in Chapter 4, there is work in progress on corpora of learner English which will specify more rigorously the nature of learners' errors. The grammar-checkers are still crude, moreover, detecting only about half the errors committed. For example, both the programmes reviewed by Granger and Meunier failed to detect error in the following:

A teacher*s has come to see you.
I will *sold it in January.

*My luggage *are really heavy.*
*What *an yacht!*
*Too *much problems have arisen.*

They conclude that a good EFL text editor must be based on authentic learner errors. This is itself sufficient justification for anyone to do EA.

3.   Match correction to student preferences

Students' preferences for certain types of correction cannot be ignored of course. Nor should they be put on a pedestal, because they are not necessarily more effective for being preferred.

Some research exists on students' preferences among the various feedback options on their writing. Leki (1991b) is a 'preliminary exploration' of ESL students' preferences for some feedback options in this modality. She established that, rightly or wrongly, these students expected their teachers to mark their errors in grammar, spelling, vocabulary and punctuation, and 70 per cent of the 100 students expected *all* their errors to be corrected. As to *how* they wanted to be corrected, they reported that they 'wanted their teachers to show where the error was and to give a clue about how to correct it' (1991b: 207). Note they did not want the teacher to write in the correction, but preferred to solve the correction problem themselves: they were not looking for the easy way out, but expected to have to work in order to improve.

Another study of learners' preferences in types of feedback on their writing is Hedgcock and Lefkowitz (1994), a study that at the same time looked for any differences in preferred feedback between ESL and EFL writers. The assumption is that for EFL students, composition is a form of language practice, so they will expect or even welcome teachers' focus on accuracy. ESL writers, on the other hand, view writing as a means of communication, so will most value functional and content-oriented correction. This was borne out by the data, which indicated 'high concern among ESL subjects for matters of content, rhetorical structure, and writing style' (Hedgcock and Lefkowitz, 1994: 157) while 'FL subjects displayed response norms which were distinctly form-focussed' (ibid.).

As for students' preferences for feedback on their spoken errors, a useful study is Kaufmann (1993). He administered questionnaires to teachers and students of EL2 in Puerto Rico and Turkey containing descriptions and examples of 12 types of feedback on spoken errors ranged on a scale from explicit to implicit. Explicit correction moves are defined as 'those where the teacher directly informs the student that he has made an error' (1993: 2). Examples of explicit corrections of the erroneous *I*go to the bank yesterday* are **negate and provide**, as in 'Don't say go, say went'; **provide in context** as in 'I went to the bank'; and **supply the rule** as in ' "Go" is the present tense'. Implicit correction took on forms such as **accepting** as in 'Really? Did you make a deposit?'. The two sorts of error investigated were grammar errors such as wrong tense, and pronunciation errors. The questionnaire responses revealed that while teachers preferred to give implicit corrections, students preferred to receive explicit ones. Kaufmann followed this questionnaire with another enquiring how learners feel that non-teacher interlocutors (friends, colleagues, employers) should respond to their EL2 spoken errors. The main finding was that overlooking the erroneous form was an acceptable behaviour 'among friends'. From teachers, on the other hand, they expected corrections.

4.   Two-stage correction

In the preceding two sections we have addressed the question of how best to do correction. Reading the research literature on correction, one forms the impression that teachers must choose between formal and functional focus in correcting. For example, Prabhu (1987: 63), describing the Bangalore ELT Project, insisted that correction must be content-focused 'taking care to exclude any sustained attention to language itself, which would have resulted in a reduction in the focus on meaning' (Prabhu, 1987: 63). In actual fact, as Beretta (1989) showed by analysing transcripts of 21 lessons taught in the Bangalore Project, quite a large percentage of form errors (65 per cent) were corrected by key teachers; by comparison they corrected 88 per cent of content errors. This dichotomization reflects the parallel one for teaching: with the discrediting of the form-focused audiolingual approach in favour of the function-focused communicative approach, teachers saw themselves as having to choose either the one or the other. I believe such exclusivity is unnecessary, and exposes a misunderstanding of audiolingualism, where form-focus was the first step (at the practice phase) and function-focus followed this in the production phase. We might appropriately call his **two-stage** approach to initial teaching. The question is: could we take a parallel two-stage approach to error correction?

Levenston (1978) proposes that students' erroneous output – their composition errors in particular – are not one remove, but two removes from the NSs' version. He thus challenges Corder's (1981) claim that the data of EA are 'two sentences: the idiosyncratic sentence [produced by the learner] and a well-formed sentence [that which the native would have produced]' (Corder, 1981: 22). These two sentences would then be compared. This is not the case, however. The data of EA comprise not two but **three** sentences: (i) what the learners said; (ii) what they were attempting to say; and (iii) what the NSs would have said (or written). Levenston's genius is in his realization that these three must also figure in error correction. Let us call what the learners say their **composition**. What they were trying to say is its **reconstruction**. What the NSs would have said with the same communicative goal is the **reformulation** of that reconstruction.[1] Reconstruction involves putting the grammar right – there is form-focus therefore. Reformulation involves what I shall call the **naturalization**, which is quite the converse of 'nativization', which involves the introduction of nonnative elements into an originally native text. Levenston sees naturalization as something that happens when we 'rationalise the paragraphing, remove obscurity and ambiguity, iron out infelicities, and generally try to turn it into a reasonable essay' (1978: 5). Notice that naturalization involves just the sorts of improvement that native-speaking writers, who are ideally at least knowers of their language, find difficult but have to edit-in to their compositions (Davies, 1991a). In the case of FL/SL writers, many of these improvements will involve the removal of L1 features that have been 'negatively' transferred. Here is an illustration of two-step correction. *marks errors in the composition that are corrected in the reconstruction while $ marks infelicities in the reconstruction that are smoothed out in the reformulation. The writer's L1 is Hebrew.

Composition: *Recently we heard about (*the) road accidents and the news (*weren't) good for us because the (*numbers) of casualties are (*growing up) every year and the people who have driving licences in Israel (*also are) growing very quickly . . .*

Reconstruction: *Recently we ($heard) about road accidents and the news wasn't good ($for us) because the number of casualties is ($growing) every* *year and ($the people) who have driving licences are also increasing very quickly . . .*

Reformulation: *We have recently been hearing about road accidents, and it has not been good news: the number of casualties is increasing year by year, and the number of people in Israel who have driving licences is also growing rapidly . . .*

This stepwise approach to correction should recommend itself to applied linguists, who have stressed that learning takes place a bit at a time, and that learners will learn (and correct) their output according to a fixed programme that gradually approximates their knowledge to target norms: see our earlier reference to Pienemann's (1985) **learnability theory**. Focus must be on form if correction is of misformations. Notice that the two stages in this correction procedure are not equitably balanced between 'formal' and 'functional' foci: at each step focus is on form.

Noticing error

We referred above to the suggestion, most recently made by Ellis (1992), but by others before him, that grammar teaching should be less immediately concerned with accurate production, and more with helping learners to **notice** TL forms receptively. Once the learner starts **noticing**, learning starts to take off. Language test designers have always known that noticing enhances performance on tests, in fact to an unacceptable degree: so they include dummy items in a test to conceal its true focus. The methodological correlate to this distinction drawn between production and noticing is to be found in the options of **practice** and **consciousness raising** (CR). Ellis (1992) sees CR as being a straight alternative to practice: 'Whereas practice is primarily behavioural, consciousness-raising is essentially concept-forming' (1992: 234). In other words, practice is for improving performance (by proceduralizing knowledge), while CR is for inculcating cognitive structure or competence. What they have in common is that both involve isolating some feature of language as an object for focused attention. Practice requires **actional** attention in performance, while CR calls for 'intellectual effort to understand the targeted feature' (Ellis, 1992: 233). CR is, in a sense, mediating direct positive evidence by saying to the learners 'Look, this is how it is in the TL!'. Practice and CR have different purposes: practice is supposed to improve performance, that is, to enhance implicit knowledge, while CR is supposed to improve explicit knowledge of the L2. Practice is to be used in initial teaching, CR in correcting. Now explicit knowledge has generally been assumed by modern methodologists, such as Krashen, to be of limited use to the learner: there is no **interface** between it and implicit knowledge. It can only be put to use in monitoring. But there has always been a lingering hope that CR will facilitate the mastery of **implicit** knowledge. There is an assumption that each piece of explicit knowledge has a corresponding piece of implicit knowledge, and that the learners, having accessed this knowledge in its explicit form, will find the connection to its implicit correlate. CR has certain other desirable features: it appears to have durability: 'Once consciousness of a particular feature has been raised through formal instruction, learners continue to remain aware of the feature and notice it in subsequent communicative input' (Ellis, 1992: 238). Another advantage that explicit knowledge has (making it quite distinct from acquisition) is that learning it is not 'developmentally constrained', which means that there is no fixed order in which it must be learnt: it can be learnt and taught in any convenient order.

Fotos (1993) did an experiment involving noticing. She hypothesized that noticing would be induced to different degrees by two sorts of teaching: teacher-fronted formal instruction, and doing grammar tasks in groups. So she gave two matched groups of learners grammar-noticing opportunities under these two conditions in order to find out which way is the more effective. The grammar points in question were adverb placement, indirect object position and relative clause position. Students were given texts and asked to underline 'anything which they considered special or noteworthy' (Fotos, 1993: 400). She found that both types of instruction increased noticing by the learners when compared with a control group that had not been encouraged to notice. She also found no significant differences in the noticing rates of the two experimental groups. In other words, traditional teacher-fronted grammar work is as effective as setting group tasks to promote noticing. This research, I suggest, puts the teacher back into the classroom. Of course it does not give teachers a licence to *lecture* to their class on grammar.

Now, what comes after noticing? According to Fotos, after the learners notice the feature in the input, 'an unconscious comparison is made between existing linguistic knowledge, also called interlanguage, and the new input' (ibid.: 386). Now, as I have pointed out here and elsewhere (James, 1990; James, 1994a), making a comparison between IL and TL forms is none other than Error Analysis. The way learning proceeds is by learners doing their own Error Analyses, something that learners are naturally inclined to do but often need teacher guidance in doing effectively. As Bourke puts it: students are 'keen to bridge a perceived "grammar gap" in their learning of English' (1992: 2). Ellis has something similar in mind: 'intake is enhanced when learners carry out a second operation – comparing what they have noticed in the input with what they currently produce in their own output' (1995b: 90). He coins a phrase for it: **'cognitive comparison'** (ibid.: 94). Clark (1982) used the term **coordination** to refer to the phenomenon, observed in L1 acquisition, whereby children gradually bring their own production more and more in line with what they hear, by bridging the gap between input and output. Snow (1977: 154) suggests we learn by becoming conscious of what we do not know, while for Klein (1986: 138) the 'matching problem' is fundamental to FL learning. Matching is what determines 'what learners consciously notice' for Schmidt (1992). Self-correction, or editing, or monitor use are all error-analytical activities based upon noticing.

There is a difference between cognitive comparison, as for example Schmidt (1992) conceives of it, and EA, which is this: when I do cognitive comparison, I first notice a linguistic entity in the TL, and then ask myself 'How do I say that? What is my IL version of this?'. But when I do EA I proceed in the converse direction: I say 'I have just expressed something in a certain way, and been informed (or myself feel) that it is the wrong formulation. Therefore I must take note of the correct formulation when it is used by the teacher, a NS, or the writer of the book I am reading in the TL.' It is not just preferable but necessary in this paradigm that the forms learners are encouraged to notice and the cognitive comparisons they are asked to make are based on their own recent learning experience, particularly where that experience is negative. This is the practice of other disciplines and Wheeler (1977), for example, suggests basing remedial maths teaching on what he calls the 'anatomy of a failure'. As Prabhu puts it, the act of noticing in FL learning should be 'self-initiated, that is, not planned, predicted, or contrived by the teacher' (1987: 76). Rutherford makes the same point with 'It is obviously best if what is to be judged emanates from learner production itself and is embedded in the original context' (1987: 161).

Ellis suggests further that cognitive comparison will be promoted by asking learners to correct typical errors of the learner group to which they belong, which usually means they have a shared L1. One such text for 'translation' by the learners into TL English came my way in Portugal. Here is a small segment of it, with the deliberate errors asterisked:

> My name*s Jorge Marques and I *have 26 years. I was born *at Lisbon *in May the *twelve 1955. My parents hadn't much money so we *all *were living in a small flat which *it was very crowded as we *were seven. None of my sisters *have spent much time in this place as we left when they *are still *quiet young. We *have lived there *during ten years ... and then we *must move to Coimbra where *was my father*s work ...

Shaughnessy tackles the problem of learner 'subjectivity', referring to the fact that 'all writers have difficulty seeing [noticing] what they have written with objective eyes' (1977: 182). As we observed earlier, one is myopic to one's own mistakes. She recommends as an exercise to 'immerse students in passages dense, even grotesque, with misspellings' (ibid.: 182). She calls this **double-spell** and here is an example:

> When I travel I pefur a plain to a care. I tak a first glass flight, have a good diner, and relax my mine wile I watch the clouds go buy and here the quite hum of the plain, which hasn't stoped yet wile I've been abored.   (ibid.: 182)

An obvious weakness of such exercises is that not every single learner in a class or group has committed all of the errors that are exposed. Those who have not made any or many of the errors might object to or be bored by the exercise.

Now, some might object that exposing learners to printed errors, produced by themselves or their peers, is risky: they might learn the erroneous forms and fail to learn, or even unlearn, the correct ones. Reviewing Clausing's *German Grammar* (1986), Alter objects to 'the pedagogically unsound practice of printing sentences full of mistakes' since 'the student is bound to remember them' irrespective of 'a tiny black asterisk prefacing them' (1986: 426). I am, however, unaware of any experimental evidence supporting this view. There are strong arguments against it. Corder is much in favour of using **negative instances** in teaching since:

> A concept is achieved partly through the illustration of what is *not* an example of the concept, that is, through *negative instances.* . . . There is a strong argument in favour of the controlled use of examples of incorrect forms so long as these are correctly labelled as such.
>   (Corder, 1973: 293)

Correction exercises are now commonplace in teaching materials: for example, Sexton, Williams and Baddock (1985: 116ff.) and Hall and Shepheard's *Anti-Grammar Grammar Book* (1991) both have error-spotting exercises based on 'negative models' that can be done as group-work activities. Similarly, Rinvolucri (1984) has a cluster of 'grammar games' that involve learners in discussing and passing judgement on sets of erroneous sentences they have produced themselves. The pupose of these exercises is to develop criteria for degrees of deviance. I have never found using these exercises to lead to an increased incidence of error.

Noticing what one knows: language awareness

I would like to say one more thing about learners as analysts. When they compare their IL version with the TL version and see a discrepancy, they are assuming the role of Error Analysts. But they can also assume the role of Contrastive Analysts. This comes about when they compare their NL version with the TL version and notice the discrepancy or the incongruence between these two. There is a good deal of evidence that this happens. In this connection I have proposed, elaborating a suggestion made by Hawkins (1984), a way of distinguishing the two concepts of **Language Awareness** (LA) (James and Garrett, 1991) and **Consciousness Raising**. They are usually treated – I think wrongly – as if they were synonyms. I suggest that LA is a learned ability to analyse one's own repertoires – be they in the L1 or in that part of the TL that one has learnt so far; it is about 'implicit knowledge that has become explicit' (Levelt *et al.*, 1978: 5). 'Consciousness' as in the term CR, refers to getting explicit insight into what one does not yet know implicitly of the L2. So LA is for knowers and CR is for learners (see James, 1994a: 209–13). LA is brought about by **explication**, while CR is the result of **explanation**. Grammars explicate, rather than explain, which is a key to why it is that grammars are most useful to knowers but of very little use to learners. Learners do not need explication but explanation, which is best mediated by teachers and teaching materials.

A lucid example and proof of how LA of the L1 can solve problems of FL learning is to be found in Roulet (1980). He describes the occasion when his daughter was having a problem with making sense of Latin *cum* ('with'). Her problem could not be satisfactorily accounted for in terms of her ignorance of Latin, but ultimately had to be referred to her low level of awareness of the corresponding preposition *avec* in her French L1. Another example is from Gomes da Torre (1985). He notes that some advanced learners of EL2 in Portugal make errors which they would not make if they knew Portuguese 'better', or, in this case, if they knew a 'better' (standard) Portuguese. The error in question reflects directly the learners' nonstandard native language (NL) grammar:

Just now [*why not thinking] of visiting London? is derived from
Ja agora [porque não pensando] em visitar Londres?

We are not saying that people ought not to speak nonstandard dialects of their NL: that is not the point at all. The point is that people should be **aware** of the forms they use in their NL, and in their preferred dialect of that NL. Such awareness would refine their insights into the NL and at the same time allow them to monitor its transfers into the FL.

Now bringing together what one does and does not know I call **Interfacing**. French didacticians (Bourguignon and Dabène, 1983) in Grenoble have been developing *l'enseignement grammatical intégré*, which is based on L1:L2 interfacing. Classical CA would assume that the English learner of German as an L2 would have a problem distinguishing the German conjunctions *sondern* and *aber*, since *but* stands for the two: we seem to have a case of **divergent polysemy**:

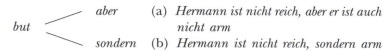

This need not be so, as Ducroit (1978) shows: there are in English not one but two *but* words (call these but_1 and but_2), having distinctive meanings and syntaxes.

(a) *Hermann ist nicht reich, sondern arm.*
(b) *Hermann ist nicht reich, aber er ist auch nicht arm.*

Compare:

(c) *He's not rich (,) but₁ poor.*
(d) *He's not rich, but₂ not poor either.*

These two are semantically distinct: *but*₁ corrects a misconception, while *but*₂ is concessive. Furthermore, they are different syntactically: *but*₁ requires Pronoun + Aux ellipsis:

(e) *He's not rich, but₁ *he is poor.*

but *but*₂ does not require this ellipsis:

(f) *He's not rich, but he's not poor either.*

English learners of German need to raise their awareness of their English for the L2 problem to be solved. If they do, they will be in a position to 'interface' L1 and the L2. Such interfacing could be conceived in terms of using the relative 'transparency' of the FL form to reduce the 'opacity' of the L1, which then makes the L2 seem to the learners to be less exotic, redundant and difficult. Interfacing would be improved if L1 and L2 teachers collaborated more, or, better still, if teacher training were less dichotomized so that the teacher of L1 was also the teacher of the L2: we need teachers with two linguistic strings to their bow.

Such interfacing of the L1 and the TL is a form of CA that is enacted in class. Its purpose becomes clear when we ask: what do we have to make a special effort to notice in the TL? Here, the notion of **markedness**, discussed in Chapter 4, comes back into the picture: we need to make special provision for what is marked in the TL. This means those forms and features that are less in evidence, less usual, less frequent. Unless these are somehow singled out as worth noticing, they will pass unnoticed. Some proof that childen learning the L1 learn easiest the unmarked forms frequently used by their parents is to be found in Larsen-Freeman's analysis of the input data of the three childen whose early language development was logged by Roger Brown (1973). Now the single most obvious candidate for noticing in FL learning is those TL forms susceptible to interference from similar L1 forms. These are the forms that bear such great similarity to one another that the difference between them does not normally get noticed by the learner. Jackson's definition of interference makes this clear:

> Interference is a largely unconscious process and appears to operate mainly in respect of the less obvious differences between languages. That is to say, gross differences, which are quite obvious to the

learner, tend not to interfere with a learner's performance in the second language and thus do not cause errors.

(Jackson, 1987: 101)

It follows that Contrastive Analysis CR must concern itself with revealing to the learner, or preferably, showing the learner how to notice unaided, the elusive, subtle – in a word **contrastive** – differences between L1 and L2.

Rules and the role of corrective explanation

In the previous section we drew a distinction between explanation and explication, claiming that while explication is useful to knowers, explanation is what learners want. Learners who are asked to evaluate their teachers often refer to the good teacher as someone who can 'explain' the TL and its difficulties clearly. If explanation is perceived as a sign of good teaching (James, 1994a; Kennedy, 1996), it must also be a sign of good correcting of error. Leki found that students preferred corrective moves by their teachers that 'direct students to a grammar handbook for an explanation of the error' (1991b: 208). To the extent that this prevents future commission of that same error type, it qualifies as remediation. Let us be clear about what 'explanation' means here. What it does not mean is **diagnosis**: it is not a question of making clear to the learners **why** they have produced a wrong form, but in what way their IL version is different (or deviant) from the target form. Explanation is, in effect, comparative description: quite simply EA. Furthermore, explanation, as Furey (1977: 9) stresses, anticipating Ellis, improves the learner's chances of **pattern recognition** (noticing) rather than pattern production. The implication is that once noticing occurs, learning will follow automatically. But it will initially be receptive learning, which will have to be converted by practice into productive control. Mistakes call for practice, but errors call for explanations, which will induce the learners to adjust their mental representation of the language item in contention. For Cook (1988: 61) explanation is another form of evidence: explanatory evidence.

I would dispute Johnson's (1996: 121) assertion that FL teachers have developed techniques for handling errors but not techniques for handling mistakes. By techniques for handling errors he presumably means linguistic descriptions of the FL. I believe that descriptions, even those labelled 'pedagogic' grammars, have been singularly unhelpful to learners to date. The probable reason is that they are too closely related to the linguists' grammars they are derived from: they lack accessibility to learners, and only make explicit to knowers what they already know tacitly. They are explications rather than explanations.

This raises the question of how explanations aimed at learners are to be formulated. In a book on expert systems Sell (1985: Ch. 7) suggests there are three types of explanation: **interpretive**, which elaborates on the terms used; **descriptive**, which describes the typical processes with which a thing is associated; and **reason-giving**, telling why such is the case. Furey (1977) suggests that every explanation has three components: the **formal** analysis of the entity being explained; its **functional** analysis; and its **lexical clarification**, which I assume to be its meaning. The most obvious way to explain, though, is in terms of 'rules' or generalizations. Rules are not in fashion, neither in linguistics nor in language teaching. Nevertheless, they are immensely useful if they are based on the learners' genuine observation of language data and formulated in metalanguage the learners are comfortable with. Littlewood (1975) points out that to be effective explanations must do two things: first, they must give the learner 'insight into the structure of the sentence he is [sic] using'; secondly, they must show the learner 'how this structure relates to other structures in the overall system' (1975: 92). These could, taken together, be a perfect definition of CR activity! There is some evidence that knowing rules enhances accuracy: Hulstijn and Hulstijn (1984) showed that learners of L2 Dutch who were able to verbalize certain rules of Dutch grammar had higher accuracy in performance than students who could not. Explanations should avoid complexity of formulation. Shaughnessy (1977: 177) suggests that rather than try to combine in one proposition all the conditions for a rule's application, it is better for the learner to 'follow a sequence of instruction'. When it assumes this form, the rule ceases to be rule-like and becomes a decision-tree or **algorithm**. For example, the learner who wishes to make a future time reference in a simple declarative must make the following decisions in the order given to arrive at the correct grammaticization:

1. Is your belief that the event will happen just based on your irrational intuition? If so, use WILL + Infinitive. Or are there

visible indications that it will? This will yield the speculative *He'll be Prime Minister one day* as distinct from *Labour have 74% of the vote: Tony is going to be Prime Minister.* If neither . . .
2. Do you wish to convey the idea that the future event has been fixed by someone? If not, use GOING TO + Infinitive. If neither . . .
3. Has a higher agency fixed the future event? If so, use PRESENT SIMPLE. Or has the doer fixed it him/herself? If so, use PRESENT PROGRESSIVE. This distinguishes *He takes his exam on 22 July* (it is so ordained) from *He is taking his driving test on Friday* (he has decided to).

These decisions can be deployed on a branching tree-diagram.

A less technical mode of explanation is the bilingual text. I do not mean 'parallel' L1 and TL texts, but a mixed text which code-switches between the two languages. An example written for L1 German speakers wishing to learn or to reactivate their EL2 is Werner Lansburgh's *'Dear Doosie': Eine Liebesgeschichte in Briefen.* Here is a short excerpt:

1 Ich biete nämlich keinem Menschen in der Welt mehr eine Zigarette an. With
2 other people, I keep my smoke strictly to myself, und zwar KONSEQUENT –
3 letzteres Wort möchte ich bitte von Ihnen auf englisch haben, und zwar
4 gleich hier, auf der Punktlinie, on the dotted line – also bitte KONSEQUENT
5 = ... [This is the dotted line: CJ]
6 Nein, nicht 'consequently', das wäre etwa 'somit' oder 'folglich', sehr böses
7 Deutsh-Englisch wäre das, nennen wir es fortan 'Denglisch' . . .

Here we have an instance of skilful explanation. First, the topic is contextualized: I don't pass cigarettes round, and *strictly* (line 2) is presented as indirect positive lexical evidence. Now the reader is asked for a translation of *konsequent*, which is equated with *strictly*: this is consciousness raising of the lexical equivalence. The instruction to write 'on the dotted line' turns the reader into a student taking a cloze test. Next (line 6), there is anticipation of error, since *consequently* is, for German learners of English, a notorious **false friend**: *don't say this*! or the provision of direct negative evidence. Fail to take this into account and the outcome will be barbarism in the form of Deutsch–Englisch or *Denglisch* for short. Apart from the code-switches here, there are what we could call **function switches**: switches from metalinguistic to epilinguistic functions.

Notes

1. Interestingly, van Wijk and Kempen (1987) also argue along similar lines that there are two mechanisms for repairing error: 'lemma substitution', when changes are made while retaining the same syntactic structure (corresponding to Levenston's (1978) **reconstruction**, and 'reformulation' (in the same sense as Levenston), meaning recasting the intended message in a new syntax.
2. I am grateful to Robert Cooper in Tampere for his insights on these data.

9

A Case Study

'Just do It'
(Name of a sports shop in Bangor High Street)

There exists an **algorithm** for doing Error Analysis that was originally proposed by Corder (1971, 1981) and subsequently elaborated
by Levelt (1977). By 'algorithm' is meant simply the specification
of the set of procedures you need to carry out, together with a
statement of the best order to follow, to perform a complex operation. Our representation of the 'phonetic route' to spelling in
Chapter 5 was in algorithmic format. The complex operation we
attempt to encapsulate now is doing an EA. In this final chapter
we shall set out the algorithm (Figure 9.1, page 269) and test it
against a small corpus of errors extracted from a text provided by
one learner of EL2. It is intended that the reader should undertake
this guided exercise against the background of information and
argument presented in the preceding eight chapters of this book.

Elicitation and registration

Step 1 is the **elicitation procedure** outlined in Chapter 1. In the
present instance, no formal elicitation was necessary, since the data
were volunteered in the form of an unsolicited letter of enquiry
in EL2 sent by a Brazilian (L1 Portuguese) student of language
whose identity has been concealed for ethical reasons. Since what
we have is an untargeted or 'broad trawl' sample, this will probably
be a prelude to a targeted elicitation of data pertaining to some
especially interesting aspects of this writer's English. The letter was
typed and is reproduced here exactly as received, but with anonym-
ity added in, and line numbers added for ease of reference:

Sao Paulo , 2nd July 1986 , Brazil .

1   Mr. Dr. Carl james :
2   My name is Santa Claus . I am psychologist and student of linguistics and
3   oriental languages . There is longtime ago I am very interested in Walsh lan-
4   guage . So , I am writing these missive for asking whether you promote
5   courses of Walsh (at the University College of North Wales , or by correspond-
6   ence, like the Open University of London) for non-english speakers.
7   I want to express myself desirous of maintain correspondence with all
8   walshmen interesteds in doing it .
9   Grateful for any assistence you can give me ,

       (Santa Claus)

Not only are we spared the trouble of doing an elicitation, but each utterance has been registered for us by its writer in its context. This includes both the surrounding language or **cotext** as well as the context of **situation** in which the letter was written. We can therefore move directly to step 3 and ask ourselves whether the letter is wholly 'normal', by which we mean does it conform to the **norms** of standard written English. 'Normal' is thus a kitemark of grammaticality, while 'usual', through its associations with language use, is a test of acceptability. Clearly this is not the case, and so we can proceed to ask where and in what respects the text is not 'normal'. This involves splitting the text into its constituent parts, which we have labelled 'utterances', but in a non-technical sense of the term. The whole letter is a composite utterance, but it is constituted of smaller segments: these we might call 'minimal' utterances, sentences, clauses, phrases – and we shall make use of these categories presently.

Error identification

We have a choice of which direction to follow in our description and analysis: either **top>down**, moving from discourse to substance, or the converse **bottom>up**. The choice is usually immaterial, but there are grounds for preferring top>down when describing receptive processing, and bottom>up when giving an account of the user producing utterances.

1. Substance-level errors

Beginning at the level of **substance** (in this case written), we identify deviances in the **spelling** and the **punctuation**. The few misspellings are: lower case *<j> in the proper name *James* (line 1) and the nationality adjective *english* (line 6); the consistently thrice-repeated *<a> in *Walsh*; and <*assist*ence*> in line 9. As for punctuation, some would object to the use of the colon (rather than comma) after the salutation. The misdivision across lines *lan-guage* (line 3), and the converse failure to divide *longtime* (line 3) suggest ignorance of punctuation. The remaining mispunctuations reflect the writer's poor typing skills, as he usually leaves two spaces before and after stops and commas. The parentheses on lines 5 and 6 are overinclusive: the opening bracket should be positioned between '*correspondence*' and '*like*'.

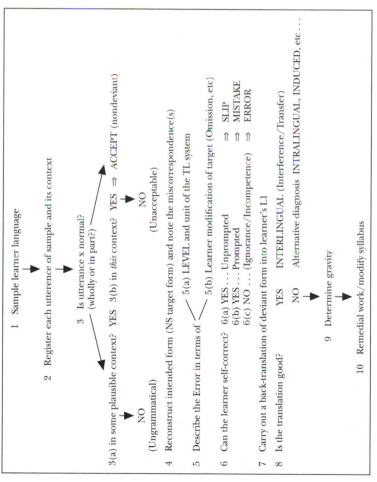

Figure 9.1   Algorithm for Error Analysis (adapted from S.P. Corder, 1981: 23)

2.   *Level of grammar*

Turning now to the text-level errors of **ungrammaticality**, there are many instances, some very challenging to analyse:

- On line 2: *I am Ø/√a psychologist* . . . is an error of **omission** of the grammatical formative indefinite article. This is required with noun phrase intensive complements indicating profession or nationality. But what then is the status of the next NP . . . *student of linguistics?* Here, since the NP is the second of two coordinated NPs, the indefinite article is optional: *a student* and *Østudent* are both well-formed options here. But the crucial question is: did this learner **intend** to use the zero article Ø, or is he consistently failing to supply an article, as he did with the first NP? Is this an error, or is it well-formed by pure chance? Or is it a **concomitant** error (see page 116), being the consequence of the writer having omitted the article from the first NP *psychologist?*

- On line 3, **There is longtime ago* . . . is a **global** error that reconstructs either as *√For a long time* . . . or as *√It is a long time since.* . . . There is **misselection** of grammatical elements used to indicate the point in past time when an ongoing state or activity began. There is a tense misselection *I *am interested* for the target *I √have been interested* on the same line: the present perfect in standard English is a marker of the semantic feature [current relevance] since he is still interested in Welsh.

- *in *Walsh language* is analysable as a **blend** error, resulting from the conflation of two grammatical options *√in Welsh* and *√in the Welsh language*. As is always the case with blends, an alternative wrong combination could have arisen: *√in the Welsh*. Note that the latter potential blend would not have been ungrammatical: it would simply have not been usual (acceptable) in this context (criterion 3b in the algorithm). Indeed, it could be argued that there are contexts where our writer's error *in Welsh language* would be acceptable: contexts such as *He's taking courses/exams √in Welsh language, not Welsh literature.*

- On line 4 there is misselection of an NP constituent: the plural demonstrative **these* for the intended singular *√this*. Another misselection on this line is of the verb phrase (VP) constituent: the gerundive **for asking* has been selected instead of the infinitive *√to ask*. This error is replayed in reverse on line 7, the infinitive (*of*) *maintain being misselected for the required gerund (*of*) √*maintaining*.

- The overinclusion of the plural -s suffix on the adjective *interesteds (line 8) is interesting, but one can do little more than speculate about the systematicity and productivity of this sort of error on the basis of this one incidence of it. Here is a case therefore for further targeted and lateralized elicitation of samples bearing on this feature.
- We have on line 9 a text-grammar error involving the misselection of the anaphoric cohesion marker . . . *in doing* *it, which refers to the antecedent *maintain correspondence*. The authentic marker here would be either *that* or *so*, and the latter could appear either before or after the verb: thus . . . *in so doing/* . . . *in doing so*.

3. Lexis-level errors

In our sample there are four interesting errors on the text-level of lexis:

- The use of the preposition head *ago in place of √*since* or √*for* (line 3) is a lexical **misselection**.
- Consider another lexical misselection:*missive (line 4) for √*letter*. The *Concise Oxford Dictionary* defines missive as either 'a letter from sovereign to dean and chapter nominating a person to be elected bishop' or 'letter: esp. official one or (joc.) long or serious one'. Clearly, in the context of our letter none of these meanings of *missive* is intended. Its use here is certainly not jocular. There are contexts where it would be appropriate, but this is not one of them: so it is a lexically unacceptable misselection, violating sense-relations.
- ?*promote courses* (line 4) and ?*maintain correspondence* (line 7) are **collocation** errors. They are 'strange' (Allerton, 1990) word combinations, despite which the writer's intended meanings (in this situational context at least) are totally clear. However, 'promoting' courses does convey the unintended idea of some courses being given preferential treatment, while to 'maintain' correspondence suggests prolonging correspondence that was initiated some time ago. In (British) English, institutions *offer* courses and individuals *conduct* correspondence.

4.   Discourse-level errors

First, we ask whether the letter is 'normal' and 'usual' in the sense of conforming to the conventions (in this case recorded in many manuals for secretaries and other letter-writers) of the written **genre** letter (Bhatia, 1993). Or are some of the conventions for letter-writing in English flouted? Since these are questions about the rhetorical or generic felicity of the text in question, we are thus dealing here with **discourse** errors. We do indeed find errors of this nature. First, in terms of **layout**. The sender's postal address (or **letterhead** or **originating address**), to which a reply would be sent, is omitted. Its vestige, showing the origin of the letter (*São Paulo, Brazil*), is mispositioned, being placed at the top left of the page, whereas it should be properly positioned at the top right. The addressee's address (or **inside address**), which should be at top left, is totally omitted. As to the position of the date, this is misordered relative to the sender's address, as well as being mispositioned on the page. Now consider the **salutation**: '*Dear*' is omitted, while there is redundancy (overinclusion) of *Mr.* as well as *Dr.* The usual English practice is to use one of these, but not both. And finally, another genre infelicity is the failure to sign off with a '*Yours (sincerely)*': omission of the conventional speech act at the discourse level. We might classify this in terms of the types of **infelicity** suggested by Austin (1962). There he refers to **misinvocations** (ibid.: 17) as those speech-act failures that occur when there exists in the TL culture no 'conventional procedure' for doing something: for example, the absence in English of the conventional procedure executed with *bon appétit!* in French, or that signalled by *de nada* in Spanish. Austin's example is a misinvocation of the utterance *I divorce you*, said to a wife by a husband in a Christian (non-Muslim) country. It would not have the intended effect, though of course it would not be without effect either! The case of our letter from Brazil is rather different: there does exist a convention (the **complimentary close**) in the TL English literacy culture, but the writer has failed to invoke it where he should: it is therefore a case of **omission** at the discourse level. Alternatively, staying within Austin's system, one might say that the writer has made a **misexecution** of the entire letter by this omission. The letter is flawed by this omission.

A mirror-image discourse error, not an omission but a **redundancy**, occurs on the first line of the body, where the writer commits the infelicity of introducing himself explicitly by name. This is not standard practice (not usual) in the English letter genre. In fact, it is viewed as an infringement of the generic conventions. On opening a letter, one usually first glances at the bottom to find the signature to see who has sent it, before reading on. Again, we must decide whether to categorize the error as a misinvocation or as what Austin calls a **misexecution**.

We should include errors of **style**, which we define in terms of the language being appropriate (or not) to the formality conventions reflecting the status relations between speakers. This letter is required to be somewhat formal, it being between complete strangers and in the professional domain, rather than being of a personal nature. It makes certain demands or **impositions** on the recipient, for example to reply, to make necessary enquiries, to send the information requested. Overall, it succeeds quite well in striking the appropriate style, except for the sign-off ?*Grateful for any assistance....* The ellipsis of the antecedent *I shall/would be...*, making it casual, almost chatty, in style strikes a dissonance with the general tone of the letter.

Categorizing the errors

We have reached step 5 in the algorithm, having elicited, identified, isolated and described the main deviances in the letter from Brazil. At this point we can begin to make use of a chart which clearly displays the errors we have identified and described the nature of. The chart could be usefully employed for purposes of **profiling**.

Note the areas of the chart in which most entries have been registered: this particular learner's errors mainly involve **misselection**, which suggests that he has accumulated a considerable repertoire for English, and is seldom at a loss to express himself, without however falling victim to verbosity. His English is generally **ill-defined**, in the sense that he has not yet defined the grammatical and semantic boundaries of his stock of English. Some noticing and focusing activities are called for.

Status: error or mistake?

We have now reached step 6, where the question arises whether this learner could have self-corrected, with or without prompting.

LEVEL / MODIFICATION	SUBSTANCE	TEXT		DISCOURSE
	Phonology Graphology Spelling Pronunciation	GRAMMAR	LEXIS	COHESION COHERENCE GENRE-FIDELITY FELICITY
		RANK: Clause-Phrase-Word-Morpheme. CLASS: Noun, Verb, Adjective, Adverb, Preposition, Conjunction, etc.	SENSE RELATIONS COLLOCATIONS	
OMISSION		*∅/a psychologist (2)		COMPLIMENTARY CLOSE INSIDE ADDRESS
OVER-INCLUSION		interested*s (8)		SELF-INTRODUCTION (2) Mr + Dr in salutation (1)
MISSELECTION	*:/√, in SALUTATION (1) *j/√ʃ (ames) (1) *e/√E in <English> (6) *a/√e in <Welsh> (3,5,8)	*There is . . . /√It is (3) *am/√have been . . . (3) *these/√this (4) *for asking/√to ask (4) doing *it/√so (9)	*ago/√since (3) *missive/√letter (4) *promote/√offer (4) *maintain/√conduct (7)	Ellipted 'Grateful for' (9)
MISORDER	lan-guage (3) *longtime (3) *(. . .) (5)			MISPOSITIONED ORIGINATING ADDRESS
BLEND		*in Walsh language (3–4)		

Figure 9.2 Profile of errors in the letter from Brazil. (Numbers in brackets indicate line numbers).

It is on this basis that we shall determine the epistemic status of each deviance. The author not being available to submit to the necessary tests, we must resort to other, less reliable, means to make this sort of decision. **Consistency** is one such check, and we have enough evidence, in the form of the thrice-repeated misspelling with the vowel <a> in **Walsh* to conclude that he is convinced that this is the right spelling, and does not even hesitate to consider alternatives. Note that the misselection of **<a>* for √<e> is limited to the lexical item *Welsh*, and he does not, for example, write <stud*ant> for <stud√ent>. Similarly, he seems to be operating on the basis of a rule that nouns naming languages take initial capitals, hence √*Walsh* (twice). In his system these contrast with the adjective, which he believes takes the small initial as in **walshmen* and *non-*english speakers*. His punctuation is also consistent: he types two spaces before and after every stop and comma except one. In fact, the one time he gets it right (the comma after *correspondence* (line 5)) might be regarded as a happy accident or a **slip**, thanks to which he gets it right just once, against his better judgement.

Diagnosis

Steps 7 and 8 lead us into **diagnosis** of the errors identified. Back translations into his L1 (Portuguese) are very revealing. In the salutation, the dual-inclusion of *Mr.* and *Dr.* is certainly congruent with the Portuguese convention of using both: *Senhor Doutor* ('Mr. Dr.') as a form of address. The omission of the indefinite article before *psychologist* (line 2) similarly could be a transfer from L1 *Sou √Øpsicologo e aluno de linguistica*, since in Portuguese such NP complements do not require articles.

Likewise the global error connected with expression of the semantics of 'current relevance' and 'commencing point of time in past' in line 3 is very suggestive of L1 transfer, since Portuguese uses the present tense verb form here, and the time adverb itself is congruent with the literal translation *Hà muito tempo*: 'there is much time'. The form *ago* looks like an attempt to incorporate a half-learnt or half-remembered bit of English: such a combination of the L1 form (*hà*) with part of the TL form (*ago*) is a complex **bilingual blend**.

One could make a strong case for the overincluded plural -s suffix on *interested**s (line 8) being a negative **transfer** from Portuguese: *todos os galeses interessad**os nisso. The L1 certainly seems to be activated at this point in our correspondent's composing. Getting right the Noun + Adjective order of *Welshmen interested* is quite an achievement, since it is a relatively 'marked' or rare order in English. In Portuguese, by contrast, this order is the commonest. The postnominal position of the adjective is doubly licensed: lexically, that is by an idiosyncrasy of the adjective in question; and syntactically, by virtue of being followed by the prepositional phrase . . . *in doing it*. Again, it is not unreasonable to suggest that he is right by chance on this rare occasion but would usually be wrong.

Very interesting is the misselection of the plural demonstrative form *these for √*this* on line 4. It is interesting because it is an example of the descriptive and the diagnostic categorizations according to linguistic levels being at variance. Descriptively, the error is to be located on the level of **grammar**, in the number system of the noun phrase. Diagnostically however, in terms of its causes, it is a **phonology** error. The English 'long' and 'short' vowels [i:] and [I] are phonetic confusibles for the Portuguese learner, whose '*mills*' become '*meals*' and whose '*wheels*' become '*wills*'. Relying on sounding as a guide to his spelling, the writer hears himself say [ði:z] for intended 'this', so spells it phonetically. The error of grammar has phonological origins.

As for **alternative diagnoses**, we could start with the pluralized adjective. While it is tempting to attribute this to the effect of L1 transfer, as we have, there is a case to be made for an intralingual diagnosis. One wonders whether this plural suffix is in some way **compensatory**, in the sense that the writer (mistakenly) believes that his *walshmen lacks a 'normal' plural suffix, so is making this good by suffixing one to the adjective. The writer is therefore operating with the handicap of a blind spot for the irregular plural formation on *men*; he is assuming regularity: it is an error of **regularization** therefore.

Clearer cases of English-based confusions are: the inclusion of *ago* on line 3, where he attempts to incorporate a form he recalls as being relevant to this sort of context. Then the confusion of the gerund versus infinitive options *for asking/√*to ask* (line 4) is probably a universal error of EL2 learners.

So much for the attempted analysis: it is suggestive, and we hope an eye-opener in places. In other places it is patently half-baked, and the main impression it leaves is of uncertainty and a lack of confidence: in a word, it is tentative. I see that as a challenge to persist with the elaboration and refinement of the whole apparatus of EA. I hope this book persuades its readers of the need for and worthwhileness of such a venture.

References

ABBOTT, G. 1980. 'Towards a more rigorous analysis of foreign language errors', *International Review of Applied Linguistics* Vol. 18 No. 2: 121–30.

ABBOTT, G. 1991. 'The English explosion: fission? fusion? or what?', *English A World Language* Vol. 1 No. 1: 17–22.

ABERCROMBIE, D. 1964. *English Phonetic Texts.* Faber and Faber, London.

ALBRECHTSEN, D., HENRIKSEN, B. and FÆRCH, C. 1980. 'Native speaker reactions to learners' spoken interlanguage', *Language Learning* Vol. 30 No. 2: 365–96.

ALEXANDER, L.G. 1994. *Right Word, Wrong Word: Words and Structures Confused and Misused by Learners of English.* Longman, London.

ALLERTON, D. 1990. 'Linguistically strange word combinations', in M. Bridges (ed.), pp. 109–20.

ALTER, M.P. 1986. Review of S. Clausing, *German Grammar: A Contrastive Approach.* Holt Rinehart, New York, 1986. In *Modern Language Journal* Vol. 70 No. 4: 426.

ANDERSON, J.R. 1983. *The Architecture of Cognition.* Harvard University Press, Cambridge, MA.

ANDERSON-HSIEH, J., JOHNSON, R. and KOEHLER, K. 1992. 'The relation between native speaker judgement of non-native speaker pronunciation and deviance in segmentals, prosody and syllable structure', *Language Learning* Vol. 42 No. 4: 529–55.

ANDERSSON, L. and TRUDGILL, P. 1990. *Bad Language.* Blackwell, Oxford.

ANDREASSON, A.-M. 1994. 'Norm as a pedagogical paradigm', *World Englishes* Vol. 13 No. 3: 395–409.

ANDREWS, S. 1996. 'Metalinguistic awareness and lesson planning'. Paper presented at the International Language in Education Conference, Hong Kong.

ASHER, J. 1986. *Learning Another Language Through Actions: The Complete Teacher's Guidebook.* Sky Oaks Publications, Los Gatos, CA.

AUSTIN, J.L. 1962. *How To Do Things with Words.* Oxford University Press, Oxford.

BAARS, B.J. (ed.) 1992a. *Experimental Slips and Human Error: Exploring the Architecture of Volition.* Plenum Press, New York.

BAARS, B.J. 1992b. 'The many uses of error: twelve steps to a unified framework', in B.J. Baars (ed.), pp. 3–32.

BAILEY, C.J.N. 1978. 'Native accent and learning English as a foreign language', *International Review of Applied Linguistics* Vol. 16: 229–40.

BAIN, R. 1991. *Reflections: Talking about Language.* Hodder and Stoughton, London.

BALDWIN, J. and FRENCH, P. 1990. *Forensic Phonetics.* Pinter, London.

BALLY, C. 1937. *Traité de Stylistique Française.* C. Winter, Heidelberg.

BANSAL, R.K. 1976. *The Intelligibility of Indian English,* Hyderabad, Central Institute for English as a Foreign Language and Educational Resources International Clearinghouse Report ED 177849.

BAXTER, J. 1980. 'How should I speak English? Americanly? Japanesely? or internationally?', *Japanese Association for Language Teaching Journal* Vol. 2: 31–61.

BEAUGRANDE, R. de and DRESSLER, W. 1981. *Introduction to Text Linguistics.* Longman, London.

BECKER, J. 1975. 'The phrasal lexicon', in B. Nash-Webber and R. Schank (eds), *Theoretical Issues in Natural Language Processing* Vol. 1. Bolt, Baranek and Newman, Cambridge, MA. pp. 70–3.

BELL, R.T. 1974. 'Error analysis: a recent pseudoprocedure in applied linguistics', *International Review of Applied Linguistics* Vols 25–26: 35–49.

BERETTA, A. 1989. 'Attention to form or meaning? Error treatment in the Bangalore Project', *TESOL Quarterly* Vol. 23 No. 2: 283–303.

BERTRAND, Y. 1987. 'Faute ou erreur? Erreur et faute', *Les Langues Modernes* Vol. 81 No. 5: 70–80.

BHATIA, A.T. 1974. 'An error analysis of student compositions', *International Review of Applied Linguistics* Vol. 12 No. 4: 337–50.

BHATIA, V.K. 1993. *Analysing Genre: Language Use in Professional Settings.* Longman, London.

BIALYSTOK, E. 1982. 'On the relationship between knowing and using linguistic forms', *Applied Linguistics* Vol. 3 No. 3: 181–206.

BIALYSTOK, E. and SHARWOOD SMITH, M. 1985. 'Interlanguage is not a state of mind: an evaluation of the construct for second language acquisition', *Applied Linguistics* Vol. 6 No. 2: 101–17.

BICKERTON, D. 1971. 'Cross-level interference: the influence of L1 syllable stucture on L2 morphological error', in G.E. Perren and J.L.M. Trim (Eds), *Applications of Linguistics: Selected Papers of the 1969 International AILA Congress.* Cambridge University Press, Cambridge. pp. 133–40.

BIRDSONG, D. 1992. 'Ultimate attainment in second language acquisition', *Language* Vol. 68 No. 4: 706–55.

BIRDSONG, D. and KASSEN, M.A. 1988. 'Teachers' and students' evaluations of foreign language errors: a meeting of minds?', *Modern Language Journal* Vol. 72 No. 1: 1–12.

BITTER, G., HATFIELD, M.M. and EDWARDS, N.T. 1993. *Maths Methods for the Elementary and Middle School: A Comprehensive Approach.* Allyn and Bacon, Boston, MA.

BLEY-VROMAN, R. 1983. 'The comparative fallacy in interlanguage studies: the case of systematicity', *Language Learning* Vol. 33: 1–17.

BLOOMFIELD, L. 1935. 'Literate and illiterate speech', *American Speech* Vol. 10: 44–59.

BOLINGER, D. 1980. *Language: The Loaded Weapon.* Longman, London.

BORSLEY, R.D. 1991. *Syntactic Theory: A Unified Approach.* Edward Arnold, London.

BOSWOOD, T., DWYER, R., HOFFMAN, R. and LOCKHART, C. 1993. *Audiotaped Feedback on Writing: Research Report No. 24.* English Department, City University of Hong Kong, Hong Kong.

BOURGUIGNON, Ch. and DABÈNE, L. 1983. 'Le métalangage: un point de rencontre obligé entre enseignants de langue maternelle et de langue etrangère', *Le français dans le monde* Vol. 177: 45–59.

BOURKE, J.M. 1992. 'The case for problem-solving in second language learning', *Occasional Paper No. 33*, Centre for Language and Communication Studies, Trinity College, Dublin.

BOWEN, J.D. and PORTER, D. 1984. 'The relative intelligibility of British and American English', *The TESL Reporter* Vol. 17 No. 1: 6–10.

BOYLE, R. 1996. 'Modelling oral presentations', *English Language Teaching Journal* Vol. 50 No. 2: 115–26.

BREMER, K., BROEDER, P., ROBERTS, C., SIMONOT, M. and VASSEUR, M.-T. 1993. 'Ways of achieving understanding', in C. Purdue (ed.), *Adult Language Acquisition: Cross-Linguistic Perspectives* Vol. 2. Cambridge University Press, Cambridge. pp. 53–195.

BREMER, K., ROBERTS, C., VASSEUR, M.-T., SIMONOT, P. and BROEDER, P. 1996. *Achieving Understanding: Discourse in Intercultural Encounters.* Longman, London and New York.

BRIDGES, M. (ed.) 1990. *On Strangeness.* Günther Narr, Tübingen.

BROWN, H.D. 1970. 'Categories of spelling difficulty in speakers of English as a first and second language', *Journal of Verbal Learning and Verbal Behavior* Vol. 9: 232–6.

BROWN, L. 1993. *The New Shorter Oxford English Dictionary on Historical Principles.* The Clarendon Press, Oxford.

BROWN, R. 1973. *A First Language.* Harvard University Press, Cambridge, Mass.

BROWN, P.P. and SCRAGG, J. 1948. *Common Errors in Gold Coast English: Their Cause and Correction.* Macmillan, London.

BURT, M. and KIPARSKY, C. 1972. *The Gooficon: A Repair Manual for English.* Newbury House, Rowley, MA.

BUZAN, T. 1974. *Use Your Head*. BBC Publications, London.

BYGATE, M., TONKYN, A. and WILLIAMS, E. (eds) 1994. *Grammar in the Second Language Classroom*. Prentice-Hall, London.

BYRAM, M. 1988. *Cultural Studies in Foreign Language Education*. Multilingual Matters, Clevedon.

CAMERON, D. 1994. 'Putting our practice into theory', in D. Graddol and J. Swann (eds), *Evaluating Language: Papers from the 1992 British Association for Applied Linguistics Meeting*. Multilingual Matters, Clevedon. pp. 15–23.

CARNEY, E. 1994. *A Survey of English Spelling*. Routledge, London.

CARRELL, P. 1982. 'Cohesion is not coherence', *TESOL Quarterly* Vol. 16 No. 4: 479–88.

CARROLL, S., ROBERGE, Y. and SWAIN, M. 1992. 'The role of feedback in adult second language acquisition: error correction and morphological generalization', *Applied Linguistics* Vol. 13 No. 2: 173–98.

CATHCART, R. and OLSON, J. 1976. 'Teachers' and students' preferences for correction of classroom conversation errors', in J. Fanselow and R. Crymes (eds), *On TESOL '76*. TESOL, Washington, DC. pp. 41–3.

CHAUDRON, C. 1988. *Second Language Classrooms*. Cambridge University Press, Cambridge.

CHOMSKY, N. 1965. *Aspects of the Theory of Syntax*. MIT Press, Cambridge, MA.

CHOMSKY, N. 1968. *Language and Mind*. Harcourt Brace Jovanovich, New York.

CHOMSKY, N. 1980. *Rules and Representations*. Blackwell, Oxford.

CHOMSKY, N. 1986. *Knowledge of Language: Its Nature, Origins and Use*. Praeger, New York.

CHRISTOPHERSEN, P. 1973. *Second Language Learning: Myth and Reality*. Penguin, Harmondsworth.

CILIBERTI, A. 1991. *Grammatica, Pedagogia, Discorso*. La Nuova Italia, Florence.

CLARK, E. 1982. 'Language change during language acquisition', in M. Lamb and A. Brown (eds), *Advances in Developmental Psychology*, Vol. 2. Lawrence Erlbaum, Hillsdale, NJ.

Cobuild English Grammar. 1990. Collins, London.

COHEN, A.D. Forthcoming. *Strategies in Learning and Using a Second Language*. Longman, London.

CONNOR, U. 1996. *Contrastive Rhetoric: Cross-cultural Aspects of Second-Language Writing*. Cambridge University Press, Cambridge.

COOK, V.J. 1988. *Chomsky's Universal Grammar: An Introduction*. Blackwell, Oxford.

COOK, V.J. 1991. *Second Language Learning and Language Teaching*. Edward Arnold, London.

COOK, V.J. 1992. 'Evidence for multicompetence', *Language Learning* Vol. 42 No. 4: 557–91.

COOK, V.J. 1993. *Linguistics and Second Language Acquisition*. Macmillan, Basingstoke.

COPPIETERS, R. 1987. 'Competence differences between native and near-native speakers', *Language* Vol. 63: 544–73.

CORDER, S.P. 1967. 'The significance of learner's errors', *International Review of Applied Linguistics* Vol. 5 No. 4: 161–70. Reprinted in S.P. Corder, 1981. *Error Analysis and Interlanguage*. Oxford University Press, Oxford. pp. 1–13.

CORDER, S.P. 1971. 'Idiosyncratic dialects and error analysis', *International Review of Applied Linguistics* Vol. 9 No. 2: 147–60. Reprinted in S.P. Corder, 1981. *Error Analysis and Interlanguage*. pp. 14–25.

CORDER, S.P. 1973. *Introducing Applied Linguistics*. Penguin, Harmondsworth.

CORDER, S.P. 1975. 'Error analysis, Interlanguage and second language acquisition (Survey Article)', *Language Teaching and Linguistics Abstracts* Vol. 8: 201–18.

CORDER, S.P. 1981. *Error Analysis and Interlanguage*. Oxford University Press, Oxford.

CORDER, S.P. 1983. 'A role for the mother tongue', in S. Gass and L. Selinker (eds), *Language Transfer in Language Learning*. Newbury House, Rowley, MA. pp. 85–97.

COULMAS, F. (ed.) 1981. *A Festschrift for the Native Speaker*. Mouton, The Hague.

COX, C.B. (Chairman) 1989. *English for Ages 5 to 11*. (Proposals to the Secretary of State for Education and Science and the Secretary of State for Wales.) Department of Education and Science, HMS. London.

CREWE, W.J. 1977. *Singapore English and Standard English: Exercises in Awareness*. Eastern Universities Press, Singapore and Kuala Lumpur.

CRUTTENDEN, A. 1981. 'Item learning and system learning', *Journal of Psycholinguistic Research* Vol. 10 No. 1: 79–88.

CRYSTAL, D. 1982a. *Profiling Linguistic Disability*. Edward Arnold, London.

CRYSTAL, D. 1982b. *An Encyclopaedic Dictionary of Language and Languages*. Edward Arnold, London.

DAS, B.K. 1978. 'An investigation of some advanced skills of composition', *Central Institute of English and Foreign Languages Bulletin* (Hyderabad) Vol. 14 No. 1: 42–62.

DAVIES, A. 1991a. 'Correctness in English', in M.L. Tickoo, (ed.), *Language and Standard: Issues, Attitudes, Case Studies*. RELC (Regional English Language Centre), Singapore.

DAVIES, A. 1991b. *The Native Speaker in Applied Linguistics*. Edinburgh University Press, Edinburgh.

DAVIES, E.E. 1983. 'Error evaluation: the importance of viewpoint', *English Language Teaching Journal* Vol. 37 No. 4: 304–11.

DAVIES, E.E. 1985. 'Looking at style with advanced EFL learners', *English Language Teaching Journal* Vol. 39 No. 1: 13–19.

DAY, R.R., CHENOWETH, N.A., CHUN, A.E. and LUPPESCU, S. 1983. 'Foreign language learning and the treatment of spoken errors', *Language Learning and Communication* Vol. 2 No. 2: 215–25.

DECHERT, H. and LENNON, P. 1989. 'Collocational blends of advanced second language learners: a preliminary analysis', in W. Oleksy (ed.), *Contrastive Pragmatics*. John Benjamins, Amsterdam. pp. 131–68.

DELISLE, H. 1982. 'Native speaker judgement and the evaluation of errors in German', *Modern Language Journal* Vol. 66 No. 1: 39–48.

DEYES, A.F. 1978. 'Textuality through translation', in G. Nickel (ed.), *Proceedings of the 4th International AILA (Association Internationale de Linguistique Appliquée) Congress 1975*. Hochschulverlag, Stuttgart. pp. 25–38.

DICKERSON, W. 1977. 'Language variation in applied linguistics', *ITL (Instituut voor Toegepaste Lingüistiek)* Vol. 35: 43–66.

DI PIETRO, R.J. 1971. *Language Structures in Contrast*. Newbury House, Rowley, MA.

DOUGHTY, C. 1991. 'Second language instruction does make a difference: evidence from an empirical study on second language relativization', *Studies in Second Language Acquisition* Vol. 13: 431–69.

DUCROIT, O. 1978. 'Deux mais', *Cahiers de Linguistique* Vol. 8: 109–20.

DULAY, H., BURT, M. and KRASHEN, S.D. 1982. *Language Two*. Newbury House, Rowley, MA.

ECKMAN, F. 1977. 'Markedness and the contrastive analysis hypothesis', *Language Learning* Vol. 27 No. 2: 315–30.

EDGE, J. 1989. *Mistakes and Correction*. Longman, London.

EHRI, L.C., GIBBS, A.C. and UNDERWOOD, T.L. 1988. 'Influence of errors on learning the spellings of English words', *Contemporary Educational Psychology* Vol. 13: 236–53.

ELLIS, R. 1985. *Understanding Second Language Acquisition*. Oxford University Press, Oxford.

ELLIS, R. 1990. *Instructed Second Language Acquisition*. Blackwell, Oxford.

ELLIS, R. 1992. *Second Language Acquisition and Language Pedagogy*. Multilingual Matters, Clevedon.

ELLIS, R. 1995a. 'Interpretation-based grammar teaching', *System* Vol. 21 No. 1: 69–78.

ELLIS, R. 1995b. 'Interpretation tasks for grammar teaching', *TESOL Quarterly* Vol. 29 No. 1: 87–105.

ERVIN, G.L. 1979. 'Communication strategies employed by American students of Russian', *Modern Language Journal* Vol. 63 No. 7: 329–34.

FÆRCH, C. 1978. 'Performance analysis of learner's language', in K. Gregersen (ed.), *Papers from the Fourth Scandinavian Conference on Linguistics*. Odense University Press, Odense. pp. 87–95.

FÆRCH, C. and KASPER, G. (eds) 1983. *Strategies in Interlanguage Communication*. Longman, London.

FÆRCH, C. and KASPER, G. (eds) 1987. *Introspection in Second Language Research*. Multilingual Matters, Clevedon, U.K.

FATHMAN, A.K. and WHALLEY, E. 1990. 'Teacher response to student writing: focus on form versus content', in B. Kroll (ed.), *Second Language*

Writing: Research Insights for the Classroom. Cambridge University Press, Cambridge. pp. 178–90.

FAY, D. and CUTLER, A. 1977. 'Malapropisms and the structure of the mental lexicon', *Linguistic Inquiry* Vol. 8 No. 3: 505–20.

FERGUSON, C. 1978. 'Multilingualism as an object of linguistic description', in B. Kachru (ed.), *Linguistics in the Sixties: Directions and Prospects*. Special Issue of *Studies in the Linguistic Sciences* Vol. 8 No. 2, University of Illinois, Urbana. pp. 97–105.

First Steps 1994. Longman Cheshire, Melbourne.

FISIAK, J., LIPINSKA-GRZEGOREK, M. and ZABROCKI, T. 1978. *An Introductory English–Polish Contrastive Grammar*. Panstwowe Wydawnictwo Naukowe, Warsaw.

FITIKIDES, T.J. 1936. *Common Mistakes in English*. Longman, London.

FOTOS, S.S. 1993. 'Consciousness-raising and noticing through focus on form: grammar task performance versus formal instruction', *Applied Linguistics* Vol. 14 No. 4: 385–407.

FOWLER, H.W. 1906. *The King's English*. Clarendon Press, Oxford.

FOWLER, R. 1969. 'On the interpretation of "nonsense strings"', *Journal of Linguistics* Vol. 5 No. 1: 75–83.

FRANCIS, G. 1994. 'Grammar teaching in schools: what should teachers be aware of?', *Language Awareness* Vol. 3 Nos 3/4: 221–36.

FREI, H. 1929. *Grammaire des Fautes*. Droz, Paris and Geneva.

FRENCH, F.G. 1949. *Common Errors in English: Their Cause, Prevention and Cure*. Oxford University Press, Oxford.

FREUDENSTEIN, R. (ed.) 1989. *Error in Foreign Languages: Analysis and Treatment*. FIPLV (Fédération Internationale des Professeurs de Langues Vivantes), University of Marburg, Marburg.

FRIES, C.C. 1952. *The Structure of English: An Introduction to the Construction of English Sentences*. Harcourt Brace, New York.

FUREY, P. 1977. 'The preparation of grammar explanations in the teaching of English as a second language', in H.D. Brown, C.A. Yorio and R.H. Crymes (eds), *On TESOL '77*. TESOL, Washington, DC. pp. 46–56.

GARRETT, P. and AUSTIN, C.G. 1993. 'The English genitive apostrophe: judgements of errors and implications for teaching', *Language Awareness* Vol. 2 No. 2: 61–75.

GASS, S.M. and SELINKER, L. (eds) 1983. *Language Transfer in Language Learning*. Newbury House, Rowley, MA.

GASS, S.M. and VARONIS, E.M. 1991. 'Miscommunication in nonnative speaker discourse', in N. Coupland, H. Giles and J.M. Wiemann, (eds), *Miscommunication and Problematic Talk*. Sage Publications, London. pp. 121–45.

GATBONTON, E. 1983. 'Patterned phonetic variability in second language speech: a gradual diffusion model', in B.W. Robinett and J. Schachter (eds), *Second Language Learning: Contrastive Analysis, Error Analysis and*

Related Aspects. University of Michigan Press, Ann Arbor, MI. pp. 240–55.

GEE, J.P. 1990. *Social Linguistics and Literacies: Ideology in Discourses.* Falmer Press, Brighton.

GEORGE, H.V. 1972. *Common Errors in Language Learning: Insights from English.* Newbury House, Rowley, MA.

GILES, H. 1970. 'Evaluative reactions to accent', *Educational Review* Vol. 22: 211–27.

GILES, H. 1979. 'Ethnicity markers in speech', in K.R. Scherer and H. Giles (eds), *Social Markers in Speech.* Cambridge University Press, Cambridge. pp. 251–89.

GLENDINNING, E. and MANTELL, H. 1983. *Write Ideas: An Intermediate Course in Writing Skills.* Longman, London.

GOMES DA TORRE, M. 1985. 'Uma Analise de Erros: Contribuição para o Ensino da Lingua Inglesa', unpublished PhD thesis, University of Oporto, Oporto, Portugal.

GOMES DA TORRE, M. 1986. 'Locally-orientated language courses', *Revista da Faculdade de Lettras* Series 2 Vol. 3: 115–26.

GRANGER, S. 1993. 'International Corpus of Learner English', in J. Aarts, P. de Haan and N. Oostdijk (eds), *English Language Corpora: Design, Analysis and Exploitation.* Rodopi, Amsterdam. pp. 57–71.

GRANGER, S. 1994. 'New insights into the learner lexicon: preliminary report from the International Corpus of Learner English', in L. Flowerdew and K.K. Tong (eds), *Proceedings of the Joint Seminar on Computers and Lexicology.* Hong Kong University of Science and Technology, Hong Kong.

GRANGER, S. 1996. 'Romance words in English: from history to pedagogy', in J. Svartvik (ed.), *Words: KVHAA Conference 36.* Almquist & Wiksell, Stockholm. pp. 105–21.

GRANGER, S. and MEUNIER, F. 1994. 'Towards a text editor for learners of English', in U. Vries and G. Tottie (eds), *Creating and Using English Language Corpora.* Rodopi, Amsterdam and Atlanta. pp. 79–91.

GRAUBERG, W. 1971. 'An error analysis in German of first-year university students', in G. Perren and J.L.M. Trim (eds), *Applications of Linguistics.* Cambridge University Press, Cambridge. pp. 257–63.

GREENBAUM, S. 1988. *Good English and the Grammarian.* Longman, London.

GREENBAUM, S. 1991. 'ICE: the International Corpus of English', *English Today* Vol. 28: 3–7.

GREENBAUM, S. and QUIRK, R. 1970. *Elicitation Experiments in English.* University of Michigan Press, Ann Arbor, U.S.A.

GRICE, P. 1975. 'Logic and conversation', in P. Cole and J. Morgan (eds), *Syntax and Semantics III: Speech Acts.* Academic Press, New York. pp. 45–68.

GUNTERMAN, G. 1978. 'A study of the frequency and communicative effects of errors in Spanish', *Modern Language Journal* Vol. 62: 249–53.

HALL, N. and SHEPHEARD, J. 1991. *The Anti-Grammar Grammar Book.* Longman, London.

HALL, R. 1950. *Leave Your Language Alone!* Linguistica, Ithaca, NY.

HALLIDAY, M.A.K. and HASAN, R. 1976. *Cohesion in English.* Longman, London.

HALLIDAY. M.A.K., McINTOSH, A. and STEVENS, P. 1964. *The Linguistic Sciences and Language Teaching.* Longman, London.

HAMMARBERG, B. 1974. 'On the insufficiency of error analysis', *IRAL* (*International Review of Applied Linguistics*) Vol. 12: 185–92.

HAMMERLY, H. 1991. *Fluency and Accuracy: Toward Balance in Language Teaching and Learning.* Multilingual Matters, Clevedon.

HARLEY, B. 1993. 'Instructional strategies and SLA in early French immersion', *Studies in Second Language Acquisition* Vol. 15 No. 2: 245–59.

HARLOW, H.F. 1959. 'Learning set and error factor theory', in S. Koch (ed.), *Psychology: A Study of a Science* Vol. 2. McGraw Hill, New York. pp. 492–537.

HARPER, D.A.L. 1962. 'Error Analysis', Diploma in Applied Linguistics dissertation, Edinburgh University, Edinburgh.

HATCH, E.M. (ed.) 1978. *Second Language Acquisition: A Book of Readings.* Newbury House, Rowley, MA.

HAUGEN, E. 1956. *Bilingualism in the Americas: a Bibliography and Research Guide.* American Dialect Society, University of Alabama, U.S.A.

HAWKINS, E. 1984. *Awareness of Language.* Cambridge University Press, Cambridge.

HAWKINS, J.A. 1987. 'Implicational universals as predictors of language acquisition', *Linguistics* Vol. 25: 453–73.

HEATON, J.B. and TURTON, N.D. 1987. *Longman Dictionary of Common Errors.* Longman, London.

HEDGCOCK, J. and LEFKOWITZ, N. 1994. 'Feedback on feedback: assessing learner receptivity to teacher response in L2 composing', *Journal of Second Language Writing* Vol. 3 No. 2: 141–63.

HELLIWELL, M. 1989. *Can I become a beefsteak?.* Cornelsen and Oxford University Press, Oxford.

HENNING, G.H. 1973. 'Remembering foreign language vocabulary: acoustic and semantic parameters', *Language Learning* Vol. 23 No. 2: 185–97.

HINDS, J. 1987. 'Reader versus writer responsibility: a new typology', in U. Connor and R.B. Kaplan (eds), *Writing Across Languages: Analysis of L2 Text.* Addison Wesley, Reading, MA. pp. 141–52.

HOCKETT, C.F. 1967. 'Where the tonge slips, there slip I', *To Honour Roman Jakobson: Essays on the Occasion of his 70th Birthday*: Vol. II Mouton, The Hague and Paris. pp. 910–36.

HOLDEN, C.L. 1960. *Written English at Secondary School Level in Sierra Leone.* London.

HOLLEY, F.M. and KING, J.K. 1971. 'Imitation and correction in foreign language learning', *Modern Language Journal* Vol. 55 No. 8: 494–8.

HONEY, J. 1983. *The Language Trap: Race, Class and the Standard English Issue in British Schools.* National Council for Educational Standards, Kenton, Middlesex.

HOSENFELD, C. 1977. 'A preliminary investigation of the reading strategies of successful and nonsuccessful second language learners', *System* Vol. 5 No. 2: 110–25.

HOWARD, G. 1992. *The Good English Guide.* Macmillan, London.

HOWARD, G. 1993. 'The state of the language', *The Author* Vol. 104 No. 3: 97–8, The Society of Authors, London.

HOWARD, Sir M. 1991. *The Lessons of History.* Clarendon Press, Oxford.

HOWARD, P. 1984. *The State of the Language.* Hamish Hamilton, London.

HUBBARD, E.H. 1989. 'Cohesion errors in the academic writing of second-language users of English', in J.B. Goedhals, M.H. van Zyl and M.A. Curr (eds), *English Usage in Southern Africa.* Vol. 20 No. 2: University of South Africa, Pretoria. pp. 1–19.

HUBBARD, E.H. 1996. 'Errors in court: a forensic application of error analysis', in H. Kniffka (ed.), 1996. *Recent Developments in Forensic Linguistics: Proceedings of the 3rd. Congress of the International Association for Forensic Linguistics.* Peter Lang, Frankfurt.

HUGHES, G.A. and LASCARATOU, C. 1982. 'Competing criteria for error gravity', *English Language Teaching Journal* Vol. 36 No. 3: 175–82.

HUGHES, G.A. and TRUDGILL, P. 1996. *Accents and Dialects of English* (3rd. edn). Edward Arnold, London.

HULSTIJN, J. and HULSTIJN, W. 1984. 'Grammatical errors as a function of processing constraints and explicit knowledge', *Languge Learning* Vol. 35: 23–43.

IBRAHIM, M. 1978. 'Patterns in spelling errors', *English Language Teaching Journal* Vol. 32: 207–12.

ISHIYAMA, K. 1982. *Common Japanese Mistakes in English: Over 600 Entries.* Jiyukokuminsha, Tokyo.

JACKSON, H. 1987. 'The value of error analysis and its implications for teaching and therapy – with special reference to Panjabi learners', in J. Abudarhan (ed.), *Bilingualism and the Bilingual*: An Interdisciplinary Approach to Pedagogical and Remedial Issues. Nelson for the National Foundation for Educational Research, Windsor and Philadelphia. pp. 100–11.

JACQUET, R.C. and PALERMO, L. 1990. 'Comprehending texts in small groups', unpublished manuscript, University of Delaware. Cited in A. Labarca, 1995 'Interactive testing: a dormant giant?', in J. Fernandez-Barrientos and C. Wallhead (eds), *Temas de Linguistica Aplicada.* University of Granada, Granada. pp. 169–91.

JAKOBSON, R. 1971. *Child Language and Aphasia.* Mouton, The Hague.

JAMES, CARL 1971. 'The exculpation of contrastive linguistics', in G. Nickel (ed.) *Papers in Contrastive Linguistics*, Cambridge University Press, Cambridge. pp. 53–68.

JAMES, CARL 1974. 'Linguistic measures for error gravity', *Audio-Visual Language Journal* Vol. 12 No. 1: 3–9.

JAMES, CARL 1977. 'Judgments of error gravities', *English Language Teaching Journal* Vol. 31: 116–24.

JAMES, CARL 1980. *Contrastive Analysis.* Longman, London.

JAMES, CARL 1990. 'Learner language', *Language Teaching* Vol. 23 No. 4: 205–13.

JAMES, CARL 1991a. Review of M. O'Malley. and A.U. Chamot, *Learning Strategies in Second Language Acquisition.* Cambridge University Press, Cambridge, 1990. In *System* Vol. 19 No. 3: 321–3.

JAMES, CARL 1991b. 'The "monitor model" and the role of the first language', in V. Ivir and D. Kalogjera (eds), *Languages in Contact and Contrast: Essays in Contact Linguistics.* Mouton de Gruyter, Berlin. pp. 249–60.

JAMES, CARL 1992. 'Awareness, consciousness and language control' in C. Mair and M. Markus (eds), *New Departures in Contrastive Linguistics* Innsbrucker Beiträge zur Kulturwissenschaft Vol. 2 Innsbruck University, pp. 183–98.

JAMES, CARL 1993. 'Accommodation in crosslinguistic encounters', *Papers and Studies in Contrastive Linguistics* Vol. 27: 39–48.

JAMES, CARL 1994a. 'Explaining grammar to its learners', in M. Bygate, A. Tonkyn and E. Williams (eds), *Grammar and the Language Teacher.* Prentice-Hall, London. pp. 203–23.

JAMES, CARL 1994b. 'Don't shoot my dodo: on the resilience of Contrastive and Error Analysis', *International Review of Applied Linguistics* Vol. 32 No. 3: 179–200.

JAMES, CARL 1996. 'Mother tongue use in bilingual/bidialectal education: some implications for Bruneian *Dwibahasa*', in G. Jones (ed.), *Bilingualism through the Classroom: Strategies and Practices.* Special Issue of *Journal of Multilingual and Multicultural Development* Vol. 17 Nos 2 and 4: 248–57.

JAMES, CARL and GARRETT, P. (eds) 1991. *Language Awareness in the Classroom.* Longman, London.

JAMES, CARL and KLEIN, K. 1994. 'Foreign language learners' spelling and proof-reading strategies', *Papers and Studies in Contrastive Linguistics* Vol. 29: 31–46.

JAMES, CARL and PERSIDOU, M. 1993. 'Learners and acquirers: compensatory strategy preferences', in J. Fernandez-Barrientos Martin (ed.), *Proceedings of the International Conference on Applied Linguistics* Vol. 1. University of Granada, Granada. pp. 344–59.

JAMES, CARL, SCHOLFIELD, P. and YPSILADIS, G. 1992. 'Communication failures in persuasive writing: towards a typology', in A. Athanasiadou and R. Parkin-Gounelas (eds), *Yearbook of English Studies* Vol. 3. pp. 174–93, The Aristotle University of Thessaloniki.

JAMES, CARL, SCHOLFIELD, P. and YPSILADIS, G. 1994. 'Cross-cultural correspondence', *World Englishes* Vol. 13 No. 3: 325–40.

JAMES, CARL, SCHOLFIELD, P., GARRETT, P. and GRIFFITHS, Y. 1993. 'Welsh bilinguals' English spelling: an error analysis', *Journal of Multilingual and Multicultural Development* Vol. 14 No. 4: 287–306.

JANICKI, K. 1980. 'Deviance beyond grammar', *Studia Anglica Poznaniensia* Vol. 12: 61–71.

JOHANSSON, S. 1975. *Papers in Contrastive Linguistics and Language Testing. Lund Studies in English No. 50.* CWK Gleerup, Lund.

JOHANSSON, S. 1978. *Studies in Error Gravity: Native Speaker Reactions to Errors Produced by Swedish Learners of English.* Gothenburg University Press, Gothenburg.

JOHNSON, K. 1988. 'Mistake correction', *English Language Teaching Journal* Vol. 42 No. 2: 89–97.

JOHNSON, K. 1996. *Language Teaching and Skill Learning.* Blackwell, Oxford.

JONES, A.L. 1966. 'The written English of Malayan teacher training college students', unpublished MEd dissertation, Manchester University, Manchester.

KACHRU, B. 1985. 'Standards, codification and sociolinguistic realism: the English language in the Outer Circle', in R. Quirk and H.G. Widdowson (eds), *English in the World: Teaching and Learning the Language and Literatures.* Cambridge University Press, Cambridge. pp. 11–30.

KAMIMOTO, F., SHIMURA, A. and KELLERMAN, E. 1992. 'A second language classic reconsidered: the case of Schachter's avoidance', *Second Language Research* Vol. 8 No. 3: 251–77.

KAPLAN, R.B. 1966. 'Cultural thought patterns in intercultural education', *Language Learning* Vol. 16: 1–20.

KASPER, G. and KELLERMAN, E. 1997. 'Introduction', in G. Kasper and E. Kellerman (eds), *Communication Strategies: Psycholinguistic and Sociolinguistic Perspectives.* Addison Wesley Longman, London. pp. 1–13.

KAUFMANN, L.M. 1993. 'Please correct me if I'm wrong', Unpublished paper presented at the 10th AILA Congress, Amsterdam, August 1993.

KELLERMAN, E. 1976. 'Elicitation, lateralization and error analysis', *Interlanguage Studies Bulletin* Vol. 1: 79–116.

KELLERMAN, E. 1983. 'Now you see it, now you don't', in S.M. Gass and L. Selinker (eds), pp. 112–34.

KELLERMAN, E. and SHARWOOD SMITH, M. (eds) 1986. *Crosslinguistic Influence in Second Language Acquisition.* Pergamon, Oxford.

KENNEDY, J. 1996. 'Classroom explanatory discourse: a look at how teachers explain things to their students', *Language Awareness* Vol. 5 No. 1: 26–39.

KENWORTHY, J. 1987. *Teaching English Pronunciation.* Longman, London.

KINGMAN, SIR J. (Chairman) 1988. *Report of the Committee of Enquiry into the Teaching of English Language (The Kingman Report).* Her Majesty's Stationery Office, London.

KLEIN, W. 1986. *Second Language Acquisition.* Cambridge University Press, Cambridge.

KNIFFKA, H. (ed.) 1990. *Texte zu Theorie und Praxis Forensischer Linguistik.* Max Niemeyer, Tübingen.

KNIFFKA, H. (ed.) 1996. *Recent Developments in Forensic Linguistics: Proceedings of the 3rd Congress of the International Association for Forensic Linguistics.* Peter Lang, Frankfurt.

KOBAYASHI, T. 1992. 'Native and nonnative reactions to ESL compositions', *TESOL Quarterly* Vol. 26 No. 1: 81–112.

KRASHEN, S.D. 1982. *Principles and Practice in Second Language Acquisition.* Pergamon, Oxford.

KRASHEN, S.D. 1983. 'Newmark's ignorance hypothesis and current second language acquisition theory' in S. Gass and L. Selinker (eds) *Language Transfer in Language Learning,* Newbury House, Rowley, pp. 135–53.

KRASHEN, S.D. 1985. *The Input Hypothesis: Issues and Implications.* Longman, London.

KRZESZOWSKI, T.P. 1970. *Teaching English to Polish Learners.* Panstwowe Wydawnictwo Naukowe, Warsaw.

LADO, R. 1957. *Linguistics Across Cultures.* University of Michigan Press, Ann Arbor, MI.

LANE, H. 1963. 'Foreign accent and speech distortion', *Journal of the Acoustical Society of America* Vol. 35 No. 4: 451–3.

LANSBURGH, W. 1983. *Dear Doosie: Eine Liebesgeschichte in Briefen. Auch eine Möglichkeit, sein Englisch spielend aufzufrischen.* Fischer, Frankfurt am Main.

LAUFER, B. 1992. 'Native language effect on confusion of similar lexical forms', in C. Mair, and M. Markus (eds), *New Departures in Contrastive Linguistics: Innsbrucker Beiträge zur Kulturwissenschaft* Vol. 2. University of Innsbruck, Innsbruck. pp. 199–209.

LAUFER, B. and SIM, D. 1985. 'Taking the easy way out: use and misuse of clues in EFL reading', *Forum: A Journal for the Teacher of English outside the United States* Vol. 23: 7–10.

LEECH, G. 1969. *A Linguistic Guide to English Poetry.* Longman, London.

LEECH, G. 1981. *Semantics.* (2nd edition) Penguin Books, Harmondsworth.

LEECH, G.N. 1983. *Principles of Pragmatics.* Longman, London.

LEGENHAUSEN, L. 1975. *Fehleranalyse und Fehlerbewertung.* Cornelsen-Velhagen & Klasing, Berlin.

LEINONEN-DAVIES, E. 1984. 'Toward textual error analysis with special reference to Finnish learners of English', unpublished M.Phil thesis, Exeter University, Exeter.

LEITH, D. 1983. *A Social History of English.* Routledge and Kegan Paul, London.

LEKI, I. 1991a. 'Twenty-five years of contrastive rhetoric: text analysis and writing pedagogies', *TESOL Quarterly* Vol. 25 No. 1: 123–43.

LEKI, I. 1991b. 'The preferences of ESL students for error correction in college-level writing classes', *Foreign Language Annals* Vol. 24 No. 3: 203–18.

LENNON. P. 1991. 'Error: some problems of definition, identification and distinction', *Applied Linguistics* Vol. 12 No. 2: 180–96.

LEONARD, S.A. 1929. *The Doctrine of Corrections in English Usage 1700–1800*. University of Wisconsin Press, Madison.

LESTER, A. 1964. 'Graphemic-phonemic correspondence as the basis for teaching spelling', *Elementary English* Vol. 41: 748–52.

LEVELT, W.J.M. 1977. 'Skills theory and language teaching', *Studies in Second Language Acquisition* Vol. 1 No. 1: 53–70.

LEVELT, W.J.M., SINCLAIR, A. and JARVELLA, R.J. 1978. 'Causes and functions of language awareness in language acquisition', in A. Sinclair, R.J. Jarvella and W.J.M. Level (eds), *The Child's Conception of Language*. Springer, Berlin and New York. pp. 1–14.

LEVENSTON, E.A. 1971. 'Over-indulgence and under-representation: aspects of mother-tongue interference', in G. Nickel (ed.), pp. 115–21.

LEVENSTON, E.A. 1978. 'Error analysis of free composition: the theory and the practice', *Indian Journal of Applied Linguistics* Vol. 4 No. 1: 1–11.

LEWIS, B.N. 1981. 'An essay on error', *Instructional Science* Vol. 10: 237–57.

LITTLEWOOD, W.T. 1975. 'Grammatical explanations', *Audio-Visual Language Journal* Vol. 13 No. 2: 91–4.

LITTLEWOOD, W.T. 1981. *Communicative Language Teaching: An Introduction*. Cambridge University Press, Cambridge.

LITTLEWOOD, W.T. 1992. *Teaching Oral Communication: A Methodological Framework*. Edward Arnold, London.

LONG, M. 1991. 'Focus on form: a design feature in language teaching methodology', in Kees de Bot, R.B. Ginsberg and C. Kramsch (eds), *Foreign Language Research in Cross-Cultural Perspective*. J. Benjamins, Amsterdam. pp. 39–52.

LOTT, B. 1988. 'Language and literature', *Language Teaching* Vol. 21 No. 1: 1–13.

LYONS, J. 1968. *An Introduction to Theoretical Linguistics*. Cambridge University Press, Cambridge.

LYONS, J. (ed.) 1977. *Semantics*. Cambridge University Press, Cambridge.

MACKAY, D.G. 1992. 'Errors, ambiguity and awareness in language perception', in B.J. Baars (ed.), *Experimental Slips and Human Error: Exploring the Architecture of Volition*. Plenum Press, New York. pp. 39–69.

MACNEILAGE, P.F. 1964. 'Typing errors as clues to serial ordering mechanisms in language behaviour', *Language and Speech* Vol. 7 No. 3: 144–59.

MACWHINNEY, B. 1987. 'Applying the competition model to bilingualism', *Applied Psycholinguistics* Vol. 8: 315–27.

MAGNAN, S.S. 1979. 'Reduction and error correction for communicative language use: the focus approach', *Modern Language Journal* Vol. 63: 342–9.

MALCOLM, I. 1994. 'Discourse and discourse strategies in Australian Aboriginal English', *World Englishes* Vol. 13 No. 3: 289–306.

MATTSON, M.E. and BAARS, B.J. 1992. 'Error-minimizing mechanisms', in B.J. Baars (ed.), pp. 263–87.

McCARTHY, M. and R. CARTER (eds) 1994. *Language as Discourse.* Longman, London.

McCRETTON, E. and RIDER, N. 1993. 'Error gravity and error hierarchies', *International Review of Applied Linguistics* Vol. 31 No. 3: 177–88.

McMENAMIN, G.R. 1993. *Forensic Stylistics.* Elsevier, Amsterdam.

MEAD, M. 1950. *Male and Female, a Study of the Sexes in a Changing World.* Gollancz, London.

MEARA. P. 1984. 'The study of lexis in Interlanguage', in A. Davies, C. Criper and A.P.R. Howatt (eds), *Interlanguage: Papers in Honour of S. Pit Corder.* Edinburgh University Press, Edinburgh. pp. 225–35.

MEDGYES, P. 1989. 'Error and the communicative approach', in R. Freudenstein (ed.), pp. 70–9.

MEY, J. 1981. 'Right or wrong, my native speaker', in F. Coulmas (ed.), pp. 69–84.

MILROY, J. 1992. *Linguistic Variation and Change.* Blackwell, Oxford.

MILROY, J. and MILROY, L. 1985. *Authority in Language: Investigating Language Perception and Standardisation.* Routledge and Kegan Paul, London.

MILROY, L. 1984. 'Comprehension and context: successful communication and communication breakdown', in P. Trudgill (ed.), *Applied Sociolinguistics.* Academic Press, London. pp. 7–31.

MOREIRA, G.G. 1991. 'The specific language needs of future language teachers', in I.P. Martins and A.I. Andrade (eds), *Actas do 2. Encontro Nacional de Didacticas e Metodologias do Ensino.* University of Aveiro, Aveiro. pp. 39–49.

NAIMAN, N., FROHLICH, M., STERN, H.H. and TODESCO, A. 1978. *The Good Language Learner.* Ontario Institute for Studies in Education, Ontario.

NATTINGER, J.R. and DeCARRICO, J.S. 1992. *Lexical Phrases and Language Teaching.* Oxford University Press, Oxford.

NAYAR, P.B. 1991. 'The ethoglossic power dynamics of interaction: English across cultures and races', *Intercultural Communication Studies* Vol. 1 No. 2: 237–50.

NEMSER, W. 1971. 'Approximative systems of foreign language learners', *International Revue of Applied Linguistics* Vol. 9, No. 2: 115–23.

NEMSER, W. 1991. 'Language context and foreign language acquisition', in V. Ivir and D. Kalogjera (eds) *Languages in Context and Contrast: Essays in Contact Linguistics.* Mouton de Gruyter, Berlin. pp. 345–64.

NICKEL, G. (ed.) 1971. *Papers in Contrastive Linguistics.* Cambridge University Press, Cambridge.

NICKEL, G. (ed.) 1972. *Fehlerkunde: Beiträge zur Fehlerkunde, Fehlerbewertung und Fehlertypologie.* Cornelsen-Velhagen and Klasing, Berlin.

NICKEL, G. 1989. 'Some controversies in present-day error analysis: "contrastive" versus "noncontrastive" errors', *International Review of Applied Linguistics* Vol. 27 No. 4: 293–303.

NICKEL, G. 1992. '"Contrastive" versus "noncontrastive" errors: a controversy in error analysis', *South African Journal of Linguistics* Vol. 10 No. 4: 229–34.

NORRISH, J. 1983. *Language Learners and their Errors*. Macmillan, London.

NOTHOFER, B. 1991. 'The languages of Brunei Darussalam', in H. Steinhauer (ed.), *Papers in Austronesian Linguistics No. 1: Pacific Linguistics*. A–81. The Australian National University, Canberra. pp. 151–76.

OAKESHOTT-TAYLOR, J. 1977. 'Phonological errors in the written English of German-speaking students', *Hamburger Phonetische Beiträge*. Helmut Buske Verlag, Hamburg. Vol. 22. pp. 101–12.

ODLIN, T. 1989. *Language Transfer: Cross-Linguistic Influence in Language Learning*. Cambridge University Press, Cambridge.

OLEKSY, W. (ed.) 1989. *Contrastive Pragmatics*. John Benjamins, Amsterdam.

OLLER, J.W. and REDDING. J. 1971. 'Article usage and other language skills', *Language Learning* Vol. 21 No. 1: 85–95.

OLSSON, M. 1972. *Intelligibility: A Study of Errors and their Importance*. The GUME Project, Research Bulletin No. 34, School of Education, Gothenburg University, Gothenburg.

OLSSON, M. 1977. 'A model for the interpretation of utterances', in S.P. Corder and E. Roulet (eds), *The Notions of Simplification, Interlanguage and Pidgins and their Relation to Second Language Pedagogy*. Neuchâtel University and Librairie Droz, Geneva. pp. 72–87.

OXFORD, R. 1990. *Language Learning Strategies: What Every Teacher Should Know*. Newbury House, Rowley, MA.

PAGE, B. 1990. 'Why do we have to get it right anyway?', in B. Page (ed.), *What do you mean it's wrong?* Centre for Information on Language Teaching, London. pp. 103–7.

PAGE, B., HARDING, A. and ROWELL, S. 1980. *Graded Objectives in Modern Languages*. Centre for Information on Language Teaching (CILT), London.

Password – English Dictionary for Speakers of French. 1989. Modulo Kernerman Semi-bilingual Dictionaries, Quebec.

PAVESI, M. 1986. 'Markedness, discoursal modes, and relative clause formation in a formal and an informal context', *Studies in Second Language Acquisition* Vol. 8 No. 1: 38–55.

PAWLEY, A. and SYDER, F.H. 1983. 'Two puzzles for linguistic theory: nativelike selection and nativelike fluency', in J.C. Richards and R.W. Schmidt (eds), *Language and Communication*. Longman, London. pp. 191–226.

PETERSEN, M. 1988. *Japanese English*. Iwanami, Tokyo.

PHILLIPSON, R. 1992. *Linguistic Imperialism*, Oxford University Press, Oxford.

PHYTHIAN, B.A. 1989. *A Concise Dictionary of Confusables*. Headway, Hodder & Stoughton, Sevenoaks.

PICA, T. 1984. 'L1 transfer and L2 complexity as factors in syllabus design', *TESOL Quarterly* Vol. 18 No. 4: 689–704.

PICKETT, G.D. 1978. *The Foreign Language Learning Process: An ETIC Occasional Paper*. The British Council, London.

PICKTHORNE, B. 1983. 'Error factors: a missing link between cognitive science and classroom practices', *Instructional Science* Vol. 11: 281–312.

PIENEMANN, M. 1985. 'Learnability and syllabus construction', in K. Hyltenstam and M. Pienemann (eds), *Modelling and Assessing Second Language Acquisition*. Multilingual Matters, Clevedon. pp. 23–75.

PIENEMANN, M. 1992. 'COALA – A computational system for inter-language analysis', *Second Language Research* Vol. 8 No. 1: 59–92.

PLANN, S. 1977. 'Acquisition of a second language in the immersion classroom', in H.D. Brown, C.A. Yorio and R. Crymes (eds), *On TESOL '77*. TESOL, Washington, DC. pp. 213–25.

PLATT, J., WEBER H. and HO MIAN LIAN. 1984. *The New Englishes*. Routledge and Kegan Paul, London.

POLITZER, R.L. 1978. 'Errors of English speakers of German as perceived and evaluated by German natives', *Modern Language Journal* Vol. 5 No. 6: 253–61.

POTTER, F. 1980. 'Miscue analysis: a cautionary note', *Journal of Research in Reading* Vol. 3 No. 2: 116–28.

POTTER, S. 1975. *Changing English*. Andre Deutsch, London.

POULISSE, N. 1997. 'Slips of the tongue and their correction in L2 learner speech: metalinguistic awareness and second language acquisition', in H.W. Dechert (ed.), *Metacognitions and Second Language Acquisition*. Multilingual Matters, Clevedon.

POULISSE, N. and BONGAERTS, T. 1994. 'First language use in second language production', *Applied Linguistics* Vol. 15 No. 1: 36–57.

PRABHU, N.S. 1987. *Second Language Pedagogy*. Oxford University Press, Oxford.

PRATOR, C. 1968. 'The British heresy in TEFL', in J.A. Fishman and J. Das Gupta (eds), *Language Problems of Developing Nations*. John Wiley & Sons, New York. pp. 459–76.

PRICE, C. 1993. *Time, Discounting and Value*. Blackwell, Oxford.

PRIESTLEY, J. 1761. *The Rudiments of English Grammar*. London.

PURVES, A.C. 1988. *Writing Across Languages and Cultures: Issues in Contrastive Rhetoric*. Sage, Newbury Park, CA.

QUIRK, R. 1968. *The Use of English*. Longman, London.

QUIRK, R. 1985. 'The English language in a global context', in R. Quirk and H.G. Widdowson (eds), *English in the World*. Cambridge University Press, Cambridge. pp. 1–6.

QUIRK, R., GREENBAUM, S., LEECH, G. and SVARTVIK, J. 1985. *A Comprehensive Grammar of the English Language*. Longman, London.

RAABE, H. 1982. 'Die Korrektur mündlicher Fehler im Spanischen: Einsichten aus der Sprachlernforschung', *Grazer Linguistische Studien* Vol. 19: 159–83.

RADFORD, A. 1988. *Transformational Grammar.* Cambridge University Press, Cambridge.

REASON, J.T. 1984. 'Lapses of attention in everyday life', in R. Parasuraman and D.R. Davies (eds), *Varieties of Attention.* Academic Press, New York. pp. 515–49.

REISS, M.-A. 1981. 'Helping the unsuccessful language learner', *Modern Language Journal* Vol. 65: 121–8.

RICHARDS, J.C. (ed.) 1974a. *Error Analysis: Perspectives on Second Language Acquisition.* Longman, London.

RICHARDS, J.C. 1974b. 'A non-contrastive approach to error analysis', in J.C. Richards (ed.), pp. 172–88.

RICHARDS, J.C. 1976. 'The role of vocabulary teaching', *TESOL Quarterly* Vol. 10 No. 1: 77–89.

RINGBOM, H. 1987. *The Role of the First Language in Second Language Learning.* Multilingual Matters, Clevedon.

RINVOLUCRI, M. 1984. *Grammar Games: Cognitive, Affective and Drama Activities for EFL Students.* Cambridge University Press, Cambridge.

RIXON, S. 1993. *Language Teaching and Learning: A Video-based EFL Teacher Training Package at Certificate Level.* The British Council, London.

ROBB, T., ROSS, S. and SHORTREED, I. 1986. 'Salience of feedback on error and its effect on EFL writing quality', *TESOL Quarterly* Vol. 20 No. 1: 83–93.

DE ROCHA, F.J. 1980. 'On the reliability of error analysis', *Studia Anglica Posnaniensia* Vol. 12: 83–90.

ROOM, A. 1979. *Dictionary of Confusibles.* Routledge & Kegan Paul, Boston, MA.

ROOM, A. 1981. *Dictionary of Distinguishables.* Routledge & Kegan Paul, Boston, MA.

ROSEN H. 1991. 'The nationalisation of English', *International Journal of Applied Linguistics* Vol. 1 No. 1: 104–17.

ROSTEN, L. 1937. *The Education of Hymen Kaplan.* Harcourt Brace, New York.

ROULET, E. 1980. *Langue Maternelle et Langues Secondes: vers une Pédagogie Intégrée.* Hatier-Credif, Paris.

RUTHERFORD, W.E. 1987. *Second Language Grammar: Learning and Teaching.* Longman, London.

SACKS, O. 1986. *The Man Who Mistook His Wife for a Hat.* Picador, London.

SAMARIN, W.J. 1967. *Field Linguistics.* Holt, Rinehart and Winston, New York.

SANTOS, T. 1988. 'Professors' reactions to the academic writing of nonnative-speaking students', *TESOL Quarterly* Vol. 22 No. 1: 69–90.

SCHACHTER, J. 1974. 'An error in error analysis', *Language Learning* Vol. 24 No. 2: 205–14.

SCHACHTER, J. 1990. 'On the issue of completeness in second language acquisition', *Second Language Research* Vol. 6 No. 2: 93–124.

SCHACHTER, J. and CELCE-MURCIA, M. 1977. 'Some reservations concerning error analysis', *TESOL Quarterly* Vol. 11 No. 4: 441–51.

SCHEGLOFF, E.A. 1987. 'Some sources of misunderstanding in talk-in-action', *Linguistics* Vol. 25: 201–18.

SCHMIDT, R. 1992. 'Psychological mechanisms underlying second language fluency', *Studies in Second Language Acquisition* Vol. 14 No. 4: 357–85.

SCHMITT, N. 1993. 'Comparing native and nonnative teachers' evaluations of error seriousness', *Japanese Association of Language Teachers: Journal* Vol. 15 No. 2: 181–91.

SCHUMANN, F.M. and SCHUMANN, J.H. 1977. 'Diary of a language learner: an introspective study of second language learning', in D. Brown, C.A. Yorio and R. Crymes (eds), *On TESOL '77*. TESOL, Washington, DC. pp. 241–9.

SCHUMANN, J. 1978. *The Pidginization Process: A Model for Second Language Acquisition*. Newbury House, Rowley, MA.

SCOLLON, R. and SCOLLON, S.W. 1995. *Intercultural Communication: A Discourse Approach*. Blackwell, Oxford.

SCRIVEN, M. 1991. *Evaluation Thesaurus*. Sage, London.

SEDGER, J. 1798. *The Structure of the English Language*. London.

SELIGER, H.W. 1977. 'Does practice make perfect? A study of interaction patterns and L2 competence', *Language Learning* Vol. 27: 263–75.

SELINKER, L. 1972. 'Interlanguage', *International Review of Applied Linguistics* Vol. 10 No. 3: 209–31.

SELINKER, L. 1992. *Rediscovering Interlanguage*. Longman, London.

SELL, P.S. 1985. *Expert Systems: A Practical Introduction*. Macmillan, London.

SELLEN, A.J. and NORMAN, D.A. 1992. 'The psychology of slips', in B.J. Baars (ed.), pp. 317–39.

SEXTON, M., WILLIAMS, P. and BADDOCK, B. 1985. *Communication Activities for Advanced Students of English*. Langensheidt-Longman, Munich.

SEY, K.A. 1973. *Ghanaian English*. Macmillan, London.

SHAUGHNESSY, M. 1977. *Errors and Expectations*. Oxford University Press, Oxford.

SHAPIRA, R. 1978. 'The non-learning of English: a case study of an adult', in E.M. Hatch (ed.), pp. 246–59.

SHAW, H. 1975. *Dictionary of Problem Words and Expressions*. McGraw-Hill, London and New York.

SHEPPARD, K. 1992. 'Two feedback types: do they make a difference?', (Regional English Language Centre) *RELC Journal* Vol. 23 No. 1: 103–9.

SINCLAIR, J. (ed.) 1987. *Looking Up. An Account of the Cobuild Project in Lexical Computing.* Collins English Language Teaching, London and Glasgow.

SMITH, L.E. (ed.) 1987. *Discourse Across Cultures: Strategies in World Englishes.* Prentice-Hall, New York.

SMITH, L.E. and NELSON, C.L. 1983. 'International Intelligibility of English: directions and resources', *World Englishes,* Vol. 4 No. 3: 333–42.

SMITH, L.E. and RAFIQZAD, K. 1979. 'English for cross-cultural communication: the question of intelligibility', *TESOL Quarterly* Vol. 13 No. 3: 371–80.

SNOW, C. 1977. 'Mothers' speech research: from insight to interaction', in C. Snow and C. Ferguson (eds), *Talking to Children: Language Input and Acquisition.* Cambridge University Press, Cambridge. pp. 31–49.

SORENSEN, V. 1981. 'Coherence as a pragmatic concept', in H. Parret, M. Sbisa and J. Verschueren (eds), *Possibilities and Limitations of Pragmatics.* John Benjamins, Amsterdam. pp. 657–82.

SPILLNER, B. 1990. 'Status und Erklärungspotentiell Sprachlicher Fehler', in H. Kniffka (ed.), pp. 97–113.

SPILLNER, B. 1991. *Fehleranalyse, Error Analysis. Analyse de Fautes: A Comprehensive Bibliography.* John Benjamins, Amsterdam.

STEMBERGER, J.P. 1982. 'Syntactic errors in speech', *Journal of Psycholinguistic Research* Vol. 11 No. 4: 313–45.

STENSON, N. 1983. 'Induced errors', in B.W. Robinett and J. Schachter (eds), *Second Language Learning: Contrastive Analysis, Error Analysis and Related Aspects.* University of Michigan Press, Ann Arbor, MI. pp. 256–71.

STRONG, W. 1994. *Sentence Combining: A Composing Book.* McGraw-Hill.

SUNDBY, B. 1987. 'Prescriptive labelling: problems and principles with a prescriptive index', unpublished working paper, Department of English, University of Bergen, Bergen.

SUNDBY, B. and BJØRGE, A.K. 1983. 'The codification of presciptive grammar', in S. Hattori and K. Inoue (eds), *Proceedings of the 13th International Congress of Linguists, Tokyo 1982.* CIPL, The Hague. pp. 748–51.

SVARTVIK, J. (ed.) 1973. *Errata: Papers in Error Analysis.* CWK Gleerup, Lund, Sweden.

SWAN, M. and SMITH, B. 1979. *Learner English: A Teacher's Guide to Interference and other Problems.* Cambridge University Press, Cambridge.

SYKES, J.B. (ed.) 1982. 6th edition. *The Concise Oxford Dictionary of Current English.* Oxford University Press, Oxford.

TANG, E. and NG, C. 1995. 'A study on the use of connectives in ESL students' writing', *Perspectives* Vol. 7 No. 2: 105–21. City University of Hong Kong, Hong Kong.

TARONE, E. 1983. 'On the variability of interlanguage systems', *Applied Linguistics* Vol. 4 No. 2: 141–63.

TARONE, E., COHEN, A. and DUMAS, G. 1983. 'A closer look at some interlanguage terminology: a framework for communication strategies', in C. Færch and G. Kasper (eds), pp. 4–14.

TAYLOR, D.S. 1981. 'Non-native speakers and the rhythm of English', *International Review of Applied Linguistics* Vol. 19: 219–26.

TAYLOR, G. 1986. 'Errors and explanations', *Applied Linguistics* Vol. 7 No. 2: 144–65.

THOMAS, J. 1983. 'Cross-cultural pragmatic failure', *Applied Linguistics* Vol. 4 No. 2: 91–112.

THOMAS, J. 1984. 'Cross-cultural discourse as unequal encounter', *Applied Linguistics* Vol. 5 No. 3: 226–35.

TIFFEN, B. 1992. 'A study of the intelligibility of Nigerian English', in A. van Essen and E.I. Burkart (eds), *Homage to W.R. Lee. Essays in English as a Foreign and Second Language.* Foris, Dordrecht. pp. 255–9.

TOMASELLO, M. and HERRON, C. 1988. 'Down the garden path: inducing and correcting overgeneralization errors in the foreign language classroom', *Applied Psycholinguistics* Vol. 9: 237–46.

TOMASELLO, M. and HERRON, C. 1989. 'Feedback for language transfer errors: the garden path technique', *Studies in Second Language Acquisition* Vol. 11: 385–95.

TOWELL, R. and HAWKINS, R. 1994. *Approaches to Second Language Acquisition.* Multilingual Matters, Clevedon.

TRÉVISE, A. 1986. 'Is it transferable, topicalization?', in E. Kellerman and M. Sharwood Smith (eds), pp. 86–206.

TROUTMAN, A.P. and LICHTENBERG, B.K. 1982. *Mathematics: A Good Beginning. Strategies for Teaching Children.* Brooks & Cole, Monterey, CA.

TURTON, N.D. 1989. *Send or Take? A Guide to Correct English Usage.* Federal Publications, Singapore and Hong Kong.

TURTON, N.D. 1995. *ABC of Common Grammatical Errors: For Learners and Teachers of English.* Macmillan Educational, London and Basingstoke.

VAN ELS, TH.J.M. 1989. 'Errors and foreign language loss', in R. Freudenstein (ed.), pp. 104–13.

VAN WIJK, C. and KEMPEN, G. 1987. 'A dual system for producing self-repairs in spontaneous speech: evidence from experimentally elicited corrections', *Cognitive Psychology* Vol. 19: 403–40.

VIGIL, F. and OLLER, J. 1976. 'Rule fossilization: a tentative model', *Language Learning* Vol. 26 No. 2: 281–95.

WALLACE, M.J. 1991. *Training Foreign Language Teachers: A Reflective Approach.* Cambridge University Press, Cambridge.

WALZ, J.C. 1982. *Error Correction Techniques for the Classroom.* Prentice-Hall, Englewood Cliffs, NJ.

WARDHAUGH, R. 1970. 'The contrastive analysis hypothesis', *TESOL Quarterly* Vol. 4 No. 2: 123–30.

WEINREICH, U. 1953/1968. *Languages in Contact.* Mouton, The Hague.

WHEELER, D.H. 1977. *Notes on Mathematics for Children*. Cambridge University Press, Cambridge.

WHITAKER, S.F. 1992. 'Why do French-speakers have difficulty with *coming* and *going*?', in A. van Essen and E.I. Burkart (eds), *Homage to W.R. Lee. Essays in English as a Foreign and Second Language*. Foris, Dordrecht. pp. 273–81.

WIDDOWSON, H.G. 1987. 'Significance in conventional and literary discourse', in L.E. Smith (ed.), pp. 9–21.

WIDDOWSON H.G. 1989. 'Knowledge of language and ability for use', *Applied Linguistics* Vol. 10: 128–37.

WIDDOWSON, H.G. 1995. 'Discourse analysis: a critical view', *Language and Literature* Vol. 4 No. 3: 157–72.

WILKINS, D.A. 1976. *Notional Syllabuses*. Oxford University Press, Oxford.

WILLIAMS, J.M. 1981. 'The phenomenology of error', *College Composition and Communication* Vol. 32 No. 2: 152–69.

WILLIAMSON, J. 1990. '"Divven't write that man": The influence of Tyneside dialect forms on children's free writing', *Educational Studies* Vol. 16 No. 3: 251–60.

WILLIAMSON, J. 1995. 'Canny writers: Tyneside dialect and the writing of secondary school students', *Educational Studies* Vol. 21 No. 1: 3–12.

WOOD, J. 1777. *Grammatical Institutions, or a practical English Grammar*. Newcastle.

WRAY, A. 1996. 'The occurrence of "occurance" (and "alot" of other things "aswell"): patterns of errors in undergraduate English', in G. Blue and R. Mitchell (eds), *Language and Education*. The British Association for Applied Linguistics and Multilingual Matters, Clevedon.

YOU SIHAI 1990. 'Persuasive writing of application letters: Chinese and English', unpublished MA dissertation, University of Wales, Bangor.

YULE, H. and BURNELL, A. 1886. *Hobson-Jobson: A Glossary of Colloquial Anglo-Indian Words and Phrases, and of Kindred Terms, Etymological, Historical, Geographical and Discursive*. Linguasia, London.

ZIAHOSSEINY, P. and OLLER, J.W. 1970. 'The contrastive analysis hypothesis and spelling errors', *Language Learning* Vol. 20 No. 2: 183–90.

ZOLA, D. 1984. 'Redundancy and word perception during reading', *Perception and Psychophysics* Vol. 36 No. 3: 277–84.

ZYDATIß, W. 1974. 'A "kiss of life" for the notion of error', *International Review of Applied Linguistics* Vol. 12: 231–7.

Index